Journey of a Lifetime

Part 1: Voyage of Uncertain Destination

David Hazell

Published by

MELROSE BOOKS

An Imprint of Melrose Press Limited
St Thomas Place, Ely
Cambridgeshire
CB7 4GG, UK
www.melrosebooks.co.uk

FIRST EDITION

Copyright © David Hazell 2017

The Author asserts his moral right to
be identified as the author of this work

Cover designed by Melrose Books

ISBN 978-1-912026-47-0
epub 978-1-912026-48-7
mobi 978-1-912026-49-4

All rights reserved. No part of this publication may be reproduced, stored in a retrieval system, or transmitted, in any form or by any means electronic, mechanical, photocopying, recording or otherwise, without the prior permission of the publishers.

This book is sold subject to the condition that it shall not, by way of trade or otherwise, be lent, re-sold, hired out or otherwise circulated without the publisher's prior consent in any form of binding or cover other than that in which it is published and without a similar condition including this condition being imposed on the subsequent purchaser.

Printed and bound in Great Britain by:
4edge Limited
7a Eldon Way, Eldon Way Industrial Estate
Hockley, Essex
SS5 4AD

Contents

Prologue	1
Introduction: A Rude Awakening	6
Taking Back Control: In the Nick of Time	12
Testing to Destruction	15
Meeting the Ghost of Inner Being	21
Ineluctable Destiny and a 'Chance' Meeting	24
Stumbling Forward To …	27
… A Massive Transformation	30
Steps on the Road to Life	34
Bioenergetics and an Awakening Body	37
Group Therapy; Truth and Denial	44
Signs Along the Way	52
The Healing Power of Nature	55
Outer World Versus Inner Being	60
Epiphany on Dartmoor	70
Doors Opening, Perceptions Deepening	72
Unexpected Revelations Within Myself	74
Inner Peace Outer Conflict; Mirrors and Magnetic Attraction	88
Calm and Sunshine After the Storm	95
The Body and its Inner Wisdom	98
Through the Wardrobe into Worlds Untravelled	100
Broadening Horizons; Nature's Gifts; Inner Canyons	109
Consolidation and Growth; The Wider World	118
Deep Stress Catharsis	129
Deep Trauma and Miraculous Transformations	134
Intellect, Archetypes and Transformation	139
Deeper Journeys; Widening Worlds	145
Searching for Meaning; Looking for Answers	154
Subterranean Symbols, Disconnected Consciousness; Ends & New Beginnings	160
'A Big Lift'	171
Hindsight and Perspective	181
The Inner World Looking Out	184
Coincidence and Inner Consciousness	194

Ocean Swells and Mortgages	209
Insights, Toil and Prophets in Back Yards	223
The Trench To …	241
… Inner No Man's Land	248
Patterns; Healing; Worlds Unseen	250
Revelation	262
Out of No-Man's Land …	271
The Bridge of Trust	276
The Wisdom of Animals	282
The Long Climb To …	289
Work, Survival and Body Wisdom	294
Perfect Health?	301
Fate's 'Sat Nav'	312
Dreamtime	318
Introducing Groundhog Day	326
Groundhog Day Effect	335
Beginning All Over – Again!	340
Old Routines; New Territories	358
Energy and the Body's Wisdom	383
The Path to Nirvana … Errr …?	395
The Power of 'Cunning Old Fury'	398
Following the Signposts	405
Toenails, Milestones, Trends and New Perceptions	418
Warnings from the Inner World are Real	426
A Matter of Balance	432
The Conservation of Energy, Intellect, Logjams and Palpitations	436
Plus Ça Change Plus C'est La Même Chose	442
Recent Times and Recent Signs	446
The Dimensions of Intellect	455
Outer Wars and Inner Conflict	458
Inner Walls and Outer Armour	462
The Wisdom of Animals	473
More of the Same	476
Coughing up Elastic Bands – Again	482
The Art of Gargling	484
'Coincidence' and Gathering Momentum	487
Rhythms, Patterns and Future Trends	492
From Part Time to Continuous Working	501

Prologue

In a time when we are drowning in 'media' of all kinds; books (paper and electronic), magazines, articles, CDs, DVDs; the whole mobile instant information 'I' culture and a clamour of voices proclaiming new knowledge, transformation, enlightenment, realizing one's full potential and a myriad of doctrines, disciplines, therapies, regimes and diets through which to achieve one's particular goal, I have asked myself many times whether there is any point in adding yet one more book to the cascade flooding out into the world over some literary Victoria Falls; or perhaps tsunami would be more appropriate.

To try and sample, much less keep pace with, this deluge is a hopeless task. Just as to want to view these Falls of such great beauty and power, standing at the base of them is to be instantly swamped and swept away. Likewise, to add to the torrent of knowledge and experience flooding out into the world in a deluge of words of diluvial proportions, I have pondered long before reaching the conclusion I should do what a number of people have been urging me to do for years now: write a book on the experience and knowledge I have gained over more than half my life. The more I have written, the less inclined I have been to publish it.

The particular reason is we are all drowning in words, written, spoken and beamed to us electronically these days. Yet how else do we communicate in our word-infested world?

In our society we are utterly dependant on this means of interacting to make sense of our own world and of others. Though at times it seems the more words used, the less we understand each other. The more we explain, the more confusion is created.

As a culture we have come to rely almost totally on words,

particularly in a written/printed form, in its turn reflecting how we use and rely on our intellect to an overwhelming extent for navigating through life.

Essential though this faculty may be, something has got out of proportion when, for example, the American Declaration of Independence (which let us not forget created a nation state), amounts to a little over 1,300 words whereas the EU Directive on the basic export of duck eggs runs to nearly 27,000!

The advent of the computer age has made the problem much more acute. More and more we interact directly with one another less and less, depending instead on what information is projected on to a screen in front of us – as I am, typing this. In some aspects it is very useful, in others absolutely maddening; when a few words with the right person could save us hours trying to fix our own computer wading through yards of verbiage which may help or equally totally confuse and we give up in exasperation. And I speak as one who over forty years ago used to build, test and troubleshoot computer systems and their operating software down to the minutest detail, in the days before they shrank to about one millionth – or less – of their current size with exponentially increasing speed and power.

In my view and experience, there has never been a greater need to balance the intellect with what our human senses tell us. *They* are the creators of our reality. Intellect may have a lot to say, but it is not the seat of our reality. What we touch, smell, see, hear and *feel*, are what ground us in our world, and in 'feel', I include the full range of the meaning of the word. Not only 'feel' in a tactile sense, but in an emotional and intuitional sense, or what people also refer to as the 'sixth' sense; and which is an aspect of our sub/inner conscious and greater mind.

Intellect may chatter away about what it *thinks* reality is, but the sub/inner conscious and its more accessible attributes IS reality.

Instead, intellect, which should be a wise counsellor listening to and interpreting guidance our inner conscious gives us all the time, has been turned into a despotic tyrant listening to no one but itself. Our culture values intellect above all else; indeed, as a culture we have not only forgotten the 'language' of inner conscious which is through images, symbols and portents, but positively ignore, disavow, shun and fear its Promethean wisdom.

Without intellect, we can still function but not focus. Without inner conscious, we cease to exist.

Having once pursued intellect and logic to the brink of self-extinction, from being as near dead as one can be without stepping off this mortal coil, I began getting my body working again and working through a huge burden of emotional repression, and this clearing process has continued ever since.

It has now reached the stage where, in some respects, I am a stranger in my own culture, because I can relate to and understand how aboriginal cultures read signs and symbols and infer meanings, understandings and courses of action I would have treated as incomprehensible – or nonsense – years ago. Their cultures do not rely on technology and the written word; both provinces of the intellect. They carry it in language, customs, ceremonies, art of many forms, story telling; a living history passed through an archetypal common heritage and by word of mouth through the generations and a connectedness to the earth. All of which relates directly to realms of inner consciousness just exactly as the Celtic culture of these islands did before the Roman invasion.

For me, the gestalt of creating a harmonious relationship between intellect, body and my inner world is burgeoning good health I would not have dreamed of even in recent times, and expanded consciousness utterly beyond any imaginings I might have harboured; again, even a few years ago. More correctly stated; I simply did not possess.

This is not about 'guruship'; I am strongly inclined to be

unimpressed and very wary of anyone who aspires to some Titanic matchless wisdom not possessed by us mere mortals. Too often I find, like the ship of the same name, they founder on their own need for power and status, for when they begin to speak, it is clear they still have not understood the difference, and created harmony, between their intellect and that vast, hidden, inner universe of sublime wisdom; their inner/subconscious and broader aspects of mind.

What follows in my book is what I have learned on my own and by my own efforts. At an early stage it occurred to me I had turned my intellect into a repressive tyrant, but creating warfare within my own self between my intellect and very badly abused emotional and intuitive nature was an exercise in stupidity. For developing my intellect had taken me further than I ever imagined possible. Nurturing my feeling nature I began to see as 'shifting gears' to a higher level. Consequently, knowledge for me is what works as a harmonious whole. To analogise with a jigsaw puzzle; the overall picture is supplied by intuition and emotion. Putting the elements into a cohesive whole uses intellect to put into context one element with another. It is an interlocking process between the two. It is not about creating airy-fairy castles in the air, nor is it about sloshing around in a swamp of emotion. But the 'jigsaw puzzle' isn't two-dimensional, nor even three, because our deeper selves transcend time and space.

This is a record, literally and metaphorically, of a journey of a life and into life 'time' which has lasted over forty years, so far, and will only end when I do.

Consequently, the title chosen might appear bland, but it masks many levels and many paths within the one. It began with what was a very rare opportunity – even unique – to visit the other side of the world, and although ending at its allotted time, it transmogrified into one of inconceivable breadth and scope limited only by my will and persistence to travel it.

Though lengthy, it expresses only a fraction of the work I have done. Even less, the positive improvements and fundamental positive changes in my body and being. Far less still, the way in which consciousness opens up as a direct consequence, at an accelerating rate providing recall, insights, intuitions and direct knowledge I never dreamed of.

Above all, I hope I can create an unshakeable conviction that life is a continuum inexpressibly beyond what we are erroneously taught is immutable reality in our completely unbalanced, intellectually dominated, lopsided culture. No less also, it does not come through fond imaginings, wand waving, feeble efforts and fear-limited toe-dipping in waters of new experience, retreating in haste and uncertainty before even taking a first step.

My aim is: if by sharing my journey and what I have lived through and learned – and it would be true to say, also, unlearned in the process as well – I can encourage others to believe in, and become trusting of, their own great inner giant to heal and improve their own bodies and lives for themselves and those around them, then what others have been telling me to do for decades will have been worthwhile.

Finally to warn; reading this book *will* rattle and pull against closed inner doors our culture teaches us to hold shut from birth onwards, against personal history hidden and held within since, that becomes an increasing burden bearing down on us as life progresses.

The wisdom of the universe also applies; namely, there's no such thing as a free lunch. Reading is one thing. Doing it is entirely another.

Introduction:

A Rude Awakening

KER-LONK THUMP! I was propelled into wakefulness with almost the speed of a gun-shot; the ill-fitting door of the flat next to mine was heaved shut with its customary sudden force.

For a moment I lay; conscious of surfacing from nowhere. Not a gradual awakening, but as if I had been propelled back out of limbo by this explosive reveille.

I collected my thoughts of who and where I was and the weekend I had spent driving around the un-metalled roads and trackways of Victoria taking me through the most delightful and often aromatic scenery. Woodland scent of gum trees and other unseen sources lacing the warm air with wonderful perfume; soothing and invigorating bitterly neglected parts of me.

The recollection of escaping from the city and out in the hot bright sunlight to countryside well to the north of Melbourne, and, driving along one of the many unmade roads past the occasional house or homestead, stopping to savour all I saw around me. Sitting on the bright, reddish-brown earth leaning against the car's side to look out at the rural scene; the paddocks and many trees greeting my gaze.

Vivid blue sky; blissful, unaccustomed silence.

Not a car, aeroplane, human voice, nor any other human intrusion met my ears. I sank into this tranquil pool, rippled only by the sibilant raspings of some vibrating insect, and occasionally the clear tones and novel discord and unfamiliar warble of bird song.

This oasis brought into sharp relief the cacophony of noise in my head. A cement mixer of tumbling, clattering intellectual debris; like empty cans, nuts and bolts roaring endlessly round and round inside my skull. The switch of inner volition to stop this awful inner clamour long forgotten. Or even its existence until then.

As I lay, cascading scenes flooded me from the two previous days. I had driven as a fugitive possessed of some desperate, insatiable compulsion to devour the wonderful scenery of this ancient, strange new continent.

Visions of winding hair-pinned roads gouged into steeply falling hillsides large enough to be small mountains. Massive gum trees of many hues and hundreds of feet tall. Clouds of dust and the car drumming itself along the earthy corrugations of grainy, wheel-scuffed forest roads to who knew where. Or cared.

Having lived, or existed, in London, with the constant roar and boom of traffic and background noise, air conditioned computer rooms, classrooms and exhibition halls in England, Germany and Italy the previous year, all this and the events of my life; these were the clattering detritus in my brain I sought to lose in Australia's endless miles. And much deeper echoing cadences besides.

Recollected sights and smells bringing a light euphoria contrasting with the leaden aching throughout my body and mind. The more I drove, drinking in all my senses brought to me, the more my head ached. I felt a deep unease and utter weariness beyond words.

Again I saw the stars above me out of the car's window on that long Saturday night spent sleeping in the cramped back seat of the little ochre-coloured Ford Escort. Perched as I placed it amongst the gum trees atop an angled earthen bank: a flood wall beside a trickling creek.

Thirteen hours I had slept, waking to turn around and use the tilted front seats as a leg rest and stretch my body beyond the confines of the rear. In turning to straighten my legs, I saw the stars turning in the sky. Somehow they reassured me and I slept as one with narcolepsy.

How difficult it had been, even after all that time, to wake and begin to journey on again wherever the road-to-nowhere led me.

JOURNEY OF A LIFETIME

Once again, a gush of euphoria overwhelming my torpid, aching, leaden heaviness within as the road climbed ever higher, I came upon a vast and beautiful blue-tinged, tree-carpeted, plummeting valley stretching to a beckoning horizon in the sunlight. This vantage point at the summit of Mount Hotham, for a fleeting instant, magically parted the glutinous fog of my life. The visceral impact of this majestic scene burst upon me, producing indescribable aching, yearning within; wanting simultaneously to cry out in joy and deep anguish, but finding nowhere in me to form the words. My eyes devoured it as simultaneously it devoured me. Its elemental beauty transcended me to a forgotten place and plane long unvisited, like a shaft of light within a parting cloud piercing dull incomprehension of how much I had brutalised my inner worlds in work; and hidden within it from all I sought to expunge from memory.

Unwell did not describe my feeling or condition. Nearly dead came closer.

All to be quickly swept aside; wonderment deepening to concern and accelerating into stark terror with the increasing angle of descent. The warning sign daubed on rocks in blood-red paint at the summit had really meant what it said about getting into a low gear. I plunged down the staircase-steep, roughly-cut, unmade track scored into the mountainside, descending at such an alarming angle the engine's braking effect was more than nullified, and the brakes, though hard applied between incessant bends, and smelling strongly so hot were they; the car instantly lunged headlong downwards whenever they were released.

Trembling and shaking with fear from head to foot and finally, relief; barely able to control the pedals after stamping repeatedly on the brakes so hard numerous times until I thought they would fail, to slow sufficiently and get in second gear before the next bend, as the sheer-sided drop on my left snaked by, perilously close.

All this and a tumbling collage of scenery welled up to inner view in those few seconds of regaining consciousness.

I was very pleasantly surprised to have slept so log-like for a change rather than my usual fitful, shallow night-time restlessness.

It had been an anticlimax to return to my little one-roomed flat in Melbourne on the Sunday evening and my mood had mirrored the weather. Cloudless, sunny sky frowned into lowering greyness and finally rain as I approached closer to the city after my motoring idyll in the fascination of intangibly inspiring landscape.

I had yearned to continue on into some realm of fantasy, untrammelled by the need to work, such was the deeply unfulfilled urge in me.

It was reassuring too, arriving safely in the pleasant familiarity and smells of my little rented habitat at the top of the three-storey block where I stayed. I was very thankful to have survived the experience of that interminable descent whilst the engine raced, the brakes stank; smoke trailing thinly behind, yet thick enough to see its warning haze in the mirror, until finally I had got the speed down to a controllable fifteen miles-an-hour.

Head and body aching, and with the same drunken feeling of fatigue, I had fallen into bed and deep unconsciousness.

Christ! The time! I suddenly grabbed my watch and read the time. Bugger! It was nearly quarter to nine. As if on springs, I launched out of bed and into the little shower room adjacent to my living-cum-sleeping area.

As I passed through the bathroom doorway, I did my usual face inspection in the mirror. I froze and stared in stark amazement; horror, and utter disbelief. Staring back at me was the face of a corpse.

The image I saw was utterly devoid of any colour whatsoever. Not even the dirty, greyish-white complexion with red-rimmed eyes I had grown used to; it was pure white. Mesmerised, I continued to stare. Could this really be me and actually alive? For it was me I was staring at. I was intrigued and simultaneously horrified and appalled anyone could appear so utterly dead from their appearance and still have the motive power of life.

For perhaps a couple of minutes, I gazed in sheer morbid fascination and even thought of trying to take a picture of this death mask, but decided that might not be such a good idea.

Instantly, an image flashed into mind of a 'corpse' I had seen in a film about smugglers on Romney Marsh in Kent in which Peter Cushing starred. For shock impact, they had an old man in a coffin who had been terrified out of his life by seeing skeletal shapes riding horses in the dark. This was smugglers dressed in black and painted with luminous skeletal outlines producing this ghoulish aspect.

When the coffin opened full in the face of the camera, this visage of horror with popping eyes, dropped jaw and stark, pure-white countenance assaulted the eye.

That was me alright. The same pure-white skin – though mine wasn't painted at all – this was 'natural', if that was the word.

The need to get to work prised me from my morbid fixation and after a shower the 'corpse' was showing some signs of life again. Perhaps that door banging had brought me back from the dead?

It was rather odd, but within myself I actually felt better than I had done since I landed in Sydney some weeks before.

I shaved, or ran the electric face mower around my jaws, hurriedly dressed and equally bolted down some breakfast, climbed into my little hired car and drove along St Kilda Road back to the Avis rent-a-car compound close by where I worked.

No one seemed to have missed me when I got into the air-conditioned offices of the company. Or even noticed my absence.

Thankful to sink into a comfortable, padded chair behind a desk and listen to the air conditioning's soothing steady hiss, for the first time since fate catapulted me into the chaos of Melbourne's outraged customers and unfixed faults; the burning fury of their anger and brick oven summer days from scorching northern outback winds, all had subsided, and I sat in temperate comfort reflecting on the long path and the many twists and turns of my life bringing me there.

Not least the awareness, had I not been transported halfway around the world and the oasis into which providence steered me, I would be enjoying respite of a different kind, though not in the body I inhabited.

Taking Back Control:
In the Nick of Time

By the time I was thirty-years-old in 1974, I had achieved more in an intellectual sense than I ever imagined possible a decade before, but equally on a human level, I was burdened with such a weight of personal history I was barely able to function.

The great age difference between my parents, combined with a poverty stricken existence, caused family break-ups and a great deal of uncertainty in which, with hindsight, I felt like a pinball cannoned around in a gaming machine. Changing homes, schools and being fostered out by the time I was aged nine, culminated in the complete and final family disintegration with the death of my father and my mother's complete breakdown and entry into a mental hospital from which she never returned.

Its impact on me was shattering, not at all helped being fostered by relatives and living with an uncle who existed on the brink of hair-trigger emotional uproar and terrifying rages. After four years I 'escaped' to be fostered and live with a spinster aunt in the nick of time. My growth had literally been stunted emotionally as well as physically, and in the year following the move, I grew a foot in height. First, catching up with classmates who had grown three or four inches taller, then overtaking them.

The trigger for this being a spontaneous catharsis a few months after my move, quite literally hitting me like a hammer blow one Sunday evening as I was washing my socks in the kitchen sink after getting wet feet earlier that day. Without warning, it was as if I had been given a heavy blow on the back of my head. I lost all strength in my legs and were it not that I propped myself on the sink with my forearms, I would have collapsed on the floor. My face, as my aunt observed, went very pale. With very long hindsight, the accumulated repressions of the previous four years and the suppressed loss of my family came gushing out with the force and suddenness of a thunderbolt. In fact, it was like a stroke, and silently reverberated inwardly for months as I hid it from everyone and to a considerable extent, even myself. My aunt had provided a sanctuary for me before as a small child, through my own family break-ups, and, more than that, was, without doubt, the best teacher I ever had at a primary level, though not a teacher herself. Again with hindsight, I very much doubt if I would have made it to adulthood but for her. Or if I had, I would have been suffering serious health and personal problems.

For three years before I joined the Royal Air Force from school, she provided, yet again, an oasis of nurture and calm in which to mend and live a normal, boyhood life.

As an apprentice in the RAF, I enjoyed the camaraderie, training and predictability of organised, disciplined life, and the excellent academic and technical training in radio and electronics. The experience in the wider Air Force, however, was a very different matter. It was back to chaos, uproar, uncertainty and moving around well over thirty times in three years until a Bedouin's life looked positively immobile and sedentary as compared with my own. An experience exactly similar to those with my uncle, but far more vindictive and vengeful, changed me in five minutes from a keen, open, enthusiastic young technician, to detesting the uniform I wore and utterly determined to rid myself of it and the service it stood for. Which I did.

I joined the computer industry and became a factory test technician for Honeywell, building up and testing computer systems and putting them into working order before shipping them to customers.

Like previous times in my life when circumstances of calm permitted, I drank from the pool of new knowledge like a traveller dying of thirst stumbling upon a desert well. I was soon persuaded to become an instructor teaching new factory test engineers and studied with avid enthusiasm at the same time as studying electronics at night school. At one point I worked, studied seven days a week and attended evening classes three evenings a week. Like a saturated sponge, I became incapable of absorbing any more, or dealing with mathematical problems, and almost repeating the experience a few months later, so great was the pressure on me to teach and study, my head felt like a washing machine full of tin cans thundering around inside; I could not find the switch to turn it off.

TESTING TO DESTRUCTION

ALTHOUGH FRIGHTENING, I didn't care a great deal; I was master of my own destiny and I was not going to let opportunity pass me by. And anyway, it only took me a day or two to recover a semblance of normality with a few palpitations warning me to be more careful in the future and have more respect for myself. Obtaining an Ordinary National Certificate in electronics when more than three-quarters of my fellow class students failed the course made it feel very worthwhile; and I had not only learned and taught a new, complex computer system to very demanding, experienced factory engineers, but learned other hardware as well and I understood just how far I could push myself; which seemed further than most.

I moved from the factory in Scotland, where I had been until then, to the company training school in London and enjoyed the opportunity to study the hardware I had taught earlier that year even more deeply. I became known as a hard, intense worker, and woe betide anyone who interrupted my studies, which earned me no friends and made me the butt of jokes behind my back.

Having been a factory engineer whose job it was to fix problems and check out computer systems quickly and efficiently – or get the sack – I was more capable than most other instructors who lacked the same concentrated exposure. Kudos, and a position I enjoyed.

So life continued, worshipping at the altar of the great god of intellect; it did not need much insight by others around me to see I buried myself in work.

After my mother's death, finally succumbing to thirteen years of barbaric, brutal 'shock treatment' administering some hundreds of volts shocks to the temples every two weeks, and a further three years of being reduced to a compliant, drug-overloaded, stupefied robot, my aunt – her closest sister – having retired and had plenty of time on her hands to reflect on the effect of the absolutely staggering load she had shouldered without murmur or one word of complaint in all those years and at other times, finally took her own life.

I might have tested myself before striving to build my knowledge and self-esteem, and taking myself to the limits of what I could carry, but the effect of this loss absolutely tore me to pieces. Sleep, peace of mind and any semblance of sense of purpose ceased to exist. It reduced me to a shattered, broken shell.

Outwardly, I functioned after a fashion; inwardly I didn't – on any level; I was a smouldering, fractured ruin.

Requirement to teach another new, more complex, computer system did not materialise and I hid in empty classrooms studying software in the minutest detail to learn how the operating system began working from the moment the system was booted up. It took months and I filled A4 notepads from end to end whilst knotted up, unable to breathe and stomach muscles clenched solid.

As I worked away in this solitary fashion, I knew I was like a piece of metal worked this way and that, until it was brittle and if worked further, fatigue cracks appeared until finally it broke. I understood the way I had treated myself, devouring knowledge ravenously, working and studying until I reached a complete standstill, at the cost of becoming rigid and brittle in myself. And, like metal, my aunt's death had created deep cracks in me. Metal could be annealed or reduced to an unstressed state. Metalwork I loved and excelled at in school taught me this, though how to 'anneal' myself I had no idea.

Perhaps there was a way? A yearning of unfathomable depth and longing filled me for I knew I could not live out the rest of my life as I was. Either something changed and I found a way to 'anneal' myself, or my life was going to be a short one – as it was for two other instructors in the training school of exactly the same age, around the same period.

♥

Breaks came in teaching and troubleshooting systems in England, Germany and Italy but neither rest nor peace of any kind were possible; not even the food and wine of the latter country that I loved made the slightest difference. My mind ached as much as my body, until, light-headed I trembled with fatigue, but sleep was still impossible.

The only respite was training with the Territorial Army, tramping over Welsh mountains and going through a selection process to weed out those who were not fit enough and I wasn't just desperately unfit; I existed on willpower alone. Running on this human 'nitro' and in spite of all, the fear of failure that had been part of my sublimated inner drive, drove me on so even the staff running the course who were very fit, tried and failed to catch up with me.

On the last occasion, battered by wind, weather and the sixty-five pound rucksack I carried, I was blown into the air like an autumn leaf, and nearly knocked out by the make-weight bricks added to my load as I crashed back on to the wind-scoured mountain top. Later, utterly spent and incapable of rational thought, reduced to the homing instinct of an animal, I stumbled in difficult terrain and knew I had reached my limit and would never make the grade.

Finally, as the year turned and January 1974 arrived, having been asked to and foolishly accepting, out of a mixture of misplaced loyalty and defiance, I taught software to a large class of engineers; some with years of experience, others less and some with none at all. The book learning and knowledge acquired through microscopic study of the actual software I had managed to gain was no match for the level of expertise some had, whilst others found it beyond them and for the rest completely incomprehensible, and the software I had studied in such great detail was being taught by someone else anyway. Fuelled only by adrenaline, working until ten o'clock at night after each day's teaching, I was reduced to a burned out wreck, until finally I left the course and apologies were made for putting me in an impossible position.

Fortunately, in the meantime, a life saver materialised in the form of a company assignment to Australia, having been chosen to help out their customer engineers who lacked experience and were overloaded with problems they couldn't fix.

It really was a life saver, for looking at myself in the mirror each morning the greyness of my skin, blood red rims to my eyes and a face I no longer recognised and even detested, all told me what I already knew when lying brick-coshed and wind-torn on the mountain top, shaking with fear and the words; there was not much of me left alive, echoing round my brain, though also caring very little for what was.

The journey to Australia in a Pan Am aircraft flying on not much more than a wing and a prayer was, in the light of subsequent knowledge, the same as me: engines that were worn out and windscreens partially shattered with fatigue, so deeply had maintenance been cut; debts rocketing as the price of fuel leapt four-fold after the Yom Kippur war, only intensified the feeling of indescribable fatigue and disorientation.

Once there, my brief from customer service management was supposed to be teaching engineers how to fix problems, though no one bothered to tell those lower down the customer service management chain anything, and to the burden of jet lag, fatigue, disorientation and acute light-headed sickness, was added the accolade of expert-in-everything and an expectation of fixing all manner of problems – and irate customers – by myself.

Fortunately, within a few weeks the heat went out of the situation and the Australian summer in Melbourne where I had been sent. The direct help I gave and the instructing I had done helped to lift the situation to a level where computer systems got fixed properly, and on the first occasion, customers stopped threatening legal action and company salesmen became visibly less nervous about their commission statements.

Having accumulated a fairly unreasonable tally of overtime hours in the uproar and pandemonium greeting me on my arrival, a hire car was negotiated in lieu of pay. My presence was if anything, an embarrassment; my British pay being below Australian subsistence level and yet, paid just a daily expense allowance, I had fixed all manner of faults, taught senior and junior customer engineers whilst the latter were earning nearly double what I was, and acted as company pacifier to some extremely angry customers!

With the hire car, I took to the countryside of the vast continent at weekends in search of something I knew not what, except that it was all new to my eyes and I wanted to see as much as I could of it. In fact, again with long hindsight, to positively devour it all.

The first weekend was a pivotal experience; it was the first time I had been out in any countryside purely for my own pleasure rather than attempting to gain even the most moderate semblance of fitness so I might better perform for the army's benefit. Waking from the first night of peaceful sleep in many months, transfixed by my ghostly white reflection in the mirror that completely immobilised me. I was accustomed to my grey visage and red-rimmed eyes, but that was something very different; I was at once puzzled, mesmerised, appalled and fascinated at the macabre corpse staring back at me.

The term 'white-faced' does not express what I saw in my reflection. It was utterly devoid of *any* colour. Along with the coffin scene from the 'X' rated horror film, it also reminded me of pictures of Aboriginals, who, when performing certain ceremonies painted their faces pure white. I remained motionless for minutes, completely hypnotised, horrified and morbidly curious. Apart from my own eyes, there was no sign of life whatsoever in the chilling visage peering back through this death-mask. Not even the red 'eye liner' around the rims.

It was a pivot point after which health seemed to take a small but definite turn for the better.

Meeting the Ghost of Inner Being

From one extreme, my days turned from head and body scrambling over-activity to its polar opposite of almost total indolence. From being sought by many for my knowledge and skills, few if anyone bothered or cared what I did or if I was there at all.

After three months I moved to Sydney, where generally my knowledge and help was, if anything, even less sought after – except when particularly difficult faults occurred on the range of machines I knew in great detail. Determined to see as much of this huge, fascinating, spectacular and indifferently brutal land, I arranged to get a hire car for some weekends at least, rather than languish in the total indifference of those I was supposed to be helping, and aimlessly wander among the burgeoning concrete and steel mushrooms increasingly lining the streets of Sydney.

One weekend I decided to visit a town a hundred or so miles to the North of Sydney.

Making my way on excellent road surfaces towards Newcastle, the autumnal heavens opened and bucketed down with rain. The leaden, winter sky complementing my feelings. At one point in the middle of nowhere, on the side of the road I came upon a hitch-hiker; a young woman. I stopped and gave her a lift. She was lucky; it began to rain so heavily the windscreen wipers could hardly keep pace. I asked her where she was going. She said it didn't matter and wherever I was going was fine.

I thought this somewhat odd, though it was no sort of invitation to make our similar paths more closely joined. She did not care about her appearance and my nose said it wasn't hard to tell she didn't have a love affair with soap either.

JOURNEY OF A LIFETIME

She began to talk a little about her life and her current circumstances. It all seemed to be meandering chaos. She had an air of total aimlessness and resignation about her.

Trying to help, I explained what I did when life crowded in. How mood could be affected positively by going for a long walk, how food could make all the difference to one's emotional state and my general approach to life. I hoped it provided her with helpful ideas.

There was the briefest of pauses and like a brick from nowhere hitting me in the head she retorted, "I have never come across anyone so fiendishly logical in all my life!"

Stunned, I said nothing. I did not see any point in offering more well-intentioned, but as it had been received, completely alien advice. I thought it a bloody cheek that here was someone who couldn't hold a job down, had been turned out of her lodgings and exhibited all the single-mindedness of confetti in a gale, throwing back in my face what I had offered in genuine concern for another human being. I decided the conversation would remain strictly polite and this smelly person and I would part company just as soon as Newcastle was reached!

Politely, and as heavy drops began to spatter the car and fall again, I stopped as we reached the town. This was where her lift ended. She still hesitated to leave the car, making some excuse of finding a hotel and stopping for rest; I was determined to be alone.

The large brick she had thrown hit me squarely in the keyboard of my life; her words crashed around my head in jangling discord. They hurt. 'Fiendishly logical' my Life's Music Book might be, but it had helped me achieve much for myself. I knew it wasn't the apogee of existential achievement. My homespun philosophy had got me so far, but now I knew I had reached a dead end. Both words resonating with the finality I felt.

Far beyond anything I perceived at the time, the head-ringing brickbat I received connected deep inside with an unacknowledged awareness, in our diametrically opposite ways, I was exactly the same as my soap-shy passenger; outwardly and logically very organised, I was, nonetheless, as utterly aimless and confetti-like as her day-to-day life in my inner worlds. In gender as in disposition, we were polar opposites: my outer world was acutely regimented and inwardly my sense of emotional identity was as fractured, and chaotic, as her day-to-day existence, whereas inwardly, her emotional knowledge and self-possession were crystal clear and unchallengeable.

Uncannily, it was as if in some manner I was not even remotely aware of, I had beckoned fate to bring me the exact mirror image of myself to deliver a projectile straight through my window on the world, and through its brittle remnants, the elements of life's weather pelted and buffeted me in shocked surprise.

Lashed by words reverberating; smarting, echoing endlessly in dark recesses I thought beyond the reach of others to assail.

Ineluctable Destiny
and a 'Chance' Meeting

AFTER SIX MONTHS, the time came to leave and return home. Deeply uncertain about going back to all I had left behind, my health was a little better but all the underlying tensions and fragility were part of my everyday existence.

In my terms, I was still very much a piece of stressed metal with fatigue cracks all over and wondering when and how I would ever find some process by which to 'anneal' myself and become supple and malleable again in my being. Or even if.

Having experienced a mad, body-scrambling trip from England via the States and across the Pacific with Pan Am, according to Australian news bulletins it also was losing great chunks off its aircraft's wings and whole aircraft at Pago Pago island in the Pacific ocean. I was therefore determined on two things: not flying with them, and given such a chance as I had, I was going to see places I had not been able to on this once-in-a-lifetime trip.

First stop was a country whose exotic nature I had been fascinated by since childhood. New Zealand fired my imagination with its native people, geysers, flora and fauna.

The best way to see as much of this as I could for a reasonable price was a coach tour of the South Island with its spectacular scenery; everything from the Canterbury Plains roasting in summer to the chilly climes of the Antipodean Edinburgh; Dunedin and the beautiful mountains and lakes of its Southern reaches.

But before this I wanted to put the couple of spare days in the North Island to good use and see the geysers at Rotoura if I could.

No matter how or what I felt, I was determined to make the most of my own sightseeing tour and enjoy it as much as possible.

My introduction to Auckland the previous evening had been absolutely bizarre. Amongst other things, walking up Queen Street, someone over six feet six in height tried to trip me up to pick a fight, whilst two policemen strolled by just as two cars roared by in a deafening flat-out drag race, without batting an eyelid!

Beating a hasty path to the safety of my hotel room, I was glad to get out of the town as soon as I could. Surprised to have slept well, and feeling an equally unexpected sense of optimism, I set off on a crisp, frosty morning in my hired car out of Auckland southwards towards my goal.

Right on the edge of town, acting on a sudden impulse almost against my own will, I stopped for a hitch hiker I had already driven past, in a squeal of unaccustomed power-assisted brakes. A few seconds later the passenger door opened and a young man a few years my junior asked where I was going, and happy with the reply got in with his rucksack placed on the back seat.

First, it became clear very quickly the expected accent wasn't New Zealand but American, and secondly, within a few minutes, that there was some rapport and a meeting of minds.

Within an hour, I had the absolute certainty this young man had given me the key to my Holy Grail quest; how to 'anneal' my own tormented being. For the rest of the day, and all the way to Rotorua, he talked more or less non-stop about the book he had come across by a Californian psychiatrist who had developed a suitably Californian form of therapy that sounded outlandish enough to be the means by which I could change how I felt very much for the better; and in doing so to change the span of my life.

It was a conviction so strong; from having cold feet and being very sluggish, a glow suffused me from head to toe. As did alternating waves of soaring elation and utter despair for how I would make it all work – for myself.

JOURNEY OF A LIFETIME

The conversation or his near monologue ranged over many subjects; diet, the occult, shamanism, spiritual matters as well as his experiences with drugs which had nearly killed him as it had all but one of the sixteen young people of his group, and which had led him to this book and therapy promising a purging out of one's inner demons. The next day was much the same; he talked non-stop until suddenly he asked to be let out of the car in the middle of nowhere and was gone.

I flew from Auckland the following day to Christchurch and within a couple of hours, much to my surprise and jubilant satisfaction, I immediately found and bought the book my travelling friend had told me about, but dared not open it and start reading. I knew the process I would be embarking upon and the coach tour starting the next morning would not mix. This was going to be something I was sure was going to take me not a few days or weeks; nor even months, but years. If I could make it work at all.

Stopping off at Fiji for a day, I passed on to California and to Boston where I met a pen friend I had corresponded with and spent a few weeks there, then flew to Nova Scotia where an old friend I had known since the age of five lived with his wife, having emigrated to Canada a few years previously.

Stumbling Forward To …

At long last there was plenty of space and time where I could begin to read this mysterious book, seemingly promising so much so far as changing my state of being and health were concerned, as my friend's wife went off to hospital to give birth to their first child.

From hiding in sleeping pills, and sometimes tranquillisers, and eating food I couldn't taste whether I wanted it or not, I sat down at the kitchen table without any of these crutches of my existence and tried to write down what I felt in a book with blank pages bought me by my pen-turned-girlfriend.

Indescribable waves of overwhelming despair broke over me as I tried to form words to express my feelings; something I had never done before in my life. As words came to me I wrote them, whether they made any sense or not. It was like standing in front of a huge tidal wave; a sense of profound futility that what I was doing would ever change anything; and yet the words in my head and the images with them said I had burned my bridges and there was no going back. This in turn would be followed with a still small voice whispering I didn't care how long it took, I was going to change and take back control of my life which I felt was steadily sliding away within, and from me.

After about three hours I decided to start reading the book I had bought in Christchurch, called *The Primal Scream,* which seemed to make sense in as much as yelling at the top of one's lungs felt quite appealing. Something I had never done; and with the fear I felt from what I had seen my mother suffer for sixteen years at the hands of barbaric ghouls who had shocked her, lacerated her brain 'to stop her worrying' and finally drugged her into an absolute incommunicable permanent and compliant passive stupor until she gave up and died, was spur enough to want to give vent to a sense of primal outrage. Words didn't matter; and anyway, there was a mantra beginning to circle in my head I had seen in the book which said: left to its own devices, the human organism is completely self-righting and self-healing.

This was guide enough for me; I might not have a clue of where it led, but I trusted to what I had read and, most of all, to my unshakeable inner conviction it *would* lead me in the direction I wanted to go – wherever that was.

These first few days of stumbling forward, trying to find my own way; reading *The Primal Scream*, going up into the large, mostly conifer woodland and forests abounding in the sparsely populated Nova Scotian countryside, were anything but easy. Allowing my body to do what it wanted for the first time in my life rather than ruling my movements with thoughts of what I 'should' be doing and just yelling for the sheer relief it brought, seemed inadequate, aimless and even futile. Time and again though, the mantra would repeat over and over in my head: left to its own devices, the human organism is completely self-righting and self-healing.

It was like waves breaking. Futile! Crashed upon my shoreline of conscious thought and my mantra would answer in the whispering drag-back hiss to deeper levels of awareness.

And so it repeated; the sense of futility, the mantra and the determination; if it took ten years before I felt better in myself than the torpid fragile embrittled state I existed in, then so be it; for *nothing* was going to stop me.

At other times, I would tramp along dirt roads consumed with a sense of complete uselessness, worthlessness and feeling dreadful, for all I now allowed to surface I had never dared admit before. Truth to tell, I didn't know what I felt. I had never opened the door to this strange place in myself before. I accepted this disturbing endless jumble of unresolved inner conflicts, but desperate also to change how I felt; which was indescribably horrible.

Soon, a pattern became apparent. In the mornings I would generally feel at my worst, and as the day progressed this would subside as I tried to give expression to what I felt – whatever it might be – and I had no idea of what that might be except to repeat the ritual of going into the woods, making noise and thrashing around; scared someone would find me. Ending up hoarse, croaking like a constipated raven and covering myself in pine needles, moss, earth, leaves and twigs; spitting and coughing out what I had sucked in between roars and avian croakings.

Sleep; my hiding place of pill-assisted unconsciousness before shrank to a cramped and uncomfortable bolt hole where, for just a few hours, the world was kept at bay… but sleeping pills or tranquillisers were something in my past, and horrible and even desperate though I felt, they were not going to pass my lips again.

... A MASSIVE TRANSFORMATION

FINALLY, AFTER NINE days, my friend's wife came home from hospital with her new son, teetering on the verge of postnatal depression and in a very fragile state.

This coincided with my first night of better sleep for days. Feeling pleasantly serene as I woke, suddenly a gush of panic erupted within me. I squirmed and thrashed around on my bed, the movement restoring a sense of sanity. Unfortunately, the wooden floor of this flimsy little wooden bungalow acted like a drum skin; the noise of the bed's agitated feet transmitting through the house and this fragile lady, who, with the usually ecstatic beagle hound which took this as its cue to slobber all over my face in rapturous greeting, came to my bedroom to enquire on the edge of brimming tears what was going on.

A hushed, equally agitated conversation ensued a few minutes later as my friend returned from building his own bungalow nearby and it was clear I was in some trouble.

Dressing hastily, I left the house without any breakfast, and a few hostile and awkward words with the distressed wife quickening my footsteps and made my way to see my friend, and hopefully mend a fairly large hole in the fence of mutual trust.

Having ascertained it was suspected I was on drugs, I pretended to make light of it all whilst feeling very raw and vulnerable, and much to my friend's unvoiced displeasure for the help he expected me to give him – felt tile waterproofing the roof of his new home – I made hastily for the woods.

It was make or break day for me, that was very clear, and giving voice to the desperation I felt, I found the best spot I could, once again letting my body move around on the forest floor until I resembled a caterpillar chrysalis coated with its detritus and yelling whenever and whatever I felt, more or less uncaring of who might fulfil the fantasy I harboured and come rushing up with a nice 'comfortable' straitjacket and strap me in it.

Amongst all this, the words suddenly formed; catatonic schizophrenic, and no sooner in my mind than launched into the weak, autumnal sunlight peering in thin beams through the pines above me.

To this was then added: I'm not a tree, I'm me!

Once voiced, the words were like nails being driven in. I understood what my writhing around was about; I was so logical in my mentality and all I did, I was becoming statuesque and tree-like as people who finally froze into whatever pose they were placed. The realisation fascinated and mildly horrified me. It served to reinvigorate my serpent-like contortions and the output of noise.

For hours, the spontaneous purging continued. My forehead steamed and sweat dripped from my hair, my tee shirt was soaked and my vocal chords, unused to such strenuous exercise for such a long time, reduced the noise to raven level once more. Finally, and involuntarily, my body arched around away from my left side laying on my back amid the needles, leaves, moss and twigs. My left arm held up in the air bent at the elbow turned pure white and agonising pain suffused it and my left side. Gradually it subsided and I dripped and steamed my way to a feeling of peace I had not experienced in longer than I could recall.

Eventually I got up and began turning from an invertebrate in the process of transformation to regaining human form as I beat my tee shirt against a tree to dislodge the forest floor coating, shook my jeans and removed debris from my underwear, finally dressing and mopping my hair with a soaking muddy rag that was my handkerchief.

Vaulting jubilation rose in me. I knew in a blaze of invigorated circulation and defiant anger I had broken through. It didn't matter to what; I didn't care. I had an all-pervading conviction I had turned the near solid, rust encrusted key in the door to unlocking my body and myself given me by my American hitch hiking friend.

I didn't need *The Primal Scream*, its author or several thousand dollars for his god-like help as he might insist either.

The mantra whispering in my head sustaining me against the crushing weight of pointlessness and futility had become a deafening roar of utter certainty.

So began my steps along the road of self-healing.

From having no energy and little sleep for days, I went back to my friend and his helper, and began tearing the cover strips off an adhesive band used to bond the felt roof shingles together, lifting several at once, resting them heavily on my arms, mounting a ladder, for them to nail in place on the roof. In less than an hour, work progressed more than it had all day. From the noises reaching my ears from my friend and his assistant, I knew I was forgiven.

Similarly, going back to my friend's fragile spouse, the atmosphere, whilst brittle, began to soften, once I cleaned the car I had been allowed to drive around muddy, unmetalled forest roads on my own. Amid all this, I began coughing up clods of yellow mucus from my lungs that I knew had been there a long time, and my urine turned a mid brown. If evidence were needed my body knew how to heal itself, I was witness to my own resurrection, for it was coming back from being lifeless and deeply unfeeling or downright dead.

This experience has unsurprisingly remained with me in the minutest detail ever since that day at the end of September 1974 when I began climbing back up the slippery slope of diminishing health down which I had tripped and slithered a very long way.

It has taken many years – decades in fact – to understand what I achieved over a few days and in that one particular four-hour session.

I found, for example, when I stood up and decided which way 'logical' me was going to go, to get back on the path out of the wood, there was another me that said even more strongly, 'you' can go which way you like but *I'm* going in this direction, and, fascinated by this new 'voice' it led me directly to the path much further on than I otherwise would have joined it.

There could be no clearer message of just how much I had developed my intellect into a powerful aspect of my working life, but also a life-strangling brutal tyrant in the wider context of deeper being. In the process, creating a massive split and conflict in myself; expressed in the spontaneous words, catatonic schizophrenic. Fortunately, there was enough of me left to realise, as I already had, I needed to 'anneal' my being. Once a deeply yearned and longed-for state, this powerfully impelled wish had become reality in almost exactly a year from this silent, heartfelt, deeply-fervent inner prayer.

In this manner, I came, years later, to understand how sub/inner conscious works through *Think and Grow Rich* by Napoleon Hill who began the 'PMA' or Positive Mental Attitude school from which flowed the gathering avalanche of everything to do with using the power of the inner mind and being, to materialise a particular result or outcome. I had no doubt whatsoever I had saved my own life whilst two of my fellow instructors of the same age in the London training school had lost theirs. But my experience was really the first step of a journey of not just a thousand miles, but many thousands along the road of self-healing and self-transformation that still continues.

Steps on the Road to Life

Returning to England, I began taking myself out into the countryside at weekends from my lodgings in Wimbledon, and suffusing the woodlands of Dorking with the same diffuse cries of inner outrage and ones of deeply felt injustice for the endless hours I spent as a young boy, dragged off by my uncle of mercurially erupting rages to his miserable workshop at weekends when, instead of playing with friends, I was used as cheap – or often unpaid – labour, sweeping and clearing up and any menial job he wanted done. Also, as a warm human 'teddy bear' comforter and butt of his hair-trigger temper to soothe him in a business he chose but detested. Shackling himself through his own lack of confidence to a dreary rust- and mud-filled agricultural business, bulldozing his real creativity and gift for engineering and mathematical talents into the ground – and himself with it.

Driven about in his rickety old vans, smelling of oil fumes and sometimes hot water where the cooling system leaked and the pea flour, literally creating pea soup, to plug the leaking radiator, wasn't sufficient to the task.

The outrage of sitting alone hour after hour whilst he chatted to his business acquaintances, sometimes late into the evening hours and more, elsewhere rang out in fury, into the woodland, though fortunately at the time autumnal gales roared their approval through the trees even louder, blowing the noise into oblivion.

Always, the outcome was I left my place under the shrouding boughs of a holly tree feeling lighter and freer yet always too, with the same consuming impatience to be further along my path of self-clearing.

If I thought what I had learned and begun by myself would quickly lead me to full health and vigour I was much mistaken. The first steps in Nova Scotia, although beyond any doubt had saved my life, were just the echoes of my fervent prayer being answered. The most basic level of wellbeing was not something I could take for granted. My breathing was always shallow and clamped – as were my abdominal regions and stomach muscles; I was racked with tensions throughout my body. Even my ankles were locked solid; there was no flexibility in them and I would stump noisily across wooden floors, unable to articulate my feet softly down.

Nonetheless my impatience drove me to be much further on than I was. I set goals when I should be free of breathing restriction or more able to climb hills without having to pause every few yards and summon up energy for another short burst by a certain month, but this as I discovered was not how my body saw things and, impatient or not, life happened according to its own agenda and not one I might have in mind.

Which is another way of saying there was still a yawning chasm between intellect and inner being. It wasn't going to magically change. I had created a muscle-bound, life-strangling intellect and was going to have to learn how to harmonise with parts of me I had badly neglected or more actively downright brutally abused and didn't understand at all.

At times I would yell blue murder with frustration in my car with the windows wound up at some mistake I made, such as missing a turning I knew I needed to take but was involuntarily impelled to drive past. This had the effect of producing a near blackout for a second or so, so rigid were the muscles in my neck. Although that was something else I didn't realise about myself either.

Sleep, if anything, became worse; to shallow clamped breathing were added nightmares of being confronted by the IRA or some other threatening presence, and struggling with my fear to act and beat off the attack more than once resulting in the bedclothes being propelled on to the floor in a heap, kicking away at them, waking myself in the process!

I would get up in the morning feeling – with justification – I had just completed a night's work.

Having been joined by my pen friend from America who had become my girlfriend, which in hindsight had much to do with escaping the pressures of her family life and the stress she visibly carried, in *Timeout* magazine she found an advertisement for a group therapy workshop that seemed to be run on Primal lines although the word 'Bioenergetics' was used which I thought was about growing plants in a chemical solution!

Bioenergetics and an Awakening Body

The beginning of February 1975 was the first one of these we both attended, and given that the first of the month is the pagan spring celebration of Imbolc when the rate of new growth of buds and shoots noticeably accelerates, it seemed a good omen. Though like so much in those days and for many years thereafter, such synchronicity as well as the actual celebration, utterly escaped me.

The workshop, run by a psychologist named Doctor Glyn Seaborn-Jones, proved to be a watershed of development. I knew I needed other people's interaction and above all presence, to help me move on and accelerate my own clearing and healing process.

This is not to say that in the short time from September to January since I had begun pursuing my own path little had been achieved. Diametrically the opposite.

Significant body changes and improvements became very apparent; including one having great impact.

Used to the mid brown colour of my urine as my body steadily rid itself of all the 'sludge' laying dormant within, one day, prior to a visit to the local pub one lunchtime whilst at work, I was transfixed to see not the usual colour but almost black. Panic stricken for a moment, I regained control with the mantra sustaining me from the beginning: Left to its own devices, the human organism is completely self-righting and self-healing.

How did I feel? The answer was better than for a long time.

Was I in any pain? No, I most definitely wasn't. The opposite; I felt good.

The panic was not only engendered by the shock of seeing such an unexpected colour descending into the urinal but reconnected with an early childhood event when I had severely chilled my kidneys and urinated colours from bright red blood to the deep brown and blackish hue I saw, as my kidneys reacted to the shock; I bled, and slowly healed over the following month.

Reassured by my self-diagnosis, a colleague in the next stall and I departed to the pub and with other colleagues, consumed a fairly unreasonable amount of beer and felt better and better for it!

That though was only the beginning. A few weeks later, whilst giving a course in Cologne, Germany I awoke with a feeling like a pneumatic drill boring into my mid lower back. The pain was excruciating and breathing, except in gasps, almost impossible as it rose to a crescendo then subsided.

Cologne had powerful memories for me, having been there shortly after my Aunt's death the year before. It was a time of barely suppressed aching sadness and deep mourning, coupled with levels of stress beyond anything I had ever experienced.

Finding a suitable space on derelict land, I had given muffled vent the previous evening to the backlog of inner outrage bottled up from that time; the direct consequence being a large kidney stone announced its eviction from its lodgings in insistent fashion in the early hours the next day. The connection between the episode of seeing black urine before going to the pub and the kidney stone announcing its presence did not occur to me for a long time. Certainly months and probably longer. In hindsight the first event was my left kidney spluttering and flushing itself back to life again and the second, the release of a lot more body stress – and the repressed emotions that had been the force clamping my body – resulted in my left kidney further regaining its function, or at least returning to growing signs of life from near total deadness like the rest of me.

The 'feel good' factor around both these events; the release of tension before the stone began to move, caused my digestion to begin working like a house full of noisy plumbing and I was propelled back to my hotel singing utter nonsense and farting like a cart horse, feeling warm and happy, signalling my body was doing what it wanted to: heal itself.

Another positive improvement was the lymph gland up under the point of my jaw (trigeminal mandibular joint; TMJ) below my right ear. One morning around the same period in November 1974 whilst travelling on the underground to work I prodded the area as I had done so many times before and suddenly realised the lymph duct that had been completely solid from the gland to halfway down my jaw towards my chin, was now soft and pliable.

There was also a delightful feeling of inner lightness and freedom when I bounded up a flight of stairs where before my heart felt as though it would leap out of my chest, pounding like a steam hammer.

I still felt very raw and physically fragile but deliberately ran up the stairs for this delicious new feeling.

In spite of these improvements I wanted to broaden my healing horizons and the 'Bioenergetics' workshop – whatever that was – seemed to have the potential to help.

So it proved.

The simple yet effective exercises to get energy moving in the body and relate body movement to stored emotional energy were very much in sympathy with what I had intuitively done by myself. Better still, 'Glyn' as he was known, was open to people expressing what they felt in their own unique way.

Kicking away an attacker in much the same manner as I had thrown off the bedclothes, whilst letting out sound – as for example kicking out at a dog threatening to bite and intimidating the animal with a bark of one's own at the same time as thrusting a foot in its direction – I found very good. But just as it was associated with fear of being attacked I would duck, once foot and voice had thrust outwards.

My legs also felt as if strong elastic restraints were attached as I found bringing my legs and feet back in far easier than kicking out.

JOURNEY OF A LIFETIME

Which was the other half of the picture; pulling my arms in. The complete posture being both arms and legs pulled in going back to the foetal position in self-protection – just as I had once done the first time I did a parachute drop, and, warned by the instructor of this, pushing my arms and legs out so I did not tumble and wind my parachute into a useless bundle of cloth, I found exactly the same – but even more difficult to overcome fear's powerful 'elastic' on my arms and legs.

At times repelling my nocturnal attacks, I had actually tried to cry out as well as kick, so 'Bioenergetics' began to make a lot of sense.

More meditative aspects I did not like. Silence and suppression was something I had practised too much in my life and walking slowly round the church hall where we were imagining ourselves to be monks in a monastery only produced the urge to yell at the top of my lungs; which was the trigger for the exercise to descend into all manner of sympathetic expressions of pent up emotion of varying degrees of noise from other people. It reflected the complete spectrum from deep rage to deep sadness and hurt, including one young woman who cried the biggest shower of tears covering the floor at her feet I ever saw.

Whilst the kicking out exercise related to a defensive response with aggression to fend off an attack, and for me, ducking in fear as a reflex action, other exercises using feet and legs, hands and arms related to the expression of fear.

Instead of kicking or a thumping gesture with fists and arms, loosely shaking and flicking hands and arms whilst making a sound as though in a cold atmosphere; 'brrrrrrrrr', I found connected well with fear that seemed to be very close to the surface in me. It did not take much of this to produce sobbing. Flicking my feet produced either wanting to duck and pull my arms in like a boxer protecting himself from blows, or the same sobbing.

The connection of the movements and the emotions I found came and went in waves.

To say my awareness was as I have expressed it here would not be true. I did the exercises or movements and I knew what my responses were but what underlying emotion was connected and expressed was not clear for some considerable time. In a short while these movements became satisfyingly familiar and in the longer run the awareness of what emotion was linked with them came clear in its own good time.

Not that this altogether satisfied me, for impatience was my constant spur.

It did not take long for emotional convention to become apparent; men were more inclined to express anger and women fear.

One exercise most women disliked and showered Glyn with requests to opt out, was pushing against a partner.

Facile though it might appear, it had both obvious as well as subtle aspects.

Many would begin timidly pushing; flat hand to flat hand held up at chest/shoulder height. Often fixed smiles accompanied this. Eventually though the social veneer would be broken by the more determined partner backing their opponent into a wall; a chair or another person, and the veil of niceness would crumble in genuine – and sometimes long stored – resentment; which was the whole point of the exercise.

Culturally, we tend to politely accept being pushed around, whether physically but more usually, emotionally. Either from childhood having little choice but live with feelings engendered by an overbearing or bullying adult, or in the hurly burly of adulthood, pretending it is of no consequence whilst seething inside.

Silence too was often the initial emotional posture, which resulted in the silent partner being easy to push around as their breathing was clamped and energy throttled with it.

Control freaks also quickly identified themselves by forcing their fingers in between their opponents instead of maintaining hands flat. Getting a better grasp of their opposition was as much emotional as physical.

The exercise also demonstrated how much energy someone had in their body – upper and lower. Whilst being able to push hard with my arms, my legs lacked the strength to resist a really determined and strong partner.

In spite of my diminished amount of strength as compared with some years before, I could still push most people more than get pushed around myself and enjoyed doing it.

It took about three years before I liberated enough energy to become an equal match for a powerful Australian who also resorted to 'cheating' in that if he couldn't budge me statically he would bounce up and down on his feet, which meant if I remained stiffly anchored to the floor he could agitate me off balance and push me as much as he wished. I quickly learned to bounce in time with him and we became respectful equals.

The stiffness, rigidity and lack of movement demonstrated attributes of character; hence as in the exercise, so in life. Being flexible and making changes of balance reacting to those induced by someone else was as much about changing my 'balance', adapting to altered circumstances in my life.

Consequently, what from the outside seemed to some as just an exercise in brute force, ignorance and aggression was nothing of the kind as it quickly exposed life and character postures, as well as the more immediate unlocking of energy clamped so as to appear 'normal', pleasant, and terribly 'civilised'.

At times, doing these simple limb movements of the different exercises, I felt a compulsion to disperse an uncomfortable sensation between my shoulder blades and would reach back over with an arm as if to pull it off or sweep it aside and rid myself of it. It would also be accompanied by tramping my feet to aide the dispersion of discomfort.

One woman thought me very amusing, and seemed to enjoy indulging her voyeurism, rather than sort out her own body which was completely split between lower and upper halves of which she was utterly unaware; expressing giggling pleasure in my movements as the behaviour of a seven-year-old having a tantrum. The deep significance of these actions and the energy associated with them did not begin to become clear for nearly twenty years and thousands of hours of work dealing with layer after endless layer of stored energy until it emerged and itself took many hundreds of hours to unblock, release and integrate. Indeed, the looming shadow of it all, whilst continuing to diminish, remained almost up to the time writing this book ceased; more than forty years from this event to its final resolution and departure.

The significance of it all originally was not even remotely apparent to me. From the beginning, completely on my own, I was content to follow my own path, conviction and gathering experience, and frightened voyeurs such as this initially registered unspoken resentment for their lack of courage to go below their shallow intellectually-dominated avoidance of fear; and its brittle put down. Ultimately she was the loser. This though was still not the complete picture, for there was yet another turn of an upward spiral of knowledge which brought me back to the original event thirty-three years later. Yet ultimately none of this expresses the depth of significance of this instinctive movement.

For in it is ultimately contained the key to and outcome of whether in later life we suffer diminishing energy and strength and the myriad of symptoms, conditions, syndromes and diseases of 'old age', or life lived in a body with all its faculties in very good working order: strong, vibrant and healthy.

Group Therapy; Truth and Denial

There was, though, only so much I could do on my own. Anger and irritation might be my response when others picked on some aspect of how I was or worked but being in a group greatly accelerated the process of becoming aware of and dismantling my inner barriers.

In interludes between activity, people stood individually with Glyn and were introduced to the group sitting on the floor in front of them and encouraged to say what they wished to change about themselves, their lives, patterns of behaviour or recurring situations they found themselves in, aspects of their relationships and generally anything they felt they wanted to explore and improve.

In working on some aspect of what they wished to change it often occurred that some response would be triggered in a member or members of the group.

One young woman stood up and was encouraged to express herself on some issue she wished to work on and with hesitating speech responded.

At the same time, very audibly, her stomach began making noises. No one said anything though, and being completely new amongst people who mostly knew each other quite well I kept silent, wondering, if this was about opening up and being honest about oneself with others, why no one made any comment or asked a question about the significance to her, of the powerful gut contractions all could hear.

Honesty, it appeared, had clear bounds and there was a tacit code of group behaviour and protocol.

It took exactly seven years to the day, and the last time I attended a group, for the same situation to arise; the same lady to stand up and work on some aspect, and exactly the same 'gurrumphing' emanating from her abdominal regions, to know the hesitating speech and gut strangled sounds were the unspoken expression of deep fear. Yet *still* no one said a word. At which point I knew I had reached the stage where I could trust my own perceptions and needed to work on my own.

But at the first group I attended, as with so much else then, the significance of this was lost to me. Though not forgotten.

I, too, had my turn at being introduced and briefly explained some of the work I had done on my own, including getting my left kidney to work, which intrigued a few people. I was also invited to do some self-assertion and the more aggressive movements such as kicking out and making a loud yell, which resulted in my 'elastic band' response ducking and pulling my leg and arms back in as fear surfaced.

A voice in the group seated on the floor whispered to the next person, "He doesn't know what he wants."

The whisper wasn't meant to be heard. I felt like retorting: "Oh yes he does; but he's frightened!" Though decided against it and settled for knowing what I felt; fear being the overriding and controlling factor.

Working one to one, one person actively working on what they wished to express, triggered by some interaction, recent or in the past, sometimes a long way back, the other person would simply be an attentive presence, offering no advice nor becoming embroiled in any way with what the partner was working on or expressing.

The only way the passive supporter might offer any help was to suggest the active one ask themselves a question, e.g., Can I suggest you ask yourself the question; am I clamping my breathing?

This could be accepted or rejected by the active partner.

Having only worked on my own until then, I felt nervous and awkward, especially if my session partner was female. I was good at yelling; but I seemed to be running out of the desire to do this, not least because my head ached having done a lot of it. Itself an indication something had changed and I needed to move on. It was becoming clear to me I was back at fear again but didn't know how to deal with its expression. At the end of the first day I felt completely spent. I ached with the physical exercise and the relationship between body tensions and emotional blockages associated with them. My tee shirt was damp and my hair a tousled mop also from the sweat dripping off the ends.

Just as I had found working on my own, towards evening time, the need to express diminished. My body and inner world perfectly regulated what I needed and wished to work through. Once completed and energy expended doing it, like a vessel being drained dry, my body and conscious level energies once depleted could not be forced into further expression without it being completely faked.

Again, the mechanics driving this were merely something I accepted at the time, but conscious mind and body are microscopically limited compared to the subconscious which once the body is re-energised in rest and sleep delivers more uncompleted experience to conscious levels. If only we will let it!

The sad thing is our society makes a fetish out of using drugs to suppress the natural healing capacity and characteristics we all possess.

The group workshop second day repeated the first with the great exception that almost any movement I made was either painful or near impossible to begin with. It took quite a long time doing the same simple movements, exercises and releasing my inner 'knots', for energy to get moving. The previous day had stirred and opened up parts of me not used or allowed expression in years. If ever.

It called to mind sitting in an empty classroom, decoding instruction by computer instruction, the workings of an operating system and my deep yearning to go beyond the racking tensions of my body; to 'anneal' myself so it was supple, filled with energy as once I had been and with the knowledge and experience of all I had gained.

The great acceleration the workshop provided my efforts to achieve this brought for a moment feelings of relief and peace. I knew I was on the right path as continual body improvements; sometimes small, others more significant, continued to occur.

The second day I found a lot quieter than my pent up noise of the first. The desire and need to give voice to the backlog of pressure inside had been dissipated; I had moved on to a new phase, and beginning to talk whilst doing one to one sessions, which still felt to some degree futile, but that was the only thing that felt right, so as ever; that was what I would do and see where it led me.

Workshops occurred every few weeks. It was the same format each time but never the same twice.

These though were only part of the picture, for I needed the influence of nature around me and in particular the energies I picked up from them.

Still very fresh in my mind was the memory of the fascinating experience in Nova Scotia when I knew I could heal myself and part of me decided it/I was going off to join the woodland path where 'it' *knew* to go, rather than the logical part of me – like computer instructions – by following directions, would lead me back to it where logic said the path had to be.

This spontaneous process I called 'walking the dog', or more correctly being taken for a walk by the dog. For just like a dog running this way and that, pulling on the lead to dart hither and thither, logical me was the master holding the lead and the other part driven by senses alone, was the 'dog'.

I would wander about in woods and fields and find myself inexplicably drawn to certain spots, often compelled to walk in a spiral. It was both intriguing and simultaneously irritating and frustrating, simply because there was no apparent reason to do so and I could not sense what had drawn me there.

Only after I learned to begin using my hands as sensors did I derive some satisfaction from the process. I could feel sensations; difficult to define, but approximating to a 'buzz' of energy; sometimes stronger as if I had brushed against the needles of a pine tree. Once on the spot, all my body wanted to do was stay there.

It began to dawn on me that it wasn't just dogs who were led by their senses; cows, sheep and other animals did the same, and chose particular spots to rest on for no apparent (logical) reason.

Energy seemed to be the only explanation and the more I 'let the dog take me for a walk' the better I became at detecting the energy, but it was still a frustrating process because logical me was also like a dog with an itch; I couldn't stay still for long, and what I could see made me curious to investigate, clashing with the ruminative instinct of deeper parts.

One thing was very clear though; there were very distinctly different parts of me that logic did not apply to.

In the earlier days, I still felt the equally irritating need to be in contact with the ground – especially in the region of my shoulders – when an urge to release energy and let out noise occurred. This went on for more than two years until I began individual therapy sessions and in the first one, explaining this was something I did as I lay on a mattress, I suddenly realised – as I said at the time, "I think I want to get out of my body!" It wasn't a logical deduction; like a bubble surfacing from deep in a pool, the realisation popped into consciousness, the connection and the words to explain it instantly there.

The therapist observed I didn't realise the extent of what I had just said. True! But then I hadn't had a chance to test it out either.

The next time I felt the desire out in the countryside to release 'pressure', yell and make noise, I no longer needed to writhe about on the ground.

As I had come to understand before this, not long after the first group weekend in early 1975, there were two ways my inner/sub conscious had of getting 'messages' through. The first was a sudden 'pop' of awareness from nowhere and the second I called the carpet slippers approach. Very quietly, like someone stealing up close in noiseless footwear, awareness would gradually dawn of a presence as if someone was quietly hovering close by, wanting to speak but unwilling to interrupt in any way.

In either case these messages from my inner conscious were not the end; they were only the beginning. These were harbingers of something new. In the case of realising I wanted to get out of my body, the reasons why were not long in following on behind. There was so much hurt – physical – but infinitely more so emotional hurt; in turn locking up my physical body, I simply wanted to remove 'myself' from this. 'Myself' I also learned was some deeper, other part of me.

My need to squirm around like an earthworm on uppers, I also realised, was driven by deep fear.

Once all this even remotely became clear, that companion of fear – like dock and nettles growing together – anger, soon began to blaze.

It was not something on the surface. This came from a well of suppression so deep down it felt exactly like tapping oil without a 'blow-out' valve to halt the erupting gusher. This was not an ordinary release of strong irritation at some event. The feeling was exactly like a screaming geyser of unstoppable force and was as nearly disturbing to me as whoever was on the receiving end.

It was not an easy time to live through and deal with all of this. It was difficult in the extreme. My girlfriend, having become my wife, it was clear we had little if anything in common; except suffering, which was no basis for relating, though as I was to discover, that was by no means the full picture.

One occasion was a salutary experience. Driving one evening with my wife beside me along a stretch of road I travelled every working day and knew the tricks people got up to, I came to a large island created in the road where a junction was on my side of it. The island split the carriageway so oncoming traffic could wait safely in between the two flows until the way was clear to turn into the junction.

For some yards at this island the road widened into two vehicle widths which people used as an overtaking area to pass slower traffic on their nearside before the road narrowed after the island.

About to pass two slower cars, suddenly the one nearest in front on my left leapt into my lane so as not to be boxed in. Having almost been broadsided before in this way, I was ready for such a move; nonetheless, at the speed the car moved out and the scant inches between us, my wife almost landed on me in the driver's seat, terrified.

It triggered the geyser of deep fear-driven anger within and at the next traffic lights I got out, ran to his car, opened the driver's door and asked him what the hell he thought he was doing and half thumped, half slapped the side of his head.

He switched off the engine and proceeded to unwind out of his car like a clock spring until he released all six feet, five inches of his fully upright height! He seemed calm except for the fact he was white faced, and shaking with suppressed rage – as my wife noticed. Looming over me he then announced he was a police officer, produced a warrant card and said he was going to arrest me! Anger morphed into fear in the blink of an eye and hardly comprehending it, I read the card, disbelieving who he said he was.

He told me my behaviour was disgraceful, and repeated he was going to arrest me, at which fear burned back into anger once more. In my turn I blurted out he was driving so as to endanger life, and explained the effect he'd had on my wife and had I not been ready for such a dangerous manoeuvre he would certainly have caused an accident that would almost certainly have killed someone.

With an indefinable flinch in his posture, he mouthed threats about recording my behaviour and, clearly chastened, went back to his car, and I to mine in a similar state.

This episode brought to full consciousness this well of deep stored fear-driven anger and gave me clear understanding of its power; and forming a police blue 'blow-out' valve in myself to exert some kind of restraint over it! But it took many months to work through this before it subsided and life threatening actions could no longer trigger such a response simply because the well of unexpressed emotion no longer existed. At least, to the same extent.

Signs Along the Way

During these early years there was more than one theme to be worked on.

With the benefit of long hindsight, 'more than one theme' does not adequately or correctly describe the process. The central unchanging theme was reducing the immense amount of bodily stress severely limiting any feelings of wellbeing and the equally immense amount of emotional stress accumulated as life progressed, sublimated and suppressed for years or from its beginning.

Dealing with it all was like dealing with a bush fire. So much pressed for expression and resolution it was an exhausting, almost non-stop process; seemingly resolving disparate things but it was still all the same, 'fire'.

Yet again at this stage as I worked through various events of my life I was not clear this was so. However, in a vague way I had a feeling what I was doing was perhaps like the movement of ocean waves.

There was the disturbed surface with small wavelets which formed and were soon gone. Then there were the major waves of the ocean swell and I also wondered if there was an even longer swell, not detectable by normal senses.

Once again the perspective of many years provided clear answers; what, at the time were just things to be worked through and the emotional – and no less physical – energy released, were connected with fairly recent experiences, or going back to my bizarre childhood of continual upheaval and emotional chaos.

These equated to wavelets or individual ocean waves but there was indeed a much longer oceanic heave; that of birth experience.

The conviction exists now though, there are even longer ocean movements not limited by the life we are living.

My process of healing felt like a slow plod once I had got going and used to it. There were no visible miraculous changes I sometimes saw in others. The young woman who covered the floor at her feet with tears at the first workshop, changed in a few months from a gaunt-faced, chisel-jawed, thin, smouldering-eyed person of brittle temperament to an absolute beauty whose eyes shone softly with life as did her skin, reflecting the startling changes throughout her being.

If I set aside my impatience though and paused to reflect, changes in my body and other improvements were readily apparent. My hair began growing faster, straightened out as it had been years before and the layer of oily skin on my scalp I could dig my fingernails into but was not dandruff, started to diminish. Digestion began to improve instead of food sitting inside me like a swallowed brick. The freedom in my chest and feeling of lightness when I ran up stairs presaged a slow rise in energy, though from a very low level.

On occasion I still received clear, even powerful, 'reminders' of how my inner self felt in the form of palpitations. The first and most memorable felt like the recoil of a howitzer; with a great thump my heart heaved in my chest. It didn't hurt and after a sensation like an elephant dancing about on springs, heart beats jumped around then settled back to normal again.

It aroused a strange contradiction of vague concern and pleasant curiosity in me. Once again the messages contained in these autonomic shocks and tremors were, on a conscious level, merely something I was an observer to within my own body, glad their effect was transitory and happy my heart regained its measured beat!

The real significance and clear understanding of what was taking place only became clear as months became years and then decades as the path to my inner self changed and broadened from being a tenuous picking of my way, like clambering through a monumental junk yard of vast proportions, steadily opening up as more and more 'junk' disappeared. Creating first a path, then a thoroughfare, the piles of junk continuing to diminish, leaving wider and wider access, eventually allowing movement in any desired direction.

The palpitations were the piles of junk being disturbed and suddenly falling. As the junk diminished so did the force of them. And just as diminishing piles of junk revealed a view in what was once chaos, insight into my inner processes and world also expanded and clarified as time and perspective lengthened.

If I did deep breathing, instead of quickly reaching a point where my body went through some crisis after which I felt dreadful, I reached a natural point where I became flooded with oxygen where it was sensible to stop. Gradually too I noticed there was less tension in my arms, which after a while ached with the gradual release.

Sleep too regained some degree of normality instead of nights when my inner world resembled a box of fireworks into which a spark had fallen, though I still had uncomfortable, sleepless times; my breathing was shallow, and 'IRA' dreams occurred as yet more fear signalled its insistent presence. Gradually too my car learned how to go on its own rather than being so tensed up it felt like I was willing the thing to move!

All these things were apparent by the spring and early summer of 1975 and telling someone else I had seen at the group workshops, her face had changed and lightened a great deal, I discovered she thought the same of mine.

The Healing Power of Nature

THE COUNTRYSIDE I loved to get out in and find out what the 'dog' had in store for me was a regular ritual – if at times not an outright obsession. Sometimes at weekends when a lot seemed to be bubbling up from within after a week embroiled in computer software; a job once seen as a holy grail but found it a bitter cup to drink from. I hated it with a passion and ended up in knots, barely able to breathe, chest aching and stomach like a clenched fist, I would get in my car and go from Twickenham where I lived, to Effingham forest and other parts, release and express whatever I felt sometimes in sound and fury, others more quietly and often 'taking the dog for a walk,' letting my body and its inner senses take 'me' where 'it' wanted and often ending up just gazing out over the beautiful woodlands and countryside.

This might be once or twice in the day, but the record was five or six times.

Regaining health and strength were an absolute priority; the same burning ambition drove me as when I sat down in late September 1974 in my friend's house in Nova Scotia and tried to put words to what I felt. Though optimism and an unstoppable determination had grown strong roots and green shoots from the seed and once barren soil of utter hopelessness, and with the following year's spring, steadily continued.

The echoes of my experiences with the Territorial Army still reverberated within and the Welsh mountains over which I had marched, slithered, been gale-blown into the air and struggled over, a bare eighteen months before, were like a magnet and I revisited the routes I tramped;

wondering where I found the strength to do it and how it had not put paid to me. Without doubt the rugged scenery administered some form of healing and inspired as much as its ferocious weather reduced me to teeth chattering fear, thrown around in its colossal indifference. The visit, as with so many things I measured myself against in my consuming impatience to free and heal myself, contrasted with my literal and metaphorical headlong slippery downward path in wild autumn and the gentle, if fragile, leisurely upward climb in soft springtime mists.

Nature gave me something I got from nothing and nowhere else, no matter what all the exercises, movements, regimes, disciplines, doctrines, therapies and wisdom from others I might soak up; find useful and worthwhile.

Connection to the earth I slowly began to appreciate was a power I needed and could tap; in fact if I don't get it something in me begins to die like a plant denied the sun's light and natural surroundings.

As I progressed during this period 1975 for four years, a trend emerged I was curiously blind to; I relied more and more on the outdoors and nature for its healing power.

A part of this even less obvious to me, was literally getting my hands in the earth, something repeated a number of times to the present day. Something a clairvoyant once told me to do I hadn't taken much notice of, but the 'dog' levels of awareness of my inner being – as always – had a lot more wisdom than my superficial outer consciousness. There has clearly been a pattern when beginning a new cycle in my life when under great stress I have instinctively sought to 'get my hands dirty' and into mother earth.

It finally dawned over years, earth *is* actually healing in the most direct sense.

In my experience and view, archaeologists would do a lot better than the intellectual head-scratching indulged in about barrows and stone 'tombs' of all kinds shapes and sizes, if they began getting inside them; giving their intellect an enema and staying there for some time; hours / days and seeing how their perceptions changed instead of regurgitating other people's intellectualising as ritual this or religious that and treating them as some inexplicable arcane oddity.

Without doubt mother earth and what grows out of it provides human kind and the animal kingdom with sustenance unseen, but more than this the earth's energy can be accessed and assimilated using underground or covered chambers to tap into deeper levels of consciousness; once the parrot farm of intellectual chatter and all the rubbish of our culture's superficial 'sticking plaster' knowledge is stilled, there is awareness transcending thought we are all capable of using as a real resource in our lives; as all aboriginal or 'primitive' native cultures know very well, and use to their direct benefit.

During this period also, starting with my routine of 'dog' walking, it steadily developed into being able to physically feel the energy given off by trees, plants and ley lines, the latter giving me a great surprise one day.

One spring weekend in 1979 I attended an interesting workshop run by a Native American named Sun Bear; a powerfully built man who shone and radiated with all the wisdom of his race.

The experience was as much worthwhile for what it stirred sympathetically in those of us who attended as for the rituals performed and the wisdom shared with everyone. Indeed, in hindsight the perception is it was his powerful aura producing sympathetic responses in the rest of us.

In talking to someone about what I did to find a ley line, another man close by overheard me saying I held out my left hand and swept across in front of me to pick up these straight lines of energy where I felt one might exist, and having done so how it produced a definite 'buzz' in my hand by which I could follow the line's course.

The man quietly suggested I might like to try holding my left hand on the base of my spine and sweeping across in front with my right.

Somewhat resistant and sceptical, on my next foray out into the countryside, nonetheless, I felt bound to give it a try. I walked along a sunken path overhung with trees emerging on to open heathland with bracken and brambles to its raised right side. Coming to a point I suddenly sensed energy coming directly from my right. Turning ninety degrees to face this, making sure my left hand was firmly on the base of my spine; right hand out in front, I got the shock of my life.

The shoes I wore were slip-on town ones, with smooth composition soles giving no grip on the dry grass and bracken, yet as if gripped by a powerful hand I was jerked up the bank through brambles and bracken, finding myself similarly yanked along once on top. Though my shoes gave no grip, making it difficult to walk on the flat, let alone climb a steep bank, this made no difference. I was invisibly hauled up it and along through bracken and brambles tearing against my trousers and ankles with gathering speed as if hitched to the end of an invisible rope.

The ground in front of me dropped steeply away a few yards further on and I seemed about to be heading for over halfway up a large Douglas fir through mid air. Amazed, fascinated, but very concerned by this time, I hastily retracted my right hand and removed my left from above my behind, uncoupling from my rapid invisibly powered progress which instantly ceased!

With bleeding scratches on my ankles and legs through my socks and trousers which were snagged and ripped, testifying to the force with which I had been pulled, I retraced my involuntary steps and slithered in my shoes down the bank to the path.

Unwittingly I had tapped into this power, though I never tried again to find out how.

Somewhere in a book by John Michell (*The New View Over Atlantis*) I recalled people in ancient times reputedly 'flying' along ley lines or the old straight tracks following them, which the Romans used with the roads they built, or rather renewed, pre-existing the invaders by centuries if not millennia.

This I verified for myself, finding the course of an old Roman road and criss-crossing it numerous times to make certain what I felt was no isolated fluke in one localised spot. Having discovered the same definite buzz of energy, not just in my hands but body also, I then walked along the road's course; the sensations remaining constant.

As with everything, the more I practised, the better I became at sensing and feeling these energies. The most powerful experience of ley line energy was at Glastonbury Abbey where the great ley line (called the Michael And Mary Line) running from St Michael's Mount in Cornwall to Bury St Edmunds in Suffolk – and which the A30 originally followed – passes right through the centre of the Nave and continues up Dod's Lane on the Eastern side. 'Dod' in this instance being short for 'Dodman' – the old name for surveyors and the two headed stick used in straight lines; measuring between points, looking like a snail's antennae and giving this sobriquet to surveyors from its country name of 'Dodman'.

Venturing out on to the raised viewing walkway erected across the Western end of the Nave, one day and reaching the centre, it felt as though I was being compressed front to back in my chest, so strong was the sensation, as I turned to face up the Nave.

Outer World Versus Inner Being

Although to some, perhaps many, healing might be about the narrow issue of feeling physically well, comfortable in their body, and content to jog along in their life, this did not satisfy me.

The more I healed and cleared myself, the more 'isms' and therapies appeared to me about erecting implicit barriers at the limits of their particular systems of knowledge.

Or as I answered a relative who questioned why Primal therapy had no rapport or any empathy with religion; metaphysical or esoteric aspects of being, it seemed to me it had its feet too deep in shit to see the stars above its head. John Lennon's song 'Imagine' being a direct consequence of his exposure to and experience of Primal Therapy.

Similarly, from the mid-seventies I became an avid reader of Carlos Castenada's books of his experiences with a Mexican Indian shaman he called Don Juan.

It became clear to me the Indian possessed abilities, knowledge, and experience utterly alien to Castenada's heavy academic intellectualism. Knowledge for one was based in direct experience of having done something and following rules producing certain repeatable effects, whereas for the other it was acquired through intellectual study.

I soaked up these books and the stories in them like water on parched earth, yet people I spoke to who had read them treated them with complete scepticism, as a pack of lies, incomprehensible gobbledygook, or descended into blind rage whilst reading, tore up the book and threw it away.

At the very least, being able to find certain spots of ground my body felt attracted to and able to feel ley line energy attested to real knowing having nothing to do with intellect.

Once again, the significance of all this was only a faint glimmering at the time. During these early years I continued to work in the computer world in software and in moving from fixing problems and supporting software to giving courses and instructing I immersed – even submerged myself – in crushing levels of technical convolution and amounts of it.

During one course I gave of two weeks' duration and gruelling complexity, by the end of the third day, whilst setting the class's evening study I paused from going through the assignment and looked up to address them directly. My gaze was met with a universal reflection of how I had looked whilst in Australia; grey faces and red rimmed eyes. But, the faces before me were the reflections of my inner self, and probably my own face also.

When the course was finished I took a long weekend to begin recovering from its effects; its reputation renowned for leaving instructor and students alike in a state of pronounced mental and physical fatigue, if not outright shock.

In a dream on the first night I saw a small dilapidated rowing boat lying in a silted up creek. The bottom had rotted away in part and there were the remains of an old tarpaulin in it. As I saw this image, little furry animals scurried in it and I tried to hit them with a thick book I held between fingers and thumb. Pinned under my left thumb was a grubby piece of paper on which mathematical symbols were scribbled. Yet again, although I was incapable of seeing the obvious message contained in the dream for a long time, there could hardly be a clearer one. The mouldering little boat had a lot to do with my inner nature; my vessel of life in fact, and the little furry animals with my feelings and emotional self and deeper aspects of being.

The book and the piece of paper had everything to do with intellectual knowledge which I was using as a weapon to beat my true nature with. If finding a way to heal myself had brought and continued to bring so many changes in me for the better, it still had an immeasurable distance to go before the equally great rift within me even remotely had the prospect of being healed and my vessel of life restored to anything like seaworthy condition.

Other dreams triggered by reading Carl Jung's book, *Dreams, Memories and Reflections*, had the same message; in one seeing two serpents with heads and bodies cobra-like sticking up out of the earth. I threw rocks at them whereupon they instantly retracted back into the ground and disappeared.

Manifestly I was in conflict with my inner self and causing gratuitous damage by what I was doing in my intellectual pursuits.

In an earlier period of particularly intense working through long buried emotions I had carried since the uproar and chaos of my childhood, the clearing of them also brought intense dreams of a similar theme.

This time my 'vessel of life' was a vehicle of life; and cars, as this symbol appeared on many occasions.

In the first of a series of dreams, I found myself following old rutted tracks curving round to my left. A few feet further on the tracks disappeared where saplings and scrub grew showing long disuse of this area. Next to the scrub was a dilapidated ramshackle old garage and through a gap I was able to see an old car inside.

As I looked, I saw the car was not empty. Someone was sat in the driver's seat. Focusing on its face, I saw the flesh was hanging off it but the eyes were still alive. It was a scene straight out of a horror film with the same ghoulish impact, and I awoke instantly; appalled, shocked, hot and out of breath.

The next dream following a night or two later was of a bandaged person with blood seeping through the makeshift dressings in a ramshackle wooden lean-to, acting as a sort of 'hospital' ward. This person or body seemed to have been rescued or retrieved from somewhere and rather surprisingly recovering – or showing signs of life in these primitive circumstances.

Other dreams followed but these first two marked the point where some near dead aspect of my inner self was remarkably regaining some semblance of returning life.

It should not be thought the words 'working through' and 'clearing' related to some vague, airy fairy intellectual meanderings of the mind in order to deal with long-stored effects carried from many years earlier.

'Working through' meant expressing a lot of sublimated outrage, anger, hurt, sadness; in fact the complete spectrum of human emotions which were the 'lid' to my inner aspects of self that had suffered as a young boy. Though definitely, there were also aspects relating directly to the crushing intellectual abuse I heaped upon myself as all this surfaced and found resolution.

These first few years of finding my own way of healing myself were a reflection of all I had learned and experienced in my life until then, and all the heritage of suppression that went with it.

Once I found my own path in the woods of Nova Scotia I became like a coiled spring released from the tensioning effect of upbringing and cultural indoctrination I absorbed through my parents, school, education and training I had undergone.

The determination to 'anneal' and heal myself wherever it might lead me meant no one 'ism', therapy, wisdom of whatever shade or flavour could keep my undivided and devoted attention for long. They all created more questions than they answered, and the mantra I carried within me – left to its own devices the human organism is completely self-righting and self-healing – never left me.

It was and always has been my touchstone of reality. Unless I could feel what was being said, taught, put across and imparted – and most of all – fitted together with what felt right to me I would keep on searching until, like some vast jigsaw puzzle, I found the piece I wanted to place where it fitted naturally without forcing and where I wanted it fitting into.

JOURNEY OF A LIFETIME

It did not make for a conventional or an easy life.

The constant theme of all this was constant change, which in a marriage meant that if both did not share the same outlook inevitably cracks would begin to appear. In any case I had had the uncomfortable awareness when I emerged from the church having got married, I had probably made a big mistake. As time passed and changes in me steadily, and sometimes rapidly occurred, the strains increased until the marriage broke.

If one person changes in a relationship and the other wishes it to remain the same, that one will make greater and greater attempts to maintain it as they see it and need it to be. There was without a doubt a bond between us with far deeper roots than I realised, but like everything else in those times, the full significance of events were not clear at the time they occurred; but more and more connections made as time passed, so it was with my marriage.

Its end became a spur for a huge amount of clearing, healing and growth, much of it painful, all of it very worthwhile and the end of the year as compared with its beginning were like night and day, or, being fascinated by aircraft and aviation from a very small child; an image that stayed constantly with me that year; from a very low ebb, like a fragile wood, canvas and wire biplane transmogrifying into Concorde as it rolled with increasing momentum down the runway of my life, such was the gathering pace of my headlong efforts as the year progressed.

Images like this, whilst metaphors, actually occurred in dreams. One series began with a tank clanking and squeaking its way along a track beside me in full 'technicolour' and sound, and as the days progressed so did the images becoming faster and faster until finally ending up with Concorde itself.

Insight into its meaning came a few weeks later. It had to do with the uproar and chaos of childhood events interspersed with periods of relative calm, but these swings becoming more pronounced and more frequent, until like Concorde what had been my sense of childhood disappeared, like it taking off over my house in Twickenham close to Heathrow with a head splitting roar leaving nothing but an echo in a final tumult of equally personal 'head splitting' uproar which was all I was left with. All sense of family and self gone just as the plane and its cacophony faded, leaving only the memory of its passing.

Not only were there the events referred to above; stark dreams triggered by a great deal of work on the emotional level – which as my own efforts from the very outset showed me and Bioenergetics reinforced – to manipulate the body is to manipulate the emotions and vice versa. But as time and experience progressed finding myself in realms I never imagined when I began.

Quite apart from the work leading directly to the dreams from which I awoke shocked, hot and breathless, even earlier in the year as buds on trees and daffodils began to burst, I gave a programming course away from the main company training centre, to students based in Gloucester. Although much more relaxed and less pressured, my teaching day often ended with my stomach in knots.

To relieve this and get to know the town, I wandered around the streets after the day's teaching; not that there seemed to be much worth seeing other than the cathedral. Near to where I stayed was a very ordinary street of terraced houses, and walking past them I slowed down at one, feeling there was something eerie, dark and foreboding about it. It was a definite and insistent sensation in me, but I pushed it to one side and out of mind; dismissed it as fantasy and forgot about it until after writing about these events. Then, gradually over several days, the recollection returned like the insistence of a dripping tap as did the names; Fred and Rosemary West. The house that gave me the creepy, vaguely uneasy feelings was in Cromwell Street and the Wests lived at number twenty five, from 1972 until police began digging up the garden in 1994 and finding bodies. Having read what took place there I know what my feelings were, though only now as with so many other things then and since, I was incapable of consciously connecting up what I sensed. Now it is clear what I registered all those years ago but blotted out; horror, sickness in the pit of my stomach and utter revulsion.

Walking past only seemed to deepen my abdominal distress …

My early practice of finding a suitable spot and letting out the pent up agony in sound and squirming around on the ground to release the racking tensions in my body was something I no longer felt the inescapable need to do as once I had, and the lack of inclination was reinforced by wet ground and cold, dark evenings.

There was no denying though, the painful knot in my gut, and driven to find some means of dealing with it. Instead I discovered, kneeling on the driver's seat of my car, having found some out of the way place, and leaning over the seat back with the top of it pushing into my knotted abdomen (in the days before head restraints) was the only way I could gain any relief, for the discomfort broke the knot of muscles forcing sobs out of me that sounded more like half chuckle, half sob. I found this posture and process strange, but if it was how I could create relief and release the painful clamping in my abdomen then, as from my very first days, it was what I would continue to do until I found out where my body was leading me in its own, perfectly self-regulated way. My head would find out when my body was ready to 'explain'. It too, after all, needed no artificial 'head restraints!'

I little realised then, and yet again, for many years thereafter, the full extent and truth of the saying: the stomach is/guts are the seat of the emotions. Like the chuckle-sobbing that came and went in waves over the better part of an hour before reaching natural conclusion and gurgling, pleasant, abdominal relief, the process changed in its expression and intensity over decades for well over thirty years right up to current times as layer on endless layer of sublimated energy worked its way out in sometimes excruciating, gripping agony.

And as always, to the unfailing positive outcome for my health and wellbeing.

After the first week of the programming course, whilst staying locally, with free time on my hands I decided to revisit the places I came to know whilst tramping the Black Mountains with the Territorial Army, which were not so many miles distant.

I felt a deep inner need to be immersed in nature, particularly at that time of year when I experienced something akin to excitement given off by the natural world's energy as new life awoke and burst from its slumbers. To be out on wild windswept hilltops, in anonymous cloaking mist, shouting and yelling as drizzle and gusts beat against me, charged batteries depleted in the classroom and its dusty intellectual grind. Not only this but the far greater enduring feelings of triumph for having regained control of my life and health, no matter what other hills I might still have to climb in their re-establishment.

Following my tradition of letting my body take me where it would, 'walking the dog', to my dismay I found I was headed for a conifer plantation, but refraining from allowing my intellect to interfere and walk in the logically sensible place along a path, I entered the tunnel of low hanging needle-fingered fronds and spent the next hour and more making my way downhill, stumbling through this cramped, dripping space until I emerged, soaking wet and 'face whipped' at its lower end.

Wondering why I hadn't overruled the 'dog' and saved myself a lot of unnecessary effort and discomfort, I treated it – as so much else I did – as a 'one off' experience never to be repeated.

JOURNEY OF A LIFETIME

Equally and increasingly as time and the years passed I was to discover nothing I did in my healing activities was an isolated event.

My body – and the deeper layers of being governing it – were whispering to me in this dismal, wet, slithering needle-pricking descent down a birth-canal like tunnel, this was a foretaste of what it needed to do.

Yet even this does not express the full extent of this deep awareness.

In this instance, later in the year I began to work through the first major layer of what I rediscovered was my so nearly catastrophic birth. Although by this time no stranger to some awareness of my birth already for about two years, in the interim a lot of work needed doing 'shovelling' away the overburden of sublimated and suppressed energy before – when my body was ready for it – the effects of birth locked away deep within began to be accessible.

Like the ancient city of Troy built layer on layer, the process of discovering each was the same; a gradual clearing away to expose the features, understanding what had been brought to view, clearing it and continuing the process.

The difference being Troy had six different layers to work through. Birth, I was to discover, had hundreds if not thousands before the elements were exposed, understood, cleared away and the trapped energy associated with each released. Even that is to understate the process owing to our simply staggering capacity to sublimate trauma and still maintain a semblance of what passes for 'normality'.

It was not a digging process either, unlike digging in the earth, releasing the blocked, locked up energy, then exposed new 'features' that in their turn became accessible, the emotional and physical energy released and put into context at a conscious level. 'Digging' in the mind occurs with drugs, either with damaging or even catastrophic consequences, as for example taking LSD; which works like archaeological site looters using mechanical shovels to loot artefacts, gouging them out of the ground with no regard for context and the greater picture. Let alone greatly damaging and destroying what is there. And further; in the brain's case, when large or massive doses have been ingested, leading to the potential of brain tumours in later life.

As happened to my certain knowledge with servicemen used as guinea pigs by their military superiors.

At the point where I spent an uncomfortable time groping about in part of the 'tartan forest' there still remained much to do before I was strong enough to even begin to embark upon sustained clearing of birth effects.

Epiphany on Dartmoor

Following the programming course I gave in March 1978 I went to Devon, savouring the prospect over the Easter period of doing some concentrated work clearing more inner wreckage, and still at a very low ebb from my marriage break up, and the relatively small amount of strength and energy I possessed compared with earlier times, of freeing up more of it amid the wonderful countryside I knew something of from years previous.

Dartmoor, like a great magnet, drew me back to places I had been whilst an electronics Apprentice in the RAF, when for two weeks of 'summer camp' in 1962, I and all my intake or Entry lived close to nature and with the knowledge of hindsight, soaked up what it offered, like human blotting paper.

Over squelching ground I found the actual spot at Powder Mills where I had camped and lain with my fellows in bivouacs and where amongst other activities we tramped round a number of tors in groups as a fitness exercise. I retraced the route I had once marched until I came to a high tor where, to check in at the rendezvous point, I and my group had to climb to the top.

Reaching it, I stood surveying the scene I once, with much regret, had no time to drink in years before. As I did so I became aware of a desire to roll around on the tor's bare stone surface.

I was torn between this inner imperative of my body and practical considerations of the stone being very unforgiving, as equally I had no desire to bruise or batter it in doing so. I seemed to be regressing to times when I had writhed around on the ground.

Having learned though my body had a lot more intelligence than what stirred in my conscious thoughts, I lay on the hard surface, and as much from inner frustration and confusion let yells rip the cold clear air that in the vastness of the moor seemed puny.

Suddenly, without precursor, a rising bubble of consciousness burst into mind and vocal expression. A spontaneous volition seemingly outside my control, and instead of just making noise, words from nowhere took form and impelled to my feet as if on springs, I began shouting almost as if in a rage: Get up! Get up! Followed by: for the first time in my life my head knows there's a body about, as I sprang to a standing position.

There was a flicker of inner confusion, the words changed and bellowed forth again: for the first time in my life my head knows what my body's about.

Intrigued, mildly dumbfounded, and enjoying this surprise from my inner regions I kept shouting for the world and the unimpressed Dartmoor sheep to hear, who neither slackened their rhythmic cropping nor took the slightest notice.

Jubilation swept through me. The message was unmistakeable even to me! At some level a connection – like two tunnels meeting to form one in an invisible subterranean cell – had occurred within.

Exhilarated, I continued to harangue the sheep for a little while, stood, then sat in silence, pondering what the significance of this revelation to myself might mean in the days to come.

Finally the breeze and spring afternoon chill crept into my clothes and I climbed down from this prominent feature in two landscapes; the one the massive natural edifice from which I viewed all around me, the other no less impressive and of even greater prospect, vantage point and view to my future, though paradoxically scenes beyond the power of my vision.

In the succeeding days the words echoing inside suffused fields and hedgerows where I walked and lay in a quiet euphoria, coupling mine with the sublime happiness of nature's vibrant blush in which I basked.

Doors Opening, Perceptions Deepening

THE DARTMOOR REVELATION made a deep and lasting impression; or better to say it shattered a divide in me between inner and outer consciousness. Not that I was able to express it this way at the time.

But the image or images coming to me as a direct result of this experience were of an infant on hands and knees peering out from a cavern in the wall of which a great jagged hole had been knocked, letting in light from the outer world.

Over years and decades the whole scene continuously evolved; the scenery changing, the cavern opening up becoming a disused quarry, passing in turn into uneven, open grass-covered land.

Then from being a rustic scene a road appeared and civilisation gradually superseded its original character.

No puzzling over these images was required; unlike others telling me of what was to come, these mirrored the profound changes proceeding in my inner world and set the future scene.

After the event, over succeeding evenings I co-supported with a fellow group workshop attendee with whom I was staying. I discovered early on in my healing activities I possessed the ability to see into others and help unlock the blockages in their bodies and past.

Indeed, the more I did it the more it came clear to me it transcended following someone's else's rules of co-supporting as much as it transcended my own ordinary awareness.

On hands and knees he attempted to express something but lacked focus. I felt strongly drawn to his shoulders to bear down with my weight and literally and metaphorically to put him under pressure. At the same time the words of an overbearing parent came to me, telling him he'd do as I said.

Instantaneously it recreated his deeply hurtful and unpleasant history with his father who beat him and who was an overbearing bully, re-channelling his own walled off accumulated hurts, outrages and marital resentments, using his son as the lightning conductor to 'earth' them.

The equinoxial weather of wind and lashing rain seemed to empathise with the squalls and storms of long suppressed emotional energy.

Finally after a number of sessions clearing more stored personal history and the nights of restful repose brought through freeing myself from considerable internal clutter, deep restlessness and shallow sleep signalled the emergence of yet more that took months of work to clear before nocturnal inner peace was restored. Though all too briefly. Together with the familiar aches, stiffness, muscular tics and spasms unfailingly signalling changes occurring deep within; not just body, as these were only the external signs of subliminal changes at an altogether deeper level, but also, what I came to call 'coughing up elastic bands'. I noticed early on as some aspect was freed and worked through within myself, I would begin coughing, clearing my throat, and spitting out thick threads of mucus from my lungs. After a day or two it would cease. I thought this merely a continuing part of the process of when I first began in Nova Scotia and coughing up clods of thick yellow mucus my whole system having being very shut down.

Just another physical thing, I thought. But then again, as has become crystal clear over decades, 'thought' has nothing whatever to do with reality. It is the drip, drip, drip of insights over time until the vessel of greater awareness is filled and realisation truly dawns of what drives such 'physical' responses.

Unexpected Revelations Within Myself

I co-supported with another group workshop attendee weekly, turning a small bedroom in my terraced home into as much of a sound deadening cell as I could. Each week we took it in turns for an hour to work on what pressed for expression, often triggered by interaction or event with someone raising echoes of previous unresolved experiences. Sometimes there would be much sound and fury that I hoped did not disturb my neighbour too much! Other times would be more introspective when little appeared to be happening. Though just as ocean waves have peaks and troughs, so it became clear did the cycles of clearing unresolved experiences and the blocked energy directly connected with them.

I looked forward each week to my time of self-expression, for as ever, impatience was my whispering companion to be clearer, stronger, freer and with more energy than I possessed.

One afternoon before we were due to meet the same evening, whilst at work, my co-supporter rang me and informed me he had hurt his back and couldn't get over and would have to miss our session.

Disappointed, I was not very sympathetic and it was left for another week. Once again the same thing happened and this time I was even less sympathetic. I knew he could hear my lack of sympathy and in my turn I could hear the resentment in his voice.

Another week passed with an exact repetition and if possible, even less sympathy.

A letter in his handwriting dropped through my letter box a day later telling me at length he was crippled with pain after he had slipped a disc in his back when he had bent down to pick up a toy for his young child. At one point underlined and in capitals he wrote: "I want you to understand I have hurt my back."

All this coincided with a book I was reading about a New York housewife named Jane Roberts who had dabbled with a Ouija board to contact 'spirits' but quickly found she could go directly into trance.

The spirit or 'entity' coming through her was called 'Seth' and there followed a number of books of the séances. One of the first was called *The Seth Material*. They contained a great deal of wisdom, some of it fascinating.

Chapter nine of the book was taken up with an episode about back pain at exactly the time my co-supporter was afflicted.

The husband had been in agony with back pain and suggested to his wife they go away for the weekend – his rationale being he might as well be in agony somewhere different as being stuck in the house in his condition.

Uncertainly, his wife agreed; they drove out into the country and came upon a very ordinary and dated 'dance diner' where they stopped for evening dinner.

Sitting at the side of the small dance floor, deserted but for one other couple sitting directly across from them, still in agony, the husband suddenly rose to his feet, demanding to dance. Looking at him as if he was mad, his wife did so. By the end of the dance all trace of the crippling condition had completely gone.

At the next séance the husband asked 'Seth' through his wife – whose voice and looks changed markedly when she went into trance – what caused his back pain to suddenly and inexplicably vanish.

'Seth' responded, saying the problem was between his fifth and sixth lumber vertebrae and was caused by a conflict in him.

It appeared the husband was in considerable inner turmoil over his relationship with his wife. The conflict manifested in energy trapped in his spine and finding no resolution crippled him.

When they sat down in the diner dance floor area, he had noticed the couple opposite and although it had not registered consciously, he had seen they were completely dead to each other. Indeed; that they were a projection of themselves.

'Seth' said deep within, the potential of the path his own relationship might take, registered and instantly choosing not to take it, leapt to his feet, his inner conflict resolved, which dancing with his wife the movement helped free the blocked energy and by the time the dance finished he was relieved of all pain.

Scanning my co-supporter's impassioned letter, I wrote a note telling him to read the chapter dealing with this episode and to get over for a session.

The next week on the Wednesday evening, our normal arrangement to meet and co-support, there came no phone call at work and a gentle tap tap on the door knocker announced his arrival at the usual time.

I opened the door to a grim, ashen-grey, angry face, the skin of which hung loosely such was his agony, and without a word we ascended my stairs and went into my makeshift sound-insulated work room.

He lay face down on the floor, unable to get any relief.

I had the strongest conviction I had been reading the 'chapter nine' episode in the book for a very good reason; that this bad back and the one in the book were exactly the same problem: conflict.

Unsure where to begin, I picked my way intuitively through what had been happening to him and quite soon, within a few minutes, I knew resolution was not far away.

To while away the time, unable to move around, he had read a book called *Julius Caesar's Campaign In Gaul*. He felt himself inexplicably tensing up more and more and increasingly uncomfortable as he read Caesar's own account of the wholesale slaughter meted out to the Celtic Gauls by the Roman army.

The Celts were renowned as I knew from having also read a book called *The Roman Conquest of Britain* years before when at my lowest ebb whilst in Australia, for being individualistic, extremely artistic, fearless, utterly unafraid of death and their culture steeped in the depths of inner being from the Druidic religion holding powerful, if not absolute, sway over them.

The Romans were polar opposites; regimented, logical, authoritarian and based in an intellectually dominated society.

I also knew the person laying face down on the many layers of sound insulation at my feet was a gifted artist, yet like so many people was persuaded to get 'a proper job' by his parents and became a journalist.

He rose to be an excellent one and work for well-known national newspapers, all of which he utterly detested; the evidence of which was a stomach ulcer. Fortunately he eventually managed to extricate himself, and began an arts degree allowing his long and deeply suppressed artistic talent – like a Bonsai tree planted in a garden and left to grow – or put on growth like a small bamboo shoot in its fifth year; sixty feet.

At this point, with rock solid certainty, I was sure beyond a flicker of doubt his back problem had the same genesis as Jane Robert's husband. For just as I had been reading a book giving the cause and effect of his inner conflict it had given me the key to my co-supporter's condition. He had been reading a book which – albeit symbolically – in relating the literal conflict between Roman and Celtic armies and their inherent cultures was showing him the polarised diametrically opposed conflict of energies in himself.

I gently asked him to ask himself a question; was there a parallel between the dominant, authoritarian, organised, intellectually-based Romans and their conflict with the artistic, individualistic, deeply intuitive Celts and his experience as an intellectually based reporter dealing in words, and his artistic inner nature?

Before I had even finished framing the question for him to consider and ask himself, he interrupted and replied, "Yes … there is."

JOURNEY OF A LIFETIME

At this precise instant he let out a cry and it was clear the agony in mid-back had reached crisis point.

Also at this point I felt a powerful desire to stretch out my index and middle finger of my right hand held tight together with thumb pressed over my two remaining fingers below.

Positioning my fingers about a foot above his back and the spot mid-spine I was drawn to, I made a small clockwise circle with them in mid-air.

Instantaneously, a convulsion as if he had been electrocuted went through him like a bolt of lightning. He continued to cry out in agony for a short while then subside and after a few minutes he lay silent; the pain completely gone.

In half an hour I had brought about the circumstances of this quite astonishing resolution of what looked like a human lightning discharge, in the reflexive convulsion faster than the blink of an eye engulfing his being.

Relief and sympathy swept over me. It was obvious when finally – still ashen faced – he rose to his feet without pain, and the immense strain gone from his face, I was definitely not his most treasured friend; the resentful glower of his dark eyes spoke all he felt.

In silence I led back down the stairs, opened the front door and passing through without a word he was gone.

It didn't matter. What I witnessed made a great impact on me; I would never have believed it had I not been there and able to help in the way I had. Nor would I ever forget.

I knew he had spent four hours and a lot of money in therapy sessions leading nowhere trying to resolve his agony; and doctors were no help at all. Yet in half an hour, and for nothing, I proved sympathy was a poor substitute for knowing where to look, and bringing about the permanent resolution to his agony.

It took years before the full realisation and significance of what I had intuitively facilitated and witnessed; drip by drip of insights filled the vessel of clear understanding.

The 'back problem' never returned – only when he was raised to anger did he get twinges expressing his inner conflict of allowing and simultaneously suppressing it in himself.

The impression might be gained from these experiences and events I have related that progress took place in a few isolated episodes. Nothing could be further from the truth or reality.

My utterly consuming desire to heal myself and rebuild my health and strength never left me for an instant. It was constantly present, no matter what I did. At times sublimated by the need to concentrate on work and its constant study, but only a thought away. Day or night, waking or sleeping it was always there; it was the reactor core of my existence. Indeed, whilst at work studying by myself to learn a new course or subject, I would also concentrate on releasing tense muscles in some part of my body. And on reflection, this was a skill I possessed from a very early age.

It served me very well, for even sitting on a course, studying, laying in bed, or almost anywhere when I was stationary, I could focus on muscles and command them to release. At the same time I found it worked best if I breathed out at the same time; or perhaps I felt compelled to breathe simultaneously. I would repeat the process over and over, sometimes for hours and over a day or two, after which the muscles learned to release and invariably that part of me would feel extremely stiff and/or ache and I would feel weary beyond description as the tension ebbed away.

I first found this ability when a small boy, out in the snow one very cold winter's day and unpleasantly aware my left foot was freezing. I concentrated on it for a short while, forgot about it; only to suddenly realise a little later it had warmed up.

JOURNEY OF A LIFETIME

I 'forgot' how to do it until years later and in Australia when shortly after arriving there feeling physically sick and utterly disorientated with jet lag added to the very poor state I was generally in, one day whilst at a very political customer's computer installation suffering from unfixed faults, muscular pain burned deep in my right side. Finding a cure for it was essential; I knew I couldn't function for long if I didn't. Concentrating on the muscles deep in this area, within a day I 'found' the one I was searching for and it finally answered with a jolt like an electric shock and began releasing as I continued to command it to let go, in agonising and deeply relieving spasms. These continued over a day or two until the agonising tension was replaced with acute weariness and profound stiffness as bodily retribution for my self-inflicted outrage.

For about the first three years I concentrated on different parts of my body below my neck, then the focus shifted naturally to working on shoulders, neck and my head.

Which, like bringing about resolution of crippling back agony, was something I did instinctively and intuitively.

Without doubt over the years and decades this aspect of healing alone amounted to thousands of hours' effort.

It did not take very long to realise once I freed up some area of my 'body armour' as Wilhelm Reich called it, emotional energy associated with the clamped muscles rose to the surface and needed to be dealt with. Reich, who began as a pupil of Freud, broke away to become much more body-centred, which Freud detested and Bioenergetics in its turn owed its beginnings to Reich and his pupil, Alexander Lowen, who came to clearly understand the relationship between physical and emotional.

'Body work', though was just one aspect of what I did completely on my own.

As related, the writings of Carlos Castenada about his experiences with the Mexican Indian shaman I found deeply intriguing and a real source of inspiration for they stood completely outside the (to me) narrow confines of many 'isms' and therapies of western origin.

It only became clear after decades of endless pondering and attempting to use some of the knowledge, reading and rereading the books, why they so utterly fascinated me.

Other people could and did concentrate almost completely on one 'ism' or therapy but I felt this was as much a hindrance as none at all.

I found to try and talk to many people about teachings, systems of knowledge and learning outside their own was to invite the complete spectrum of sometimes witty though often deriding humour, a cryptic response; compressed lip silence, scorn, derision and hostility, or even outright rage.

It never mattered to me and never would whether something appeared ridiculous, bizarre or downright incomprehensible if it seemed to have some practical utility; it was worth investigating and using.

Putting it another way, as someone prosaically once did; pouring cold piss on someone else's ideas never proved how good your own might be or advanced them very far.

Something that in my view the hopelessly intellectually dominated scientific fraternity might do well to ponder. Demonstrating scientific 'open-mindedness' is as fragile as the glass-brittle limits of the intellectual greenhouse cultures they nurture to the exclusion of all else outside it.

And as a reminder to myself not to throw stones at other's greenhouses from my own!

JOURNEY OF A LIFETIME

The end of 1978 came with perhaps a fitting culmination to a tumultuous year and my efforts over more than four years to not only heal myself and improve my health but expand into a much broader approach to this and of being generally.

Apart from the general rubric of freeing myself of my personal history locked up in my body, directly impacting the amount – or the complete lack of it – of energy of all kinds I possessed: physical, emotional and mental to use in all aspects of my life, the particular aim for the year was to prepare myself for the advent of divorce and all it might demand of me.

From earlier years I progressed through a period two years previously of fatigue so intense, for much of the time I felt as if I had been kicked squarely in the crutch. By early 1978 the internal plumbing of my digestive system was definitely giving some kind of heave manifested in gut pain rising to an uncomfortable climax followed by considerable farting relieving it.

Intuitively it occurred to me my pancreas was beginning to work better or perhaps even to function moderately well at all. One undeniable effect was considerably more physical energy. In particular it began to dawn as this symptom progressed how little energy I had from my waist down before and how much more vigorously I was able to push back against my Australian adversary in the hand on hand pushing exercise, with my legs, than I had been able to until then. They had much more energy which before seemed to diminish markedly from the small of my back downwards. It felt like learning to walk all over again and I savoured being able to stride out conscious of this new power.

Yet, when following someone over rocks on a seashore, I was acutely conscious of just how weary and heavy I felt, barely able to keep up even though the person concerned was much shorter.

Another milestone came later in the year, which although utterly trivial, marked a change on a mental level rather than physical. For months an irritating inertia I seemed powerless to overcome meant my car tax disc slid backwards and forwards across under the windscreen until finally one day I bought a holder for it and put it inside and stuck it to the screen.

The satisfaction was out of all proportion to this insignificant gesture, but as cars appeared often in my dreams representing me – or my 'vehicle of life' – the inner significance was much more about creating official recognition of myself to the world; of anchoring diffuse inner parts of me together as one.

As with so many – if not all – seemingly piddling events, they are the visible part of the iceberg of total reality. The rest of which we are taught to deliberately ignore, disavow and even exterminate in ourselves.

Calling this 'normality'.

At the point where the divorce began, the emotional strain coupled with very demanding intellectual study and exertion giving technically demanding courses, caused me to go completely blank in the middle of a sentence and lose track of what I was saying, when explaining some related point.

Somewhere within, 'fail safe' shut down was beginning to takeover and continued right up to current times and only as of writing has this 'circuit' begun to be deactivated and the faculty to pick up the main thread again and continue with it has reasserted itself; though still not completely.

The young solicitor I used proving utterly useless in negotiating terms of settlement, I wrote a letter to my ex wife and with it still hanging in the air, went to Paris to teach for the first time the two-week course reducing students and instructor alike to haggard visages and debilitated condition. In this instance the class was very small with the added bonus of doubling in duration due to language considerations for foreign students.

A month in the city I had wanted to see for many years healed me on a number of different levels.

JOURNEY OF A LIFETIME

It coincided with finding a book by Bhagwan Shree Rajneesh, an Indian philosopher turned Guru, called *The Hidden Harmony*; and his reflections on the wisdom of Heraclitus, a philosopher who treated Aristotle's cerebral outpourings as lacking in any kind of solid reality being the result of his febrile intellect. In his turn Aristotle found Heraclitus a baffling enigma and could only disdainfully label him a 'poet'. The essence of the book and of Heraclitus' philosophy was whatever you do, do it a hundred per cent; do not cut across yourself with a hundred different thoughts, recriminations, guilt, anguish, regrets and conflicting 'what ifs'. Be completely in where you find yourself. It is, after all, your own decisions that have placed you there, be it good, bad or indifferent.

Reality is experience and with existence comes experience – theorising about existence is not reality. It is simply a lot of intellectual chatter. Doing 'it' is real; thinking about 'it' is not.

Which was nothing if not appropriate considering my divorce, which spun within me like a tornado.

But infinitely more, something I was incapable of harbouring even the merest flicker of consciousness concerning myself then; all my work and so much of my life was nothing else *but* thought.

An expanding inner peace and perspective grew from the book's wisdom tramping around different parts of the city; its markets, shops, boulevards; more ancient parts and along the Seine under bright lights twinkling in the frosty air of winter evenings after the day's teaching.

With each day and mile, I explored new parts; menus, wine and restaurants and with this the clamour in my head and body began ebbing away, as did my compulsion to writhe around on the ground. Yet again, although I had connected consciously a couple of years before, the writhing around was a deep desire to get out of my body, I was incapable of connecting with the real wellspring of understanding then – and for decades after – what really drove this need to get away from my physical body.

Only after many years and many thousands of hours' work did clear perception and real understanding begin to arrive. Deep hurt might be one level of connection but far, far deeper, buried under a mountain of sublimated suffering, was the realisation fear drove the writhing around *and* the desire to get away from my own body. It was not until much of this had been cleared I gained anything like a clear insight by becoming free(r) of fear. At the time when I was under intense intellectual and emotional pressure through work and impending divorce during 1978 it acted exactly like a huge physical weight on me. The deep, involuntary and entirely natural response to being crushed under a great weight is to try and escape it. But if the great external 'weight' was as invisible as that sublimated within me; what then?

So my inner distress expressed itself in attempting to escape from where it was felt; deep, deep within.

Writhing around was by no means anything like the full picture either. After the dismal experience of emerging soaked and moderately thrashed about the head by the tunnel of fir tree fronds doing my 'dog walking' exercise in early springtime up on the Black Mountains, letting my body go where it wanted rather than my head deciding logically where I would walk, it was not very long before, as the summer came, so did a very much more focused expression of escaping a huge weight on me: my experience of birth.

Beyond a vague sense, groping my way downhill through the barely navigable tunnel created by lines of sitka spruce trees crowded together was similar to the process of birth, I had no clear idea of its significance at all. I was irritated with myself for having indulged my instinct in a completely pointless, time-wasting and deeply uncomfortable pursuit. Once begun though, as I discovered, retracing my steps up the steep muddy slope was near, if not completely, impossible.

Like birth; it was a one-way journey.

JOURNEY OF A LIFETIME

In so many ways our deep inner consciousness always finds a way to fit an allegory of our unresolved life's experience *exactly* to what needs to be brought into waking consciousness; expressed, released and, finally, resolved. Placing these mirrors before us happens all the time, but we confuse 'mirror' with 'mirage'; and blunder on unheeding of our own inner wisdom we are face to face with.

Only when, a few months later, as I began ramming my head face down, and shoulders deep into a large cushion and kicking out behind me with my legs and feet, like a breaststroke swimmer, in an individual therapy session, did it spontaneously connect the fir tree tunnel episode was anything but pointless. Neither was it just an isolated event. My body consciousness was telling my head what it needed to do. But the twittering aviary of thoughts was not listening. The epiphany on Dartmoor soared far higher on eagle's wings of clear perception and further into my future than my own incessant 'bird-brain' noise allowed.

Once begun though, there was no denying the deep impulse to use my legs to kick my way through against my mother's utterly unyielding muscles. Worse yet; they clamped me solid. Such was the force of my kicking out at times, the only parts of me in contact with the mattress I was on were my head and shoulders.

Just as with others I helped release and resolve a great deal stored and sublimated energy within themselves, this had nothing to do with thought whatever; it was what my body needed to do and it was accompanied by a fog of terror. The sensation was not only of being clamped solid; but crushed as well.

As waves of this swept over me a bubble of intuition surfaced; exactly as on the Dartmoor occasion, the words bursting in a sentence: This is where I split into two parts. My head and thinking processes were simply observers to all this. From deep within, my body was following a long delayed agenda of exactly what it needed to do; thought had nothing whatsoever to do with the overwhelming volition to kick and fight my way out of the nightmare that was my birth.

This revelation to myself of splitting into two parts confused and disappointed me; I thought it should be exactly the reverse; the point where this occurred should have been; this is where two parts become one within me.

Even so it needed no explaining, nor anyone to tell me what this was about, I knew exactly what I felt; vague yet profound terror, and the cause of it; an absolute implacable, crushing, iron resistance against my progress to be born.

By the end of an hour's session I had run out of steam. I knew I had begun to tap an unimaginable amount of fear from somewhere within me. That this was the first of many sessions dealing with the same process and the same feelings surrounding it I also knew. But no idea whatsoever of the colossal effort and countless thousands of times this would be repeated. For whilst I felt some relief for the effort I had expended it was superficial. No sense of resolution accompanied it at all. It felt like there was a lot more my body needed to do before I had any clear perception of where it was all taking me. To reiterate; at the time; as ever, my mantra: the human organism is entirely self-righting and self-healing, left to its self and the utter conviction this was so, sustained me. Concomitantly; in its own good time my body would let me know what had driven my manic squirming, as it had. What I wanted to get away from was the unimaginable amount of fear I had sublimated and stowed somewhere deep within me. It had done this from a depth of intelligence and awareness far surpassing any rational explanations and theorising. As *The Hidden Harmony* expressed it: doing it is real; thinking about it is not. And the figures of Heraclitus and Aristotle could not have been clearer symbols of the huge divide in myself. But I was as incapable of bridging that chasm of understanding as Evil Knievel was around those times of jumping the Grand Canyon in a car powered by rockets – or anything else! And just as wide.

Inner Peace Outer Conflict;
Mirrors and Magnetic Attraction

Towards the end of the course and my stay in Paris, I decided one Sunday in mid-December to sit in on a church mass. Quietly observing from the back and if possible to knock the gears of mind into neutral and coast along with all the sights and sounds around me, staying in each second as it passed but without wandering off into thoughts of anything; past, present or future.

At first my mind was like a dog off the lead running this way and that and having to retrace steps back to its master of stillness and inner silence. Surprisingly quickly, I found I became steadily quieter until I could watch and listen, all inner distraction silenced. Somewhere I floated weightless in a conscious state of bliss and peace.

Leaving the church after quite a long time in euphoric inner silence, I wandered in the weak winter sun; meandering towards the Seine, as if pulled along with many others, like polarised iron filings to the magnetic influence of Notre Dame's great towers.

Entering the cathedral I found to my surprise it was packed solid. I began listening and trying to see what was happening from behind this forest of people; a service appeared to be starting.

Quite suddenly, within a few seconds of having arrived, a small group of men walked down the nave handing out leaflets. Continuing on until they reached the officiating priest and the choir chanting some cerebral liturgy; a thin, distant sound full of human frailty amongst the forest of pillars and lofty spaces. The interlopers had their own liturgy they chanted; what they said or sang I had no idea. One grabbed the priest's microphone and continued to give voice to the protest he and his fellows were plainly making. Leaflets were thrown into the air, scattering like autumn leaves.

The congregation, until then comatose, rose as one out of their universal detachment, craning on tiptoe over others to see what was happening. From supine disinterest the atmosphere buzzed with electricity.

Abruptly the organ thundered forth in a way I never heard in any cathedral let alone church. It crashed out. An exploding battleship-broadside of sound. The establishment and the organist's wrath determined no protest should hijack their service. The impromptu recital shook the rafters; the whole vast space pulsated; people began standing on pews straining for sight of this heretical spontaneous 'worship' unfolding before them.

The hair on the back of my neck prickled and goose flesh rose on my arms. It felt like a gladiatorial stadium with music.

The organ's apocalyptic resonances continued to break in thundering waves for some minutes until the recital ceased as abruptly as it had begun, propelling a shower of notes from the final chord; scouring gloomy recesses.

The chanting continued; though the confiscated microphone had been silenced.

A brief interlude of voices weakly attempting to fill the distant spaces ended abruptly. A musical Saturn Five blasting off; its chords of hostility bursting through the congregation with colossal force like scouring steam clouds, rent the air.

Like the rocket's crackling breath, the organ's near deafening efflux hit congregation and church with physical force. Frightened, blocks of stone might come crashing down as the roof disintegrated; I retreated, standing close by the side entrance. The noise was so overpowering I felt it would propel the vast stone columns and the whole cathedral fabric skywards. Being in the centre of this volcanic musical eruption; if the atmosphere had been electric shortly before, it exploded into pulsating incandescence. The musical cadences took on a viscous quality. People were visibly affected by it. All the liturgical chanting, singing, and organ sounds of all the cathedrals I had ever heard concentrated as one, failed utterly to compare with this profane, anarchic, devotion; and no service I ever witnessed roused the congregation to such rapt attention. Its impact far surpassed all institutional priestly piety.

I realised, until then, I had never heard an organ speak with even a fraction of its voice.

Simultaneously, at a raw gut instinct level, standing in this great symbol of Christian devotion, the chasm between bloodless intellectual worship and the scalding emotional power boiling through it like launch pit steam from this keyboard driven rocket, engulfed me. Unable as it unfolded to form or find the words, nevertheless the extreme polarisation between the two, was voice enough to be understood.

Completely choked with emotion, trembling as this tsunami of harmonies drowned everything and me with it, I witnessed it as all who on tiptoe strained for sight of it did and those standing on pews.

Finally, sound-battered into submission, the protesters silently left, and the Jericho-levelling chords ceased; though their penetration plunged so deeply through every last stone and crevice, I felt the recollection of it all would last in them for as long as Notre Dame did.

Finding an area softly blazing with candle light, lighting one, I placed it amongst tiers of others; said a silent prayer for myself for all that the day, my year and its shattering climax had been; for those who mattered to me, and slowly left, pondering what unseen whorls and eddies of fate arranged to take me into a peace and silence not experienced before and the earth shaking meditation and 'religious' celebration that in some inexplicable way seemed to mirror my life and all I had lived, struggled and grown through over the year dwindling rapidly to its close aboard a projectile of ascending prayers into the heavens.

Like struggling out of a dark crevasse of life-threatening decline, it marked a natural culmination of at least beginning to rebuild and regain health from the frayed and tenuous thread by which all too recently had hung my fate and life.

In parallel with it, my relationship having become marriage, was climactically also, ending.

The first service I attended had, after all, been as an observer – very like I had been before I had begun healing myself. My contact with life then being very fragile and slender. The perception and feeling of not being part of what I was living through, being just about able to coast along; but was completing in the second 'service' in a tumult of clashing themes; discord, conflict and harmony competing powerfully together and the act of placing the candle with silent prayers finally reaching a point of stillness, calm and resolution.

The year had begun at a very low ebb and progressed at a faster and faster pace of non-stop work on all levels, commencing with emotions welling up like an oil gusher about to blow its rig and feeling suicidal. At the same time the experience of intuitively sensing my pancreas was regaining proper function in sharp gut pains, bloated with trapped wind, and gathering energy and strength.

Later on in mid-year, being painfully aware although I still possessed a powerful conviction of being able to heal myself, I had really only just got the process going and I had a vast amount more to do and my perception was like a child with a glimmering realisation of what growing up meant. Blinkers suddenly fell off and I moved beyond cosy delusions of self-imposed timetables for how and when I would progress on some imaginary Maslow-esque existential staircase to nirvana.

Simultaneously coping with the increasingly heavy demands to learn and teach more courses at work having deeper and deeper technical levels. Of reaching a point as my divorce occurred, of somewhere in my brain the 'plugs' being pulled out and connections lost with the sentence I uttered, as inner turmoil clashed powerfully with my need to impart intellectual knowledge to students, and having to take time off. Though finally, teaching the most complex course of all, as I had done, to foreign students.

In parallel, working non-stop through powerful, sometimes barely containable, emotional history surfacing in dreams of starkly graphic imagery and breath-clamping heart-pounding impact, triggered by the deeply significant experience on Dartmoor early in the year, of my body and deeper levels of being at last beginning to co-exist with intellect and heal the brutal suppression and divide existing until then. Yet having to study harder than ever as the demands of my work increased. The Notre Dame experience expressed in its clashing elements, mind against mind; intellects conflicting with emotions and overall the force of some far greater will in all this, drowning everything in harmonies of gigantic power. A catharsis of sound purging away the discordant clamour of all preceding it, until finally after the headlong pell-mell rush, my year's efforts were closing, having mastered an Everest of intellectual endeavour together with a tectonic heave of healing and inner personal growth. There could be no more fitting symbolism than all I witnessed and been part of on that memorable day. For in long retrospect it seems the strong polarisation within myself finding deep inner peace and perhaps projecting out into the world its polar opposite; the uproar and chaos of my daily life, I was indeed attracted to a place of deep spirituality; the great cathedral, becoming a part of its tumultuous conflict whose spark ignited the instant I entered.

Impossible too, to believe the church wherein I had strived and found a pool of motionless serenity, dedicated to St Sulpice, was mere chance. Completely unknown to me at the time and for decades after, I had sat within a few feet of the Rose Line – the Zero Meridian based on Paris – marked by a brass strip running across the floor, and aligned to exactly mark Easter sunrise.

Moreover, the line projected out across France through what was central to and once Cathar Christian territory and deeply bound up with the mythology of the Knights Templar and its inner circle the Priory Of Syon.

In turn spinning together many threads centring on Crusades, Jerusalem, Jesus, and his first wife, Mary Magdalene who voyaged and preached there, bringing – in my belief – a much more enlightened Christianity of equality; savagely stamped out later by Rome, residing on the Herodian estates, and the subsequent bloodline of Jesus.

No less also the art of Nicolas Poussin whose pictures; their content and encoded geometrical symbolism in Les Bergers D'Arcadie (The Arcadian Shepherds) amplified echoes of these loudly whispered traditions.

Strangely enough, not knowing any of this until many years and much reading later, the one thing I felt was no coincidence, was yet both the most ephemeral though palpable aspect. For a brief time, the sun's rays shone down through high windows lighting the spot where I sat, and to my inner stillness added a pleasant insistence and in its continuing presence, a pulse raising warmth.

It would be hard if not impossible to imagine so many tangled threads of myth and history combining conflict and spirituality woven together and around me. And being merely pure chance.

About which I was in total and literally blissful ignorance. Let alone what Notre Dame had still to show me, and for me, its symbolism although deafening and staring back at me like a vast distorting mirror, I felt only vague stirring notions I was being shown things about myself beyond my grasp.

Finally if what I picked up from what little I understood of French, the cathedral service was to mark International Human Rights Day, tempestuously clashing as it had, with Breton separatists. Could there possibly have been a more direct, potent symbol concerning conflict and harmony and its enactment right in front of me.

Though able to sense threads of subliminal consciousness weaving all this together as parts of myself and my own spinning vortex of inner harmony and projected outer conflicts, let alone to give it any form or expression in words, to me all this was vanishingly remote beyond any ability I possessed to articulate.

If my year's climb into the light of renewing life began with the Epiphany on Dartmoor, it had ended with a light of Damascenean power; neither of whose significance or symbolism I understood, yet both presaged great changes in my inner worlds.

CALM AND SUNSHINE AFTER THE STORM

FOR THE FIRST time since my Grail quest of healing began, the final year of the decade commenced outwardly with rigidifying Arctic cold but inwardly feelings of vibrant wellbeing and health not experienced in years. In fact I had seldom if ever felt as inwardly free as my body had become. The experience of a few years before of running up stairs to savour and remind myself of how my chest felt compared with before when my heart pounded like the rebound of a trampoline feeling as if it would leap out of me, became a condition I enjoyed throughout my body. And yet, as much as I had long since got various bits of me like left kidney and lung to work better or indeed at all, I was conscious physical energy was not as it once had been.

That it had improved out of all recognition and beyond all expectation was clearly evident, but as ever an inner impatience to be moving on to some greater nirvana was rather like the donkey pursuing the stick-dangled carrot; I was always striving to be further on than I was, in my quest.

Little seemed to be happening. Viewed from my understanding then I simultaneously enjoyed how I felt and was disappointed as compared with the previous year, nothing was.

But with long perspective 'nothing' as I have come to understand, was merely a superficial perception taking no account of what my body and inner being with its far greater wisdom than my clucking squawking intellect understood and knew it needed to do, which was to gather strength and consolidate my inner 'edifice of mind' to move on to other things in their own good time!

There was though, also an awareness my intellect did after all put a roof over my own head and provide me with a certain status I also quite enjoyed or more accurately, I was addicted to.

In spite of being dedicated to healing myself, intellectually I was striving as much or more than I had ever done, and it had brought me the chance to travel not least to Iraq to teach a course as well as the healing experience of Paris I had so recently greatly enjoyed.

The year also brought a desire to explore more mystical subjects and I visited a festival of mind, body and spirit at Olympia to poke around and pry into areas, even years before I had been drawn to. Not least amongst other books of esoteric nature, reading the vast work of George Gurdjieff, entitled *Beelzebub's Tales to His Grandson*, a mind bogglingly convoluted book, though utterly fascinating in parts, not least in its peculiar vocabulary, apparently designed to make people question what was written and fathom deeper truths buried in its pages. As much of it dealt with the ancient history of the Middle East it kindled the fires of my imagination, soon powerfully stoked by teaching in Iraq and being lucky enough to visit the ancient ruins of Babylon and actually climb the steps of the Great Ziggurat in a whirling dust storm and brick oven temperatures, at what had been the ancient Sumerian city of Ur; Abraham's birthplace.

The country utterly fascinated me and its palpable aura of ancient civilisations was inescapable; as indeed it was for Egypt I was lucky enough to visit as well. I positively burned with a desire to learn more about each.

Nineteen-seventy-seven had given me a first chance to see both and fan the sparks of abiding fascination for them since childhood, into flames. Whereas 1978 had been a year of non-stop work on personal horizons, by comparison 1979 seemed one of exploding consciousness into cosmic realms. In an inexplicable way then and now it seemed like a further reward for the work I was doing within myself. I indeed found whilst my feet might be wading around in some primal swamp of my inner worlds there really were stars above my head; and why limiting myself to one 'therapy' or 'ism' seemed merely to trade one transcendent straitjacket of inner being for another as many people seemed to do. For me at least, the more I freed myself from my inner shackles and healed my body the more consciousness and aspects of my mind seemed to expand exponentially.

To limit myself to John Lennon's world of 'Imagine' seemed to make as much sense as choosing to take sandwiches and a packet of crisps to a banquet and eat them, ignoring all else.

Although I still continued to do healing work at a body level there seemed much less needing to be dealt with than before. The focus had moved more to the level of mind and hardly coincidental that I was concentrating on releasing the tensions in my upper body including my head. Though at the time the connection between the two areas of focus and interest never even remotely occurred to me!

THE BODY AND ITS INNER WISDOM

THAT OUR SUB/inner consciousness is our perfect protector, healer and 'nothing happening' regulator was shown to me – if only I had known it then – in experimenting with Rolfing.

This very deep form of massage was developed by Ida Rolf, a brilliant teacher and natural scientist, who in teaching Yoga, began manipulating people's bodies who were unable to adopt a particular 'asana' or body position. By administering this deeply probing manipulation to cause realignment of muscles and overall body posture, people were then able to adopt positions impossible before.

My Australian friend of pushing fame took a course and became a qualified Rolfer, and I decided to undergo a complete body realignment with him. I knew the process could be deeply painful as fingers and knuckles used to do the muscle realignment, dug into muscles and tissue; and so it proved to be, particularly on the legs and neck regions. Being a strongly built person his technique was particularly vigorous.

The working week of giving courses in software in the training school finished at midday on Fridays when students were given time to make their way home. I and other colleagues gathered, thankfully relieved, in the wine bar conveniently next door to generally unwind from the considerable stress everyone experienced in their work. Lunch, often a large bowl of chilli con carne, was consumed and its effects in the mouth pleasantly moderated with a pint or two of cooling lager. Being free time it also coincided with appointments I arranged for the next instalment of body realignment. The convivial lunch helped overcome a certain vague inner resistance I felt at the prospect of probing digits and knuckles and the red wheals they raised.

In a curious way I looked forward to each session and yet once we got in the wine bar I also felt somewhat reluctant to leave its atmosphere of alcohol lubricated good humour, witty badinage and camaraderie.

Not until over a year later when my Rolfer and I met to clear an atmosphere of non-communication between us did he express considerable annoyance at the smell of beer on my breath when, working close to my body he began the manipulation I had chosen to put myself through.

In my turn I explained a direct consequence of his work on me was experiencing a powerful reaction in being unable to go near him. I felt like an animal having been given a beating and I reacted the same way; when I saw him I felt a powerful desire to distance myself from him – and did so, and also like a beaten animal to snarl at my tormentor. It was not something I thought about; the response was instantaneous, deep and automatic. He found this difficult to understand or accept and I could only say these were the after effects his Rolfing had on me.

It was not until at least another year passed and I began another course of massage that the disparate parts of this experience were finally put together.

It took me much longer though to realise my lager 'anaesthetic' of Friday lunches had been the way I coped with the physical agony of the body realignment. Still longer to understand how even this was nothing like the full picture, for it evoked deep powerful fear at a body level I was years away from even remotely connecting together consciously.

Through the Wardrobe into Worlds Untravelled

The break-neck intellectual mountain climb, wintry personal struggles and tremendous efforts to heal and grow of the year previous having passed into history, a sunny spring rose within me from winter's frozen inertia, exactly as it did in the outer world.

I savoured life and all around me and as recounted earlier, interest in matters beyond the mundane in the unseen worlds of earth energies, esoteric and spiritual realms absorbed and captured my curiosity and imagination.

Like Narnia thawing, I found my own magic wardrobe of life to explore worlds dormant; waiting for human presence of mind and mobilising energies to unfreeze them. For uncomprehending though I was then, my year saw a great blossoming within as well as aspects of my ordinary life. The one inescapably driving the other.

Having reached the summit of technical complexity in the software courses I taught, the pressure at least eased teaching what I had learned and taught at least once before, though the sheer scope and complexity was beyond anyone to say they knew or would ever know everything about all aspects of it, and it was still a heavy burden to shoulder and carry. In fact, far heavier than I ever realised at the time, and long after.

I was still more or less completely blind to the fact, whilst fascinated and absorbed by the world of intuition and aspects of occult knowledge, I was as deeply involved as ever – if not more so – in worlds owing everything to intellect, reason and rational thought as it was possible to be.

Heraclitus and Aristotle still resided in me; each side having little understanding of the other, and the likelihood was it was set to continue.

Being out in the countryside and sensing earth energies; those of trees, rocks, places and nature generally I derived great pleasure and satisfaction from just as I had when in my early teens, and I discovered a talent for divining water. I also became interested in an esoteric society calling themselves 'The Emin' or 'The Eminent Way', run by a remarkable man notable for a great deal of occult knowledge, as well, it appeared, as being a particular focus of attention of the Inland Revenue owing to the fact that belonging to the society as a new person cost nine pounds a week, and after the probationary period of three months membership rose to thirteen pounds a week!

Whilst acquiring occult knowledge particularly of a practical nature I found well worthwhile, fifty-two pounds a month for membership was not a great deal less than many people's mortgage payments or monthly rent!

In the interim between my Rolfing experience and its effects working their way out to a conscious level, several months later I discovered the Australian and I shared similar interests, except perhaps his propensity for the odd puff of 'waccy baccy'. From an early age, before I was five when I discovered I had an uncle who had emigrated there and lived in Victoria, I was fascinated by what I was told and somehow what I felt about the country. My fascination later fed by tales in the 'Dandy' comic of Barny Brennan and Digger Merry, related through the picture serial there each week with their exploits prospecting for gold in the outback.

Whoever drew the little black and white sketches with their balloons of words spoken by the two characters managed to convey to me the harsh unforgiving rawness of the outback – whatever that was – and the toughness, resilience and resourcefulness of these two imaginary people. For me, they lived and breathed.

Having been to Australia and lived in Melbourne and Sydney for a short while, my childhood fantasy experience was, if anything, strengthened by going there, and my antipodean friend, although in some ways very cultured and sensitive, seemed to possess an aura; an indefinable hard-bitten quality imbued by the vast unforgiving reaches those imaginary prospectors of my childhood had.

Apart from our similar physical build and strength, we shared interests in the books and teachings of George Gurdgieff, and some of his acolytes; P D Ouspenskey and others and the esoteric subjects ranged over. Remarkably also I had actually been to the 'town' – more like a village – and driven five hundred miles across Queensland into the outback from Brisbane to get there, where he had been brought up!

More pointedly I helped him relive the experience of being given electric shock treatment. With his direction, I positioned my fingers applying gentle pressure to his temples each side of his forehead; just as the electrodes had once been, his body convulsed, twitched and shook powerfully as the stored experience of this electrically induced epileptic seizure racked him. And with equally powerful cries of what to me were fear and terror for the electric sledgehammer blows of some hundreds of volts he was forced to suffer.

It graphically reminded and brought home to me the unspeakable medieval battering my mother had been subjected to and endured for thirteen years and stoked further fires of rage so profound for what she suffered they will never be quenched.

He introduced me to an American who ran workshops somewhat similar to the ones we already attended, but these seemed to be less centred in pure bodywork and more wide-ranging, bordering on the esoteric, spiritual and psychic regions as well. He was evidently a devotee of Swami Muktenanda, someone who appeared to me quite similar to Guru Maharishi Mahesh Yogi of Transcendental Meditation fame, who became well known after the Beatles beat a path to his door.

A weekend workshop brought together numerous things I was familiar with; birth for example but there were none of the simple exercises and movements featured with Glyn Seaborn-Jones. It seemed to be much more fluid and less structured, working with the clues people gave about themselves in what they said. For instance, someone might say they had a thumping headache, the response being; who do you want to thump? Or saying they had a very sore red raw throat; to which the question would be: who do you want to roar at? In each case the underlying emotion driving the physical condition, i.e., suppressed and sublimated anger. The clues of what people felt leaking out through the subconscious puns in their speech. Something which has passed into common speech when people make a 'Freudian slip' – and being Freud and his theories of just about everything having an underlying sexual motive, remarks having a strong double entendre. One instance I recall from many years ago being one of the 'Any Questions' panel in giving her point of view on one of the audience's question; whether nudity was a good or bad thing, began by saying that a fellow panel member 'put the finger on it' by his answer. Which reduced him to near uncontrollable laughter as he pointed out her Freudian slip was showing.

Chanting a Muktenanda mantra accompanied by a recording of himself and 'choir' chanting it in the background, seemed to produce a subtle, pleasant and definite shift of energies within and something I had not done before.

As the title of the workshop was 'Rebirth And Sexuality', part of it was no contact mingling, on all fours, naked in the inky blackness with all lights extinguished in the large cellar where it was taking place.

Though from what I sensed there seemed to be something else occurring…

A very simple and illuminating activity right at the beginning was making a crayon sketch of oneself with left and right hands. People were then paired off and each read the other's two versions and I found myself face to face with the clear divide between my rigid intellect expressed in hard clear lines and much softer emotional character in less distinct ones indicated by right and left hand versions.

JOURNEY OF A LIFETIME

The difference between people's faces and their bodies and the messages they gave illustrated how experiences of life had been sublimated. It was pointed out to me my face was young (even that had changed and lightened markedly as my healing progressed in the first few years; and from hating it as I once had, I was happy with how I looked) but my spine showed clear signs of age in a slight, but to an aware observer, definite 'S' bend front to back. This was the only observation but to add for clarity; carrying a large burden; manifested by a slight but definite curve in my spine as if shouldering a load.

Silently, it rankled and irritated to be told of my spinal shape and my posture, but the evidence soon became clear; and like so many, many things about myself, at the time I was completely unaware of the connection.

At the end of the first day I went home in a stilled, reflective mood and arrived back on the Sunday morning even quieter, aware my emotions were close to the surface; if not already brimming over.

Standing in a small group, arms linked together, some shared their perceptions and effects of the previous day's experience. One woman felt she could see men for the first time as something other than sex objects, which mirrored some of my own feelings for women I had not realised before.

As chance would have it, some John Denver music was played. The clarity and tone of his voice always created reverberations of recognition deep in me. But of what I could not say. Perhaps somewhere in it there was a sadness and if so, spontaneously I found myself sobbing deeply; and equally spontaneously my 'motto' of life came out without conscious effort, almost mantra like: I won't give up and I won't give in. Simultaneously I felt as I had, aged nine, desperate to shoulder any burden if it would only keep our family together instead of disintegrating all round me.

If it meant carrying the house, everyone and everything in it on my back then I didn't care what it did to me.

Surprised at the words I uttered and their visceral power, I became racked with aches and pains, barely able to breathe as my cries and sobs continued.

This catharsis subsiding, I felt I understood what I had been doing for many years and the unseen burden I had carried with me. The reality was I understood some but by no means all. At the coal face of change within me, wider context simply did not exist. Instinctively I had simply wanted the unimaginable hurt of being an impotent observer to stop, as the crumbling destruction around me symbolised the loss of my childhood and overwhelming desperation to find some way to escape the inescapable. Though as a child of nine, I was as incapable of giving form to the words as I was of describing the diffuse agony consuming me. Yet deep within I knew.

There had been break ups before but as the end approached I indulged in equally symbolic activities, such as trying to clean my father's dulled and almost rusty Naval dress sword and create a smooth neat strip of lawn along the back of the house. Though completely exhausted by the latter, neither it nor any temporary lustre on the ageing blade bearing my father's name produced the slightest flicker of response. It merely fed the inner ache I hid even from myself.

The connection between 'load' and 'body posture' was a chasm away from anything I could put together in our small group and long after.

As the day wore on, I thought somehow I had put my back out as it became more and more sensitive and difficult to sit or stand. By close of the day I could only walk with some difficulty. Getting into and out of my car was excruciating. Over following months I regained mobility and also awareness the chronic back ache I had suffered for years standing for any length of time had completely gone.

I knew I had shed a huge load within me. But I was years from seeing that the disintegration was taking place inside as much as outside me and that was the burden I was really attempting to carry.

JOURNEY OF A LIFETIME

In fact it took decades for anything like understanding to fully begin dawning and only in attempting to describe the path to healing myself are all the strands weaving into one complete thread. It may have been increasingly difficult moving around that memorable day but when it came to the 'Rebirth' aspect of the workshop I discovered feeling very delicate was one thing; facing a brick wall of fear was entirely another.

I enjoyed the eclectic mixture of body, mind and emotional work of the group workshop; the sketch reading, and signals in people's bodies as well as the words they chose, and the background music played at times and mantra chanting. Yet in all this there was one element clashing in its lack of subtlety.

Our group conductor picked out expressions and words a few people had used concerning birth. In distinct contradiction to the unpressured way everything else proceeded he wanted to literally create pressure to resolve what he perceived to be unresolved aspects of birth he intuited from these conversations.

People were wrapped in blankets and four or five people put their body weight on to the person concerned.

Coming to me the process was repeated. I had felt both curiosity and a vague unease; enjoying being the centre of attention for a short while, but nervousness also.

On went the blankets and on top of them came the people, including our group leader. In all there were five; male and female. As the pressure came fully on to me laying flat on the padded mats, especially in the upper half of my body, a switch was thrown. Having done much work in the preceding year especially, I thought I knew how frightening, indeed terrifying, fighting against my mother's clamping and crushing resistance to entering the world was. Moreover how much of it I had worked through and resolved.

I didn't.

Very few seconds passed under their weight and I hit a brick wall of overwhelming fear; the image instantly springing to mind. Stricken by the accompanying wave of utter panic, in a single heave I lifted them off as if they were rag dolls; blankets and all.

Perhaps it was useful to find I still had a very large amount of working through to do to dissipate such a powerful and unexpected response. I was very relieved our leader invited me if I did not want to continue to say the words; I really, really don't want to continue, and he would stop.

Seldom ever refusing a challenge, having five people averaging about ten stone each and straitjacketed in blankets I knew was far beyond what I could stand and gladly said the magic words and received a reassuring hug from my well-intentioned tormentor.

I later discovered he had been born weeks prematurely. Clearly, his own birth had been an abrupt, climactic experience forced on him without choice or warning or being ready for it.

Unsurprising then he used the technique of forcing resolution of unresolved birth experience in others; having manifestly not worked through and resolved this shattering experience in and for himself; still projecting it out!

Perhaps also signifying the huge gulf of experience in him between his life of perfect nurture and protection in the womb and a brutal entry into the world, we returned from the brute force of this sledgehammer-induced catharsis, to the gentle sensitivity of all the other activities of the weekend. The workshop finished with a well-known rock band's music – not hard discordant clashing sound but soft, gentle and pleasant. Suddenly he raised a finger directing our attention; "Here come the first birth contractions," he warned.

Brief puzzlement instantly transmuted into understanding; just then into the music intruded a barely noticeable subtle muted jangling shudder, lasting a mere couple of seconds. A few seconds later it repeated; louder, more insistent and disquieting.

It needed no explanation whatever. It brought home in the briefest of moments without a single word how we imbue not only our speech and actions but music and other forms of expression with our unconscious or subconscious experience of birth.

It occurs to me now in a perspective gained of well over thirty years since taking part in these events the great sensitivity he had developed and acute awareness of the precursors of birth our group leader showed, exactly expressed his own attempt to come to terms with the terrifying nightmare suddenly thrust upon him with only two possible outcomes; he would either survive it or die in the attempt.

Learning all the subtle signs of impending birth and telling others about them was his way of surmounting and gaining control of the unimaginable raw terror of being forced out into the world; lungs not yet ready to breathe oxygen and his entire body measuring the length of an adult's hand. The lady who told me about his premature birth also thought it no accident our group leader had a habit of making arrangements to run workshops then cancelling them or failing to turn up before they took place on the appointed date.

Exactly like his birth, scheduled to take place at a certain date and time – but never happened as or when it was meant to!

Broadening Horizons; Nature's Gifts; Inner Canyons

A FRIEND AND colleague of our group leader, a psychologist and an adviser to President Jimmy Carter, ran a presentation we were recommended to attend. Not knowing quite what to expect I discovered this bridged the worlds of the unseen and the physical in that most of it was a video created using thermograph technology; a camera super-cooled by liquid nitrogen so it could 'see' heat patterns of the human body.

The noisy metallic whirrings of its cooling apparatus were the background to a session conducted as much as purely experimental as for any predictable results.

Our presenter explained the man whose fuzzy body heat pattern we viewed in many shades of grey, from white for hot spots deepening into murky graduations, suffered from impotence and chronic constipation and was married to someone he characterised as a shrew.

The voice of the man conducting the experiment could be heard above the equipment asking the subject to go back to early times in his life. He obliged; going back to the age of six months and an experience with his grandmother.

She had been left to look after him and at some point changed his nappy, or as Americans call them, diapers. At the point where the grandmother held this man as a six-month-old infant, her hands holding the sides of his torso, the presenter stopped the video tape.

Although the picture was only muddy grey and not at all clear, it was possible to see the pattern of large whitish blobs in the picture were the heat prints of the grandmother's finger pads down each side of the man's body. The size of the prints were in exact proportion to an adult's fingers on the baby's sides; they occupied most of his body between just under the arms to waist level.

Though it was given, it needed no explanation to understand the picture we saw; the heat patterns showed it was the man actually living the experience as a six-month-old. Reinforcing the message, if it were needed; sub or inner consciousness transcends time. We carry the bodily reality of our lives completely independent of time.

The video was resumed and the subject continued to describe what happened. His grandmother laid him on a table and unpinned his diaper, and found he had filled it. Questioned what happened next, the subject replied his grandmother had hit him for soiling it.

Asked what he felt about his grandmother the subject spat back with venom: "Fucking shit!"

Instantly our presenter's finger stabbed the stop button and he said: "What are his two problems?"

As the video resumed, the subject was encouraged to vent the long-stored hurt, anger and outrage at this brutal treatment, thumping the treatment table beside which he was standing naked and the heat patterns showed focal points of stress on and in his body.

Unsurprisingly, there was a large heat flare centred on his rectal regions.

The video completed, our presenter told us the corollary of all this was the subject cancelled an operation to have a section of his colon removed; his impotence was cured, he divorced his wife and found a loving and harmonious relationship.

He ended by saying: "We need the machines to show us we don't need the machines."

The presentation might have ended there, but perhaps to reinforce the message, he went on to tell of other experimental sessions. Rather than play another lengthy, indistinct and noisy tape, he told of a husband and wife couple filmed using the heat camera, standing side by side. Amongst other examples of seeing their body heat patterns, two stood out. On one occasion one of the couple complained of a headache. The other was asked to send energy to heal it, to see what the camera would show.

As energy was sent to the sufferer the camera showed its progression through the arm and hands linked together into the arm and on into the body of the other and the head. The headache duly ceased.

The camera having proved the ability to send and receive energy between people, a more ambitious experiment was tried. Standing together but making no contact with each other, the couple were asked if they could go out of their bodies. They replied they could.

Before long the camera showed their body heat and energy pattern beginning to retreat upwards in their bodies and finally from their heads. At the point the camera showed energy had completely left their bodies, the machine blew its fuses and ceased working.

Demonstrating beyond doubt humans can affect machines and confirming the law of Quantum Mechanics, which states observer and observed are inextricably linked no matter what the distance between.

Understanding Americans' propensity for using machines to do what they could just as well do without them, it took me back to my mantra: left to its self the human organism is totally self-healing and self-righting.

But the psychologist's remark also showed the schism between the mentality of the East Coast/New England establishment versus the 'wacky' West Coast/Californian approaches, consequently himself and the 'far out' therapies of people like Arthur Janov and others.

The latter had already shown in his 1960s book, *The Primal Scream* how brutal experiences are sublimated in inner/subconscious and consequently in the body by the example of someone who bruised very easily for no apparent reason until they consciously re-experienced being cruelly dangled upside down by the legs and ankles at birth, after which the bruises of the experience physically appeared on the person's legs exactly as they had been gripped and they were in exactly the same proportion as the thermograph's subject heat patterns had been of an adult gripping a baby's body.

Bringing the experience to conscious mind and releasing the agony and organismic outrage suffered, the person was no longer inclined to bruise inexplicably either.

Such events as these, together with the bioenergetic workshop weekends, provided spaces of 'green' in between the parched intellectual landscapes I inhabited in my working world. The need to teach imposed its unrelenting burden and at weekends I often spent time in the countryside soaking up its healing energies.

A spot I was often drawn to for its beauty, energy and atmosphere was the wooded ridge overlooking the valley running between Dorking, west towards Guildford.

I often sat looking out across it, content to let my eyes wander over the enchanting view of woods in every direction with fields and the occasional farm house nestled in at the foot of the hills.

At times I walked the path along the ridge's top edge, enjoying the feel of being shrouded by the soft, light energy of small beech trees.

Evening times I liked the best for the stillness and the absence of other human traffic along the paths and particularly in the summer the woods sometimes echoed to the noise I made as I lay on the ground. Unfailingly the place healed me.

Yet there were still reminders all this might be picturesque, but equally in the Second World War the valley beneath this ridge and the hills opposite the other side of the Dorking/Guildford road would have been of great significance if there had been an invasion. Brick built pillboxes were set at intervals alongside the path I walked. One nestling under a yew tree, I sometimes climbed on the roof to peer through the yew branches and ponder how those in the Home Guard must have felt manning these places.

One Saturday afternoon I decided to crawl inside; the entrance having become half filled with earth. Making my way to the front overlooking the valley I looked out through the window slot a machine gun would have poked its fire-spitting presence through less than forty years before.

Wondering what echoes persisted of the endless watches of first angst then boredom as the war progressed, I lay on the hard dry clay invading the cramped space.

From some inner volition I decided to strip off and lay naked; unconcerned. No one ever came near these places.

After some time, and almost dozing off but for the odd annoying insect intent on making a meal of me, I suddenly heard the approach of a child's footfalls.

Almost before I realised it, scuffling feet on dry clay announced I was about to get a visitor who began chattering to himself as children often do.

Most concerned this young interloper should not be scared out of his wits suddenly coming upon me, let alone stark naked, I began pulling on clothes as rapidly as possible but it was clear from the noise of his approach in a second or two he and I would be face to face.

I let out a loud cough and like a rat up a drain pipe the child shot back out of the entrance yelling: "Mum! Mum! There's a monster in there!" After a short delay a woman's hesitant voice uncertainly asked if there was anyone there.

Feigning as best I could unconcern I definitely didn't feel, I replied there was, and made my way out, hoping my frantically donned clothes didn't appear too awry and my bootlaces trailing undone would go unnoticed.

Greatly relieved, the mother calmed her alarmed offspring, letting him see there wasn't a monster in the pillbox, and bid me a nervous hello. Wondering what to say I said quite truthfully I was just sitting inside wondering what it must have felt like, but added, hoping it might end the conversation quickly and she and her by now once more chattering son, would make a hasty retreat, that I was a trainee psychotherapist and had gone inside to see what I picked up.

It did the trick; mother and approaching father with small daughter, with garrulous monster-free son climbed down beside the pillbox, disappearing quickly along the other tree-covered path below and in front of it.

Out of sight but distinctly still within earshot, the mother in a slightly brittle voice and higher tone than before still showing nervousness said quite loudly, "Do you know, I felt so horribly *normal* talking to that chap."

Tempted to make some rejoinder about normality being very fragile if it had to be stated, I thought better of it, tidied myself up, tied my boot laces and also beat a somewhat nervous retreat, vowing *never* to venture into the pillbox again in any state of dress!

From a very early age I was instinctively drawn to trees and woods for their healing effects – something else I didn't know or could put into words. I knew I felt freer under their leafy influence and carried a memory of the time sitting on a bus aged four longing to get back among them in woods where I lived.

Once home I made a beeline for them and after a short while I suddenly realised how warm and happy my body felt and how free, running around under them.

Colour too I instinctively used whilst at school to heal myself without knowing what I was doing, only that my body felt very soothed by its effect. Rehearsing a school play I would stand on stage in front of a spotlight having a rotating disc of primary colours in front of it and stood breathing deeply as blue came round, soaking up as much as I possibly could before the colour changed. After a few repetitions I felt completely limp. In the summer I would stuff my pockets with lavender flowers as much for their colour as for their fragrance I also found instinctively soothing.

Increasingly as the years progressed and study and intellectual endeavour came to dominate everything else, this natural awareness of how nature healed me became more and more suppressed.

From the beginning of my efforts to heal myself and rebuild health and strength, re-connection with the natural world was almost like picking up where I had left off; my body knew what it needed and wanted, so also like 'taking the dog for a walk' and allowing my body off my intellect's short controlling, choke-chain lead, I indulged its need, but increasingly conscious of what I picked up from nature; the particular energy of different trees and the effects of plants.

Together with my frequent forays out into the countryside – with or without relics of the Second World War – I found myself drawn to books about herbs and plants for healing.

Used to and even expert though I might be in the realms of computer hardware and software, intellectually 'vacuum cleaning' words off pages in books for the facts and knowledge they might impart, I quickly realised it was a completely pointless pursuit if I was to learn what effects plants had. So I began experimenting with them to discover what their effects were.

One delightful book by a Frenchman named Maurice Mességué – a world renowned healer to princes, potentates and even the Pope – called *Health Secrets Of Plants And Herbs*, appealed to me as much for its beautiful pictures, drawings and written information, as for the inspiration it gave me to an open door of nature to begin using plants, learning directly what their effects were on me.

Wondering where to begin, my supermarket of frequent use obligingly came to my aid by beginning to stock small tubs of cooking herbs; the usual sage, thyme, rosemary, marjoram and mint.

Trying marjoram, two effects were quickly apparent; having tipped a tub full in the bath and soaking for a while I emerged looking as though I had fallen in a duck weed covered pond; speckled all over with the herb. The second was I felt as though my head was about to fall off my shoulders. The herb has many attributes for curing or alleviating head conditions; eyes, nose, mouth, throat etc. as well as other parts of the body.

Very apparently it affected head and neck muscles also. And mine were rigid.

Mint, as Mességué says, is a cousin of marjoram and has some similar effects.

Quite apart from its well-known culinary association with lamb, I found it wonderfully relaxing and soothing to the point of only stumbling out of the bath when it had gone completely cold, being unable to stay awake after a couple of minutes of immersion. As I struggled unsuccessfully to raise leaden eyelids, I heard my stomach start working, gurgling like badly designed plumbing.

Relating to a manager and work colleague how useful I had found mint after driving hundreds of miles two days in a row and bathing in mint each evening; experiencing pleasant, restful repose instead of driving my car all night in my sleep, he looked at me as if I was mildly mad and laughed; slightly scornful and disbelieving.

I suggested he try it himself, the mint working for sceptics and open-minded alike.

One Monday lunchtime some weeks later, walking to the pub, he said, "Well, I did it!"

Irritated by his obscure remark, "Did what?" I asked tetchily.

"I had a mint bath," he replied.

Asked how he felt, the response was, incredibly drowsy.

After writing a long essay for his Open University degree one weekend and feeling tense and tired he had done as I described, put some mint in the bath and got in. He too in a very short time found it very hard to stay awake.

Such things as these widening interests; the esoteric, occult and reconnection to the natural world were all things happening in 1979; the year I impatiently thought of as 'nothing happening' on my path of healing.

Yet patently to my inner wisdom this was healing also. Connection between my head-long pursuit the year previous, working almost completely on my emotional and inner worlds and deep inner intelligence having nothing to do with intellect, was almost non-existent. In fact 'body' intelligence and intellectual strivings operated on distinctly separate parallel tracks within me.

My Grand Canyon inner divide clearly still existed. And I lived on opposite sides in my life.

Perhaps to make the point more forcefully, when I attended a crash course in Arizona as the year ended, such was the intellectual pressure to assimilate and absorb a completely new operating system, it caused me involuntary hot flushes as I rammed far too much information into my brain, knowing I would soon need to teach others, my own polarised inner chasm of being was why I stood staring across its vast incomprehensible reaches a few months later. Though the experience, like a great shout sending echoes around its ramifications was soon lost in this unimaginable outer void, the wisdom it symbolised continued to reverberate within.

Even if I persisted in simultaneously living on opposing sides; disavowing the massive divide in myself and its equally unbridgeable span I thought to bestride. Heedless of the cost.

Consolidation and Growth; The Wider World

As already related, I had felt a growing and instinctive need to mend damage I felt had been somehow caused after the invasive pummelling and prodding my body sustained in the course of being Rolfed.

A deep unease seemed to permeate me within, and yet I found it difficult if not impossible to do anything about it for well over a year.

It was only when a friend told me about a very gentle form of massage she had undergone, I felt instinctively it was probably what I needed. Though the curious unease and its inertia caused weeks to pass before I did anything about it. Whatever it might be I was very determined this would be a completely different experience to Rolfing.

This massage was Rolfing's polar opposite. It consisted of a light gentle touch, using as its barometer of activity, a stethoscope placed low down on my abdomen; the purpose being to listen to the peristaltic gurgling of the gut and use this as a means of knowing when a part of the body being massaged responded with a degree of shock and gurgling rhythmic contractions of the large intestine instantly ceased. This indicated that part of the body triggering the response was to some degree traumatised and needed careful treatment.

At the end of the first very pleasant massage by gentle female hands I explained to the lady I had climbed on to her massage table like something that had crawled on to a fishmonger's slab and died.

"That's interesting," was her considered response; "Your body was in a mild state of shock!"

Explaining my Rolfing experience months before, the pieces suddenly fell into place: I understood my animalistic response to my 'tormentor' and the vague resistance I felt coupled with the beer I drank when facing the prospect of more painful probing.

Again; like an abused animal I had reacted on a deep unconscious level exactly like one; my response propelled by an equally deep recognition of the 'body fear' all the discomfort and pain the Rolfing inflicted at what was very clearly a level well beneath any conscious awareness.

My impatience to progress in my healing had caused me to venture into experimenting with my body in a way I never should have done. It was an object lesson and the first time I began, to some degree, to understand the difference between my ranting goal-obsessed intellect which thought all manner of things and the reality and deep intelligence of my own body.

It knew what *felt* good for it; when 'nothing happening' actually meant my body and subconscious and inaccessible inner selves knew time was needed to heal and consolidate before anything else would float up from these fathomless levels of my existence and signal their own sublime agenda in their own good time, something else needing resolution and integrating into conscious mind and experience.

It was an object lesson in thought not being reality. What I felt was something with a far deeper and incomparably broader foundation of inner wisdom. Equally it was something I could not articulate then either.

The Grand Canyon's opposite edges might be many miles apart, but the ground beneath was, after all, what gave it all its form and united these extremes. Parts of me might only be in distant communication but where before it had been nonexistent it was a faculty of growing, if hesitant; even tenuous, common understanding in myself. Not easily or quickly traversed; just as anyone attempting to walk the Canyon's Bright Angel Trail down to the river bed knows – let alone the many miles to the canyon's distant rim.

These first flickerings of understanding created stirrings of awareness of just what a gulf I had created in myself and the consequential damage I was also inflicting within and the stark dreams which told me what I had been – and still was – doing. But quoting an old speech by Charles James Fox MP, a vociferous anti-slavery campaigner, in response to ending slavery – but by degrees – it was like giving up rape and pillage slowly within and against my own self.

Consequently even these first streaks of dawning awareness took many years before the light of real understanding lit my thoughts and the chasm between muscle-bound intellect and sublime intelligence really began harmonising.

Like a junkie addicted to strong narcotics though, I might have a very strong desire to improve how I felt, but intellectual kudos was just as much a drug as anything one might sniff, smoke, inject or swallow.

Over Christmas and New Year, spent with friends, I had plenty of time to sit around enjoying doing very little; it was a welcome chance to re-emerge from beneath the deep drift of brain-blizzard intellectual overload sustained on the arduous crash course in Phoenix.

For some months as the crippling stiffness gradually receded in my lower back following the workshop I attended months earlier, over the holiday period I concentrated on relaxing my left shoulder. I was well aware it was a lot less mobile than my right.

Doing nothing was a good opportunity to use the skill I developed over the years, of concentrating on tensed up muscles in a part of my body, and getting them to release.

After a day or so my efforts were well rewarded; my shoulder definitely freed up, though I hadn't bargained for indescribable tiredness and fatigue surfacing as the tensions diminished. At night I slept soundly – a most welcome luxury I delighted in – but by 9.30 the next morning I felt weary as if I hadn't slept for days.

Repeating the experience for a few days I soon regained normal wakefulness and composure. Unsurprisingly, in their turn came quite powerful dreams and some palpitations signalling my body's inner reaches expressing their resentment at the tyrant in my head for abusing these regions of myself; and of more sublimated, blocked energy crossing the opening inner door towards the threshold of conscious expression.

A curious situation I was used to being an observer of – as was so often the case – and not at all concerned about. My mantra never ceased to echo in my head: left to itself, the human organism is completely self-righting and self-healing, and it was this that gave me a focus for what must always have been – whether I realised it or not – my complete trust in my own body.

In turn it showed what a yawning chasm existed before I began healing myself and this great rift of continental proportions there had once been when 'head' ruled everything I did, and I punished my body like a cruel jockey lashing his obedient, long-suffering steed.

Releasing the tensions in my shoulder and my sublimated deep fatigue with it were of course – and as always – only the start. Infallibly as my body opened up, behind the opening sluices of energy flowing again in stagnant parts, flooded other body symptoms, of which the dreaming and palpitations were the first 'trickles' before the broadening gush began in earnest.

Soon, gut and abdominal discomfort and pain signalled more work to be done and digestion and sleep were thrown into confusion. Just like the confusion of waters, flotsam and jetsam boiling and swirling downstream from previously long-closed sluices; abdominal uproar was accompanied, then succeeded by, swirling emotions needing to be expressed and released before anything like normality was restored. Not least in the spectrum of outrage, to hurt was more on the 'chuckle sob' theme progressing from intrusive car seat back in my abdomen to a rolled up towel or cushion pushed there; and changing much more to sobbing then a dry 'chuckle'.

JOURNEY OF A LIFETIME

For a few weeks I felt quite physically delicate as considerable changes progressed. Other aches and pains flickered around my body; some small, others very sudden and sharp.

On my next visit for more peristaltic monitored massage the lady quickly noticed the shape of my shoulder had changed. She declared it much less 'full' than before, which I didn't understand except there was undeniably far less energy locked up in that region as I could feel, and no doubt as her stethoscope detected in my colonic activity.

Ultimately the wider outcome of consciously commanding my shoulder to open up and release was more usable energy. Part of my healing process with the peristaltic massage was not actual massage itself. My very observant masseuse was acute at gauging my state of mind when entering her domain. On occasion she would say something needed to be dealt with before any attempt was made to work with my body energy and musculature.

A great deal of this at the beginning was the massive overload of unintegrated emotional energy gouged out by my Rolfer's fingers and knuckles.

Part of the utterly unexpected consequence and follow-on from this deeply invasive body assault were powerful images from life before. But not this life.

This was not some vague, woolly mental meandering; I was propelled into it, wanted or not, after only the first session or two when the Rolfing began.

I found myself having to deal with insistent and very powerful images from a life in Roman times.

Although she said nothing I sensed she was sceptical; but in sympathy with the brutality my body experienced in Rolfing I was pitch-forked into images of gladiatorial brutality without a choice, and no option but to deal with them.

Some were extremely detailed. Indeed from them I corroborated a considerable amount over subsequent years about the dress, weapons and some of the gladiatorial techniques for reducing an opponent to mangled meat. The passing of many years have done absolutely nothing to change; except to reinforce, clarify, and further extend these images.

The wonderfully soothing peristaltic-governed massage helped a great deal to put my body back together again; to heal it; resolving some of the deep body trauma and 'body' fear.

Integrating and putting insistent past life images into some sort of context were completely beyond its scope though. They came to me once the Rolfing began and have never left.

I had already experienced a scene sitting at home in darkness beside my living room gas fire in the early autumn evening, enjoying the quietness as the twilight deepened.

It drifted into mind; fragmentary at first, but quickening, insistent and gaining rapidly in detail. As a Roman soldier I was returning home. As I walked towards what appeared – and still does – to be a vine covered pergola I could see a young woman sitting in the twilight on a raised stone step into the house beside it. It was my daughter. But this was no ordinary home coming. She sat naked up to her waist, holding her slit abdomen to keep her entrails from spilling out.

Approaching close, even in the twilight I could see the sadness and utter disbelief in her eyes; she knew she was dying, but like all young, believed she was immortal. Death was incomprehensible.

My home in upper Galicia – Northern Spain or perhaps what is now Southern France and the Pyrenees – had been ravaged; and her with it.

As this scene came upon me from nowhere, I was filled with choking, aching sobs so strong I could hardly breathe; my torso racked with the pain of them. They continued for nearly an hour.

It was as real to me as the grief I felt for the loss of my Aunt.

JOURNEY OF A LIFETIME

The only difference being hers I was able to work through, this other scene perhaps I never will; it still produces indescribable aching tears and paternal sadness at seeing someone I thought the sun rose for, being taken from me. As she slipped away it coalesced into a desire for bloody revenge, its burning so strong beside which the sun's rays were like a dwindling fire.

Which is where scenes of later butchery have their origin; and many, many others also.

No surprise then, around this time I also heard about a man who specialised in past life work. Just as the lady whose gentle touch helped soothe my body and deeper aspects of being was American, so was this man. In fact, as my wife had been American and those running the rebirth and sexuality workshop and thermograph video presentation were also; not to mention the company I worked for. I seemed to have some inexplicable affinity with them. But that too was decades away from discovering what threads of past existence I had become entwined with in this one.

If I expected my past life guide to produce a parting of clouds and shafts of divine wisdom beaming down on me I was very disappointed.

The sessions – held in what looked like a hastily built bank vault of massive red brick walls built into the first floor of his dwelling to avoid causing his neighbour's hair to fall out with strange blood curdling noises – did not inspire me. It all seemed a bit off the cuff and made up as we went along.

To get into a relaxed state where images of past existences might be acquired along with keys to their understanding, simple exercises similar to counting sheep were used. But the sessions did not produce anything of significance.

It seemed in spite of myself things really would surface in me only if they were appropriate.

Deciding it was a waste of time; the effort of driving from West to East London and back and the cost of sessions, I was about to call it a day when once more images came to me as undeniable as they were sudden and unexpected. Spilling over with this we ascended the stairs to the bank vault, its massive door pulled shut from the inside, and trusting we would not die of asphyxiation, I once again fell apart in floods of barely breath-sustainable spontaneous racking sobs.

This had nothing to do with family – at least so far as relatives went – but instead were scenes of a military ambush and subsequent slaughter.

The images were of a column of Roman soldiers in a mountain pass defile attacked by a hoard and being completely overwhelmed. A feature of the rout and subsequent slaughter being dogs used and trained by the attackers to get in under any shield wall and create as much confusion and disarray so the column would be caught between using weapons offensively and having to fight off dogs attacking their legs and any exposed parts.

As a Centurion and responsible for men under my command, somehow I survived. Exactly how is unknown but the enduring image is of a few figures in black; women? picking over the corpses of soldiers on the slope of a very high rounded mountainside and smoke of one or two small fires mingling in a pall over a scene of desolation and atmosphere and smell of death.

At one and the same time I felt relieved at a battle survived as a hardened soldier skilled in the arts; simultaneously consumed with excoriating guilt and shame at having failed completely to protect those under my charge.

The loss of so many of my military family driving the unstoppable gush of aching tears of outraged futility at my own skill counting for nothing and seeing all I knew and loved strewn about; hacked, bloody and silent.

JOURNEY OF A LIFETIME

The next several days following this were almost surreal. Indeed at times they *were* unreal. Waking in the morning I felt as if I was a diver rising from a great depth. I had no idea who, where or what I was for a few seconds and none of which day either.

Going out in the countryside to an old pub, perhaps a couple of hundred years old, in the area I used to frequent, when I sat down, if I closed my eyes the place simply disappeared; I was among thin saplings in a wood. It was as if I was there seeing the place a long, long time before the pub or anything else there existed.

I seemed to be in two worlds; my day-to-day world around me and some other simultaneously. The one I could see, touch and with other senses, interact with; the other equally as real and just as equally something I could not grasp at all. If I closed my eyes I felt I was somewhere – perhaps even someone – completely different. The only thing anchoring me in one place was work and the hard intellectual grind of study and teaching software. It was not until getting on for two years later and deciding to have a tarot card reading, the lady who gave it remarked there had been an 'updating' in my recent past which immediately connected with the earlier experience of finding it difficult to know precisely what reality I was in.

The only description fitting what I had felt was bits of me floating around in different realities which were also connected together by some thread of consciousness that was also me.

The cards in the reading seemed to me to be a dog's breakfast of so many different aspects of me the lady called it one of total being, there being so many, to me, disparate aspects; and yet all of it *was* still me.

Perhaps another image describes it better; of feeling stretched in all directions to just about the limit of what I could stand; or beyond it.

At the point in my life where I was dealing with the powerful after effects of Rolfing, each day was a small adventure; getting on with my life and work, wondering what else might insist on elbowing its way into mind. Rather like wandering through a darkened place and suddenly different film scenes appearing on different screens coming and going randomly. Just images without sound, yet in a dreamlike state.

That there were changes going on within I was certain, but what they were I had no idea. Just getting through it all was more than enough to cope with.

Walking around and being in the woods I had come to know so well felt very different.

Certainties about them and the familiarity of wandering in them, enjoying sensing different energies of various parts, trees and whatever else I had registered, melted away. Perceptions changed and kept on changing as the weeks and months went by.

It would be easy in long retrospect to make comments about what I did or did not perceive at these times; all would be false. Being in scenes of a play is very different to seeing pictures of it all. Only being able to view all of them is it then possible to put the whole thing in perspective. And perspective was only possible with the distance created by time. Not days or weeks; nor yet months or years but decades. Whether I fully realised it or not – and I didn't; or didn't want to – the intellectual burden of the teaching work I did was a heavy one. It demanded a great deal of mental and physical stamina; as all other instructors found in their own work.

I seemed to be driven to test myself in all directions. To struggle in vastly disparate endeavours; on the one hand dedicated to expanding my emotional horizons and casting off my own self-imposed intellectual tyranny and simultaneously shouldering even larger loads in learning and teaching of such knowledge.

I found fulfilment and satisfaction in each of these fields; in healing my body and my inner worlds and the opportunities, kudos and status afforded by deep technical insight.

JOURNEY OF A LIFETIME

The 'vehicle of my life' as symbolised by my dreams in which I was driving a car appeared to be something over which I had ultimate control as it hadn't crashed with dire consequences, but as the images persisted perhaps they were showing me I didn't seem to know how to stop the thing; I was a passenger in my own life.

Deep Stress Catharsis

A COLLEAGUE AND good friend who worked in the department shared very similar interests to my own. The books by Carlos Castenada and Gurdgieff he found as interesting and 'magical' in his own words, as I did. The world of astrology interested me more and more; something he was exceptionally good at.

He also shouldered heavy technical responsibilities in the work he undertook.

Through discussions on topics of emotion, he was well acquainted with my involvement with growth, development and healing. He was committed to developing a new course in interactive computer access for commercial business and though it afforded time in Paris – a place we both loved – to gather information he needed, it was clear from his face and his complexion it weighed increasingly heavily, and steadily took its toll on him.

One lunchtime we walked to a pub not far away beside the Thames. The strain of his work clearly showed in his face. It was also apparent his stomach and digestion were in turmoil. He suggested a healing/therapy session with me might be worthwhile.

Wanting to empathise, carrying similar burdens, myself developing new courses in my desire to help, my mouth ran away with me which, like the car in my dreams, I didn't seem able to stop.

Letting him know a few days later, I knew he was thinking; why doesn't he shut his ****ing mouth, it was clear verbal diarrhoea and was the last thing he needed to add to his own inner state; he told me how 'tragic' he felt.

Reassured, and somewhat surprised, I did understand his inner turmoil. He joined me in my small, sound-deadened room I used for opening up channels of blocked, suppressed and stored emotional energy.

At my suggestion ,he laid on a large mattress; as much for the relief it gave him as to see what direction the session might be headed in. If I hadn't worked with someone before, instinctively, I let their body express what, if anything, it wanted to in exactly the same way as I had done myself when I began my own journey. Whether it be sound and fury for the heavy pressure of deadlines and weight of responsibilities he carried or perhaps quieter and more reflective content, to allow his body some peace for once. But even before we began, the tumult in his digestive system had to be placated with a visit to the loo.

Initially he lay on the mattress quietly. After a few minutes his left foot gave a small twitch. Repeated a few times I suggested he allow the tremor without trying to control it in any way.

It was not long before his complete leg became part of the movement and invisibly within his body it spread; not only involving both legs but upper body as well, and developing from a convulsive movement to a rapid rhythmic side to side motion. Finally, his whole body from head to feet, including arms flailed from side to side. He was utterly silent. Not a sound came from his lips. Reaching a crescendo of thrashing, it subsided until only the original twitch remained.

To use a mechanical analogy, it reminded me somewhat of an engine stuttering into life, gradually warming up until it was running flat out, then gradually slowing until it regained its spasmodic 'tick over'.

Steadily, the tremor grew again; taking over more and more of his body until it thrashed like a flail with such force even his cheeks and mouth moved from side to side, very like a dog shaking itself having emerged dripping wet after swimming. Again it climbed to a manic crescendo descending into stillness a second time. The complete cycle lasting more than five though less than ten minutes.

Words and any guidance from me did not seem appropriate; his body spoke its own needs more eloquently than any superfluous verbal drizzle could. So I kept silent.

Yet again, the cycle repeated, if anything with more force and vigour, until I wondered if his head might detach from his body. The extremes of movement and its power causing saliva to be thrown out of his mouth. Almost on the point of intervening in case he dislocated a limb or caused himself a neck injury, I was relieved this human whirlwind-cum-thrashing machine once more subsided into quiet repose. The mantra I carried; left to itself the human organism is entirely self-righting and self-healing being the only thing by which I maintained my silence.

In fact, the process continued repeating for nearly an hour. Still he said not a single word.

Eventually I brought him to his feet to ground him and regain his bearings.

I did not question what had happened, refraining from any inappropriate musings on what I felt about his experience. Not unnaturally, he seemed somewhat disorientated and tired in the release of so much suppressed energy.

About two weeks later he came for another session. This time he left his car at work. He had found it difficult to concentrate after his experience, which was not surprising, and I offered to 'taxi' him back home.

Once more, without words the same cycle repeated, with equal ferocity, over and over.

Delivered to his door some miles away he looked in no fit state to have driven. He departed with the compliment I could get a job as a taxi driver anytime as he had never got home most of his usual route so quickly and smoothly! He did not realise I felt not dissimilar to him; except I was wound up like a clock spring with tension; hence the driving so I could get back home and unwind. Although difficult to recall at this distance events occurring in 1980, at least another session repeated the same cathartic release of energy.

JOURNEY OF A LIFETIME

It finally found its resolution in a truly memorable occasion.

Yet again the same amazing release of energy proceeded; it was like watching a human elastic band wound round and round, held under tension, suddenly released.

Such was the sheer violence of complete body movement at one point it would have been just possible to put a hand under his body touching neither mattress or him. For a fleeting instant, whilst completely horizontal, he levitated a few inches above it. He had told me he might be thinking about the price of a bus ticket from Hammersmith to his home; it made no difference to the thrashing at all; it continued with a volition all its own.

If before his gyrations had made a considerable impact on me, this time they were spectacular and I was very concerned and only kept from intervening by his assurance he did not feel in any danger from what happened in these sessions.

Finally, the human elastic band stilled and for the first time, actually began to say a few words.

As he stood up he looked as he described himself; pole-axed. The flesh of his face was loose; a great deal of tension had gone. At the same time he looked haggard, drained and very tired. Feeling not unlike him, I let him drive himself home, having arrived in his own car, admonishing him to drive carefully.

Seeing him safely at work in Hammersmith the following day I heaved a sigh of relief, learning his wife, on seeing him looking so drained and haggard, wondered what on earth he had been doing.

It would be easy to say I understood all that had happened as it took place. That would not be true.

Whilst I knew I had been able to facilitate a remarkable release of energy and culminating in profound relief, it took a great deal longer for complete understanding of the full picture to arrive. It did not take long however, to realise in witnessing the release of a massive amount of bottled up energy, I had also facilitated the catharsis of a great deal of fear, in much the same way as I had writhed and thrashed around over many months until I connected with wanting to get out of my body.

Ultimately just as his stomach had been the barometer of his inner uproar before, this huge gush of energy unleashed from within and manifested through his body, it did not take long thereafter before he regained abdominal normality, the strain in his face subsided and his sharp wit and sense of humour returned.

At the outset of the sessions with me, he opined he was in a much worse condition than I had been when I began healing myself. Little did he realise I envied him for the way in which he was able to unload such a colossal amount of stress in such a short time and concentrated manner.

Even a year or more after I began, and many body changes and improvements had occurred, a clairvoyant who wielded a very sharp scalpel of insight, twice told me I had the potential of a long life, which in clairvoyant speak meant at that time unless things improved I was unlikely to have one.

For me the process of regaining health felt like a very slow climb up a very high mountain and it even irked me I seemed to have a talent for creating leaps of positive change in others, whilst plodding slowly on myself.

Another such example occurred some months later.

Deep Trauma and Miraculous Transformations

One afternoon, sitting in a quiet empty classroom studying, away from the noise and distractions of our main lecturer's open office, the door gently opened and a female colleague asked if she could come in.

Welcoming her, she pulled up a chair opposite the desk at which I sat, sat down and said, almost as if she was heaving a deep inward sigh, she thought it was time to have a word with me.

It had been some considerable time since I had spoken with her at all. I had felt as though she was perhaps avoiding me. I noticed she had lost weight; she looked run down, thin, unhappy and not at all well.

She knew of my keen interest in healing from the conversations we had on the subject and very soon I understood why she had not spoken and looked as she did. She knew her face mirrored how she felt; even more, she said she was aware there were two halves to it and in the difference between left and right I saw, I knew what she meant. Moreover, just how thin, haggard and rather sad she appeared. She began by saying she was beginning to get involuntary shakes and this had been the catalyst for her to pluck up the courage to speak to me.

She told me she had become pregnant and her boyfriend had in so many words dumped her. She did not want the baby and her body had expressed this by being sick after almost everything she ate. She realised she was trying to symbolically rid herself of the baby no matter how she tried or how careful about what she ate.

After an abortion she immediately ate a plate-full of egg and chips without any reaction and could eat almost anything without any adverse effects.

The emotional effects though continued to take their toll; she could see the split in her own features between left and right side and when the shakes began she knew she needed help and so had come to me.

I felt deeply touched for her plight and also the trust she placed in me. In my earnestness to assure how I felt I could help I realised I was letting my mouth run away with me as I had with my other colleague, but arranged for her to come for a session and hopefully begin sorting out the emotional tangle weighing her down.

Living close by in Richmond, a few days later we drove to my home together from work.

In relating what had happened to her, I was quite struck by how little hurt, sadness and anger she expressed for all she had been through and endured.

Instinctively I felt these emotions were like being in a fog; unable and perhaps unwilling also, to focus clearly on any one aspect; of being beset by it all and not knowing quite where to begin or not to.

Instinctively also I suggested we begin with the exercise of pushing hand to hand against each other as I had done many times in the weekend groups with Glyn Seaborn-Jones.

This unfailingly focused the one getting pushed around on what emotion was uppermost in them. Symbolically to compress this diffuse fog into a single 'pool' of emotion; consequently to be able to deal with it in whatever way she wished to express her feelings.

Quickly, and after only brief hand against flat hand pushing, she asked to stop.

I sat opposite her on the thickly padded floor and in a remarkably gentle way the hurt and sadness began to be expressed with an equally if not even more remarkable absence of outrage and anger for all she had endured.

In stark contrast to the whirling flail of bodily released energy witnessed in my male colleague in my little room where we were, this session was just as notable for the near total absence of powerful outpouring energy.

With a sense of anticlimax, even disappointment I had not been able to help more, I ferried her back to her flat.

Next morning she arrived back in the office nearly an hour late.

Putting her coat on a hangar she came straight over to me and placing her hands on the book case in front of my desk she fixed me with her gaze and said with a quizzical look in her eyes expressing a flicker of a smile and mild optimism; "Funny thing. *Both* my alarm clocks were twenty minutes slow this morning!"

And the imperceptible flicker of humour burst into a smile then light, happy laughter when I responded: "Boy! You were letting out some heavy energy weren't you!"

Being a very heavy sleeper, she explained she had two alarm clocks; one mechanical the other electric, the latter as insurance should the first fail to rouse her as was not uncommon.

I was extremely pleased and frankly amazed at what had happened. Mechanical clocks I had heard of – even experienced myself – being affected by an invisible 'gluey' energy released in sleep but I had *never* heard of an electric mains powered clock being similarly affected.

Further confirmation if it were needed of the effects on the thermograph machine of people leaving their bodies. At which point the thermograph machine sympathetically followed suit; all energy leaving *its* 'body' as well when the fuses blew!

Over the next few weeks I witnessed as no doubt others did, including my colleague who almost levitated into the air with his thrashing, a near miraculous transformation of this young lady. Indeed it *was* miraculous.

The visible divide in her face reflecting her deeper state dissolved. Her skin and complexion, from being a mild yellowish grey, transmuted like the dawn, from leaden hues into delicate pink-flushed cheeks as her inner sun rose, shining softly in her eyes. Her peals of laughter were heard much in the days following; almost to the point of irritation as I strove to concentrate on my studies and work in the open office.

In long retrospect, as laughter and tears are such close bedfellows, I have no doubt whatsoever her laughter was her way deep within herself of transmuting her depth of hurt and sadness into this open and spontaneous release in a manner she could permit in herself. Simultaneously *safely* distancing herself from the expression of her own depth of feeling.

Her face filled out as she put weight on again and she transformed into a picture of glowing health.

I was not simply amazed by this metamorphosis; I was perplexed to the point of irritation. It was near unbelievable I had helped bring about this unimaginable change of state. It clashed; indeed once again it actually hurt; here I was plodding on my way and yet had been a catalyst for this alchemical magic.

Sitting in a local pub one Friday evening after work about three weeks later, as we often did, sharing as lecturers a sense of common identity, and release from the week's work stresses, I turned to my levitating colleague sitting next to me and said he might have wondered why our mutual colleague who at that moment was laughing fit to burst at some comical remark, was looking so well?

Slightly caught off balance he said he was right on the point of remarking to me how well she was looking in the last few weeks and how she had changed almost out of recognition in a very short time.

I knew he could be trusted with what I told him because of his own experience with me.

Once more, this transformed lady came over to me one afternoon and said she thought she would like another session. Again, by my standards it was very low key, even by comparison with the first occasion and she was a very different person. I said how difficult it had been for me as an

JOURNEY OF A LIFETIME

observer to watch the spectacular changes in her. I had deliberately kept my distance at work avoiding influencing her in any way.

Dropping her back at her flat, as she got out of the car I told her to put both clocks on twenty minutes so as not to be late the next morning.

She arrived there on time and came straight over to my desk.

Smiling and laughing she explained the mechanical clock had been twenty minutes slow but the electric one was on time.

Intellect, Archetypes and Transformation

THERE WAS A remarkable difference between how I and my other male colleague released energy and how she did and resolved experience internally. There was the patently obvious difference of gender but also with decades of hindsight, how her character expressed in her astrological birth sign affected the way she processed and resolved personal experience. The psychologist, Carl Jung, being from a family of clergymen and mystics, found astrology a far more reliable means of understanding people's make-up and inner selves than any sex-centred theorising of Freud from whom he unsurprisingly became alienated; strongly disagreeing and clashing with.

Personally, I have no doubt whatever in Freud's relationship with his own mother; patently dominated by and afraid of her translated into his theories where so many disparate threads of motivation and experience like flotsam in a whirlpool. Not related with one another but under intellect's gravitational force inescapably compressed together with one inevitable focus: sex.

Deeper than this, *exactly* how Jung describes, the effects of disowned and dispossessed 'shadow' aspects of ourselves; for a male the shadow being feminine energy and principle or archetype, called 'anima'. For a female; animus. It is clear Freud was doing precisely what Jung had witnessed in many patients over years of practice. Namely what we reject of our inner being; the image and archetype of the feminine in himself, Freud projected out into the world, seeing everything reflecting back at him as aspects of sex.

Which was true; he was seeing the feminine aspects – his anima 'shadow' – reflected back at him because he was rejecting his *own* anima *unconsciously* because of his relationship with his own dominating mother!

So he saw sex in *every* kind of inter-relationship, incapable of seeing he was locked in a struggle with his own inner being, locked in his own hall of distorting inner mirrors!

Over many years it is clear to me, not least by becoming acquainted with Jung's knowledge and use of it, astrological signs are a very good way of understanding the *characteristics and balance* of someone's energies; emotional, mental and physical. And in the hands of a really good astrologer a great deal more. Even more so one trained as a Jungian psychologist; as for example Doctor Liz Greene and discussed in her very insightful book, *Relating*.

Looking back, the way my female work colleague resolved a huge amount in her deeper unseen regions of emotions, mind and being was in exact sympathy with her strong Cancerian nature. Cancer the crab; a water inhabiting animal, being represented by the moon – whose reflected light upon the earth is 1/250,000 of the sun – and is characterised as *the* most emotional sign being seen as the 'shadow' side of our nature and the *archetypal* expression of the feminine and emotional aspects of self.

It is – literally and metaphorically – the reflection of the sun; a pale shadow of the sun's vast output. And truly the two are polar opposites; the sun is nearly a million miles in diameter, spews out four million tons of *light* every second and colossal solar winds of energy. Being also inexpressibly and colossally, the greatest influence on the earth's weather through the massive magnetic storms created by sun spots, themselves generating vast streams of charged particles counteracting cosmic radiation which otherwise causes clouds to be generated within the earth's atmosphere. And which the lying hysteria of global warming being man-made CO_2 generated, is deliberately using to institute a UN centred worldwide dictatorship and worldwide punitive taxation disguised as a 'carbon tax'.

The moon conversely is dense, solid rock having no internal source of energy. Generating no light; reflecting only the sun's, and being a mere 2,160 miles in diameter. And only influences the earth indirectly through its gravity. 'Coincidentally' appearing in the heavens as exactly the same size as the sun being only 238 – 240,000 miles from earth to the sun's ninety-three million miles.

Consequentially in every way being the obverse of the sun and seen as passively feminine; complementing the sun's powerfully active masculine principle.

The moon, it should not be forgotten, not only creates ocean tides; it is well known in hospitals that people bleed more after operations at full moon. It also causes earth tides of about two-and-a-half feet.

Also affecting the germination of planted seeds – as true farmers who work to moon phases and the rhythms of the earth – testify.

If this is still thought of as ephemeral nonsense, a power station engineer once told me a study was carried out on why the boiler tubes in power station boiler complexes when cleaned using the same procedure in every case, experienced such varying degrees to which scale was removed, to the extent sometimes the procedure worked perfectly but at others it only produced partial de-scaling and sometimes having almost no effect whatever.

The study eventually revealed the efficacy or otherwise of the process was directly related to what phase of the moon existed when the boiler cleaning was undertaken.

Once this was understood and boiler tube cleaning synchronised to the right moon phase, de-scaling worked perfectly every time.

I also recall one Friday evening when there was an eclipse of the moon. Apparently, according to a policeman there was 'absolute carnage' on the roads at that time. As John Michell relates in *The New View Over Atlantis*, lunar eclipses have been a source of ritualistic activity and fear for thousands of years. Not least because the earth's magnetic field is radically affected by lunar eclipses. Demonstrating the direct link between light and magnetic fields, see *The Bridge To Infinity* by Bruce Cathie.

Similarly the crab has a hard shell protecting its delicate – and usually very tasty – insides. At work I have seen Cancerians surround desks with an almost complete wall of books; an intellectual 'hard shell'.

It appears the astrological sign for Russia is Cancer. Little surprise then Churchill coined the phrase 'the Iron Curtain' to describe Communist Russia's erection of an impenetrable border; "from Stettin in the Baltic to Trieste in the Adriatic," which like the crab's hard shell was designed to protect it from injury. The western border being from where invasions had once swept across the country; and its military 'pincers' to protect it from attack.

As creatures crawling about and feeding on the sea bed, they eat any suitable detritus and transform this 'junk' food into delicate tasty flesh. The human gestalt of this is that they are *symbolically* potentially great transformers of the *food of experience*. Exactly as this lady so startlingly did in transforming the deeply hurtful and traumatic experience she went through. Also in the incessant peals of laughter during the time she conducted her own miraculous transmogrification.

Also with the benefit of hindsight, my intuition of the diffuse emotional 'fog' of unfocused hurt needing to be concentrated, and in focusing it, to back off and let her resolve it for herself, in her own way, proved to be correct.

It might also be said the pushing released the blockage in her emotional/spiritual 'digestive' processes which were then able to transform the 'food' of experience from something indigestible to something transcending all the hurtful energy she had sublimated within herself, from something which instead of poisoning her being could be processed into life sustaining vigour and wellbeing. Which manifestly and to a staggering degree it had.

And I have no doubt whatever in coming to me for help she

instinctively was communicating with her own inner male animus or shadow through me. In choosing someone who understood intuitively how to *relate* to her inner being.

Again, to use the analogy of this hard-shelled animal itself, trying to approach it full frontal or head on only results in painful bleeding fingers from its sharp, powerful, pincers.

So in humans; trying to pin down or hammer home a solution to a Cancerian; intellectual or emotional, will only generate tremendous resistance at best, or the inflicting of a painfully administered emotional and/or intellectual 'pincering' or all of it together! *Exactly* as pushing did and which focused the 'fog' in her as I intuited. It brought to the surface and *focused* her need to protect herself; the reasons for doing so concomitantly, what her experience had meant to her. And in backing away, to let her, in her indirect way, deal with what – and how much – she chose to as she felt able; and what to sublimate and transform in herself; like tears of laughter from tears of hurt.

Succinctly; to gain a Cancerian's cooperation, just as the animal moves about sideways, approach them 'sideways' with ideas and suggestions. Similarly be prepared for inscrutable little comments and deductions to themselves and others, and to need to work out where all their internalised meanderings came from in what they say.

Yet once more, at the time I helped this young lady colleague I followed my intuition and instinct, as I had done for myself from the very beginning of my own healing. Putting it all into words at the time was simply not possible.

Why mention astrology and astrological signs?

Unfortunately 'scientists' and those such as myself, who pursue intellectual attainment and prowess not only to the exclusion of all else, but in doing so – just as I did – create *immense* damage within themselves turning by far the lesser function of consciousness into a merciless tyrant with which to brutalise themselves. Not content with this; they then project out into the world – exactly as Carl Jung so clearly demonstrated through his work in psychology – the immense conflict in themselves by deriding, sneering and attempting to expunge astrology as a bogus pseudo science. Ranting at their own inner mirror image. And further blindly deepening their own damaging conflict.

Deeper Journeys; Widening Worlds

Doctor Liz Greene – another American! and coincidentally in my view one of the best astrologers in the world – has written some excellent books dealing with psychological types and astrological signs in her books: *Relating*, already referred to and *Saturn: A New Look At An Old Devil*.

I once read out a description of a typical Sagittarian and some of their scatter-brained tendencies from *Relating*, at work, which had the lady who transformed so miraculously in helpless fits of laughter for it so exactly characterised another Sagittarian colleague as to be almost a caricature.

A good example being when the police stopped him on the motorway. He showed them his driving license and insurance, put them back in his wallet – and drove off leaving it on the roof of his car.

There are some academics who regularly deride astrology in TV programmes. Unfortunately demonstrating only total blindness of their own inner make up and the hidden reaches of themselves that because they can't be viewed through a telescope, a space probe's cameras, mathematical formulas; or theories do not exist.

One has only to see and listen to their delivery of speech to know they are damaging their own deeper nature, which ultimately means as life continues, bodies will show the punishment self-inflicted within and which will be attributed to chance and misfortune when it turns to 'disease'. To listen to them railing against astrology and kicking it to death is to see those who have not the faintest flicker of understanding of the great conflict in themselves between domineering intellect and their sub/inner consciousness they treat with such unconscious, bitter cruelty. Perhaps they imagine they are infinitely greater and vastly more enlightened beings than Sir Isaac Newton who when once sneered at by Sir Edmund Halley – discoverer of comets' trajectories – on the subject of astrology responded; "I have studied it; you have not." Quite so; and not simply with just his intellect either.

To be fair, perhaps the 'scientists' are cosmically beyond anything the combined knowledge and understanding of Newton, Tycho Brahe, Johannes Kepler and Carl Jung aspired to, rolled into one? Who all counted astrology as a real and valuable resource.

However, these are names that will endure long after all those who make burnt offerings of their inner natures at the shrine of the great god of intellect, disappear into the background microwave hiss of the universe.

As one who could crush diamonds like grains of sugar with the massive weight of intellectual study and brutal abuse I heaped upon myself to the point of near extinction, the lesson to be learned was intellect is merely a servant and wise counsellor – or should be – to the real seat of consciousness; our sub/inner consciousness. Intellect is where synthesis occurs; knowledge and understanding as Newton put it in the words of his time, was something to be sought and it would be provided; but not through thought alone.

There were no reference books on gravity he could turn to; once inner consciousness delivered the inspiration intellect asked for, it could then create the language to describe the understanding. And Newton was also reputed to take note of what the ancients – like the Egyptians – had to say about gravity *and use it*.

A salutary lesson of the difference between the two came after reading a book and seeing a play about a woman who was part of a small community run by the psychiatrist Ronald Laing and others in the East End of London where the woman, named Mary Barnes, and others were able to put together their own lives and selves after the damage done to them emotionally and their deeper inner worlds in early life.

The community was based at Kingsley Hall; Mahatma Ghandi's lodgings on his visit to Britain in 1931.

Everyone there wore ordinary clothes; there were no white coated doctors, resulting in comical situations where the patients were spoken to by visiting psychiatrists as equals, and doctors, and Laing and his colleagues condescended to as the befuddled inmates, to the visitor's great confusion and embarrassment.

Mary Barnes, in working through the traumatic effects of her upbringing developed a rather unpleasant predilection for smearing the walls – and herself – with her excrement. She was not prevented from doing so, which caused the place to stink and endless work cleaning it off her and the building. The excrement being symbolic of what she felt about herself and her deep, imploded anger, eventually as she progressed in her own healing, externalising and transmuting into anger for what she suffered in her upbringing; the constant denial of recognition and right to be, in the 'don't do this / don't do that' syndrome she experienced and lack of any warmth and love, ultimately turning people into an incandescent fog of diffuse, confused, unfocused rage.

More pointedly; the loveless, disrespectful, degrading and excessive potty training she endured with growing suppressed anger and rage meant she created an exact equivalence between anger and excrement and projecting her anger out initially was to project it on to the walls as a means of stinking revenge against her mother's mechanistic, loveless, and ultimately degrading treatment of her.

A more elegantly apt allegory it would be impossible to create! She was in effect saying; you demand I shit; you treat me like a mechanical shit machine. Alright! *I'll* give you *shit!* A more perfect mirror image from deep consciousness it would be impossible to fashion.

Unable to stand the smell any longer, it was suggested she might like to use paint and put her feelings about herself on the walls rather than covering them in it.

Paint was provided and this she did, not only transforming the smell of the place but providing her with a creative outlet aiding her path to recovery, externalising her feelings in the process. The pictures coming of course, from deep within her repressed creative true self.

And in using her hands to daub paint rather than excrement she was in the most direct manner possible transforming her blocked degraded creativity from the downward spiralling path creativity *always* takes, in becoming destructively expressed anger, into an ascending celebration of light and colour.

In treating astrology like shit, 'scientists' are smearing themselves with their own mental excrement!

At this particular time at work, like my colleague whose bowels barometrically expressed the great stress and pressure he was under to produce a new course – but which fortunately only generated nasal discomfort for others in the toilets if their visit coincided with his – I too was developing a new course concerning the functional principles of a new, very complex operating system. Only just having attended the very concentrated, achingly detailed crash course in Phoenix, Arizona; rather like studying the operating system with a powerful microscope, my task was then to transform the detail into its concepts whilst also comparing it with its predecessor which I knew and taught to the minutest level of detail.

Mentally it was like wringing out a sponge that had been mangled dry and trying to get more drops of inspirational water out of it.

The idea of painting with my hands seemed very appealing and with a friend one Saturday, and pots of primary colours plus black and white, we spent a very liberating and creative time daubing with bare hands, what we felt on the walls of my little therapy 'cell' accompanied by glasses of wine, cheese and biscuits, and near inedible, lip-splittingly salty 'poor man's caviar': lumpfish roe.

It was no accident on the left of my seven-foot-square wallpaper-obliterating mirror of mind, down at floor level in the extreme left corner, a vague bubble of black mingled with bright yellow, grew into a bright red rearing serpent across and vertically up the centre of my 'canvas'. A long, equally bright red reptilian forked tongue thrust straight at the uraeus – the serpent crown – of a six-foot Egyptian face bearing a Pharaoh's head dress, on the right-hand side of my 'picture'. In fact the red forked tongue exactly bracketed the uraeus, itself in the centre of the crowned forehead which in turn was also the representation of a rearing hooded cobra. All of this done with almost no real conscious thought; just following impulse.

Symbolically it could hardly have been clearer there was a powerful clash existing in me between my emotions and other aspects of mind. The artist whose back problem I steered to a resolution of his inner conflict between intellect and his creative nature, took one look at the picture and said in his hesitating manner; "Your intellect ... is ... er ... interfering with your emotions."

At the time it jolted me for I was basking in an unfathomable feeling of relief and even pleasure at this image I created. Yet something also nagged at me as if there was more his explanation did not touch and put in words.

Again, with the telescope of long hindsight, it didn't only show 'interference' between these two aspects of mind his own back had shown of his inner conflict between creative energies and the repressive 'lid' he had screwed tightly down on these artistic talents developing a powerful intellect as a journalist.

JOURNEY OF A LIFETIME

My wall hieroglyph of self showed precisely the same thing in me as his spinal energy showed in him.

The serpent; spine and emotional and creative energies; the crowned head; intellect.

Once he understood the clash in himself the blockage released like, indeed exactly as, a dam bursting, in the convulsive bolt of energy that shot through him from head to foot with lightning speed.

The difference between the two of us though, was he was healing the divide in himself by nurturing his powerful artistic talent and I was still years away from understanding the 'painting' I had created, could hardly have been a more exact mirror of the same conflict in myself. And whereas he hated, even detested, his journalistic work, I derived satisfaction from sticking my nose deep into the complexities of electronics, computers, their software and how they worked. The problem was the rate and the sheer volume of facts, information and its complexity I needed to absorb to perform the job I had taken on.

Had I the eyes to see clearly at the time they would have shown me the damage I was doing. I was though, an information junkie, far too busy sniffing heady aromas of kudos from the glue pot of fleeting intellectual status, but as computing's break neck progress evolved and new technology quickly faded into history, the mesmeric contents I thrust my nose into, and its intoxicating qualities, rapidly ossified to incubus to which I was shackled in a vise-like grip.

The following Monday morning when I sat down to create more course material from purely mental understanding of the operating system I had just gained, for a while inspiration came quite quickly without having to wrack my brains. Noticeably, as the day wore on the 'sponge' was wrung dry again of creative juice and metaphorically it was back to chipping ideas out of granite with a bone antler.

It created the first faint glimmerings in me of the vast difference between creative impulse and intellectual synthesis and more acutely, what I was doing mangling facts out of my intellect was not good for my wellbeing. But no telescope of perception I possessed at the time and for long afterwards could penetrate my inner infra red intellectual haze masking outright damage this addiction created.

During this period from exactly the end of 1979 into the '80s, I became interested in not only using herbs including marjoram and mint already mentioned, but pure essential oils.

If the word 'aromatherapy' cropped up in conversation people looked puzzled and were inclined to conjure up images and enticing smells of freshly ground coffee wafting out from cafés.

I doubt if I had even heard the term myself, and if I had, it meant nothing to me, and excited no interest whatsoever.

A few years earlier a clairvoyant directed me to Watkins bookshop just off Charing Cross Road and I found it a fruitful source of spiritual, occult, and esoteric literature.

Some time in 1979 I made one of my visits and as I was walking out from its second-hand department through its small, rather shabby looking front room where new books were displayed, out of the corner of my eye to my left I saw a colourful display. I did not stop to look, nor read what the display and book were about, but something inside said; that's the book I'll get when I next visit.

In early December of that year, I went back to the shop, straight up to the display, took a copy of the book, bought it and looked at the title which read *The Art of Aromatherapy* by Robert B. Tisserand.

Curiously, it seemed to excite my interest and as I flew to Phoenix in Arizona for the brain mashing crash course I attended, I read about the attributes of the different plant essences listed in the book.

I very quickly realised intellectually 'vacuuming' words off the pages as I did with endless software books and course literature was a complete waste of time; using the essences and doing it was what mattered and was the only way to begin to understand what their effects were; only then using the book to understand more about their properties.

From the beginning of the new decade I began using them, experiencing their effects and soon appreciating they were not to be messed about with for even very small amounts; a drop or two could have potent effects on physical sensation but much more so at an emotional level.

This was a doorway to a secret garden within me; somewhere I could enter and escape the unrelenting, overwhelming weight of study and grind of my workaday world.

Indeed, in retrospect I am sure they were of considerable help in healing the deeply wounding uproar created in me by my Rolfing experience.

Their potency was amply demonstrated on someone whose eyes were streaming with 'hay fever' – in late November! This was mentioned to me by the fellow weekend group attendee I visited in Devon. He also mentioned the man had told of a recent bereavement, which seemed to me like some suppressed grieving going on. The sufferer was a farmer and very much a Devon son of the earth.

My group fellow asked me if I had anything that might help the man's condition.

Not having Cypress, which I read somewhere was associated in legend and folklore with the afterlife, I recalled Juniper essence oil having similar properties, according to Tisserand, so swore the farmer to only put a single drop in a glass of warm water, into which a good dollop of honey was stirred, to drink the mixture.

A few days later the farmer's reaction and condition was relayed back to me, along with the small dropper bottle he had been entrusted with.

The farmer did as instructed and the 'hay fever' miraculously disappeared, saying in his broad Devonian accent: "That there stuff you gave me; it were a proper job!" Repeating himself a number of times so impressed was he.

Similarly, single drops of basil, and when I got some, peppermint oil, in a glass of warm water and honey instantaneously cured two separate cases of fairly acute stomach ache. As even before the mixture was completely swallowed, in each case the ache simply vanished.

Yet again when my unexpected interest in these oils developed it was something I not only got relief and pleasure from myself as well as satisfaction at helping others, I felt vaguely there was some other aspect to this but pushed it to the back of my mind or out of it.

That there were other aspects is very clear now, instinctively and as a consequence of the 'order' that came out of nowhere to get the Aromatherapy book, this adventure took me into a world of gentle yet powerful healing, literally a door to a garden within me which broadened in equally unforeseen ways into taking an active interest in plants, flowers, herbs and trees for the healing qualities they possessed. And not only these, for with oils came massage and reflexology. In short, some unseen influence was directing and re-connecting me with nature and the earth so utterly otherwise lacking in everything else I did at the time. In a literal and metaphorical sense I was being 'grounded' almost in spite of myself. A more fitting counterbalance and antidote to the rarefied intellectual atmospheres I floated around in would be difficult to imagine. Not least also a continuum in which I could continue to heal myself and recover from the sledge hammer effects and damage of Rolfing.

Searching for Meaning; Looking for Answers

P ERHAPS IT MAY appear this burgeoning interest in healing from the outside of my body inwards signalled a turning point and changing focus from work in my inner worlds working outwards. This was not the case, though time and again I met people who thought delving into my emotional and inner worlds was one step from madness, witchery or other demon possessed activity and was as frighteningly taboo as black magic.

I never stopped to ponder at the time what my own different approached signified, but as the iceberg of undiscovered 'me' has melted into conscious awareness over many years, a perspective is available that wasn't then; I was following my instinct and intuition and simply doing it. Now, as expressed, it was not only a 'grounding' in the physical world; it was the yang of external healing meeting with the yin of internal healing, creating a complete whole.

I learned to accept people would rather have their knee caps drilled than look into themselves for the seat of a condition, for to mention an emotional and deeper unseen dimension to illness and disease was often to see the whites of their eyes as they opened wide with fear and the conversation was either dragged off in a different direction or ended in shifty looks and an edgy, brittle, silence.

Always and right from the beginning when I questioned whether what I was doing was leading me anywhere, I would reflect on and review the long and growing list of beneficial and permanent changes for the better they brought in their wake as I freed up my inner worlds.

Without doubt chief amongst these was the invisible load I carried from my birth. There was no denying it; I might think I had freed myself from its effects on me but what I thought and what I felt was the difference between myth and reality.

So in the early '80s I would be brought back to reality and dealing with yet more from this unresolved store of experience.

As a general rule, driving in London traffic always brought up a deep feeling of impatience and I would find myself going rigid; clamping my breathing and struggling to beat the traffic flow I was trickling along in.

It wasn't a mild discomfort or irritation many seemed to experience; I absolutely hated being caught in the tin 'snakes' of which I was a single 'scale' as they writhed slowly along the roads. Although even that was a great improvement on seeing red with every traffic light blocking my progress a few years previously.

Unfailingly – especially if I was up against a deadline to reach my destination – I would end up just yelling with frustration in my car.

It would often result in a session on my own writhing around, thumping with my fists on the mattress in my therapy room. Or in an individual therapy session. As I found right from the very beginning, once I released the outrage and clamping in my body I would find my thoughts taking off in other directions and it was a reliable barometer I had shovelled a bit more out of my path. Precisely what, how much and whether it related to birth I had no idea except I knew I had been born a week late. And I absolutely detested being late for anything.

There were innumerable times when I felt I was plodding painfully slowly along a road with no end even remotely in sight and very disheartened by the wearisome repetition of what I felt compelled to do to free up my body. At the same time I still possessed a profound and utterly unshakeable conviction I *knew* what I was doing would ultimately lead me somewhere and my body would tell me in its own good time where it was taking me.

On one occasion my manager held a lunch meeting on a Friday. I calculated by the time it finished I would still be able to get to my pre-arranged individual therapy session, only to find the roads all around Hammersmith where I was, choked solid with traffic. I arrived for my session about three-quarters of an hour late, feeling like an over heated pressure cooker with no safety valve and about to explode. It brought to the surface not birth but powerful feelings of there never being enough time in my early childhood, which was true; for after I was five until nine years old was an increasing repetitive cycle of break up and moving like a pin ball cannoned about in one of these machines with my parents as the flippers, by which time the 'gyr-antics' were so extreme, to continue the pin ball analogy, the 'ball' split into fragments; both 'flippers' disappeared, and if the machine was a sense of family it was a shattered, splintered, wreck. All too soon the session ended. Inwardly I felt a strong sensation of heat and surrounded by an inner image of the colour red tinged with black at the edges. A burning sense of hurt consumed me with deep, aching sobbing for want of trying to express feelings of utter futility and impotence to somehow grasp time and still the whirling cataclysm I was in. The therapist remarked there were black rings under my eyes and my upper chest was deep red and asked with some concern if I was alright. Until then I had no idea my body showed any physical signs at all but such was the extreme frustration and pressure to make my appointment, my inner state; images and perceptions, very evidently showed in my outward symptoms.

That evening these crystallised into images of a clearing in the wood we owned; it was scorched and blackened where my father had burned off dead bracken. Others floated in of delicate little wood anemones I loved, that survived, or appeared after the fire. Aged five at the time, the woods and everything in them were a magical if scary place; I felt sublimely as one within them, I was part of them all and they with me. These contrasting and conflicting scenes of destruction and delicate new flora seemed inextricably bound up with the chaos of my childhood.

It never occurred to me for a moment the rings round my eyes and the deep redness of my upper chest as if I had been burned, were an allegory of the fires of uproar sweeping through my childhood with frightening speed; just as the fire fanned by a fatalistic providential breeze, flashed through the tinder-dry clearing out of his control leaving my father decidedly red, unwell and visibly shaken and his tar-stained old flat cap and boots, singed, as he fought desperately to subdue it, just as quickly dwindling to extinction as all too soon did he. The capricious fire and its effect on the ground and some of the tree trunks exactly symbolised the sudden, out of control flash-fire existence I was in with my parents. Things I took for granted; expectations of life, incinerated in an instant, leaving only a blackened 'negative' and ashes of all that was before.

Regenerative anemones were what was left of me after the conflagration.

The images fitted uncannily as much as they did unconsciously; they could not have been more exactly symbolic of everything about my family, my life and existence; even to the aspect of my father's suppressed volcanic anger, burning frustration and bitter resentment of how he had been treated over his inventions, and made him mercurially unpredictable. When roused he burned for hours with an incandescence like the Chernobyl reactor meltdown disaster, and I could really feel it if I happened to enter his 'radiation' zone.

As much as the images were of my childhood, the physical symptoms on my body showed an even deeper level of uproar within me. It took many years and thousands of hours to work through and understand from having done so, just what these meant, were inextricably connected with, and that they were symptoms of my birth.

This whole episode was exactly like being in the middle of flash fires; it was impossible to focus on anything and maintain a sense of continuum in my life for just like the actual experience, attempting to tackle one thing was immediately swamped by another until it was completely overwhelming and the emotional conflagrations around me burned themselves out in their own time and whatever consequences fate decided regardless of anything I said or did.

In retrospect I can only wonder how I wasn't overwhelmed. But then I couldn't even recognise that either; for it took decades before I even began to realise although I was in one skin, it was filled with a jumble of bits and pieces. These were the words a palmist used to describe my experience of people around that time of the early eighties and his way of telling me what my inner state was.

His name was Mir Bashir PhD and was apparently consulted by princes and potentates.

Forwards and backwards he ran an ink roller on a pad for what seemed minutes until finally he asked me to hold out my hand, inked one, pressed it on to a clean sheet of white paper and repeated the procedure.

He produced a small six inch steel ruler and began marking off parts of my prints and asking questions as he went. He asked about my marriage, separation and break up, prompting for my comments, and ended by saying; "You should never have married that girl."

He asked more questions about my life, and my answers confirming his expectations, as he wielded his ruler and biro over my prints; he finally said, "So we seem to be on the right lines then."

Then in twenty-five minutes, propping his head with his hand spread across his temples and right elbow leaning on his desk, without repeating himself or so much as looking at me once, he told me a great deal about my life; past, present and future.

He picked up I was "ill treated or ill affected by childhood," and the effects still remained.

He also talked about a new relationship I had developed with a lady and its potential, though his comments on its potential were not easy to follow. In a decade or so I understood why.

Of my work he advised keeping a low profile for a few months after which things would be better and I would experience a 'big lift'.

To understand what he meant by this did not take long. I began to clash with my managers and feel an increasing sense of impatience and frustration, only cured by moving out of the education department with the dawning realisation I was completely wrung dry, and latterly, whilst I could understand and remember deep technicalities of subjects I taught, I was near incapable of assimilating and using software requiring keyboard usage and thinking as I went.

I knew – as a later Tarot reading put it – whilst I was good at and much involved with communicating, it was communication to the point of damage. True; when I became tired and stressed, if I tried to make a related point in mid-sentence, I would lose the thread of my original point and only after a struggle to reconnect with it could I do so. Moreover from the sensations in my head of slight sickness, pressure and disorientation I realised my blood pressure was almost certainly being affected.

With the usual hindsight, it is clear my impatience and frustration registered the conflict in me between what I was doing to myself with my own intellect and my inner and subconscious worlds. The longer I stayed doing what I was; the worse the symptoms became. My own nature was telling me; even forcing me to change by creating this deep dissatisfaction to remove myself ending my disgruntlement with management.

Subterranean Symbols, Disconnected Consciousness; Ends & New Beginnings

It felt very much as if everything was breaking up around me in my life in mid-1981. Even before my work became the burden I increasingly knew I had to shed, a similar upheaval had taken place as I continued to work through the even more burdensome effects of my birth.

Gradually after the delightful lull of 1979 following my non-stop efforts to free up my inner worlds the previous year leading me deeper and deeper into my experience of birth, its effects – like deeply rooted weeds reappearing once again – demanded my attention.

The question was what attention.

For the first time since I began my journey of healing and 'annealing' myself I seemed to be running out of something to work on. In this frame of mind I went to one of my individual therapy sessions feeling vaguely uneasy and mildly irritable with myself. I was encouraged to lie on the familiar foam rubber mattress that bore indifferent witness to my raging, thumping outrage, tears and hurt as well, at times, of humour over the years.

Amongst other rambling thoughts, those of a friend shuffled quietly in and stories she had told me. First, came that of an aged lady who lived in a flat in the house where she also lived. My friend would drop in on her to see she was alright and had on at least one occasion been regaled with a tale of the lady seeing underground trains making their way on their worm-like way along tunnels around her room.

For some peculiar reason it appealed or connected with something in me.

And just as these strange inhabitants plied their invisible way around her room yet having for her a definite presence; origin and destination, perhaps they echoed deeply inaccessible perceptions in me; things invisible even to myself and yet somewhere – like the denizens clattering along deep beneath the superficially accessible reality of London's streets – a real beginning, purpose and end to their journey.

The image amused me, and simultaneously like a train endlessly traversing the Circle Line, sending its metallic clicking, singing along the lines of its predestination; somewhere it clattered over points of imperceptible awareness; intangible harmonies, nonetheless as real as the steel on which such rails bore them on their unerring way in pitch blackness.

I pushed it all aside and in its stead thoughts of my friend's experience with a New York Jewish boy named Raun who had been born autistic.

She had read the book of his and his family's journey together in these strange worlds locked together by gravity's pull of birth and family and yet revolving separately. Isolated. Spinning on their own axes in unbridgeable emptiness.

The story was of the family's struggle to span this gulf of being and to journey into their son's cosmic insularity.

First, they took him to a doctor for a clear and unequivocal diagnosis.

The doctor with the authority of his knowledge and professional status read the runes of their son's condition in the clearest of terms, warning them with great gravity of the absolute certainty they could and should *never* expect to have any contact with him as between a normal parent and child, and sought to drive home the nails of finality with the weight of his wisdom.

They took Raun home and if anything their resolve was stronger for the damming prognosis for their and their son's future together.

The boy exhibited all the usual symptoms; avoidance of any physical or eye contact, no communication or the usual progression of sounds turning eventually to words. Also an uncanny ability to spin objects on their centre of gravity; be it boxes, plates or anything he laid his hands on.

They decided if Raun could not come to them, they would journey to his world and join him; so they began spinning objects with him.

This they did for a considerable time. There was no recognition at all but very gradually he began to speak the odd word as they talked to him, attempting to follow his deft spinning abilities.

The process quickened with his expanding vocabulary until one day, suddenly, he seemed to regress right back to his original state. No contact; eyes or anything else and no words. The parents decided he was weighing up and choosing what he wanted to do; was he going to stay completely in his own silent world or join the one he had been shown?

For three days he remained the same. The next morning his mother went into his room. Raun was standing up in his cot facing the door. As she opened it she was met by a flood of words; they gushed over her in a torrent; all those they had ever taught him in all the patient hours of loving devotion over weeks and months as they spun on the edge of his mysterious planet. Raun had decided which one he wished to be in; theirs.

She ran to him crying and hugged him for this joyful catharsis embracing both in a single world.

As he quickly became a normal, even precocious, very aware and articulate child, the parents took him back to the same doctor.

Suddenly the tables were completely turned and there was a lot of utterly unconvincing huffing, puffing and backtracking about it not being autism after all but some other condition.

Having written and published a book called (from memory) *Raun; To Know Is To Be Loved By*, my friend read the book and was so moved she got in contact with the parents and went to see them and Raun in New York.

Walking round Central Park with her, he saw a young girl he seemed to like; my friend asked if he'd like her to go and speak to the girl and perhaps she could join them.

The response was quick and direct: "Don't be silly, you'll embarrass me!"

Which from a five-year-old struck me as a pretty startling statement of mature articulation and self-awareness!

Some time passed and the parents were contacted by a Mexican family. The parents explained their own son was autistic and they thought, having read their book, Raun's mother and father could help them.

Their reply was equally direct; No! *You* are the only people who can help him; and we are happy to show you how.

First, they insisted the son be diagnosed in the same way Raun had – with exactly the same outcome. They then showed them how to join their own child in his world – with exactly the same outcome yet again; and an equal degree of similarity in the doctor's blustering discomfort at the previous certainty of diagnosis and his subsequent glaring personal contra apotheosis.

Laying on the familiar mattress perhaps the only things I mentioned were the lady who we both knew and the outcome of Raun's autism.

Out of nowhere; propelled along inky tunnels of my deep inner consciousness; thrusting like the rush of air before a train, clattering into a brightly lit platform of conscious awareness, came words, form and voice to them, I said: "I was the autistic child who escaped the sensory net."

The image of a net came to mind; rather like the Roman Retiarius Gladiator who fought with net and trident, attempting to ensnare his opponent in it.

On a sensory level, avoiding being caught in a web of overwhelming, all-consuming confusion in which I felt the autistic child was bound at birth. Locked, as I had been in mine, in an iron-rigid muscular grip repetitively crushed; having no control over this seeming endless nightmare. Either completely overwhelmed and unable to maintain clear consciousness; stuck permanently like a record in the same groove of repeating agony, terror, and outrage, or through the strength of being and faculties endowed by Great Nature, surviving the brutal onslaught. Not completely and *permanently* submerged when finally thrust into the world, but still able to react to it.

Putting words to the image I found difficult if not impossible; it remained, and the feeling of somehow escaping being caught; bound up and at the mercy of fate, persisted. The words from nowhere also remained and I repeated them with difficulty; I was the autistic child who escaped the sensory net, as if I was still on the verge of being caught in its inescapable enveloping web of confusion.

Like a tube train reaching buffers in the blackness, I could get no further with it and gave up.

For the first time ever I could get no further with anything else either.

My therapist suggested I find a talisman from my childhood to take with me wherever images of mind might take me.

I chose 'Fuzzy Freddie' as my mother called him. A teddy she had made for me out of scraps of dark material; black trousers and body, a jacket of grey and white check, dark rabbit's fur for hair and face made from buttons. 'Kid's toys' never attracted me and 'Fuzzy Freddie' had been slung around; the arms and legs being very useful; like an aboriginal woomera, to get a good leverage to throw 'it' further, inevitably causing them to come unstitched. Consequently also why it was shiny in places with grime and dirt and smelled of them, which was the only attribute meaning anything to me.

Silently, if somewhat grudgingly, I accepted the suggestion to take him with me – wherever I might be headed, and invited to see where it took me.

I found myself on the edge of a pond and sliding down in to it. As I slid under the waters of imagination I could see the wall of a dam to my left.

The only feelings coming to me were of dissatisfaction and mild irritation. As I slid deeper, defiance replaced vague disgruntlement.

I felt I was on a journey on my own – as so often seemed to be the case in my life – so that was what I would do and fuck the world at large; I would go on my own regardless.

Still with the same feelings, the session ended. It seemed a nebulous floundering around going nowhere and pretty well a complete waste of time – and money.

Just as time and hindsight showed the 'pointless' exercise of groping my way through fir fronds was not only not pointless but a deep inner awareness of what was to come, thousands of hours' work and decades of hindsight also demonstrated the exact opposite was true in this case.

I learned later my therapist seemed quite moved by the ramshackle talisman I chose for my solitary journey, which in a way was touching, though for me the feeling of not *consciously* knowing where my path was leading me was my overriding preoccupation. There didn't seem any point in having sessions if, as was the case, they became the same as I did on my own or the work I did with a partner – each working on what they wished for an hour – in my little hand-painted, soundproofed bedroom.

The only thing I felt 'fitted' or right was tedious, repetitive aspects of birth.

Long gone was my experience of being held down by five people, and, wrapped in a blanket as a makeshift strait jacket all simulating the constriction of birth, and hitting a wall of overwhelming fear; lifting the whole lot off in a single move.

The 'wall' was gone and replaced by a positive compulsion to stick my head and shoulders between a mattress and the padded floor. Quite rapidly though, the lack of air and rising temperature in this cramped oppressive space brought sympathetically, a rising tide of panic and extricating myself from this self-inflicted re-enactment of birth I would involuntarily sob with relief.

Yet as ever, the same premise sustaining me from my very first times; my body would show me where 'I' was going in its own good time, still remained; and it was as utterly unshakeable a conviction as ever. The one certain thing about the seemingly pointless, endless, purposeless repetition of feeling compelled to repeat what I knew to be my birth, was although exactly the *same process* every time, nonetheless each was a *different experience*.

That being the case I kept patience with myself – as always – and would go on doing it until it changed into something else, which as I unfailingly found, it always did.

To use an analogy of bailing out a reservoir, I didn't care if it was a bucket – or even a thimbleful – at a time; I would continue doing it until eventually the 'water level' of fear and panic receded and I could begin to see what features were there as I continued to bail.

To say this was a rock solid conviction and what sustained me from my very first efforts to clear, 'anneal' and heal myself is to say Gibraltar or even Everest are quite large stones. Though they were mere bricks by comparison with the utter certainty I gained right from the outset and over a lengthening span of years. Nothing and no one would or could ever change it simply because I had proved it to myself over and over again.

So tedious, repetitive, boring, plodding, pointless, endless it might appear from the outside, but to use another analogy; if plodding through the same old endless emotional scenery for a few thousand miles was what it took, it mattered not the slightest to me; for every step taken was one nearer a different view coming into sight.

And anyway; every step was over new ground. No two steps were ever the same just as no two sessions were.

For weeks in my own sessions and with the therapist the process remained the same. About ten weeks went by from the time of the autism session.

The therapist – who by then was feeling angry, excluded and useless – decided to wade in without warning – letting me know, as this had been going on for *such* a long time, she thought I was avoiding something as verbal contact was almost completely absent.

This coincided with my re-appearance from between two cushions with all the same feelings right on the surface; awash with colossal, overwhelming, diffuse aching hurt and fear, and only my usual reflexive sobbing being the one channel of release and relief.

The abrupt verbal invasion felt like a red hot poker being stuck into an open wound. It engendered indescribable emotional agony and evoked an equally reflexive high volume response.

It was instantly clear I had reached the end of any useful work in one to one sessions. Helpful input and guidance was one thing, to be summarily 'bounced' with someone else's perception and expectation of what I needed to do – or not to do as they saw it – was quite another. To use the Everest analogy again in a different way, I felt as if what I was attempting to work through was exactly like having its weight on top of me – indeed there were times when exactly this image came to me, and with it a feeling of aching hopelessness for ever being able to shift this crushing load I invisibly carried.

If for 166 hours a week I managed to stagger around in my life carrying it and whose dimensions were incomprehensible beyond imagining, then for the remaining two hours I would follow my instincts working with what felt right.

Exactly as I had been doing since the very first minute when I began.

To reuse another analogy; if this was bailing a reservoir with a thimble then it did not matter to me; I simply didn't care, I would go on doing it for as long as it took, and if that was for the rest of my life then so be it.

JOURNEY OF A LIFETIME

Whether thimble, bucket or any other fitting symbol and image for what I was doing, the fact was however little or much of this inner burden I succeeded in shifting and releasing from within myself, I would be that much freer as a consequence.

What effects it might have I had no idea but it couldn't be any worse than being swamped or flattened as my own images, instinct and intuition told me.

Curiously enough, I already had another insight into the ephemeral nature of what I had been doing – indeed we all were – however much we might think we were making vast changes in ourselves and lives.

I took summer holidays in Devon; a place I found magical. It oozed an energy, beauty and indefinable palpable history and atmosphere. I was dry blotting paper in its influence; I simply soaked up all it gave, unable to get enough.

Dartmoor I had camped on and tramped over many years before with the RAF and its fascination never waned.

Each summer I visited stone circles, stone rows and old settlements up on the moor to the West of Chagford and I could feel the energy of them in my hands and body. Once in an absolute bucketing downpour standing at the centre of a small triple stone circle with stones and stone avenues radiating from it, suddenly the scene opened up in a vision and I saw it as it had been in times past.

Loath to tear myself away from this magic, in the end feeling near frozen; water running down my legs and completely drenched to the skin, I could stand the frigid soaking no longer and left. A path led across the moor from near these ancient features to Grey Wethers; re-erected twin stone circles and I would walk and run, sometimes barefoot, to them a couple of miles or so and lay in the middle of one or the other, absorbing the atmosphere and letting my imagination and perceptions wander. The area was covered in settlements, hut circles, field systems, tumuli and an atmosphere that though those who had created them all were long gone their presence was all-pervading.

Returning once from Grey Wethers, I stopped at a point where I was attracted to the energy of a particular spot and sitting looking around, quite suddenly the clear perception came to me that all the work I had done and been a part of, on my own, at group weekends or in individual sessions was mere fumbling in the dark and if I or anyone was going to achieve any sort of fundamental change within, it was going to take ineffably more concentrated work than was fondly imagined.

This may create the impression I understood what was happening but actually living in it was like swimming; it was impossible to get above what I was in; work; a constant pressure, had to be done and courses given. Nonetheless, I had a growing feeling of a head of steam building and need for change.

In late autumn 1981 Devon again provided a haven to recover from the most arduous course I gave. I seemed to be in a bubble of my own, close company was not something I sought; quite the reverse, I was happy to be on my own for most of the time, almost like a Trappist monk. Chiselling words out of my brain brought a deep desire to be silent most of the time in its wake.

I continued using and experimenting with herbs and essential oils. As much for an outing to see more of Devon's magnificent countryside at leisure, one day I drove across much of the county to a place selling herbs, passing through the majestic hills of its eastern side. Strains of songs from Georges Canteloub's 'Songs of the Auvergne' echoed constantly in my head. The words were mostly unintelligible, being sung in the Auvergne dialect by Netania Devrath; a Ukrainian Jewish singer of remarkable linguistic ability, speaking eight languages plus the Auvergne dialect; a matchless soprano, who trained for six months in the regional Oc language (differentiating the Langue De Oc – as in Languedoc – from the Frankish 'oui' used for yes) to give these Shepherd songs their true expression.

Her extraordinarily powerful voice and contrasted great delicacy, her soaring range, theatrical expression and the orchestra's magical sound-scape evoked powerful feelings and images as I drove through equally inspirational towering hills, steep-sided valleys and aerial chariots; wild, sunlit pastel-painted wind-ripped clouds racing by. Deepening to brilliant streaming fiery cloaks in the waning sun.

The reverberations within not only resonated with all I was seeing but things in me I could only perceive like wraiths in the dark.

Some part of me was in another land and other times. Feelings and clear images of a Roman age haunted me. They were not something I chose. Ineluctably, the music I was captivated by on first hearing brought into focus a deluge of scenes.

Experiences in the wake of Rolfing serving only to broaden, deepen and extend these. I could not reconcile nor deny them; just as the voice and music embraced a vast range of expression so in me it evoked rugged high-flung hilltops; plunging harsh terrain in concert with emotions of equal span and power from sublime to savage.

None of which has never changed. Except to deepen and grow.

But on reflection from the time I was nine years old, things Roman lit my imagination like nothing else. Once, aged about thirteen, I read a historical novel about a Roman soldier in Britain at the end of empire. For the time I read it I lived and breathed the story. I wasn't merely absorbed by it, I *was* it; sights, sounds, smells, atmosphere. I didn't need imagination; I was there.

It is also clear over my lifetime, when under extreme pressure, Roman images trickle out from my inner world like juice from trodden grapes.

'A Big Lift'

Finally as forecast by the palm reading I had with the incomparable Mir Bashir, I arranged my departure from the company's education department with a great inward sigh at the end of the year and spent Christmas and New Year in Devon. As may be familiar by now; and even clear to myself, the pendulum of inner imperative reasserted and swung towards re-immersion in nature; herbs and essential oils quite apart from aspects of work on the emotional front.

Like a fugitive pursued, in the previous few months horizons instinctively shrank to pure survival and all else pushed aside, including the relationship with the new lady in my life.

There seemed so much I needed to clear out of my way before I could even think how I related to anyone else.

In my meanderings I found a rustic little shop selling organic food which didn't interest me, and also dried flowers including chamomile, lime blossom and eye bright; which did.

I bought these and made a late breakfast tea from the latter two. From past experience I thought the strength of this was reasonable and in any case, even with some honey, it wasn't the most appealing drink I ever tasted and considerably less than a cupful sufficed.

The effects of all my studies and teaching beginning to work their way out produced a weariness I had lived with for years; indeed some people thought my complexion similar to the sweater I wore; mid grey. I took a welcome afternoon nap.

Later than expected, darkness having arrived, I awoke but the expectation of feeling rested and refreshed was instantly dispelled in a headache so powerful it felt as if my complete skull was being trepanned and lifted off.

JOURNEY OF A LIFETIME

The tea – and in particular, the eyebright – had apparently produced the effect not so much on my eyes, but my complete upper head musculature.

Fortunately, after about an hour, I subsided into sleep again as the pain ebbed away and awoke the following morning no worse for my skull-expanding experiment. Somewhat gingerly at first, I gave my head a rub and sat up. All seemed in order; my head even felt definitely looser and muscles, I hadn't realised I possessed, perceptibly freer. I decided future eyebright teas would be considerably weaker and more or less put the experience to the back of my mind.

New Year's Day of 1982 having arrived, after a restless, dream-cluttered night some days after my eyebright experience, I lay half waking and conscious dream images came to me.

I was standing on a completely flat expanse of solid rock quite high up. Suddenly a mechanical digger appeared over which I seemed to exert a kind of remote control, though not as someone physically manipulating its functioning. I, or it, began gouging away at the rock almost in a frenzy and a river suddenly appeared underneath. No calm flaccid stream this; looking down on to its surface, I saw a powerful swirling dark rapid, parts of which seethed with eddies and flecks of foam many feet below. I recoiled from the sheer edge of the changed image, but in the next instant, overcome by a feeling of defiant abandon, I ran pell-mell and leapt into its tumbling, boiling currents and words in my head said: I have no idea if I'll survive this or not; and I don't even care.

I didn't bother to fathom its meaning, I simply accepted the images but was to some degree at least, also more than a little unnerved by my actions still seeing myself in my mind's eye being carried away in this maelstrom.

It was not until about three weeks later I understood its meaning and the overpowering sheer raw force of what I had positively gouged open within myself.

One Sunday afternoon I found myself in an unstoppable gushing flood of emotion.

Suddenly also I recalled and understood the words of the Tarot reading I had that meant nothing to me at the time, a few months before. Interpreting one of the cards relating to the near future the lady giving it said: "Around this time I think you'll have a pretty terrific access of feeling."

No kidding!

I was in the mad rapids of my dream image alright! I was no stranger to expressing tears of hurt, sadness, grief or even outrage but over this unstoppable torrent I had absolutely no control whatsoever.

I was white water rafting in my own unleashed tidal bore of roaring rapids, except there was no raft!

It went on for hours. Every time I felt it might subside another wave of uncontrollably hopeless sobbing broke within me.

I rang a fellow weekend group attendee with whom I had stayed and done co-supporting work with and not least opened his own eyes to his own unexplored continent of emotions, for some support whilst this flood swept over me. Unfortunately I discovered this proved utterly impossible; he appeared to regard it as a competition as to who could extract support from whom and as useful as a rubber walking stick.

I called a lady I did not know well who also attended the group weekend workshops, but who drove across much of London and using an A to Z map guide found her way to Twickenham.

In her quietly dispassionate presence – neither distant nor sympathetic – the flood finally slowed and ceased. I was immensely grateful for her help at the time. And still am.

To repeat phrases used before many times; at the time, although I have threaded together the words of the Tarot reading and my own dream, there was only the faintest glimmering of awareness of cause and effect. Put another way; understanding and listening to what my own subconscious was telling me if I had but been able to 'hear' what it was saying.

These were not the only straws in the breeze of prior warning. I attended a group weekend workshop at which precursors of what was to come became apparent. I seemed to be able to resolve nothing, my confidence drained away and I felt cocooned in dark heaviness.

At another small group workshop similar feelings and gloom and inadequacy were my unwelcome companions.

That there were much wider ramifications to this powerful catharsis was even less apparent to me.

Again, long hindsight and perspective brings into sharp focus the sudden lifting of the massive load I carried in my work; a visiting instructor from the company's training school in Phoenix Arizona who taught courses of the same depth and complexity once remarking he did not know how I stayed 'up' as he put it. Meaning how I carried the sheer weight of the very wide span of courses I taught.

Once this immense load lifted; like a balloon squashed flat under great weight, regaining its shape. My 'squashed' inner worlds suddenly asserted their rightful influence *especially* after experimenting with eyebright, which not only worked at the physical level on muscles but after the release of physical stress the effects permeated to much deeper levels as evidenced by the waking dream of using *a mechanical digger to gouge through my own inner protective layers,* resulting in a release of emotion in which *I was not clear whether I would survive.* The dream could hardly have been clearer in its imagery; a harbinger of what was to come, that in using eyebright I was using my intellect as a mechanical tyrant, treating myself as if my own survival didn't matter in the words spontaneously accompanying my dream. Which also showed the depth of need I hid from myself to end and get away from my self-inflicted brutalising and massive polarisation between intellect, emotions and deep inner being.

Perhaps it is worth saying I have known acupuncture when used without regard – or even understanding – of the *emotional effects* rather than the purely physical, produce *exactly* the same overloaded deluge of emotional release that, to quote the person directly, "thought they were going to die," such was the tsunami of feeling consequently overwhelming them.

I might have thought after such a powerful purging of my inner regions, calm would be the natural outcome of the experience; but thought is not reality; living it is.

Just a week later I attended another group weekend workshop which happened also to be exactly seven years to the day since the first one. I found the heavy cloud of recent times still bearing on my shoulders.

Though it was also abundantly clear a wall between me – my conscious self – and my inner world had gone.

People who I knew, worked and co-supported with were the same as ever and I was acutely aware I wasn't. It was like the difference between watching a film and actually being part of it. Before there had been something separating me or distancing me from other people like an invisible barrier. Indeed it *was* an invisible barrier. One that had been within me and the tremendous gush of feeling had been the breaking of this dam in myself.

Although I had put out of mind the image of months previous in the therapy session of sliding defiantly down into deep water and seeing the wall of a dam to my left, it was a clear message from my own inner conscious of what was to come.

Did I connect this image and my own 'dam bursting' experience? Not in the least.

JOURNEY OF A LIFETIME

It was painful to work with people who were still chipping away at things within themselves, the resolution of which had suddenly become achingly clear to me.

The clearest example was the young lady who exactly seven years to the hour had stood up to be introduced to the group by Glyn Seaborn-Jones who once she began to hesitatingly speak, the sound of involuntary gut clenching spasms could be loudly heard; gggrrruuuumph ... gggrruuuumph! Seven years before, I did not understand exactly what propelled this visceral language so audibly: more particularly, why no one, including Glyn himself, made any mention of it. But at the point, I had reached seven years later when this scene was re-enacted, no words were necessary at all; I could *feel* she was frightened.

Though as before, if neither Glyn or anyone else felt inclined to ask her what her own gut noises signified I was not going to take it upon myself. My perceptions and sense of humour got me enough stick from others including at that weekend.

One member of the group; an artist in his seventies exuded a rather pious and priestly persona and whilst sitting on the floor in time honoured fashion as Glyn introduced and worked with people on some aspect of themselves they wished to change or express, somehow the subject of cats occurred in a gap of activity. Being a cat lover I pretended to be one; something I had never dared do before, moving around on hands and knees, putting on a 'cat' voice and rubbing against people as cats do against ankles and legs when after food. I came to the bespectacled pious gentleman who I knew quite well, leaned towards him, shuffled around him brushing my shoulder against his, saying in a soft friendly cat voice, "Me-e-e-o-o-o-w-w-w. Hello Archbishop!" And making suitable feline noises; causing a ripple of suppressed snorting sniggers and stifled laughter among the group, but the 'Archbishop' was stonily silent and anything but amused; thick spectacle lenses magnifying cold, humourless hostility in his eyes.

Only in the group closing circle at the point where it came time to express resentments and appreciations towards and of others did he burst into vocal expression, spitting out jagged shards of his displeasure though completely unable to clearly express open anger; much less his hurt.

Times before I would have met the intended bruising with a loud direct riposte to say he was angry, but no longer; I felt completely defenceless and vulnerable. Emboldened by the 'Archbishop' and my silence, other faint souls began baying like a pack of hounds smelling blood, provoking a fierce clash with others who understood I could or would no longer respond and defended me.

I felt a deep sense of resignation and overwhelming futility. I had worked extremely hard for seven years to free myself from the hapless whirling downward spiral of emotional uproar and chaos of my childhood and even harder to vitiate and dispel the effects of my birth.

As foretold by the graphic image of digging through solid rock and leaping into the torrent exposed, I had gouged open a deep channel to my inner self. Indeed I had positively leapt into these uncharted depths.

The direct consequences of which I witnessed all around me. I no longer needed the artifice of any protocol intended to help people make contact with their emotional and deeper natures. Beyond any volition; that was where I had come to dwell; rules, rote and restrictive intellectual frameworks were as utterly superfluous as discussing whether flight was possible with aircraft filling the skies above.

Once an oasis of free and seemingly honest expression the group had morphed into a prison and I knew, whether I liked it or not, I had moved beyond its restrictive conventions and also with individual sessions I was set for the uncharted uncertain waters of my own choosing.

Though I had clashed with the pious and slightly pompous artist, nonetheless he had shared his perception with others; although he knew

I worked with my head he could see very clearly I needed to work with my hands. At school I had, after all, excelled at wood and metalwork and had the opportunity if I wished, to become a silversmith but chose electronics. It was something I realised right at the beginning of my own crusade to unburden and heal myself but time and again I drowned my awareness in a heady narcosis of intellectual 'glue sniffing' – the 'glue' being the paralysing aroma of software facts and understanding I absorbed and taught.

Without the slightest flicker of doubt the seven years I attended every single group workshop had not only provided me with a continuum in which to release and resolve a lot of blocked and suppressed emotional energy within myself, it had perversely enabled me to continue to abuse myself with an even greater degree of intellectual 'glue sniffing'.

It is said this planet resonates to the law of seven; perhaps in the seven deadly sins I might discover I was guilty of the sin of pride; for what I did was inextricably bound up with self-esteem, intellectual kudos, and status was very much a part of it. So was primal insecurity and the unimaginable burden of fear driving it.

Less abstractly the law also relates to the body; the seven major energy wheels or chakras as they are known in Sanskrit – a language and musical system associated with the law of seven.

Not least the author of *Supernature,* Dr Lyall Watson who discovered the office he worked in made him feel ill because it vibrated at seven hertz a second.

An experimental whistle was made resonating to the frequency and when blown using an air compressor the operator was killed and an autopsy discovered every organ in his body had been ruptured by the blast of seven hertz energy.

Not for a single second did it ever occur to me at the time the law could not have been more accurately attested to than attending the first group workshop in the first and second of February 1975 and the last exactly seven years to the day and hour later, and similarly beginning on my own and individual sessions also embraced the same time span to within a few days.

Ignorant though I might be of the planet's influence on me of its unseen circles of fate, it marked the point where I began a new phase of my life.

Moving on to a non-teaching position I soon became aware of the effects of a massive load having lifted; with the constant need to teach and for perpetual learning having ceased.

For a while every day every few minutes or even less, I experienced small heart irregularities or palpitations.

At the time, completely blind to cause and effect, it really did not clearly connect my heart beat's uncertain rhythm was my inner regions; my inner consciousness in fact, letting me know what abuse I had heaped upon myself. Even less the understanding had I not experienced the massive gush of a huge backlog of brutally suppressed energy, and made a long overdue liberating change of job; it likely would have been a gripping seizure. Understanding of all this and the deep trends of inner consciousness rising into conscious expression, were not only absent; to put the whole picture together took decades to become completely clear.

Just as seven years previously, a few months into getting my body to 'wake up' – my left kidney to work; left lung and other positive signs of improving health, powerful palpitations had occurred when for the first time in years I began to rest and actually feel rested; both were showing me what I had been doing to myself and to put it clearly; showing me what an absolute tyrant I had made my own intellect into.

If anything demonstrated this great divide I had created, it was my heart speaking its truth.

Did I understand then the deeper significance of its healing reproach? Not even remotely.

I accepted its signals with a curious kind of detachment; somehow I knew I would be alright.

I did realise in the wake of the massive gush and backlog of suppressed emotional energy I had released, I was 'bailing with a thimble'. Where before I experienced a definite desire and need to vent emotional pressure, exactly the reverse was the case after. Instinctively I felt I needed time to heal; for empty spaces I had created with this great clearing out, to begin filling up. With what and how much I had no idea but I knew the outcome would be greater strength within.

Hindsight and Perspective

In attempting to convey the seven years of my continuous attempts to heal myself my intention has been to show the trend, from consciously destroying any way back or bridge to my past, how, once I established my own template and model to begin again from scratch, of the steps I took and insights into some of the events along my way marking my progress 'shovelling' away the incomprehensible amount of inner burdens I carried, and which, if nothing else changed, then my life was not going to be a long one. As indeed had been the fate of two of my work colleagues of exactly the same age.

In sharing a few of my experiences, I have endeavoured to illustrate some of the features of this new and developing landscape of my life. To show some of the signs and milestones along the way marking the diametric change in my approach. The end of one model that had got me a long way but I was acutely aware was not going to take me any further, beginning completely again, and reversing my previous process of my inner worlds being a gigantic pit into which I cast more and more unresolved history and experiences. Or better to say, in the process of my birth and for the first nine years of my life, having no other choice than sublimate in myself every shade of emotion attempting to be a 'normal' happy child in the face of repeated downward spiralling chaos – until like a crashing aeroplane, family and self were dispersed, fragmented, shattered, wreckage.

JOURNEY OF A LIFETIME

It is not, nor has it been my conscious intention to describe the minutiae of this day to day and often hum drum process of clearing this burden. It was – and is – a journey of one step at a time and to describe it would be to describe the ground under every footfall.

An attendee of the weekend group therapy workshops I once chanced across in a bookshop and who had been frightened by the noise I made in expressing outrage and gave up after only one or two weekends, told me with gleeful relish I really liked making a lot of noise. In effect, I was addicted to it and this was all I understood or did. He received a very swift reply which was; if there had been a different way to do what I needed to do *at the time*, I would have found it. I did what I needed for the time I needed to do it and when it was worked through I moved on to whatever else demanded to be resolved.

Lacking utterly any sense of continuum or self-awareness of what he wanted to achieve, much less understanding of his own fear paralysing any expression of it – or anything else – he completely confused 'kicking and screaming' as a mindless, pointless exercise for its own sake rather than the release and integration of long stored outrage for a very specific reason and cause.

To begin a journey one must have a clear destination one is aiming for and he had not the faintest idea where he was going; where he was coming from or even what he was doing. Still less a sense of his own inner continuum and trust in it to lead him to a destination metaphorically completely beyond his vision but within the compass of a burning desire to reach it.

My intent is to describe as my experience increased, germinating and growing awareness; my body had intelligence of a kind and to a degree not possessed by intellect which I relied on totally before.

Right from the outset I profoundly trusted my all-consuming desire to 'anneal' myself. In the terms of my original perception, sitting in an empty classroom years before, burying myself in work going through the workings of operating system software exactly as the computer would; instruction by instruction in minute detail; tens of thousands of them, and being acutely aware I had been and was working all the stress in myself to the surface and what I achingly yearned for was some way to release myself from the prison my own mind and body had become, other than dying as two of my colleagues had.

Such was the power of this silent prayer its materialisation was predestined – as anyone who has acquainted themselves with the works of Napoleon Hill and all who have come to understand the power of a burning ambition will know. And mine burned with an intensity beside which the sun was a guttering candle. The choice was simple; free myself or die.

The Inner World Looking Out

WHEN I ALLOWED the inner vision to play, of the digger gouging a deep hole in the rock exposing the churning river beneath; charging headlong and leaping into its frothing boiling dark waters, I knew within a few weeks it symbolised forcing my way into my own deep inner waters of emotion and being. I had no idea of its much broader and deeper significance; that once done my perception of the world had turned inside out. For good.

There was no going back.

Up to that point I had lived dominated by intellect and as an outsider to the world of inner being. Once, like in the Film 'Butch Cassidy and The Sundance Kid', when they jumped off the cliff into the river below, the life they had lived to that point was gone forever as, remarkably, they survived and were sluiced along in its turbid waters to a new and uncertain future, as I had, in my leap of ineluctable fate.

It has taken decades to see the full meaning; not only how – using eyebright – I had mechanistically gouged a hole through to my inner consciousness, but heedless of the consequences jumped in and three weeks later finding myself swamped by overwhelming currents of emotion.

I had no idea it marked the point where my perception changed to seeing my world from inner being to looking out on the world of intellect I had previously inhabited and called 'reality'.

Thus what follows is written from this perspective and of my journey into this inner universe.

I have attempted to describe my process of 'annealing' i.e., of unburdening myself of the stress and inner burdens I carried; to get my body working again and return myself to an unstressed state like metal that is worked, is embrittled and then softened to a malleable condition. In human terms to reverse the inexorable decline in health, strength and bodily wellbeing and rise in rigidity in body, mind, emotions, attitude and every aspect of being.

As far as is practicable I have written as I created and experienced my own progress – like an external observer on a journey – who observes what he sees and experiences – at the same time as doing it. I have specifically and deliberately avoided wandering off into theories of what might or might not be, though on occasion to put into some kind of wider context what I perceived as events took place, in order to maintain coherence and interest in what otherwise would be a dreary recitation. A 'then I did this and then I did that' litany of crashing boredom or describing a long journey through scenery and vistas completely new, different and fascinating only describing every step along the way.

We live in an age of overwhelming intellectual fog. A limitless propensity of creating names for everything and profound understanding of nothing.

In particular my experience of anything remotely dealing with human perception, emotion, the psyche or inner workings of mind and interrelationship of mind and body is like venturing into a murky dungeon. A place of indiscernible features filled with cloying, clinging webs of intellectual theorising, spinning ever greater confusion, lacking even a spark of light-induced certainty born of real knowledge.

This has been described best by the incomparable American scientist, Robert Feynman, who in a televised interview of his long and outstanding career gave an example of the naming culture quoting an anecdote told to him by a teacher of his. The story was the blackbird is present all over the world; he then gave the bird's name impeccably in five different languages, from memory; Spanish, Italian, Chinese, Korean, and Japanese. He went on to say being able to give the bird's name in all these languages would only mean one would know something of the different languages and cultures but absolutely nothing whatsoever about the blackbird.

Indeed, the 'psycho industry' seems to have an unparalleled ability to create names, deliberately obscuring clear understanding.

For example; what used to be called 'manic depressive' – opaque in itself – has now become 'bipolar'.

Bipolar *what*? Meaning one has two ends perhaps; a head and feet. Or hot head and cold feet perchance?

Neither provides even the slightest flicker of insight as to the genesis of this condition; merely an intellectual 'sticky label' some poor unfortunate gets stuck with; pigeon-holing them – often for life.

Similarly 'counselling' has become 'CBT' or Cognitive Behavioural Therapy or as I am inclined to call it, Complete Bloody Tripe.

Nature heals by creating a scab either physically or at deeper levels and invisibly. Picking it off or poking a wound around either physically or with intellectualised rationalisations; gratuitous motherhood and symbiotic gloom spinning, does nothing to aid nature's process. From here my intention is to reverse the approach to this point, because in my journey extending over four decades that is exactly how my own perception has progressed. From being an observer on the outside, awareness has progressed at an accelerating rate to deepening levels of understanding.

Consequently what I may have viewed originally as unrelated 'features' along the way I have come to understand are part of a cohesive whole; and not just some localised inner personal landscape. As sentient beings we are *all* truly vast and unfathomable.

To repeat and extend what one American psychologist said back in the mid-twentieth century; the subconscious is the last unexplored continent on the earth.

It is a single step in the right direction but unfortunately it also neatly encapsulates the myopia afflicting the whole of psycho culture; in likening the subconscious to a continent it is as near to expressing reality as was the nineteenth-century speculation of how many angels could be got on the head of a pin!

Which, believe it or not, this *was* a serious topic of philosophical discussion.

In my experience our overwhelmingly intellectually dominated western culture tries to quantify the subconscious from the way intellect works; it attempts to 'dimensionalise', categorise and to set finite rational limits; rules, laws and structures because *that is the function intellect is designed to perform*, for our physical outer consciousness and world.

Which is why the psycho industry – beginning with Freud – has theories for everything and psychologists/psychiatrists and many others seldom agree on anything.

Our sub/inner conscious cannot be quantified and 'dimensionalised'. It is not an unexplored continent nor yet a complete world, solar system, galaxy or even the physical universe because the sub/inner conscious transcends space and time. It is our portal within us to the infinite and other dimensions.

Some people are inclined to liken the mind and working through our sublimated and repressed history, as a process of peeling away layers from an onion.

I did myself in the early days, but the more clearing and integrative work I have done the less adequate this analogy has become. Indeed, I have found it to be an indication of how little someone has done. For the further I travel the more it dawns just how staggeringly, unimaginably vast and limitless this portal to the infinite in us is.

The dichotomy being beautifully expressed in Bhagwan Shree Rajneesh's book, *The Hidden Harmony*. It is subtitled *Reflections on Heraclitus,* who was an absolute enigma in his own Greek culture.

Sometimes treated as a bafflingly inscrutable philosopher, labelled and belittled as a poet or simply plain mad.

In the book's introduction is an anecdote illustrating the cosmic gulf existing between Aristotle and Heraclitus.

To paraphrase and capture the essence of it, Aristotle, much concerned with his own thoughts, was walking about on a sea shore, passed by a man – not named but meant to be Heraclitus – walking backwards and forwards to the sea, dipping a teaspoon in and returning to a hole he had made, tipping the contents in.

Aristotle, roused from his ponderings, eventually became aware, and puzzled by these antics, asked the man what he was doing. The man/Heraclitus responded he was going to put the complete ocean in the hole.

Letting out an unaccustomed, and no doubt scornful laugh, Aristotle told the man he was a fool and mad if he thought he could empty the ocean into the hole, telling him to go home and rest.

At this, the man or Heraclitus, let out an even louder laugh, saying he would go because his work was done.

Perhaps taken off balance by this bizarre riposte, Aristotle asked what he meant.

The man replied, exactly what you're doing; and you're even more foolish; your head is smaller than my hole and your thoughts have less substance than what I carry in my teaspoon, yet you act as though you could put the Divine and all Existence, let alone the ocean, into the hole with your thoughts.

In essence; and if you'll excuse the vernacular; Aristotle had his head so far up his arse, he'd lost all contact with reality, imagining all that mattered was his capacity to think.

Exactly the difference between them being one; Aristotle, was completely intellectually dominated and the other; Heraclitus demonstrated that the compass of the sub/inner conscious is indescribably more vast.

Or to put it in terms of an ancient analogy I recently coined, it is like attempting to put the subconscious in a doll's house of the intellect and treat this as immutable reality, and is why western 'psychotherapy' is very limited in its ability to heal; because it is forcing the intellect's reasoning, logical, finite rationale on the infinite and why people who have spent years and decades in 'psycho-the-rapy' have to my knowledge continued to suffer from serious physical conditions and dis-ease, showing the flow of energy within them is anything but liberated, harmonious or complete.

And before it is imagined I think I'm standing on some lofty perch of cosmic imagined illumination, far from it. I'm only too aware of my own 'doll's house' and what a colossal amount of effort it takes to undo catastrophic body effects acquired – for example – in an equally nearly catastrophic birth.

To coin another equally ancient saying that came to me recently; I don't make the rules, I simply make the effort.

Which exactly expresses my journey from seeing things from an intellectual standpoint – because that is the way our western culture sees everything and the way I was taught to perceive reality – to moving more and more into a level of the sub/inner conscious; which is the way native or aboriginal societies view reality.

The difference being the latter perceives what otherwise may seem isolated events and experiences as having a consistent continuum; an integrated whole when one understands the rules of this kind of communication and is familiar with their workings. By definition, sub-conscious means that which is below the level of ordinary consciousness. Intellect deals with that which is immediately at a(n) (outer) conscious level and focuses on these experiences as discrete, disparate events.

The problem arises that these two are polar opposites. One cannot be explained in terms of the other. The rules of each are absolutely antithetical to the other.

But in unifying as opposite faces of the same faculty; consciousness, they create *integrated* unified consciousness which is how it is meant to be and function.

And why western society treats native cultures as superstitious, quirky, and too often utterly incomprehensible. Hence as 'savages' and stupid, and native cultures see westerners as a stunted subspecies bafflingly incapable of understanding the signs and portents which our world and events of life continually and constantly present to us and which we ignore to our diminishment at best and at worst to our cost and peril.

In native societies there is no distinction between what we call intellect and subconscious – or worse – *un*conscious.

Their societies, art, history and complete cultures, have no divide as has been created in our western one, which has come to us as mentioned, from the Greeks in general and Aristotle in particular.

(See *Zen And The Art Of Motor Cycle Maintenance* by Robert Pirsig – not separately referred to here.)

Consequently why native cultures untainted by western culture live harmoniously as *part of* nature and why western culture is *detached from* it and treats nature and the earth only as a resource to be exploited lacking any sense of connection with our own inner nature and concomitantly with Great Nature as a whole.

Chief Seattle of the tribe giving its name to the city in the extreme North West of the USA expressed it with the simplicity born of deep understanding; "Man did not weave the web of life – he is merely a strand on it. Whatever he does to the web, he does to himself."

Curious isn't it, we now have something called The World Wide Web…

What follows therefore expresses my journey into inner/sub conscious and consequently creating a broadening channel of communication and *integration* of these two types of consciousness we *all* possess, but which our society and culture doesn't just neglect nor even misunderstand but systematically sets out to demonise and extirpate the function of inner consciousness which is the portal of the universal within, from our earliest childhood times onwards. If one were to be told fifty per cent of our brain was superfluous and this should be surgically removed, no one would willingly submit to such an operation. Yet one Falkland's veteran soldier who was hit in the head by a sniper's bullet and had forty-two percent of his brain removed but survives disabled with his faculties startlingly intact, testifying to the staggering capacity of the human brain to function in spite of massive loss.

In treating the intellect as the sole seat of wisdom we are denying not just our rightful heritage but in my direct experience causing very real damage to ourselves suppressing the energy and vital perceptions; the signs, signals and portents inner consciousness communicates to our outer conscious rational level of existence the whole time.

The more we insist on treating intellect as the alpha and the omega of consciousness, intelligence, and seat of all wisdom and knowledge, the more we create profound conflict within ourselves.

This manifests itself in a myriad of illnesses including, for example, 'bad backs'. It is no coincidence, over ninety million working days are lost in this country every year through this condition.

It does not mean people do not experience crippling symptoms or that they are faking them; the spine is after all the body's 'super highway' through which the spinal cord delivers nerve signals to the whole body from the brain. *And* receives feedback from the world around us by which we sense and understand it.

Once we create imbalance in the workings of our consciousness – in our culture's case by massive and selective over emphasis, focus and reliance on the intellect – and deliberately suppress the rightful and *essential* functioning of inner consciousness, we inescapably create imbalance in the brain's energies and ultimately a conflict in the body's energies. Spinal energy being the primary focus of this and in turn throughout the whole body.

Balance of energies and the maintenance of it within the body is fundamental to Indian, Chinese and Eastern medicine and philosophy and however incomprehensibly it may be expressed to western minds, within native cultures also.

There is no doubt either the further back into the past of our own culture we travel the more artefacts, discoverable rituals e.g., burial practices, wood and stone monuments and legends tell us the same thing about our ancient ancestors.

To repeat the original point; no one would accept having half their brain removed for no reason and if given a saw and invited to saw off a leg or arm the response would be immediate and direct!

And yet this is *exactly* what our culture is doing in concentrating on the centres of the brain dealing with the intellect to the systematic and deliberate suppression and dysfunction of our *real* consciousness.

Life is energy and both are like water; given the opportunity, it flows to some form of completion. Dam a stream or a river and water *will* find a way round the blockage.

Energy within humans is *exactly* the same. As indeed it is in all life and existence.

When water flows freely in a stream or river it possesses a harmony within nature, but when prevented from pursuing its intended course becomes endlessly complicated and creates all manner of problems. Humans – and *all* life are no different. When energy flows to its completion in humans we see healthy, happy, creative, fulfilled people – children and adult. When it is suppressed and blocked we see all the health, personal and cultural problems our society is wracked by.

The American, Shad Helmstetter in his book *What To Say When You Talk To Yourself*, illustrates the problem very well. He says, "During the first eighteen years of our lives, if we grew up in fairly average, reasonably positive homes, we are told No! Or what we could *not* do more than *148,000 times!*"

Conversely that he had had people tell him they could not remember more than three or four times in their lives being told what they *could* accomplish.

Once a course is embarked upon of suppressing an essential and natural part of ourselves – our creative energies driven by inner consciousness – one might as well chuck bricks in a river with 'NO' stamped on every one because the energy of inner consciousness will express itself in the same way the river will continue to flow; however fractured, fragmented and tortuous the process.

To complete the analogy; a stream or river flows as a whole. Half of it doesn't suddenly end up going nowhere or ceasing to exist.

So why in the name of the most rudimentary common sense does western society attempt to do in humans what the rest of nature *and* the universe shows is utterly impossible and doomed to fail?

Rhetorical question…

Coincidence and Inner Consciousness

In 1974 as described earlier, by 'coincidence' – which simply does not exist – I was given the key I desperately yearned for, to unlock and return everything about and within myself to an unstressed or in metalworking terms once more, to an 'annealed' state.

Whether one calls it a desperate yearning, burning desire; or simply a prayer – they are all the same – it is a command to our inner consciousness to act and it *will* be answered.

I use this elegantly simple metalwork analogy because it is precisely what I originally used myself. I loved metalwork at school as something at which I excelled and for the pure pleasure it gave me. It was not only metal I could return to a malleable condition by following a simple procedure; working with metal returned me to a contented and unstressed state.

Perhaps a pity I did not follow the wisdom of my creative – and inner conscious – instinct.

Then again, if I had I would not have learned all I have and none of this would ever have been written.

And fortunately; like having once learned to swim, the skill remains.

Although at the time as I sped in my hired car out of Auckland bent on seeing the geysers at Rotarua and suddenly having gone by a lone hitch hiker outlined against the low, pale winter sun dazzling me, standing on the power assisted brakes – and the car near on its nose – as whimsically it seemed and in spite of myself, I changed my mind, stopped and picked up the young American and within an hour – or less – knew I had been given the secret I so deeply sought.

I was completely blind at the time to what I had experienced – much less as it was actually happening – the absolute battering deluge he gave me of the occult, esoteric, shamanic, magical, spiritual, holistic, dietary and other topics for nearly two days as he talked non-stop propelled by his own inversion from piratical plunderer of his inner nature to its evangelical protector and disciple; was exactly like a dying person being given a hefty heart-stimulating psychic cortisone 'injection' to revive them as longer term resuscitation and treatment was being put in hand.

Moreover, what was being 'administered' was by someone who was an absolute mirror image of me. He had powerfully abused his body with cocaine, heroin and other class 'A' drugs and had it not been for someone who realised a package of drugs he swallowed; attempting to take it into the USA from South America, made from rubber finger-wound protectors stuffed with the narcotic that burst in his stomach, and had treated him; filled him up with salt water making him vomit and forcing him to walk and keep moving, he would surely have died.

As I have written I was as much a 'junkie' as he had been; my narcosis was as greatly damaging in nature, though slower acting and intellectually induced.

He had taken himself to the brink and the ghoulish visage lacking any sign of life, save for the eyes, peering at me; like a wraith in the mirror, I had incredulously witnessed of myself in Melbourne, testified I had too. Of his circle of friends in Los Angeles fourteen of the sixteen were dead and two colleagues in my department were also. Both groups destroying their body's energies with addictive narcotics: the one class 'A' substances, the other a culturally approved implanted killer; imbalance-inducing, stress-creating, tyrannical intellect.

The verbal deluge from him filled me up with psychic/spiritual emetic and his verbal battering made sure I was woken from my cataleptic state creating life-sustaining mind-moving consciousness arresting my life-threatening decline. This subconscious allegory delivered in microscopically-complete detail to my externally conscious world could not have been more finely drawn as this mirror of my being gushed his cathartic geyser driving towards those at Rotarua.

Were I capable of doing so at the time, if I had written out a specification of how I wanted to change my life beginning with my body, and set out the requirements of the sort of person I felt could put me on the right road, it would not have come close to matching what was brought right to me by a string of 'coincidences'.

Which was nothing whatever to do with chance; but the way inner consciousness set in motion a chain of indirect events leading to the answer being manifested in the physical world.

These conspired to bring me to the other side of the world in the first place. Also put me on 'the right road' at exactly the right time and place to stop and pick up this hitch-hiker; something I very seldom did and *never* males, and presented to me someone who realised if he did not change his ways his fate would be – and so nearly had been – that of so many of his erstwhile friends.

He delivered not only a profound wake up call to me – which might have faded – but the book to guide me on my way by someone from the Los Angeles area where he lived, as a lasting reminder and record.

Where once I stared mesmerised by my own reflection in the mirror I was meeting someone who did I but see it was my butchered inner consciousness answering my deepest wish with a reflection of me.

Even more than this, as he had told me, he and his girlfriend had actually stood in front of a mirror and seen what their life and drugs were doing to their bodies and at that moment decided to change their ways.

When Jack Frost – his actual name – got out of my car in the middle of nowhere, was it 'coincidence' I suddenly felt impelled to stop a short distance further on, get out and take a photo of him?

What I actually got was a tiny figure in the wild landscape centred under massive glowering craggy rocks and lowering storm clouds right in the middle of a vibrant rainbow overhead.

For those with eyes to see and senses to appreciate there could be no clearer magical allegory of what I had been given and portents of my past, present and future.

For everyone else of a western left-brained disposition – including me at the time – it was a mundane picture taken with a pedestrian camera.

But all I have said still does not exhaust what 'chance' had brought to me as it took me nearly another twenty years to see it had an even greater dimension and realms and power of my inner consciousness was the mirror's reflection but not just what I was experiencing.

That all this was pure 'coincidence' and whimsy was as incontrovertibly so as were events immediately after, when I flew to Christchurch in the South Island prior to joining my coach tour. Having a day fallow before it began I wandered to its centre; the little cathedral with residential bungalows nearby in this delightful city in miniature, showing signs of acute twentieth century steroid-induced sterile, muscular development in overpowering new concrete, bricks and steel Charles Atlas bodies clashing incongruously with the callow diminutive frames of its short history.

Wishing to find a shopping centre but sparsely trafficked by humans for a city, I watched for 'ant trails'; the tenuous but telltale signs of people's patterns of movement indicating a direction in which concentrated activity could be found.

Following tracks of others I came to the outside of a blank-walled steroid enhanced structure and finding an opening ventured into this human analogue of the insect world.

Only a few steps further I came to the entrance of a department store; exactly what I was seeking, my intention being to buy a thick knitted sweater in anticipation of going further south, deeper into the colder reaches of the island's winter on the tour.

Crossing the threshold, less than a dozen paces directly in front was a tiered book display demanding attention. It was impossible to miss it or mistake its theme, only one book was featured from bottom to top; the one Jack Frost mentioned as being the key to his own renaissance and repudiation of his drug saturated past. Picking the top one from its Perspex stand, without pausing I walked towards the nearest till to pay for it and again not more than a few steps later came to light grey knitted sweaters with a repeated motif in brown and green up the sleeves of kiwis and ferns – the New Zealand animal and plant emblems, found the size I needed, took another few steps straight to the payment desk and bought both.

Jack Frost had been rather vague and evasive about *The Primal Scream* by Arthur Janov but from what he told me I knew it contained the key to unloading the crock of shit, as he picturesquely called it, I carried.

Coincidence I had been drawn like a compass needle to the North Pole and exactly what I needed in the same oblique way I had come across Jack Frost in the first place, travelling to the hot springs and geysers?

Then going to colder climes looking for clothing to keep me warm I had obtained in an exactly similar way precisely what I needed?

Yes, pure 'coincidence' to be sure; in exactly the same way as whilst typing these exact words, a radio news item said the small Anglican Cathedral in Christchurch New Zealand will be demolished due to the damage sustained in the 2011 earthquake making repair unviable!

'Coincidence' without doubt I'm certain …

As coincidental as a 'high protein' steroid-fed sharp, angular quake-proof design in all likelihood supplanting the charm of its predecessor.

Just exactly as 'coincidence' arranged Jack Frost to be standing waiting for a lift as I passed by, it also provided the perfect timing and opportunity to take my first uncertain steps on the road of self-healing.

When I bought *The Primal Scream*, just its possession was confirmation enough I had all I needed to begin reversing the trend of stress accumulation and suppressing my inner feelings. I had to battle hard against the powerful urge to begin as soon as I got it. I was positively bilious with Jack Frost's inner being purgative all the time until I reached Nova Scotia where a friend I had known from the age of five lived.

Moreover, as his wife went off to hospital to give birth within four days of arriving, I had the house to myself during the day, and as related I sat down in the small kitchen of the little wooden bungalow and began to try and write what I felt.

'Coincidence' this synchronised exactly with my arrival there, naturally…

Paradoxically I found it all but impossible to write anything sensible which exactly described the no holds barred wrestling match of intellect and emotions in me.

The difficulty being there was such a competing mass of feeling my 'fiendishly logical' intellect – as my unwashed female hitch hiking passenger had once described my approach to life and me – wasn't about to give up its throne of tyrannical authority and years of training expended putting it there.

I might have a book that was ultimately the model I sought but making it all work only came by doing it and as I hadn't really begun I was a blind man in an alien place without a stick; much less a guide.

I had no idea where my burning desire to free myself from my state of leaden, acutely miserable, dysfunctional fragility was leading me; if anywhere, but alternating with the waves of cosmic isolation and utter despair of ever changing this were the images I held in mind of smoking ruined bridges I had deliberately destroyed and the equally powerful conviction I was not going back to where I had been for it was a very short cul-de-sac of life – another image endlessly repeating in my mind.

JOURNEY OF A LIFETIME

What I felt at the time as my greatest lack; a sense of continuum and understanding of what I was doing or trying to achieve and no one to guide me, was, did I but realise it, also my greatest asset, for I wasn't slaving to someone else's view of what I needed to do.

Looked at from a very long perspective in trying to write what I felt and eventually going into the woods and attempting to give vent to it; yelling/vocal vomiting – when I dared to – for the sheer sense of relief from the immense suppression I felt, could not have been a better example of doing what I had never done before.

In writing what I felt – or attempting to – in so doing creating a bridge between intellect and emotions and releasing the tremendous pressure in sound and fury and opening sluices of self-expression, mobilising all the energy I clamped solid within my body. All I lacked was a sense of conviction and perspective which took a mere ten days to acquire.

When my friend's wife returned from hospital as a mother with her new son my little refuge disappeared and her fragile condition acted on me as a maternal shove to a fledgling in a nest on a precipice; it was time for my beating of wings and thrashing around in twigs and detritus to end; to spread wings of my own sustaining perception and fly. Or crash.

But having achieved it, was precisely the boundless soaring elation I felt.

Arising from the forest floor not so much like a phoenix bird as a transmogrifying chrysalis to human form, in following just my own inner wisdom I understood I could trust it utterly; I knew how to change myself, my body and my life, and curiously having bought what I had felt to be the key to it all, *The Primal Scream*, it too transmuted from distant grail goal to the tales of others tapping their way in the dark. Following the voice of someone else's method and agenda which had as its founding inspiration a quirky Californian 'comedian' who, at the end of his act stomped around the stage repeating 'mummy daddy' until he vomited into a paper bag he carried.

Blind catharsis might be one thing but it is a fetish if it is not accompanied by a clear awareness of what need propels it, and what gestalt derives from its indulgence.

Kicking and screaming as it might be characterised is merely the beginning; it may well and usually does create relief and release of blocked energy; provided it connected with real inner need and is not faked or artificial. Unsurprisingly people often – as I have/do – become warm and energised as energy clamped for so long in the body is mobilised. Indeed in my experience there is invariably a general streaming of energy of all kinds within the body; fluids, muscular, mental activity, heightened awareness and a flow of insights.

And if this doesn't occur then it is all 'kidology' and self-delusion.

Exactly describing the point I reached after ten days of following my utterly alien-feeling routine of thrashing about and saying but more usually yelling whatever came into mind in the woods of Nova Scotia. Never mind what anyone else might have thought; it all felt suspiciously like being barking mad to me also; though having embarked upon the voyage of self-liberation – wherever it led – I wasn't about to give it up.

After about four hours on the tenth day I found I had opened up a 'space' within me and profound understanding I possessed the key to trusting my inner wisdom and processes and unlocking the huge amount of repressed energy and stored history associated with it, I carried within; funnelling me down towards extinction.

Did I understand precisely what I'd achicved? No. Until then 'I' and my subconscious – or at that time my poor, horribly self-abused *un*conscious, were almost complete strangers to one another.

Consequently why I then just enjoyed or perhaps was mesmerised would be a better word, by this startlingly unfamiliar part of me leading me through the woods and urging me to drink what was, after all, ditch water.

What then was impossible to understand because no dialogue worth the name existed between my intellect and the regions of me I had brutalised, savaged and suppressed with it, are now as clear as day.

Unburdening inner consciousness, is, over four decades of work, exactly like bailing out a colossal reservoir the size of an ocean – perhaps several oceans. One bucket full makes no perceptible difference; it is the sustained continual repetition of the process gradually lowering the level until submerged features begin to become clear to conscious view.

In retrospect I can say with absolute certainty in one concentrated effort I liberated a great deal of energy which in hindsight meant my inner consciousness could begin to communicate without my own tyrannical intellect suppressing it, though unsurprisingly, it still interfered because I and others had taught it to. What it communicated was direct understanding of a depth intellect can never provide because that is not its function.

Intellect is as two dimensional as the print on this page; inner consciousness is multidimensional as it transcends space and time. It is our portal in us to the universal within and where we all exist together. Without the former we can survive; without the latter we do not exist.

Once I stopped or at least moderated, the pogrom against my inner self the inevitable consequence was physical healing began immediately.

Because at higher and unseen levels it had already occurred, driven by my all-consuming, burning desire to find some way to 'anneal' and heal myself for more than a year.

As at least one tribe of Aboriginals put it; healing is instantaneous but because we live in a *physical* body it takes *time* to manifest. Which means inner consciousness speaks to us the whole time through our bodies. Consequently why in our unbalanced society which is so completely intellect dominated, there is so much illness and dis-ease.

If we would only take notice, illness and dis-ease is inner

consciousness's way of showing we are creating blockages in the flow of energy in our bodies using our intellect to inhibit it.

Compounding this, allopathic drugs are yet more bricks being thrown in the river again; invariably all they do is sledge hammer and/or suppress symptoms; mess up the body's chemistry and subtle processes and create even greater problems, by screwing up the flow of energy of all types even more within us. And poisoning our system.

Do we take notice what our bodies tell us and the 'language' by which they do so? Rhetorical question again; of course not! Intellect is an *outwards* facing consciousness towards our outer physical world on our *outside*. From birth our culture trains us this is where all reality exists, not only ignoring what our *inwards* facing – though paradoxically universally connected consciousness – our inner consciousness – is telling us what is happening *inside* but positively suppressing what it is trying to communicate within our bodies.

So when I began to allow my inner consciousness to 'speak' it *immediately* caused my body to start waking up. My urine turned a mid-brown, I coughed clods of nearly solid yellow mucus out of my lungs and although the processes were hidden from sight and clear awareness my left kidney began stirring from total torpor, as did my pancreas though these took weeks and years respectively to communicate their recovery. Lung function, whilst beginning to improve, continued not just for weeks or months, but years and decades and still continues currently.

It might be tempting to say from that point on it was plain sailing. Living in a culture of intellect and instant fixes; instant knowledge/ self-realisation/empowerment and a blizzard of other instant transformational mastery it is easy to be blinded by mirages of the intellect. The reality was it took about four years and a great deal of work to learn

JOURNEY OF A LIFETIME

I was only just at the beginning and that long for my body to even begin regaining some semblance of wellbeing as related previously.

Deeply ingrained habits did not magically dissolve and clear like morning mists and the deepest of these was the opium of intellect. It was as much about curing a profound addiction to it as weaning away from long use of the actual narcotic. Again as earlier explained, having found the key to healing my body, if anything I abused myself to an even greater extent in the massive intellectual load I took on wading around in the deepest depths of how computer operating system software worked, learning and teaching the range of topics that at their most complex made students often look and feel distinctly unwell only a short way into the course. And which at its end left all – including me – in a state of adrenaline saturated, brutalised, mental and physical exhaustion.

In attempting to show how my own perceptions progressed; widened and deepened over the years and how it was like building a Millau bridge of the mind from the two sides of the canyon within me; the one my intellect, the other my subconscious, was a process like pushing out from both sides until they met in a union of harmonious understanding in the middle, I will endeavour to show the trend as I experienced it and the changes and effects in mind and body.

The intention is to provide an overall picture; a sketch of the process its trend and thereby how I came to heal the divide within me and, fuse together a bridge of harmony between these previously disparate conflicting aspects of my being.

In 1978 as described, near the beginning, teaching a programming course at Gloucester, after a day's work I would end up with my abdominal region in knots. I discovered in not wishing to lay on the cold wet earth – assuming I could find somewhere suitable and generally give vent to whatever expression felt appropriate – I discovered leaning over the back of my seat in my car, causing it to dig into my abdomen and letting out my acute discomfort in sound it was a mixture of half dry chuckle, half sob.

As also explained many times; if that was what created relief in my body, as it did, then I would continue doing it until it became clear what my body wanted to express; no matter how long it took and wherever the process led me.

It continued over the years and steadily gathered in strength, and 'dry chuckle' morphed into sobbing which with the seat back – or as time progressed – something pressed into my abdominal area until after the great gush and release of a backlog of pent up emotion in early 1982 it became dry vomiting.

Did this mean I suddenly understood what drove it? Definitely not. Then – and for years after – I simply accepted this was what my body needed to do, and just as it had evolved into a much more distinct body response, if my abdominal area had a 'mind' of its own and this was the way it unburdened itself and freed knotted muscles and brought relief, that was reason enough.

Conscious also how I clamped my breathing, tensing up driving my car, taking a few breaths, not even deep ones necessarily, soon brought the same reflexive desire to vomit.

It was a tedious process but the unfailing result was from being knotted up and feeling like a hand gripping my entrails, the dry vomiting would release it and I would hear my digestive 'plumbing' begin to gurgle again as the natural peristalsis rhythmic contraction of the large intestine was restored.

Unsurprisingly breathing also became freer and no longer felt as if my chest had a weight pressing on it.

But it was not a magical 'born again' one time event; far from it. Having made the choice at the outset of taking notice of what my body needed to do it was as much a part of life as other body functions.

Depending on whether there was a particular cause driving my knotted state, the amount of vomiting might be short if just a feeling of discomfort or repeated over some minutes if for example I had had a hard day's stressful work, or suffered some kind of unpleasant shock or experience.

Often it was interspersed with anger and outrage at life's accumulated frustrations and clashing of egos.

Gradually over time – years – driving my car became a less gut-strangling experience but it continued nonetheless testifying I had sublimated and suppressed a huge amount of energy within me and focused in my abdominal regions.

There were periods when I fondly imagined I had worked through it all; symptoms having left me. But as surely as one wave follows another in the ocean, there were times when far from declining they would return, as for example in 1990 it deepened into excruciating gut gripping. This being an acutely stressful period trying to start up and run a small business. There came a point when alcohol triggered agonising spasms only released by stuffing something in my mouth and pushing it against my throat, did it break the deep clamping of my abdominal region, producing as much a low roar as simply a reflexive dry vomit.

It took a while – certainly some months and maybe a year or two – before I began to realise this very unpleasant abdominal sensation was something I recalled from childhood after the demise of my family. Instead of feeling hungry I would feel a most unpleasant sensation; a sort of hollow, growling, vaguely-burning gut. In turn it dawned what this was went by the name 'Irritable Bowel Syndrome' or IBS. Yet another misnamed, misleading, wholly meaningless 'medicalism'.

I also recalled times when I had been working extremely hard in the computer industry; building and checking out mainframe computers in a factory, alternating weeks of day and night shift whilst studying three nights a week at night school and several hours on a Sunday for thirty-one weeks of the year.

On occasion my abdomen swelled up painfully as if I was suffering from malnourishment or driving along in my car my gut region became a detached rocklike centre of pain.

Also, my digestion had been adversely affected by this deep gripping knot I carried in this 'seat of the emotions' as the abdominal region is well known.

At times and still years later – invariably at night – I would occasionally have to deal with a sudden welling spasm feeling as if my entrails were on fire and someone had reached in, grabbed and twisted them around. As before, the only way I could break this acute involuntary gut contraction was by rolling up a face cloth/flannel into a plug and sticking it in my mouth to the back of my throat. The resulting instinctive need to clear my throat by vomiting would break the gripping spasm with a reflexive roar and immediate or near immediate relief followed.

To repeat; this was not some arcane, whimsical fetish I indulged in. Energy only goes one of two ways; inwards or outwards; it implodes or explodes; involutes or evolutes and it is as true in the universe as it is within the human body.

At opposite ends of the energy spectrum, a sun spews it out and a black hole does the reverse. With all other existence in the universe somewhere between these two extremes.

Fear – or for that matter anger; the emotional highest priority demand for action, or alternatively the other side of the same coin – either gets expressed in some kind of externalised catharsis but if not and it is for some reason suppressed or repressed then it is sublimated in the sub/inner conscious and the resultant clamping of the emotion produces a clamping in the body. Either in the abdomen or the chest and usually affecting both directly and the whole body overall.

Common sayings have an unerring ability to identify its location and nature within the body.

For example:

- The stomach (abdomen) is the seat of the emotions.
- So and so is a pain in the neck.
- So and so is a pain in the arse.
- Getting something off your chest.

To reiterate; when I began, I had no idea where some form of expression might lead – only that it *would* lead somewhere. I didn't need to know what it was; merely to accept my body had its own intelligence and wisdom far beyond anything chattering, squawking intellect understood. Be it the chirping 'bird cage' on my shoulders or a therapist's tree full of twittering starlings; endless competing parrot noise of book learned theories of what Freud, Jung, Rogers, Adler, or legions of other theorists and therapists evangelised as the portals to inner bliss, and a thousand other motivational tomes of guaranteed nirvana-in-a-cup bouncing around in the brain.

Freeing myself from what, all too clearly, I could *feel* had to be dealt with and cleared first was my highest priority and other things came after.

Simply following my body's unerring ability to express what it needed to in the way it needed to do it for as long as it was required always led as surely as a train on rails to a destination of clear intuition and understanding of what the process was about.

Wandering off into thoughts and speculation of what it might be about being the surest way to suppress with interfering intellect the release of blocked energy and prevent inner conscious wisdom from asserting itself.

Ocean Swells and Mortgages

When I began my own journey and crusade to heal and change my life, as I have said, I followed my instinct and intuition tenuously at first but after ten days and my great release of blocked and locked up energy bringing an explosion of liberation and inner conviction, I knew I – and no one else – held the key to my own wellbeing, progress along my path to it and utterly unshakeable trust in my body's and my inner wisdom.

To reiterate yet again; I did not know where it would lead me, only that my body and inner being would unfailingly lead me in the right direction, wherever that might be.

I did the exact opposite of what I had done – and been taught to do – all my life until then; I let my body tell me what it needed to do instead of overruling its wisdom with my intellect, exactly like someone driving a car, shooting out traffic lights at red and charging on regardless of the signs and signals telling me what was right and what was wrong for it and my wellbeing.

In the early years and for much longer it was exactly like bailing a leaky boat, trying to make the vessel of my life – me – more sea or 'lifeworthy'. I listened to what it and inner conviction dictated.

An inescapable corollary of this as time passed was trying to understand and see what patterns there might be to this process; like watching the sea and looking for wave patterns and long swells amid the short chop and frisson of individual crests. At one and the same time, 'I' was the process and also a dispassionate observer of it all.

For many years – in fact for decades, apart from going through periods when a great deal seemed to be going on in my body or periods of abdominal and inner calm and changes in muscular tension accompanied by emotional release – I had little if any perception of patterns of cause and effect or the relationship between the expression of one emotion and the rise of the next wave into bodily awareness and its breaking on the shoreline of clear consciousness.

There was more than enough just to work through, integrate and maintain focus in my day-to-day world of personal relationships, work and being.

At the back of this though I always felt there were patterns, but just as if swimming in the ocean; the wave I was in was the only one I could see and deal with.

Unlike being in an ocean though, the analogy should not be taken as sloshing around aimlessly and wallowing in a sea of bodily sensations and emotion. The computer industry I worked in and the work I did were the polar opposites, being completely intellectual in nature. Whilst also expressing the divide in me, their heavy presence meant keeping my wits about me which at times of great emotional stress – as happened not infrequently over the years – could be very difficult but was also a very useful discipline in staying focused and rendering to Caesar that for which Caesar provided my 'salt' at the end of each month!

I did not share the view of people I knew who in clearing their history and emotional paths equated it with brown bread, organic goat's cheese, wearing clothes thrown out by Oxfam, puffing on 'waccy baccy' and living in a squat.

To me it is merely to trade one social group for another and a means of feeling comfortable in some soothingly familiar milieu.

Tyrant I might have been to my own inner nature, but striving to build a bridge of harmony across the canyon of my own unresolved needs was ultimately an excellent discipline because awareness of this clash never left me; and never has since Friday 20th September 1974 when I began the task of healing it.

Wallowing in 'touchy feely' was/is as deluded as being an ungrounded intellectual ivory tower recluse.

As time and the years progressed there were distinct phases, but it is only well within the last decade the 'ocean swells' of changes; of growth and developments crystallised into clear perception; moreover the ocean currents of which they were and are a part.

Like those who navigated the globe leading ultimately to a clear charting of the movement and cycles of the seas, I can look back not simply at changes within me but as part of an overall continuum; a connected whole and continuous process.

From 1974 it took over four years before I gained a sense of pleasant wellbeing.

Beginning from this time the pace of change and growth within accelerated so as explained briefly previously; 1978 was a year of headlong, continual nonstop clearing.

On a purely personal level the failure of my marriage had a great impact and made it difficult to function at times, but looked at from the perspective of healing myself, once the bond had been broken it was like the brakes releasing; the energy I had devoted to it became available for clearing my inner world.

With gathering momentum I worked flat out, spanning the complete spectrum of emotions from deep despair and sadness, through hurt, fear, anger and outrage also spanning my marriage but much more so aspects of my life and in particular the effects of what I began to understand as the unimaginable burden I carried from my birth, generously endowed with chaos, uproar and final disintegration of my childhood. And subsequent foster care.

Just as in nature; once the storm of outpouring energy was spent by the end of 1978, with the coming of 1979 it brought calm, tranquillity and a fair amount of inner peace.

Perhaps as related, my experiences in Paris in mid-December

1978 of finding stillness within myself in Saint Sulpice church, followed later in the day by tumultuous uproar in Notre Dame may appear mannered, melodramatic, or pure fantasy in the telling but our subconscious constantly provides us with its imagery in our day-to-day *physical* world.

Times beyond number we see athletes who are 'taught' to visualise achieving their long laboured-for goal as if it was something extraordinary.

It is not. Realise it or not, we all visualise things all the time. But our western culture insists on standing true reality on its head.

Our society is like someone running amok in a colossal telephone exchange, scrambling all the connections so almost nothing crops up where it should – and such is the level of utter chaos, when it does we miss it completely in the maelstrom of inner confusion.

The someone running amok in our 'telephone exchange' is the utter confusion created by our society's insistence on using our intellect to scramble all the 'connections'/dialogues of our subconscious never ceasing to occur, no matter how intellect is trained to act like Rambo exterminating all opposition in its path.

Consequently we possess no means of understanding cause and effect in our lives and live in a swamp of 'random' happenstance; chance this and coincidental that.

At the time, I felt the experiences of that remarkable Paris Sunday were definitely related in some way.

Returning to the analogy of calm after the storm; there is also a calm before a storm and in endeavouring to exist only in the present disconnecting from all the thoughts, fears, clamour, and internal conflicting noise, I had ordered my own 'telephone exchange' to a passive state where dialogues of my subconscious could – for once – get through.

Well, what a surprise! It led me to the clearest possible allegory of how my life had been that year and was ending.

Far from being in the least imaginary or stilted, this 'dream' enactment projected into physical reality right in front of me the conflict of energies in my inner spiritual world in a thunderous deafening clash of wills like nothing else except perhaps a Saturn V rocket taking off close by. As at times that year when I felt I was coming apart, that afternoon, I feared Notre Dame would erupt skywards and bury all in some pyro-plastic religious deluge. Hardly surprising I also became completely choked with emotion.

My inner and outer worlds had meshed completely.

Not only have the patterns, the waves, swells and currents of the subconscious become clear, in retrospect I have found healing is exactly the same as paying off a mortgage.

To explain, it is necessary to review the patterns of my progress; the patterns of my inner 'ocean' over the decades.

As I have related with a few events from the early years – mostly the first seven – like a swimmer moving stroke by stroke through the ocean waves and swells, the changing patterns and rhythms of energies within my own being were something I dealt with as they happened; there was no real sense of perspective. It was a case of simply getting on with it all. It *was* clear day-to-day how my body felt; the energy or lack of it transitory or more sustained aches and pains I experienced and in this sense mostly on the physical level what progress I felt I was making.

On an emotional level changes were less clear; if at all, precisely because these took considerably longer and in any case were actually the longer motion of the 'ocean' that was also me. Expression of emotion was one thing, perception of the underlying pattern of energies driving it were quite another, linked and driven as they are by sub/inner conscious.

It is perhaps a statement of the obvious, physical and emotional energies are inseparable; feeling physically well feeds emotional wellbeing and vice versa. Things weighing us down emotionally directly affect the body.

As step by step I cleared the weight of emotional history and intellectual punishment I had heaped upon myself I gradually became less edgy, tense, short-tempered and reacquired my sense of wit and humour.

Unblocking the streams of emotional energy directly opened up my body.

For example, for many years from my early teens I suffered from pain and tension in my lower back. To stand for a long time always brought on a dull continuous ache. In 1979 I reached a point where a massive amount released and it took about three months for the muscles to recover from being clamped solid the whole time during which period I could hardly bend at all to begin with; gradually becoming more pliable and finding back ache had gone for good.

These were the kinds of changes I was aware of as milestones along the way but seeing trends between changes was not really apparent. Thus I did not see or even think about a connection between having done a great deal of work on the emotional front over four years and increasingly in 1978 as related, beginning to discover I still carried powerful effects of my birth. Discovering as I did in 1979 when wrapped in a blanket and five people pinning me down to focus me on releasing my inner demons from birth, I hit a brick wall of overwhelming fear I did not realise, until then, I carried within me.

To clarify; I did not connect the four prior years of work with the first sense of bodily wellbeing in 1979 I had enjoyed in years, with the inescapable consequence; what was still buried in my sub/inner conscious had risen to become much closer and accessible to clear consciousness, only finding this out when literally and metaphorically being put under great pressure – exactly what transpired during my birth.

Even less did I make any connection between investigating birth and personal relationships, over the weekend workshop and in a few hours my lower back being so tender I could hardly move.

Though birth was only a small part of it.

After a day's activities and their emotional impact, on the Sunday morning I felt as if I had been run over by stampeding elephants and I was leaking emotions like a sieve. We stood together in a circle and some of John Denver's music played quietly in the background. The quality of his voice and a tinge of sadness in it always brought emotions close to the surface in me.

Suddenly a barred door of memory was opened and I was back as a nine-year-old and an utterly consuming desperate desire to do anything to hold my disintegrating family together; seeing my father's inexorable decline and my mother unable to carry the emotional burden any longer; weighed down and well past breaking point, crying all day for weeks on end, not only for what she was enduring single-handedly but the immense legacy of repression bequeathed her by her mother, who in her turn had been subjected to a savagely suppressive Victorian upbringing. The words and mental image spontaneously forming; if it meant carrying the house on my back and everyone and everything in it I would do it, I didn't care. I would do *anything* to stop the endless excruciating nightmare we were all in together. Like a motto under a family crest the words expressing this I uttered without thought: I won't give up and I won't give in.

The 'family crest' was the house and everyone and everything in it and the 'motto' carrying it underneath, was me.

As this wave of perception broke into open consciousness I could hardly breathe or stand as we stood linking arms in a circle, the warmth and support of other's arms around me filled me with indescribable agony and I was wracked with pain and aching sobs for what until then I had hidden within myself.

As until now also has been the full measure of this symbolism.

JOURNEY OF A LIFETIME

Which is nothing if not an exact allegory of having carried a great 'weight' within me, and having finally put it down, my back feeling as the day wore on, this was what I had actually carried for more than a quarter of a century! No accident either the load I carried could be seen in my body as a slight 'S' shaped bend in my spine.

To restate; at that point I was still very much the swimmer in the ocean; just getting on doing it.

Or it is better to say in 1979 it was much more a case of floating along in the current and at least to some extent just enjoying it and as mentioned in broadening interests and dabbling in the realms of the spiritual, occult and esoteric knowledge. For the first time I had cleared enough 'space' in myself to have free energy expressed as expanded consciousness.

It was no accident/coincidence I travelled again that year to Iraq as I had in 1977 to give a course and take advantage of stopping off in Egypt. Both of these places recharged the fires of my interest and imagination, that from school days and boyhood times held me fascinated until I ached with their history.

The years following the great gush and logjam of energy releasing in finally giving up my addiction to punishing intellectual striving in computer software; learning and teaching such a burden of courses I was in danger of repeating the debilitating effects I had created within myself by 1974, unsurprisingly, brought a repeat of the calm following the build up to and manic clearing of 1978.

The same or very similar patterns of improved physical wellbeing occurred and for a while in 1982 I found my body more supple and pliable and for a while doing some Yoga, finding postures possible my body would not bend to before.

It was testament though to the intellectual burden I previously shouldered, once I consigned it to history a great wave of deep exhaustion and tiredness lasting not just a few months but years overcame me. For months at lunch times when I would leave the office and get out in the air, a desire to speak utter nonsense always pressed for expression and so, taking care not to be in earshot of others I would give vent to this non-language bringing inner relief.

I realised it was an antidote against having to make sense the rest of my working day, but it didn't occur to me until many years later it was not simply that, but was propelled by all the years I had stood in classrooms making logical sense and having stopped flattening my subconscious under an intellectual Everest, the direct consequence was a compulsion to speak *illogical* utter nonsense not even using recognisable 'words' doing it. It even became a source of irritation my 'vocabulary' was fairly limited and the pattern of sounds I 'spoke' – or even shouted given a suitable human-free place to do it – soon repeated.

There was simply a huge pressure to right the tremendous imbalance my left brain addiction had created.

It took nearly five years until mid-1986 before health and wellbeing really recovered.

Not least as the year progressed within a couple of hours of sitting down at my desk each morning my solar plexus region reminded me how much tension I had clamped there as it steadily released; accompanied by weariness beyond words, finally resolved by an early summer holiday.

At the beginning of the year I changed my job within the company, still moving from a technical sales related, to a marketing function.

It marked a period when a number of factors converged; a couple of years previously I had remarried. I moved out of suburbia into the countryside, which having been born and lived in either very rural surroundings or a village felt very liberating. The change of job to a much broader mixture of technical topics and related marketing activities all brought about a feeling of more energy and buoyancy not felt in years.

Work felt like riding a surf board – a delicate balance between keeping ahead of a wave of things to be done and at times on the verge of being overwhelmed by it all; being busy but not constantly weighed down in deep technical minutiae as had previously been the case.

At times deadlines pressed heavily but I was surprised, to use the surfing analogy, I managed to keep on the crest of the wave and not become swamped. I wondered why I was driven by this powerful compulsion to do so much, and to use different symbolism; like an ignited firework rocket without a stick; earthbound and rushing hither and thither. Though fortunately once the shower of creative sparks subsided, unlike the pyrotechnic a more measured progress returned – but not by much.

Simply put, I experienced a creative surge doing all that I did and yet strangely blind to seeing creative fulfilment was what sustained me during this period. Perhaps not surprising; extreme hard work was a family tradition I was brought up in and inured to and creative fulfilment was not a word in its, or my vocabulary. I simply did not understand its existence.

By now it might well be asked; what has any of this to do with paying off a mortgage in an emotional or personal sense?

In sketching briefly progress in healing myself and bridging the great divide of energies and the powerful predominance of intellect I had cultivated in me, I fondly believed for some years in the 1980s I had cleared the great burden bringing me to a state of acutely miserable existence years before.

I was wrong.

Or perhaps it is better to say I *had* cleared a huge amount but this only led me to open the throttle of my 'engine' and stretch myself further. So it comes back to the analogy once again of being like a piece of metal; the more it is worked and stressed the more brittle it becomes, requiring once more to be annealed and brought back to a malleable state.

Except it was not quite that simple either!

Yet again with the great telescope of long hindsight it is clear there were two distinctly different processes occurring in me. At distinctly different levels.

The more superficial was my need and ability to express my creative urge and find fulfilment in the work I did and in my life generally. I ran with foot hard down on the throttle of my life – which is no doubt also why I suddenly saw blue flashing lights in my rearview mirror on the motorway one day – and narrowly escaped being banned from driving for a while!

At another level there was a great heave taking place deep within me.

Having worked extremely hard in the seventies and early eighties to redress the massive imbalance between intellectual, emotional and sub/inner conscious energies in myself, Great Nature reasserted its laws and in a direct sense I was catching up on the normal pattern all human life instinctively attempts to follow against the clock of our existence. Put simply, nature's primeval urge.

Underneath all this, like a deep sub-ocean landmass gradually rising to appear out of the sea, were even deeper levels of my personal history pushing upwards to a conscious level for expression and integration.

On one level I lived and existed like any other man.

But such was the overwhelming power and strength of my desire to clear from my inner worlds all that weighed me down and had so nearly ended my life by the time I was thirty-years-old, I had conveyed this unstoppable imperative into the depths of my inner world and my sub/inner conscious, and it was not something I could then deny –

without (re) creating an all-out unwinnable conflict within myself.

Did I understand this was what I had done?

I had not the foggiest idea this was so. Only decades later is this now crystallising into clear conscious perception.

Consequently, in much of the 1980s on a deep inner level it was as if I had taken a payments sabbatical on a 'mortgage' of buried history and energies I still carried that nonetheless were steadily rising and pushing up towards the need for conscious expression.

Just like a mortgage loan, 'interest' was piling up and unless I took action to begin paying off what I 'owed' serious repercussions would follow. Which is exactly what happened.

Just another 'coincidence;' in the late '80s I also missed some actual mortgage payments...

Another way of saying it is; I put my inner worlds on 'care and maintenance'. I had no intention of living my life in what I came to call and see as 'therap' land.

Earlier I mentioned someone at the first weekend group therapy workshop I ever attended who, standing in front of the group and asked what things she would like to change about herself, in beginning to focus on an aspect had begun to emit clearly audible abdominal sounds and yet no one in the group or its leader with whom she was working made any mention of this and yet most already knew each other.

The identical scene being re-enacted exactly seven years to the hour – if not the same minute – later and *still* no one said anything. Pure coincidence again no doubt ...

Just as the same symbolism of it being repeated on the day of Imbolc; the first day of pagan spring – the first of February and the same day of the week as before; a Saturday (Saturn-day) and both marking the end of one cycle/level of events and the tipping point into the start of a new one (on the Sun-day).

Just another load of meaningless mumbo jumbo 'coincidences' *any* left brain dominated person would know made no intellectual sense whatsoever. And any person with clear sub/inner conscious access would immediately connect as being one complete turn of an upward spiral of self-development on the road to self-fulfilment.

Right from my first weekend – and the first ever workshop to be run – having risked bringing the roof down on my head for what my openly voiced perceptions might provoke in others I saw no reason to take everything on my shoulders. Consequently, as also related, it became increasingly clear that 'therap' land had its own social conduct code as much as any other group social identity. And to me honesty was an early casualty yet was supposed to be the *sine qua non* for healing depredations the world might have inflicted upon those present.

If others were content to mark the boundaries of their lives with bean sprouts, unorthodox dress, henna hair dye, patouli incense and mists of wacky baccy smoke, I wasn't; and if these were the limits beyond which fear lurked, then for me so be it.

To me it was as restricting as the intellectual iron rigidity I had once fenced the frontiers of my own life with; having cleared (at least some) of my own spoil heap of Himalayan proportions from its crushing effect upon me – or so I thought – I wanted to use the new lease of life and energy I possessed and grapple with new challenges.

Which meant my world ran on parallel rails; as much as one took me beyond the shunting sidings of bumping and clattering against other people's sensitive dispositions, the other was my working world. It too took me beyond a similar clash but the shunting was the interminable clash and grind of egos, politics, departmental and personal rivalries.

What once at work I thought of as my university and appeared a limitless route on which to travel, grow in knowledge, personal and intellectual capacity, gaining professional experience and kudos, also evolved into overcrowded sidings. Corporate plans were like marshalling yards where organisations and departments were formed, broken up; disappeared only to re-emerge later in a different guise.

JOURNEY OF A LIFETIME

The same head of steam driving dissatisfaction with both, meant an unstoppable urge to change points and move on to different rails whatever uncertain destination they might be headed for.

Never one to do things by halves, I went from the corporate vastness of a multinational and thousands of employees in December 1986, to the other extreme: just one other person who owned the business. Moreover, expecting to be working in a technical capacity, aspiration for selling being only slightly closer than the edge of the known universe, I found myself expected to do both – the colleague salesman I had expected to join with me disappeared off elsewhere!

I had well and truly set out on a journey into unfamiliar scenery and strange new territory.

Insights, Toil and Prophets in Back Yards

I WISH I had been capable of heeding insights I had from time to time; they would have led me on tracks to a very different destination. Twice, before I slammed the door of corporate solidity behind me to set foot into pitch black uncertainty, I had uttered to others prophetic words and utterly ignored them myself.

The first time was saying to an American colleague in early 1984 I felt Honeywell would be out of the computing industry within three years. That, it appeared, was less likely than the earth reversing its rotation. Not satisfied with my own powers of prediction in 1985 talking to someone who knew nothing about electronics or computers, I tapped into some passing cloud of intuition and the wisdom of its ethereal wisps formed words without conscious effort; electronic technology had reached a watershed. The ubiquitous chip had reached the point where so much could be condensed on to one, both the non computer electronics industry as well as all computer manufacturers were going to be affected. It was going to cause a complete sea change across the whole spectrum of electronics. The complete field would become a consumer industry, just like light bulbs were I felt.

By the end of 1986 all computer manufacturers reported staggering losses, whilst the sales of personal computers rocketed skywards along with Bill Gates' personal fortune; marking the time when IBM and the other computer dwarfs as they were called alongside IBM's overwhelming dominance could no longer lock customers in to huge expenditure based on their own systems.

It marked the start of a corporate mass extinction event to rival the dinosaurs passing.

But it seemed I had a long held singular talent for steadfastly ignoring my own insights boardrooms would have killed for; and were summarily 'executed' for after the event.

In my resignation letter I felt the time had come to launch into the unknown; telling myself this was something I was ready for and a great opportunity, and ignoring a very senior manager who shook his head in disbelief when he read it. Underneath it though were the echoes of deep uncertainty I would not admit, connecting directly with an event when I was five years old.

Trying to keep up with other boys who were at least two years older, climbing from tree to tree along a line of birches close to one another, I could neither climb as high nor span the distance between interlacing branches of one tree and the next as they could. Standing on a bottom branch I got as far out as possible just able to grasp the fine fronds of the adjacent tree's shoulder level limb. Then, knowing perfectly well what the outcome would be, I stepped out on to the ends of fronds from the next tree's branch no squirrel would have even considered trusting its weight on, and closed my eyes. With a thud sending shivers up the tree felt by the others, I landed waist deep in brambles and soft earth underfoot, from a height of five or six feet.

Shedding a few tears of hurt and shocked surprise at the raking inflicted by the briars on my bare legs from knee to thigh; the bottoms of my short trousers pushed up by them, and the sudden descent, I quickly suppressed them to show no weakness.

Had I been able to admit it, there was an uncanny resemblance between that childhood event, my intuitions about the industry I had come to know well, and the step I was taking from secure employment into what instinct said would be an equally certain grazing, shuddering landing. The driving compulsion though being an even more deeply denied desire to free myself from the repeating corporate process of interminable departmental reorganisations; the bickering clamour of their clanking ego-shackles of coupled alliances and fragile bonded empires that politics, rivalries and top management just as rapidly shoved off into the buffers of history.

Deeper than all this was the fusion furnace fuelling the heart of this chain reaction; the need to express my own creativity. But willingness to admit this and the stygian inner gloom with which I deliberately obscured it from conscious expression made it as accessible to me at the time, as distant reaches of the universe.

And even this was removed – though not as distantly – from the need to *act* to extricate myself from the feeling of restriction hemming me in.

The seemingly small gap between 'creativity' and 'restriction', only revealed decades and thousands of hours work later.

Having set out into unknown territory, the immediate result far from being one of trepidation was a feeling of immense relief at having left the corporate ego farm behind with all its bellowing and braying, aware of the tremendous amount of energy I had suppressed as part of its internecine factional struggles. What I came to describe only slightly tongue in cheek as five thousand one-man companies all working against each other towards a common aim.

Technically, my new job within computer networking was not difficult; but faced with a cold telephone, a bare desk and no customers for the equipment I was now also selling, and with no direct experience of having done it, felt like tackling the north face of the Eiger dressed in business attire, armed with a briefcase in one hand, and an instruction book on mountaineering in the other.

Not that I was capable of admitting that to myself either.

If I had made a conscious decision to find a role where I was starting from scratch completely on my own I could not have bettered the situation chosen. I thought my boss, as the only other person in the company, would show me the way and be hard on the phone cold calling companies and people as I had begun to do, but this was not so. He liked talking to people on the phone, making grandiose plans, creating an aura of bustling lofty authority about him but cold calling were words and actions absent from his daily routine. Which meant each nerve-wracking call I made was like a single drip into a plugged sink. Dialling a number not knowing what I would say or how I would create any kind of connection or rapport with the disembodied voice at the other end.

Call by call and drip by drip the sink of conscious awareness began to fill with fear. Drop by drop the reservoir of my inner conscious was leaking its contents and more and more the level rose.

I began to realise I might have thought I had cleared a huge amount of my personal history and its effect on me reflected in my body but it steadily dawned as days turned to weeks I was running flat out.

It did not take long before I could only eat porridge for a period of about three weeks and I became so frightened I could barely maintain my balance walking along the narrow corridor to my office one morning.

In turn it began to focus me back towards the need to release the tension and discomfort of clamped breathing and knotted abdominal regions.

At night before I went to sleep my eyes would flood and then dry out.

Throughout all this and ever since having remarried I had made a deliberate and conscious decision and effort to keep my inner world separate. I was determined not to slosh around in a confused swamp of emotions so redolent of 'therap' land.

As time passed it became clear the burden of the cold hard graft of generating business rested completely on my shoulders, and the skills to do it I would have to develop unaided for myself.

Having always been involved in technology and technical aspects, never having, nor indeed ever expecting, to become directly involved in selling; still less as the *only* salesman in a company, the burden of creating sales and the need to confront a cold phone every day showed me I might have made considerable strides in liberating and healing my inner world, but the grit, determination, mental dexterity and courage it took to generate interest; let alone make a sale soon proved to be a task demanding elephantine stamina.

Someone working for the company in whose building we had office space talked about the cold calling he had done and compared it with the rigours of the SAS he experienced himself. Arduous as this had been he found a day on the phone more exhausting. He went home mentally as well as physically drained.

Having had similar contact in the Territorial Army myself I could only agree.

Months of effort produced no sales, but as the 'novice' it was my own ideas and contacts that began to open up the prospect of actually getting business.

Innovative ideas of mine creating a chance to sell into an organisation, far from being welcomed by my boss and company owner, more often than not provoked palpable dismissal, resentment and jealousy because he had not thought of it himself! Yet if some other company's product coupled to our own produced positive results he attempted to engage in a 'joint venture,' by which he meant them putting money in our business and indulging in interminable telephone conversations, visits, meetings and grandiose deluded proposals.

Which I came to realise was exactly like watching a hot air balloon being inflated; attempting to take off only to be grounded and deflated in the face of unfavourable winds.

JOURNEY OF A LIFETIME

I also experienced effects on my body of the effort and strain imposed by the relentless need to keep up the sales effort. The powerful disorientating fear gripping me once all I had taken on in my leap into the unknown finally sank in, gradually subsided into a background spectre as day after day; call after call, the scales of hard experience gradually grew and I began to learn to talk *to* people over the phone rather than *at* them.

Working at my desk, a dull nagging pain in my right sciatic area ached its way into conscious awareness. I recalled as a young teenager when on any car journey of more than a few minutes this would happen and the only way to relieve it was to push the seat cover down so I wasn't actually sitting on it for a while and restoring the circulation, only to repeat the process later. Eventually driven to distraction by this aching misery every day, it came to me perhaps I was depleted of vitamins I needed and intuitively bought a selection of common ones taking my fancy. Dosing myself with these, to my surprise and immense relief in two or three days the symptoms vanished.

I wished the growing undercurrent of tension with my spouse could be as easily dispelled. Though all this I found gruelling in the extreme, the total absence of incessant corporate political guerrilla ego warfare I had left behind constantly came back to me, and as hard and gritty as working for all practical purposes on my own was, the contrast between the two still felt like a huge burden lifted from my shoulders. Creativity might not be something I consciously understood but it was strangely consoling to me, whatever the outcome of what I was doing, I was standing on my own feet and succeeding or failing by my own endeavours.

Having reached what I thought was the end of my efforts to clear out my personal historical baggage, and all its emotional repressions,

I put all my efforts into my work and relationship and bar venting frustrations in a few bellows to the unsuspecting wildlife and trees in local woods around my home I had become a conventional businessman. Or so I thought.

Creating contacts, getting meetings with people and generally covering thousands of miles in the process and trying to maintain a sense of optimism though at times a wry smile flickered across my face pounding the motorways in my attempts as an 'ant' trying to get the attention of the corporate elephants I sometimes opened doors to. Deriding myself as the 'boy' executive dashing around creating the illusion of movement as I had seen young salesmen do; appearing very busy and important but not actually achieving anything much; and I wasn't a young salesman.

But having set myself upon the course I had chosen, the Rottweiler gene in me would not let go once I got my teeth firmly into the work I had taken on. 'Giving up' was missing from my vocabulary.

Much changed in a year; I learned a great deal, and the subterranean processes of consciousness maintained the pressure within almost outside my volition even though no sales had been made, a glimmer of light on the New Year's threshold pointed the way. An idea of mine to introduce thin, flat-screen terminals into the Lloyds Underwriting market, eradicating the need for bulky cathode ray ones saving vital space on tiny cramped desks, along with the communications equipment I sold, opened up a stream of business and a flood of relief in me.

Initially this had been a case of working against the resentful, almost burning, blank dismissal of my boss; but once sales potential in breaking into the prestigious Lloyds syndicate market became clear to him, so did ego potential and lofty lengthy discussions ensued on 'joint ventures'; with equally predictable nose-out-of-joint rebuff.

JOURNEY OF A LIFETIME

It should perhaps have brought to consciousness an experience as a child; though the degree of grudge-consumed creative denial was more like a volcanic eruption, when just before my fifth birthday I made a little boat out of flimsy plywood and thin, wooden battens.

My father's vocal venom felt like it had the power to cause spontaneous combustion. Fortunately extinguished by my mother's encouragement. The little craft looking more like a large shallow box with a closed in pointed end when completed.

Though the plywood was so thin, nails were useless – they just went right through – I quickly learned to sandwich it between battens of wood and that way it all held together. To nail it still required two hammers; one to hit the nail and a small sledgehammer the opposite side to reflect the blow, like riveting, otherwise the shock of it on the nailing I had done before ripped the plywood to shreds.

I cut up large cocoa tins for paddles, fashioning them into circular discs with my father's very large tinsnips – or tinman's shears to give them their correct name. Being small I stood on one arm of the shears and used both hands on the other. Finding a thin light birch branch I cut for the paddle shaft, split when I tried to nail the now shiny polished paddles to it, I slid each paddle into the slit and tied the end so the wood clamped it in place.

Giving it all a coat of green paint, which was actually decorating distemper, with difficulty I carried it on my back, with me half inside it, and with trepidation launched it on the small, near empty pond we had, and with even greater uncertainty; its 'seaworthiness' needing to be proved against the smouldering, silent rebuttal my shipwright skills received, I stood in it and to my delight and satisfaction, though leaks immediately sprung under my weight, it floated and for a few strokes I propelled it along.

I stood in silent reflection, basking in my achievement. The idea had been good; it was only the construction needing improving a bit. And I had succeeded against my father's incinerating silence.

His barely dormant welling Vesuvian outrage scarcely needing an alighting gnat upon this human volcanic analogue to trigger a seismic cataclysm for the immense outrage he in turn held for his thwarted genius, having his inventions whilst serving in the Royal Navy treated as 'crackpot' by a certain Winston S. Churchill – First Lord of The Admiralty.

The first of these being the rotary engine predating Dr Wankel's by more than thirty years. He invented, designed, built, and ran it on heated, pressurised tar (the residue left at the end of the distillation process and the fuel 'oil' the Navy were converting to from coal), all by himself.

More than this his ideas had progressed from rotors to compressors and turbines and consequently jet engines – decades in advance of Whittle's. Another 'crackpot' idea.

The capping irony being his design – being an equally brilliant gunnery officer, sailor and sublime navigator – of the mechanical gunnery computer fitted to all HM ships, providing them with pinpoint accuracy of fire in the Second World War they badly lacked in the First.

In selling his design to the Admiralty after leaving the Navy their Lordships opined he should have given it to them considering his long – almost thirty-five years – period of service. Flogging may have finally ended in 1870, but class-ridden arrogance was still an endemic culture; along with rum and sodomy as Churchill once responded on the Navy's 'tradition'.

Having a boss who begrudged my ideas leading to the introduction of flat screen technology to the computer world pre-dating its general usage by fifteen years, was a light adverse breeze compared with the early experience I had contended with. Though at the time my childhood triumph remained stuck fast in a deep crevice of memory.

Had I understood the way I was repeating my own history, struggling in near impossible conditions no doubt my path would have been more rewarding but as I came eventually to fully understand, my entry into life had been against odds, making all of this trivial by comparison. Creativity; the crustally suppressed magmatic pressure in me would continue to exert its irresistible expressive force, though as explained numerous times already, such perceptions concerning creative expression were still far enough away from conscious understanding, locked in inaccessible depths of inner being, the Hubble telescope would have easier located it, had it existed then, than I could. Even Hubble would have struggled to pinpoint the deeper reaches of my inner universe …

With this as an ever present unacknowledged backdrop to my efforts to succeed and build a prospering business, a clash between myself and my boss would be the inescapable consequence of my growing experience of selling and knowledge of the business I was in.

It does not need a large crystal ball to see there was a price to be paid in the amount of effort I expended.

I might have turned my focus away from my inner world but, to continue the Vesuvian analogy, there were forces in me I might deny like an inhabitant of Pompeii, but it made not the slightest difference to the inexorable pressure building up within.

There were times when the sheer effort and long hours spent in the car left me feeling completely wrung out and I could feel my body protesting under the strain.

It was very clear also there was a widening gulf opening between us in my marriage.

Which was agony. For I could feel I had grown, and was continuing to do so and my growing confidence and experience in selling were its index. It fed some almost foetal aspect of me like the unborn that has no other choice than to grow. How accurate this perception – like so many others I pushed aside – was, has taken nearly thirty years to alight in conscious awareness.

I felt I was in a race against time and myself.

I was desperate to make it all work, not just for myself but for us both and to create the security each of us needed and I also craved with an all-consuming unacknowledged passion.

Many times driving along in my company car I would play the music of Gerry Rafferty. There was something in his songs and voice exerting a deep magnetic pull on me. Like mantras I played them over and over.

Haunted by their visceral quality; a deep rooted Celtic identity, yet a profoundly disturbing struggle for his own; a complex mixture of unresolved strands of being. Songs of present life and daily struggles; some philosophical; craning spires of aching unattainable ambition. The striving of a restless spirit; endlessly reaching for a metaphysical grail of inner peace and bitter irony at its illusory grasp. All like whirling spirals of an ancient Celtic stream of consciousness carried in music at once contemporary; and ancient beyond recorded origin. Palpable; simultaneously indefinable.

Under these influences my car possessed volition of its own. Sometimes driven by a thumping beat and refrain including Celtic pipes, it surged forward like a war chariot or Highland Charge. Others, floating serenely in a current of ageless harmonies… "Spinning on another wheel; going round in s-l-o-w motion…"

Oblivious to all this at the time I too, with the music, was searching for myself as the wheels and tapes carried me along; one to certain destinations, the other; an unknown destiny.

At times it would open up yet another, until then, inaccessible shuttered cell of blocked emotion and sadness would well up and flood me with tears until I could barely see.

Increasingly, came the excruciating agony of knowing we were growing apart and aching helpless desperation to know what to do to change it; crying so hard I could barely breathe, and the car continuing to cover the miles as I did so, was all an allegory of my life. Whatever I felt made no difference; I was on a road and path of my own choosing and once begun there was no stopping. Destinations awaited me in my journey as in my life. Putting the brakes on and stopping in either only increased the pressure to reach them. I was both the one driving and a hapless passenger in my own 'vehicle-of-life'. As so many of my dreams were no doubt trying to tell me with this oft occurring symbolism but which I could not divine or in waking hours even recall.

I spent so many hours in it combing the motorways, in retrospect it is not surprising it became a metaphor for my life as well as something I still drove at times in my sleep.

It was a Tardis of life rather than time, although it definitely transported me from place to place rather than different ages and strange worlds.

It was an office in which to strategise, a place to meditate where the background rush of air and drone of engine noise were like an endless Tibetan Buddhist temple chant. A mobile sound-proofed room in which to bellow; yell blue murder and rave at daily events and much deeper currents of inner outrage as well as traffic jams and comatose other drivers.

The songs might tell of another's quest for illusory grails; but those I clutched at were sales orders, and gilded with pound signs that no matter how good prospects might seem at the outset, failed to come to fruition. It almost seemed as if some hidden hand of fate was intervening; as though deliberate obstacles were being placed in my path over which I had no control. And I raged against these too.

Not until years later I read Napoleon Hill's experiences researching for the American steel magnate, Andrew Carnegie, for whom he worked, what made some people successful and the many not. Hill wrote that every time he veered away from this project which took him twenty years, things might start out well but would unravel until he returned to the quest he had set out upon. Once he did his fortunes improved as if points of destiny had been switched, putting him back on rails of preordained achievement rather than the dead end shunting yards and buffers of personal ambition. Repeating the same pattern each time. As I repeated mine.

I came across other business people who seemed to have striven a lot less, were no more capable and knowledgeable than me, yet fortune had smiled upon their efforts.

At the time only a vague nagging question of there being something else of which I was not aware, flickered in the shadows of consciousness.

Somewhat less indistinct was the path of healing I set out upon years before. Instead of being a clear track to the future it was one increasingly neglected. I still attempted to maintain contact with my inner world – mostly in my car – but my desire to succeed in the work I had chosen meant the time and energy devoted to it was far less than previously. Perhaps the picture right in front of me was so large I simply couldn't see it – like South American natives, who when Darwin's ship the *Beagle* anchored close by, they simply could not bridge the gulf of understanding between their canoes and this – to them incomprehensibly vast – structure, also being a boat.

Neither could I see the analogy of ocean swells, currents of inner being and mortgage payments.

Never mind valuing the insights I had into and prophesies I made to others about the industry I was in. Burying them instead under crushing mountains of self-diminishing work for want of realisation of my own self-worth.

As I had done before, I could see the very clever box of American designed communications technology I sold, although years ahead of its time, lacked the essential ability to connect directly to exploding populations of personal computer networks. Instead its mercurial designer had seen that telephone networks would become *the* network to which everyone would connect and had focused on high speed – or 'broadband' telecom interfaces for it. But there were none for connecting directly into personal computer networks, and linking them out into the wider telecom world.

I questioned this and, given the chance, I would ask if this was going to be done and received vague responses; hints that it might be, or could be done but it was like chasing a mirage.

I even called the company in the States to have a word with the managing director but was unable to speak with him. Probably a good thing; because it became clear the response would likely have been reminiscent of my father's explosions at anything questioning his ideas and perceptions.

Somewhat needled by my questions about the interfaces I knew we needed to win business, my boss went to America to find out if they would be provided and returned saying all objectives had been met; I knew then for certain; nothing had changed, and I could have any interface I liked – so long as it was broadband digital telephone network based.

Increasingly, otherwise good prospects simply melted away, and in particular a large one that after much effort appeared to be a certain order, expired leaving a yawning gap in the sales forecast.

Skeletons began to rattle loudly in cupboards and previous admonitions I needed to spend more time on this erstwhile prestigious prospect, like a switch being thrown, reflexively reversed into recriminations about all the time I had spent or wasted concentrating on it to the exclusion of finding other new business!

Which was not even true.

So began a 'Dance Macabre' of long-suppressed skeletal dissatisfactions out of closets though entirely lacking in any harmony.

To his crimson-flushed embarrassment I pointed out I was the only one out on the road doing any selling, and it couldn't be had both ways. If he said I needed to concentrate on the prospect I couldn't be blamed for not giving time to creating other new prospects and business.

Then deepened crimson at the mention of all the negative 'encouragement' my ideas and suggestions had received that nonetheless had brought us business we never would have won otherwise.

There is a saying; there are many ships to be on, but the worst ship of all is a partnership.

I drove home from this confrontation of paradoxical pugnacious blame and contrite inadequacy so tense the car never once touched the road nor my feet the ground; or so it felt.

As the junior partner in the business the outcome was never in doubt. Strive though I might to try and bridge the canyon created by the loss I was blamed for, I departed a few weeks later.

Healing and inner growth might have been the poor relation before, in my quest to succeed in my day-to-day life, work and endeavours but this inner self had suddenly shrunk to an ostracised recluse.

Strangely sympathetic to these events as 1988 ran towards its end, and their deep impact on my inner world, were my efforts to plumb my house on to mains drainage rather than the cesspool my wife quietly disliked and disapproved of.

This occurred exactly as events at work were building up to erupting into the open. Connecting to mains drainage was no small-time do-it-yourself project, digging a trench, laying a few pipes and coupling up to the main sewer. It meant going down about eight feet to find the pipe and digging a trench 120 feet long to bring it to the house. Definitely not a job for pick and shovel, especially as not far under the clay surface was a deep layer of solid shingle spanning the area for miles.

I hired a mechanical digger and spent a sleepless night wondering how I would drive the thing.

JOURNEY OF A LIFETIME

The answer, to begin with, was like an electrocuted frog. The great long muscular arm jerked as I nervously twitched the controls and swung the big bucket around like a hammer thrower at the Olympics, spewing earth and shingle across the ground.

Very aware my coordination showed me what a bundle of nerves I was, trying to drive the three-ton machine like a manic stick insect, I resorted to my time honoured, though badly neglected, routine of letting my body speak for itself.

The answer was immediate; as from years before I felt a compulsion to lay on the ground and arch my body upwards so my shoulders and head pushed harder against it. Instantaneously I felt a strong urge to vomit but both of these instinctive actions had evolved from their original form years previously into something more consciously driven than thrashing around and yelling. What came out was still vocal but somewhere between a powerful dry guttural croak, a yell driven by reflexively clenched abdominal muscles, and simultaneously with it; fear.

Yet it was not a paralysing sensation; if anything the sheer relief in allowing my body to do what it needed in the context that felt right, was far stronger than feelings of fear.

It evoked a barely admitted reproach that I had returned to my old patterns of my head ruling my inner instincts and my body, in the sales work I had chosen and wrestled with doing something, if I could have admitted it to myself, was remotely distant from my real creative nature.

In reality the wrestling match was deep within me, between fear and the desire to overcome it and in doing so ensure my survival and the real me within.

But this background inner 'musak' of my life, like an irritating tinny noise emanating from some anonymous speaker and corner of a lift was, as ever, something I continued to actively ignore.

A few minutes spent letting my body express what for so long

I had denied it, and I returned to the digger. The shovel began to glide smoothly over the ground; the bucket to carve a graceful arc as it gouged out great scoops of spoil, rising effortlessly into the air; pirouetting balletically to drop the load like a gardener's spade turning soil.

Whispering guilt still recited its monologue in my head, for the time I had taken off work, but for that moment it was drowned out by sheer satisfaction at being part of this mechanical beast. Its gleaming hydraulic arms hissing their approval as rhythmically the bucket filled; was lifted, and turned to lightly set down its load, the engine humming its monotonous refrain like a son of the soil lost in his work.

It may appear my activity was merely an ephemeral event; a distraction and nothing whatever to do with any 'deep meaningful' symbolism. Put bluntly; whimsical nonsense.

In long retrospect it is even clearer to me it possessed a symbolism going far beyond anything written about it here. Never mind what I perceived at the time.

Working at the bottom of an eight-feet-deep trench took me back to potholing days clambering around in caverns cloaked in stygian gloom beyond the prying fingers of my acetylene helmet-lamp's bright flame. Or worming about in tight spaces; removing my helmet and pushing it in front of me to stop the light being smothered as both otherwise jammed between floor and 'ceiling'. Inching forward, needing nearly every time I did to pull out rucks in my overalls around my shoulders as they snagged on the rough surfaces, bunched up, and held me fast.

In these places, as in my trench; so in my life the same feelings of uncertainty wrapped me in their thrall. There was also a recurring pattern not apparent to me until much later. When I began a new phase of my life, or when under great personal pressure I would literally get back in contact with the earth, and with this perspective, now it is also clear, the greater the need to do so the deeper I went.

Perhaps it is true to say it was and is an attempt to get to the bottom of things, literally as well as metaphorically.

Yet as introspectively detailed as these perceptions are, they are as distant from exhausting their symbolic nature as the opposite sides of the Grand Canyon are from one another.

As will become clear later.

The Trench To ...

BEAUTIFULLY SHADED DELICATE crocus blooms peered in at me from the edge of my trench, as the old year rolled over and died and 1989 announced its presence in balmy weather. Perhaps it was a good omen like the pipes in my trench advancing up a gentle slope ensuring drainage?

There was great satisfaction seeing the long ascending line from the main connection, a hundred feet back to the house. But, like the year ahead, much remained to be accomplished before all was in its proper place and the house connected to mains drainage.

Might this tangible sign of progress in my outer world from my worm's eye view of the one above my head at its deep end inspection pit to its shallower cousin, mark a similar ascending path in my life and work from these subterranean depths?

Would all the things I wished and prayed for to myself come to fruition? Would everything blossom like the crocuses from which I derived such sublime pleasure, marvelling at their miniature resplendence a few inches from my face, cupped petals like supplicant arms spreading at the sun's behest, smiling in a welcome of near rainbow-span perfection?

For all I hoped for the culmination of things unseen in my inner world, they might as well have been red poppies shaking heads in uncomprehending confusion at bloody struggles over the Somme.

The year was without doubt the most unrelenting struggle and inner conflict on every level I ever experienced.

The sense of foreboding at events in the company I strove so hard to build was amply rewarded within a few days. In the best scapegoat tradition, the many sins of failure were heaped on me and I was duly banished to the wilderness to find my own way in the world. My place filled by someone possessed of infinitely greater experience and powers of salesmanship; or such was the fanfare trumpeted about him, though whose halo I felt lacked a certain permanence of lustre and would quickly fade; and did in three months, presaging the failure of the company; my boss and the company whose equipment I sold, from all the ills and failings I had foreseen and more besides.

More even than all the shortcomings, with increasing concern, I warned of.

The American company lost control of its own product development, hid it from my boss who went to see what was happening at my chiding, returning having 'fulfilled all his objectives', wearing his new tinted glasses and Hans Christian Anderson emperor suit of finery. In due course finding it left him as naked as his bank balance when all failed.

Metaphorically, I was back at the bottom of the Eiger's brutal North Wall again, dressed in a business suit clutching my briefcase in one hand and my mountain-climbing instruction book in the other.

The differences were instead of feelings I harboured the first time, of nervous optimism; having no experience of sales, this time I knew what it felt like to scale what looked like insurmountable faces of bleak attainment to precarious ledges of respite on a relentless route to higher sales.

Crashing back to the bottom, reminiscent of the tree from which I had once stepped forward into space from, or a Walt Disney cartoon figure falling out of the sky ending up a millimetre-thick flattened shape in the ground I miraculously regained my former shape and was still intact and my 'instruction book' of experience was dog-eared and torn with the lessons learned in two years of solo climbing.

That was the outer side of the picture. The inner, symbolically, was my struggle to build confidence in what I did and so in myself; and this part of me felt battered, bruised and struggling to maintain a persona of normality. Like being at the bottom of the mountain again, or the bottom of my trench I had dug for myself actually and symbolically, confidence could hardly have been at a lower ebb.

I was also back among the phantoms of the first occasion; or one phantom in particular, the salesman who should have joined the company with me who found another job, reappeared apparently having set up a company with another ghostly presence and what they needed was someone to run it for them: me for instance.

In retrospect, if in healing myself and unburdening my inner worlds of the history I carried which in turn my body showed, I was stripping away layers of past repressions, it felt very much my outer world answered in stripping everything else away from me.

The harder I strove to build a sense of self-worth, security and personal achievement the more I resembled Sisyphus. The more I struggled with the stone of creative endeavour I pushed and shoved up the hill of hard won experience; the faster it slid back down.

Like the Greek king of legend, I seemed doomed endlessly to repeat this task.

If I had read about Napoleon Hill's quest for the attributes of success before, perhaps life would have presented a flatter landscape in which to achieve lasting success.

But just as Hill's boulder of struggle was not to find its resting spot of final achievement until the lessons of his own greater destiny were understood and not simply the task set him by another, the same was true for me. Chicken and egg; I would only permanently lodge my own burden of back breaking interminable toil when I began to understand what deeper forces drove me.

No accident I only read Hill's book once I began to change…

Changing, in turn, only came when the boulder of nugatory toil deep within me began to be exposed to the weathering of clear consciousness and begin crumbling; this wasn't some metaphoric or metaphysical instant transformation like gulping down a magical draught of born again enlightenment. It was, as I had discovered right at the very beginning more than a decade earlier, a slow grinding plod of effort letting my body express what *it* needed to in the context that felt right for as long as it took for awareness to dawn; and for my body to let 'me' – my rock like intellect – know what it was I needed to do rather than what I *thought* I needed to do.

There was no Damascenian blinding flash of light and everything changing for the better.

It was a year of bitter struggle; finding the new company's fifty grand 'fully paid up capital' was fantasy and outright lies, trying to build it up from scratch – in a business sector I had no experience of; computer media. Finding the expert I relied on who knew it, was less capable than I, and incomprehensibly, with another, seemed not to care and even work against what I was doing. Both, moreover, were the biggest stakeholders in the business!

It was also apparent my efforts to provide more 'suburban' amenity by plumbing our house on to mains drainage counted for nothing either. As did the delightful woodlands and countryside all around.

Before, I had trodden the woodland paths and fields around home at the end of a working day in search of peace, feeling as if my head was encased in cotton wool and walking on cushions. With the new venture came a sense of inevitability of its ultimate demise, cold sweat often dampened my forehead and physically I could find no relief.

My once cherished routine of letting my body speak through its language of physical movement; jumping around to release the tension in my spine and body generally, flicking hands and arms to likewise free my shoulders of the rigidity there and letting out growls and roars of deep frustration, fear and outrage, shouted recriminations, and finally sobs of hurt, had all but died and been suppressed. Increasingly it was enough just to stagger through my days trying to carry the burden

I had perversely shouldered in what appeared mindless self-martyrdom.

Though I didn't need to look very deeply within to hear reverberating whispers of self-reproach at my own lack of self-worth driving me to struggle repeatedly against insurmountable odds.

In trying to plumb the ultimate depths of motivation for my own struggles it was like a pothole I once entered; of all those I clambered and squeezed my way through, this one had an aura of deep foreboding and even menace all the others lacked. For shifting boulders above the deeply obscured entrance had already claimed one life.

There were no spacious chambers of respite after narrow and pipe-like crawls and worming progress. It was all splits and angled fissures with rough edges leading straight down until our small group came into a wider opening, in the floor of which was another fissure some inches wide.

A light shone into it revealed nothing. Its darkness resembled black viscous fluid; it devoured light, defying investigation. A stone dropped into the treacle gloom to sound its depth spoke its eerie message; Clack! … clack! … clack! … tick! … tick! … tk! … Until all sound was quenched; no telltale thud or splash signalling its limit of descent. Whatever lurked beneath our feet was disturbingly vast. Attempting to explore it with short ropes, no steel cable ladders and without a powerful lamp, was out of the question. The light of conscious awareness I probed my motivation with, similarly revealed nothing except a vague fear in the pit of my stomach as had once the void beneath my feet.

Years passed before I could begin exploring this cavern of my unknown.

All this may give the impression of wandering so far off the path I set out upon many years before of clearing personal history and its physical effects that had all but done for me, and healing myself in the process, had long ago been ditched in my struggle for illusory success and security. In fact it was never far from mind in everything I did, and in spite of the toll it increasingly took of me, still somehow against the current of all the gnawing uncertainty, doubt and outright fear I lived with most of the time, some part of inner self still continued to grow.

In many respects it was the one constant thing in my life and the inner fire sustaining me and my reason for being; though it flickered and guttered under the incessant drizzle of discouragement and failure. Its flame was an involuntary St Vitas dance of persistence. It spoke my childhood mantra silently abiding in this dancing tongue of hope; I won't give up and I won't give in.

Finally, after seventeen months and effusive promises of help by the main supplier that never materialised, mounting adverse cash flow finally engulfed the company and product was repossessed.

In a way it was a relief, for physically I had reached the end of my endurance and left the company.

My body was seizing up. At night my eyes did not simply close; as had begun in 1987, increasingly they clamped shut and I would wake with what felt like welder's 'dry eye' caused by exposure to ultraviolet electric-arc light. In daylight I looked like a ghost.

Not only was I involuntarily clamping my eyes, but my whole body. Breathing in my sleep, as my wife observed, was more like some furry animal's squeaking. Physical relief had become impossible.

My abdominal regions were often consumed with gnawing pain, and any alcohol lit what became a furnace of agony; only relieved by stuffing a face cloth into my throat to induce dry vomiting which instantly relieved at least some of the gripping, gut-strangling tension and pain.

As so often before – and increasingly as time has passed – an allegory of what I endured and struggled through came to mind.

At school I won a prize for music and had chosen the book *Cockleshell Heroes*, the true story of the canoe raid on Bordeaux in the Second World War, not the twisted pathetic travesty of it shown in cinemas.

To mount this utterly gruelling raid the Marines taking part underwent equally gruelling training. In the course of this someone in higher authority had wanted to know how long a fit soldier fully dressed for battle and carrying ammunition and supplies could stay afloat.

Conjecturing how long this might be, someone said: "Only one way to find out; get someone dressed up in full kit and jump overboard." It was done and into the sea jumped one of their number complete with rifle, all his personal and battle kit, and wearing standard 'ammunition' leather boots.

For nine minutes the volunteer kept his chin above the water until finally his steel helmet sank from view.

I finally 'sank' after seventeen months of bitter struggle to build and keep the company afloat, the only difference being there was someone to pull him out of the water. I was going to have to make my own way to 'dry land' and I resembled something cast up by the tide; washed out, looking more dead than alive as someone obliquely observed.

... Inner No Man's Land

It may be recalled I indulged in a little – to some at least – whimsical comment about the law of seven relating to my progress in healing myself and events, synchronised with cycles based on this number.

Once again; all those of a rational disposition and who apply a little logic will know this is simply coincidence and merely perception. One can, after all, pick and choose events to suit one's own agenda of proof.

Or that is the way some may see it.

Seven years previously in 1982 I had left behind the 'therap' world; realising it had regressed to become a prison of intellect limited rigidity, to find my way on my own as I had right from the beginning, with the 'tools' I made for myself through my own efforts to clear and heal myself; possess and take full responsibility for using them in my wider world.

Using the telescope of hindsight again, it has come into focus I was setting out on a completely new path, for prior to that time I had followed 'safe' options, the overriding factor being security.

Although still very much in the corporate fold, instead of immersing myself – or perhaps drowning – in oceans of purely technical knowledge and teaching, I moved or rather fell blindly, into a sales related technical role.

To the question that might reasonably be asked of why? At the time and for decades after I would have said it was the logical progression so far as career within the company was concerned.

Now it is clear, however blindly at the time, I was nonetheless trying to find some means of expressing personal creativity that was more about me than being purely a technical 'shoveller' of facts and words.

It was not however a great leap on to a stage of 'self-actualisation' as the American psychologist, Abraham Maslow, characterised complete self-fulfilment. Far from it.

I was – as had been observed so adroitly years before when in teaching – still 'square pegging it'. Although I had moved away from increasingly prostrating work under its punishing intellectual load.

It was actually an even harder path to follow because however I might smother it in myself, there was a faint glimmer of personal creative ambition flickering in the corporate gloom. A recipe for growing dissatisfaction with what I was doing and personal clashes with those I worked for.

Thunderclaps of amazement and surprise; exactly what happened of course!

Did I realise this was the course of inevitable destiny I had set myself upon? I was as capable of seeing it all as the Titanic was of missing the iceberg.

The only difference being, wilfully blind to my own inner wisdom, I steamed smack into it which meant the vessel of my creative intent got a powerful battering – yet again; but not sunk – and neither would the Titanic have if it had done the same!

For unlike the ship, my 'nose' might be bashed in but the rest of me was still afloat. Just!

Patterns; Healing; Worlds Unseen

An old saying goes; if at first you don't succeed try; try, try again.

Or to repeat and adapt it to the motto discovered buried within my subconscious, the words spoken spontaneously without conscious thought: I won't give up and I won't give in, seemed to apply. Whether I knew it consciously or not – and it was certainly not something I was able to articulate at the time – there was some part of me aspiring to greater things, rather like a thistle finding solid tarmac above its head, if this doesn't cause indigestion from my varied menu of mixed metaphors. It pays no heed to the obstruction; only the need to grow, and as I discovered one year when plagued by an epidemic of them in my small garden, they were more than capable of pushing through this weather-hardened solid crust.

Similarly, having moved on from teaching at the end of 1981, a volition deep within to grow further, was as irresistible and as automatic as that impelling the thistle. Consequently the pattern of moving on into a role and position offering more freedom to explore and express my own talents and capabilities was equally inevitable. Perhaps that's why I became 'prickly' if someone questioned if I had made the wrong choice or questioned whether I could do the job!

With long hindsight it is clear I hadn't really learned anything since the childhood experience of closing my eyes to reality; taking a blind gamble and pressing on regardless. Stepping into the unknown knowing, though denying it to myself, the end result might be delayed in the job I chose to take on, but it would be no different than attempting spanning from one tree to the next without the necessary support under my feet – actually or metaphorically. The compulsion to act in the same way still governed me.

After seven years of 'stepping out' into new and uncertain territories, I still hadn't learned my lesson; by 1989 I was repeating the cycle. I had already landed with a shuddering thud out of the company I strove to build, for all practical purposes on my own, my boss showing no inclination to get out and do the hard graft of selling himself. The difference was at the start of the next seven years there was no cosy corporate 'cushion' on which to land as there had been previously. Although one of many metaphors I have used, it really did feel like being bruised, battered and back at the foot of mountainous insurmountable difficulties.

Alternatively, given this propensity for imitating thistles it shouldn't be surprising the next seven made the cycle just completed look easy. Growing through 'tarmac' might be an achievement; but if it happened to coincide with being a well trafficked road, getting repeatedly flattened in consequence was to be expected.

The outcome should not be a surprise!

Before briefly describing how I arranged to acquire 'tread marks' across my head, of what may have seemed to me at the time as immutable fate, perhaps I should restate what it was propelling me along what seemed a path strewn with obstacles – though I would have absolutely denied it at the time – I put in my own way.

It goes right back to my utterly consuming desire of cosmic proportions to release and divest myself of the life-extinguishing load I knew I carried within me back in 1973 when the image came to me as I worked through endless pages of microscopically detailed software; I was like a piece of metal, worked until it began to fracture under the sublimated stresses, being unable to absorb anymore without beginning to disintegrate; and I was.

The image coming to me of copper I fashioned in metalwork at school and annealing this; heating it until cherry red, and, as copper does not harden when suddenly cooled; quenched in an acid solution to cool as well as clean it.

Something that could not be done in today's sick world without three fire appliances in attendance, and wearing nuclear/chemical/biological warfare clothing, in a sealed stainless steel, airtight room, with live video links to 'elf (Health) and Safety H Q.

And its equally insane purely human analogue of filling people so full of dangerous chemical shit to quarantine them from their own nature and render them 'safe' in mental/emotional 'elf and safety' terms as to equally make them toxic hazard zones.

Copper once softened and returned to its malleable state, could then be beaten, bent and worked once more until it became brittle and the process repeated. In life I was no different; and neither is anybody else.

Whilst understanding the physical attributes of copper and finding it an agreeable and ductile metal to work, broader significance than this did not exist. In considering belatedly, long after this was originally written, what deeper attraction might have drawn me to this metal known from an age when God and the earth were feminine, a quick search reveals certain metals are symbolically associated with particular heavenly bodies.

No prizes for guessing gold is equated with the sun and silver; the moon.

Copper is identified with Venus – which apart from being the goddess of love – also bears the astrological glyph for female.

If there was ever a case of trying to unite with my own psyche and unlock the creative inner feminine or 'anima' being – but blindly – it is perhaps no surprise all I achieved in life was to beat myself into the ground; becoming completely rigid and brittle in the process. A more brutal allegory of how I symbolically set out to achieve union with my inner being it is hard to imagine. Except my hair being the colour of copper when it first grew as more so was my beard; perhaps also I mistook myself for a tent peg of the metal.

Still less I understood what the ultimate impulse driving this bitterly reproachful treatment of myself was; only becoming clear as this book ends.

I knew from the time I was less than a month old, when I tried to turn over in my uncomfortable 'crib' – a wicker washing basket – and do it myself owing to the booming thunderstorm of verbal denial of my father in his responsibility for my existence and my mother's equally vocal rebuttal of these fantasies – I tore my left ribs from my breast bone as I did so and was instantly deluged with unimaginable pain.

This though was a single minor link in the chain of disaster I recalled in clear detail, from that time culminating in the shattering cataclysm of my Guardian Aunt's death.

Einstein's elegantly simple proof – actually plagiarised and attributable to others – proved whilst matter and energy are interchangeable, energy cannot be made and destroyed; it can only change its form.

Human life is not exempt nor an exception to this immutable law. In humans, energy can go in one of two directions; it either evolutes and is released by a person in a state of contentment and happiness, leaving them free and 'malleable' on every level; or it involutes and is sublimated and clamped within when confronted with struggle, suffering and the powerfully repressive aspects of culture and religion, affecting them on every level making them rigid, brittle and stressed.

Put simply, at its extreme limits we either explode with energy or we implode, and in normal life existing harmoniously well within these.

A release of energy in humans is the 'annealing' process leaving us ductile in our lives and actions. Sublimation of deeply unpleasant experiences and their suppression in humans is the worked, hardened, rigidified state where subsequent 'working' by life's experiences stresses us until we literally crack. Mentally, emotionally and physically.

The 'working' and 'hammering' I experienced over the next four years acted exactly like creating an artefact from simple sheet copper.

Evolving through repeated working and annealing it transforms into something having shape and function, and I was clearly aware I was evolving within, in spite of the 'hammering' I got because although limited in extent, nonetheless I still knew how to 'anneal' myself back to at least some semblance of normality, though to say unstressed would be far from the truth.

Through various endeavours and tribulations between 1990–1994, there was a slow, steady gathering sense of confidence no matter what adverse experiences came my way; and there were several.

It was clear from earlier, my efforts plumbing our bungalow home on to mains drainage; all the space around us of fields and woodlands as well as the large size of our property was not to my wife's liking, so we moved from rural surroundings to a village close by. Though in 1993 when I left the work I was doing in circumstances dictating no other choice, there was no desire to see through difficult times together; only that I wasn't earning a salary, and we went our separate ways.

Although the slow, steady increase in inner confidence still continued in spite of all, bodily speaking during this period, 'progress' was in reverse.

I noticed a distinct decline in the energy to my lower body, to add to the sometimes extremely unpleasant painful gut gripping sensations, officially diagnosed as 'IBS' or Irritable Bowel Syndrome.

A medical 'label' as useful and illuminating as a spent match.

Lessening energy, and in winter, warmth, in my legs and feet, I didn't seem able to do a great deal about. If I sat in any kind of a draught during the cold months I felt as if air cooled by dry ice was being blasted at me. Once my feet went cold they remained blocks of chilled meat to up above my ankles and the only way to warm them was to get in bed with a hot water bottle on them. Otherwise they remained frozen for hours.

'IBS' gut-strangling pain I broke and at least moderated using a face cloth stuffed in my mouth and pushed back into my throat forcing reflexive dry vomiting, usually producing instant release of my gut muscles and with it relief.

Mentioned a number of times before, as bizarre as this may be to some, its history lay originally in the 'chuckle sobbing' leaning over the seat back of my car well over a decade previously, which pushed hard into my abdominal region, producing this effect and relief from the solid painful knots there. Continuing to do this and wherever it led me over the years, also as related previously, it evolved into something resembling a deep croak and a reflexive 'bark.' Finally it seemed the 'sound' or the symptom of release was regressing down my throat deeper into my body. Consequently the only way to stop excruciating gut pains was to 'follow' the sound down my throat, hence having to use a face cloth.

It was not something I enjoyed doing in the least – I hated having to do it. But if that was what my body found relief and release in and it worked – as it unfailingly did – I followed my precept of doing it until 'my head knew what my body was about' as the words spontaneously voiced also many years before on Dartmoor had told me.

That fear was a primary focus of these extremely unpleasant symptoms I felt was beyond doubt; though it was irrelevant so far as I was concerned. What really mattered was knowing how to stop the agony and doing it when I needed to – as circumstances permitted – and time and repetition would eventually lead me unerringly to the real root cause and fully conscious understanding of its true origin and driving force.

Which it consistently and unfailingly has done.

There was no fudging it; times beyond care or counting I wished this were so. No matter what my 'head'/intellect said, my body's wisdom allowed to assert itself, infallibly provided the answers; not just from the subconscious but from much deeper parts it communicated with; as I sensed it, the brain's brain relating directly to my autonomic functions of my body. Neither was it a 'one time wonder' born-again-miracle of deluded belief and wish fulfilment. It was just a hard steady grind of effort repeated over and over hundreds or even thousands of times *as necessary* until my body showed me it had released the energy knotting it up in one part and moving on to some other symptom reflecting more sublimated and suppressed energy and the need to release and integrate it into accessible consciousness.

It was in this period when life was at its most stressful I returned instinctively and literally, to getting my hands in contact with mother earth.

I noticed my lower back was becoming more and more delicate until it reached the point where turning over in bed caused very unpleasant pains to radiate out from it. As ever, at the time I dealt with it as best I could, which wasn't very well, until I began processing a heap of earth spoil, sieving flint rubble from it using my bare hands to stir the mixture on the bed of my sieve made from multiple layers of close mesh netting.

Eventually my hands becoming cut and abraded by doing so, I put gloves on to belatedly protect them.

It dawned on me – but only in the vaguest fashion – and after a few weeks, my lower back felt better. I found turning over in bed became easier and certainly less painful.

Yet I *still* never connected it was the Great Mother's body healing me. It perhaps only began to reverberate around my brain some time later after I went to see a Tarot reader who said many things but the one thing I most clearly recall was her admonition to get my hands into the earth – I would find it healing.

Only after months and probably a lot longer I realised I had instinctively done this over a number of years once I had begun the journey of healing myself.

Even that does not encompass its full extent though. For typing this it suddenly occurred to me to go back through my life and see if there were other times when getting my hands – or all of me – in the earth coincided with periods of great stress. It does; aged five I became a 'good little gardener' as it was said. First, destroying – probably the best word – a rockery at my Aunt's home where my mother had (reluctantly) taken me instead of my older brother, after the first family separation.

I dug the stones out from the earth to leave a flat garden border, and my Aunt with her usual tremendous kindness wisely left me to do this. From there I did something more constructive; weeding out a flower bed; forever having to re-plant daffodil bulbs I disturbed in the process.

Digging up the rockery helped me stay sane. I felt like a plant ripped out of the ground by the roots. My mother's intention to dump me with relatives I thwarted by being uncatchable until my brother volunteered to go instead, and it left me extremely frightened and very insecure.

Digging, weeding and replanting the bulbs wasn't easy, or particularly enjoyable, but it served two purposes; first, it was my way of repaying my Aunt, for she also told me in her gentle manner she preferred the rockery. Second, and beyond conscious understanding; the hours I spent with my hands in the earth calmed and healed me.

The deeper the stress and chaos around me, the deeper I dug. As all disintegrated of what had been my family, aged nine, I dug right through a bank of earth created by my father as a consequence of the pond (of my boat sailing fame) he dug, to make a 'camp' for myself. With a 'roof' over the top it meant I could surround myself with earth. To this moment I recall the curious sense of relief, stillness and peace

I felt sitting inside.

Again, in my teenage years approaching leaving school, with other lads, all of us boy scouts, on our scoutmaster's large estate we cleared a bramble infested orchard and as reward were allowed to dam a small stream and we dug a relief trench to one side of it controlling the water level so it didn't over-top the dam and erode it.

Or at least that was what I *thought* it was about; but looking back it is no accident I went home plastered in clay on the outside and suffused inwardly with happiness and contentment.

A year or two later my curiosity was aroused as a young apprentice learning electronics in the RAF, by a friend who went off on 'sports afternoon' each week, to disappear into the earth and return with tales of the caves he walked, crawled and wormed his way through in the Mendip hills; returning, not unusually, with mud-caked overalls.

Curious and attracted by his exploits recited at length, I joined him and was given a crafty introduction to a cave he reassured me was 'classed as easy'.

It was. To begin with. The first two chambers; one under the other could be walked through – easily.

Then I was introduced to a dry mud slope down which one slid head first. No problem; plenty of room.

Leading me forward he then disappeared like a rabbit into its burrow.

For about fifteen seconds or so a hollow muffled booming echoed back to me, after which his friendly voice yelled: "OK, come through!"

Laying flat I slithered my way downwards head first, until I found myself in an increasingly narrow space.

Very soon my caving safety helmet with its naked flame acetylene lamp, jammed solid between top and bottom of this now very tight space.

Burning my fingers getting it off and relighting it in the impenetrable blackness, putting it in front of me to push along and light my way; with arms outstretched, I snake-slid forward using hands and toes of my boots. I quickly jammed as my overalls rucked up and held me fast around my shoulders. Telling my friend I was stuck I realised I had, with some difficulty, to pull the rucks out for myself to move on; no one else was going to help. It was stay stuck and jammed solid; or un-snag myself and get moving again. Only to repeat it less than a body length further on, until steaming with sweat, I emerged after about thirty feet and four minutes later at the other end, into a gratifyingly, moderately large domed space – like a cupola – in solid rock.

We stood talking until vapours ceased rising off me in the cool subterranean air and I asked: "Where to now?" Seeing no obvious hole through which to proceed. The reply was simple and direct: "Back through that!"

My friend being a lot smaller build and height than I, had shot through this like the proverbial rat-up-a-drainpipe and did so again and I repeated my slow shuffle-stick, shuffle-stick journey until I re-emerged from the 'drainpipe' as it was known, and we made our way back through what felt like cathedrals of space around me to the outside world.

It was only then he told me he deliberately put me through this 'test' to see if I panicked in the drainpipe.

On subsequent forays into the earth I felt tired and would happily have gone to sleep underground. Without doubt I slept soundly after venturing into the underworld and the more I did the more dormouse-like I became until I found it very difficult to stay awake. There was no denying its soporific effect, during a time when we were all under considerable stress from the pressure of study and the regular progress tests, which if persistently marginally passed meant being re-classed to repeat training, and failing, a rapid exit from the RAF.

Without doubt, although potholes were a good deal less than womb-like, being completely enveloped in the Great Mother distinctly soothed and healed me.

Finally it was Monty Don of *Gardener's World* renown who in recent years reconfirmed this not once but twice. The first time recalling when the successful business he and his wife built collapsed taking everything with it including their home, and leaving him deeply despairing.

He instinctively turned to gardening and horticulture and to use his words he found it very healing.

The second time being when he ran a project he financed himself and filmed for BBC TV, of helping young drug addicts to mend themselves and their lives through creating a garden. Though as it proved they needed not a kind and very perceptive mentor but as he realised and said towards the end, someone who ruled with a rod of iron to prevent them from lapsing surreptitiously into drugs and infuriating deviousness to obtain these powerful body-energy destroying substances. Not least it was evident there was a definite need for such a project to last years to break deeply destructive habits rather than a few months, and for the earth to work its magic on them.

In the early nineties, being in direct contact with Great Mother did not just symbolically keep me 'grounded;' there is no question earth is healing in the most literal sense. Like a lightning conductor on a building, driven into the ground, getting hands and body into the Great Giver of all life 'earths' our human energy.

It was no miracle cure though. It helped, but it did not address the deep underlying stress locked up in my body for years and decades requiring a positive and consistently applied effort to address *all* the elements of the human equation.

To use a word I detest but serves to illustrate; we are born as one complete 'package' in one skin. We are not born as a kit of parts bolted together, energies and fluids added becoming human like some assembled flat-pack.

We are born as an integral being of body, mind and emotions.

If one element is damaged then it affects the complete person. From the womb and birth itself and subsequently in our lives.

Oh yes; we can kid and pretend to ourselves a physical injury is 'purely' physical, but experience tells me bashing my head against a low door lintel is not merely 'physical'; it sends signals of pain right through one; and not simply nerve signals of the impact; a sense of agony suffuses us. Perhaps we even cry, such is the sense of outrage in our body and from the shock of impact.

Pains inflicted by criticism and verbal abuse are as equally excoriating as having flesh ground away. And being repeatedly crushed for hours on end whilst bound and gagged at the same time would be something we might associate with Guantanamo Bay brutality but is actually what legions experience in 'normal' birth.

There are though, no human rights lawyers who would attempt to bring a case of torture against the perpetrator.

Whatever words, illustrations and examples used, we are back at my simple analogy of annealing metal; and I wasn't keeping pace, or anywhere near, with the 'hammering' I was getting and my body showed it from head to feet by late 1993.

My digestion barely worked. If I dared to comfort myself with a good old English fry up; bacon, egg and tomato, shortly after I felt as though there was a furnace in my belly only relieved by the inevitable rapid visit to the toilet.

My feet froze and remained so for hours at the slightest excuse, and such were the acute, agonising, clamping tensions throughout my pelvic region, urinating was reduced to a feeble trickle, having to get up during the night, and often to sit down to do so. Gut-strangling pains gripped my abdomen as bush fires of 'IBS' raged around my intestines all too often during the day.

Emotionally, at times I felt suicidal – especially when I had to push my small motorcycle for thirteen miles uphill and down dale, but mostly the former.

REVELATION

ONE EVENING AFTER moving, to live on my own once again, I was sitting in bed feeling at a low ebb in every way, musing over some words in a motivational book supposed to imbue inspiration, wealth, a cornucopia of success, and realisation of one's heart's desires. My thoughts meandered off to memories of my time in Australia in 1974 when, feeling even more profoundly weighed down emotionally and physically; daily dragging along in my life, I drove north, miles out into the silence and solace beyond Melbourne's expanding presence, into perfect stillness, comforting proximity and delightful scent of eucalypt forests.

Seeing again the high flood bank by a tiny stream atop which I perched my little, hired ochre-coloured Ford Escort and the stars passing by, peering at me between gum fronds, watch-keeping as I slept. Waking occasionally to reposition myself in the cramped back seat. Comforted to see the softly twinkling celestial denizens above. Finally, just able to throw off my drunken narcoleptic state, barely managing to stir after thirteen hours, feeling half dead and I could sleep for as long again undisturbed, and not see or hear a single vehicle rumble past on the dirt road close by. I got out of the car, stretched myself, breathing in the sublime, cool, essence-infused woodland air. Getting back in, feeling the slight clamminess of the plastic seat cover and steering wheel from the morning mist, I started the car and drove it gingerly at an angle down the steeply-sloped embankment hoping it wouldn't topple over, and drove off – just as a car came up behind me!

Perhaps symbolically it was fate's prodding finger pushing me forward in my torpid stupor!

Curious to know months later where I had once stopped, I was amazed to see the 'stream' was called 'King River'.

Not surprised it was called a 'river'; I knew all too well how trickles one could step over in dry periods could become deep raging torrents sometimes hundreds of yards or even a mile or more wide in winter rains. An eerie sensation flickered through me. The name 'King' was my Uncle's name. He lived in Victoria many years before and from the time I first set foot in the country thoughts of him had been a constant shadow in the back of my mind.

Propped up in bed I remembered what my Aunt, who had been such a comforting and protective influence in my life, told me about him over the years. How 'Art' (Arthur), her older brother, had lied about his age and joined the Army in the First World War aged sixteen, and gone to France.

Coming home on leave their mother washed his clothes and ironed his trench coat. Not so much to make it look smart, but kill the burgeoning population of lice multiplying in the seams; the frying stench of which, she said shaking her head, laughing, and with a deep grimace, was '*awful*!'

The tales he told as a Service Corp driver, driving munitions up to the lines; and the steady stream of wounded back to hospitals, often seeing shattered, horribly mutilated bodies, having a live soldier at one end and offloading a body at the other, and the blood and gore of it all. The effects all this had on him; of never being the same again and in the Great Depression of the 1930s emigrating to Australia to sail far away from the lack of work and the brooding spectre of his past. Of his Art-istic nature, musical talent, love of poetry; and much else.

Ultimately, all to no avail and he died tragically; old before his time on the farm where he worked. Alone; deeply lonely, and a mountain of suppressed sadness on his shoulders.

These were the whispering shadows I carried driving around the Victorian tracks and roads wondering where he lived and worked.

I recalled what seemed Aunt's favourite anecdote; how, when off duty, Art with his mates in their makeshift billet, he or later, someone would say: "Come on; let's all go mad for five minutes."

Which they did. They rushed around banging pillows, shouting, yelling and generally 'going mad'.

"After that," he said, as Aunt recounted to me, "We all felt better!"

Like a flash of lightning and clap of thunder, sitting in bed a thunderbolt of revelation hit me!

Reflexively I waved my arms, barking out loud; "Christ almighty! It was *you*, Art wasn't it! *You* were the one who led me to heal myself! *You* were the one who showed me the way and how to go mad."

Choking with aching tears of long delayed understanding; barely able to speak, shaking my head I said: "Bloody hell! Its only taken me *nineteen years* to realise and for it to dawn you've been trying to get through to me, and tell me it's you who's been leading me and with me all this time!"

As this realisation burst over me, for a moment I thought I was about to see my bedroom absolutely torn apart as the most indescribable sensation of knowing and feeling came to me – but not seeing – Art unleashed like a tailless pyrotechnic rocket performing astonishing aerobatics of liberated, pent up frustration, sheer delight and relief.

It was a certainness of knowing transcending any experience I ever had – before or since.

Like seeing the picture uniting a collection of seemingly disparate jigsaw puzzle pieces, this startling revelation – for it was nothing less – created, like a dam bursting, a torrent of perceptions.

Suddenly, leaning back into the pillows propping me up, everything snapped into its place; I did not know how, but I felt a knowing certainty of utterly profound, unshakable depth.

I thought it was 'Arthur' Janov's book, *The Primal Scream*, that was the key given me months later in New Zealand by Jack Frost that was *the* turning point in my life without which my future was destined to be a very short one.

This was true – and false – at the same time. The book was tangible; it possessed a definite authority. With my normal senses I could touch it, feel it, open it and read the print on its pages. I and it existed in the physical world, indeed as my smelly hitch hiker later forcefully spat back at me with venom, when attempting to help her; I not only lived in the physical world but a *fiendishly logical* one too.

Anything outside this and the logical computer hardware and software world I lived in so deeply, simply didn't exist.

So what chance did the words of my Uncle have, who I never met, indirectly relayed by my Aunt to me, of influencing me in this intellectual, brick-wall-rigid materialistic mental prison?

None.

Yet equally, like being hit by a brick wall of solid certainly, pondering there in my small bedroom, I could see a chain of events whose links of inevitability were forged together with such cosmic force of certainty beside which gravity, holding unseen the earth in its orbit, was a cotton thread.

It might have been a book by *Arthur* Janov triggering the volcano of life-erupting catharsis in me, but I was deluged with a conviction beyond any disputing, it was my Uncle *Arthur* King's influence and wisdom, unimaginable forces magnetically attracted me to right around the world like an iron filing into his invisible ambit, that was *the* fundamental genesis of this chain of events.

A feeling of awe swept through me at this thunderbolt epiphany of the staggering power of the inner hidden world to fuse together what in my intellectual prison I had thought of as pure chance; random events.

And far from a bizarre borrowed spectacle of someone stomping round a stage reciting 'mummy daddy, mummy daddy', culminating in vomiting into a paper bag, my Uncle's wisdom had far deeper invisible foundations in surviving the insane shrieking horror of war. The antidote for which was, to 'go mad for five minutes'.

No bridge ever built; not even the great Sydney Harbour, whose massive support I stood beside a day or so after arriving there, could span the gulf in me between the mental prison of brittle logic I inhabited and my desperately harboured desire to bestride this chasm of being.

The recollection of standing in evening gloom beside this huge, towering pillar quietly saying to myself; 'well I'm here Art, I wonder if you stood here and what it was like for you all those years ago, when you first arrived in this land,' came echoing back.

The picture and puzzle fused in resolving the paradox; without going to Australia and my Uncle's orbit of influence would I have picked up another hitch hiker; Jack Frost and in less than an hour knowing with the same kind of certainty as that I had just experienced, would I have gone on to begin clearing, in the woods of Nova Scotia, the crushing weight of history and repressions buried in me; and from which control of my life was ebbing away?

The more I pondered the more I gradually slid down the pillows until overwhelmed by this racing deluge of perceptions, I gave up, put out the light and lapsed into thankful sleep.

If these were the gush of tumbling realisations forging some new path of understanding in me, not even they completed the near incomprehensible puzzle pieces-of-fate which occur to me even now. Not just nineteen years after my first stumbling efforts to begin clearing myself of the weight of inner repressions I knew I couldn't carry anymore, but thirty-eight years later the picture still broadened and expanded.

For example and in particular; the two hitch hikers I picked up – the first the young lady – who as described, was like human confetti whose life was a scattered confusion of disparate elements.

Completely aimless, motiveless; utterly devoid of self-esteem, swept whichever way the currents of her daily existence propelled her.

But as also remarked; in long retrospect realising she was the ineluctable mirror image of my own inner world.

In being a mirror image, externally, her life was utter confusion and unresolved in every aspect, though inwardly she *still* possessed a sense of emotional cohesion and self-knowledge I completely lacked. In short; my inner world was exactly the same as her outer. In the rapier thrust of her perception of my 'fiendish' logic, she drove the point she was making straight through me, creating an extremely painful wound of focused self-awareness. Lancing an invisible boil of deep, painfully-suppressed inner knowing.

Or more aptly expressed; smashing a great hole, in my brittle shell of intellect.

That was one aspect of this hall of mirrors of my inner world.

The other was picking up the reversed 'reflection' of this young woman; in stopping for the second hitch hiker as also described, whilst I might stop for a female I *never* stopped for a male. Yet I had for Jack Frost and strangely against my own will; slamming on the brakes, standing the car on its nose. Just exactly like an occasion years before in Zambia, when I froze; poised in mid-step – foot in the air – immobilised as if by a magic spell. Looking down to see a small snake exactly where my foot would have landed, slither by, and finding out later from those that knew, it was a silver crate, which had I stepped on it, would have been my certain end within ten minutes.

The first – female – smashed the *intangible* brittle shell of my inner world; the second – male – gave me the *tangible* means of dealing in the outer world, with the jagged gap of *reality* opened by the first.

Reverberating reflections of inner mirrors of mind/Yin; Yang/masculine; feminine/inner and outer/inner consciousness; outer consciousness/intangible; physical; one can use and put together a complete 'kaleidoscope' of mirrored images attempting to illustrate the symbolism of these uncanny dualistic metaphors driven by the unseen or subconscious world – or simply 'fate' as many might see it.

For good measure, one can stir in the difference between women and men as John Gray describes it in *Men Are From Mars; Women Are From Venus* in the mirror image approach to resolving problems.

Summarised this is: women seek external confirmation for internal resolution, and synthesis. Men seek internal synthesis for resolution and external action.

Consequently it was a woman who confirmed in the outside world the problem she instinctively pinpointed in my inner one. Whereas it was a man who later gave me the (re)solution to my inner world problem, giving me the physical means to take action in my outer world.

Or summed up in the immortal words; woman to silent man who she tells all about the problem she has:

"Oh you're such a good listener! I feel *so* much better already."

Alternatively; woman describes her problem, the man becomes more and more agitated seeing a clear means of action to resolve the problem; interrupts and tells her what to do. To which the woman replies; "You're not listening to me!"

Conversely; woman to man; "What's the matter; you're very quiet?"

Response man to woman; "*Nothing's* the matter! Leave me alone!"

However I attempt to describe the sequence of events, and their symbolism, to western-culture intellectually-dominated minds, these are simply a meaningless jumble; a pig's breakfast of disparate unrelated random, coincidental events having no relationship whatsoever to one another.

Consequently meaningless drivel and utter rubbish.

The intellectual equivalent of filling a metaphorical washing machine full of words and turning it on. What comes out being just random bits of nonsensical mental 'confetti'.

But seen from the perspective of a deep clear connection to the unseen world inhabited by aboriginal peoples and those who have not lost the connection with their own sub/inner conscious, there is a continuum of cause, effect and outcome as inevitable as a train on rails running into the buffers.

Which is the proper state of all human consciousness where there is *no barrier* nor distinction between 'intellect' and 'subconscious', or outer and inner consciousness.

Consequently, what appears to be incoherent tripe to an intellectually educated and totally dominated person, to one who has not had their real consciousness sealed off such that a multi-megaton blast would fail to even dent the armoured wall dividing the two, seemingly unconnected or 'random' events have a continuum and relationship as links in a chain of inevitability in the manner already described.

The sub/inner conscious and its little brother's 'intuition' and 'instinct' (or as the Reverend Dodgson, better known as Lewis Carroll called them so far as I'm concerned, Tweedledum and Tweedledee), provide us *unfailingly* with an added dimension as to what is real, true and workable. It is the difference between a picture of something and the real thing itself.

Intellect is a comment about reality; it is *not* reality.

Reality is what our senses tell us directly, including instinct and intuition which when properly nurtured also cease to be differentiated from what western society calls the 'subconscious' or even worse; the 'unconscious'.

In fact *any* distinction between what western culture gives separate names to, to describe aspects of consciousness, ceases to exist.

Ironic isn't it – I am using words and the intellect attempting to describe the part of us that deals *only* in allegories, pictures, portents, signs and symbols, as Carl Jung showed in his books and long years of work and exploration of the mind. Which Freud with his deep dislike of the rawness of fractured emotions unlocking, and his matriarchal dominated society upbringing and mentality, never got within a galaxy's width of; but who had the great courage to take the first step.

And in my own direct experience neither of them got to dismantling and eradicating the wall between 'outward' facing consciousness; intellect, and 'inward' facing consciousness; sub/inner conscious.

Unlearning and undoing what western culture and education does to us, isn't something that happens like making and drinking a cup of instant coffee. This is part of the fatal flaw and wish fulfilment delusion of intellect. Again in my direct experience it takes decades and many thousands of hours' work to get near to it.

The process in essence is simple. But it should not be confused with easy. It is not. Anyone attempting to dismantle experience of life predisposing them to function as a 'normal', westernised person needs to possess an acute degree of self-awareness, without which it is like booking a travel ticket. The first question that will be asked is: 'Where to?'

If one's answer is: 'I don't know', the politest response is likely to be: 'Come back when you've made up your mind'.

Deciding to 'give it a try', 'have a go', 'why not; got nothing to lose', etc. and many other expressions of non-committal tentative interest, are a near total waste of time, effort and money. And worse; self-deluding.

It is the equivalent of 'giving it a go' to become an Olympic gold medal winner. Nothing less than total commitment, dedication and an all-consuming desire to achieve one's goal will do.

My choice was starkly simple; change or die.

We are back at Napoleon Hill's first principle of success; a burning desire to achieve one's goal. No ifs or buts, no half hearted compromises, just an utterly consuming desire. *Nothing else* will suffice.

Out of No-Man's Land ...

In the best tradition of apocalyptic revelations, like celestial fingers of fire burning the Ten Commandments into tablets of stone with Charlton Heston standing majestically on the summit of Mount Sinai (film set); the wind machine blowing him around, my world changed forever...

About as much as the actor's did once it had been shot and was 'in the can'.

Almost nothing changed; except, like Heston's improving bank balance, a path opened up before me between the floods of bills to be paid, threatening to overwhelm me. From wondering how the hell I was going to pay my way, having by good sense, considerably more good fortune, and a modicum of cunning, I got the all important mortgage I needed and my new home, where at this latest low ebb of my life, and with no even moderately certain source of income, this inner-consciousness expanding experience occurred.

At the point where I left the work I did in IT recruitment some months before, precipitating the terminal rift between myself and my wife, one day I was walking in local conifer woodlands; wandering in a state of comatose fatigue from stress-filled sleeplessness, wondering where I was going to find work and sustain myself.

Being nearly fifty years old, jobs were very difficult to find. All this churning over in my mind, my thoughts turned to someone I had contact with previously in recruitment with non-committal results.

I tried going within myself; to find a quiet place in my febrile state of mind and 'feel' my way forward and see what answers – if any – I came up with.

The more I tried – with considerable difficulty – to calm the cement mixer of thoughts like clattering brick bats churning over and over in my head, the more a certainty came to me the inconclusive contact I once made, held something for me, as I said to myself threading my way between pine trees off the main track, very conscious the dead under branches of them and the uneven ground impeding my progress were an exact allegory of my path in life at the time. Very uneven and uncertain.

I decided to call the man and arranged a meeting.

On one level it still seemed very non-committal, certainly so far as anything to do with recruitment was concerned, though it appeared there might be the very tentative possibility of a venture selling magnetic fuel-saving devices, purely as an agent for him.

My options not exactly brimming over with choice, I took up the challenge and began selling them.

The first day marked the absolute nadir of progress in my working life.

After leaving the safe corporate world I bumped my way downwards in bruising falls and tumbles in pursuit of a 'career' finding myself on a day of heavy rain riding around on my little motorbike getting absolutely waterlogged up to my waist, tramping round an industrial estate with squelching shoes, frozen feet, even though it was summer time, sodden and miserable trying to sell these devices.

Spending a dripping fruitless morning, I felt as if the ground would open and swallow me.

Returning in the afternoon – having mostly dried out purely through my own body heat and the blast of cold air as I rode home and back again on my motorbike, miraculously, people I badgered in their offices – and anyone else I could find to inveigle into conversation – began showing interest and actually *buying*!

Suddenly the world became a heart-warming and nicer place and the sun smiled its approval; for a while at least. I felt buoyed up by the genuine niceness of people and faith in human nature took a distinct upward turn.

In following weeks I sold many devices and equally miraculously what had seemed a cul-de-sac of my life began looking like a narrow footpath between past experience and failures to a broader future thoroughfare – if only a fairly tentative one.

This enabled me to get my crucial mortgage for the new home I was going to on my own, and created the opportunity to work with the man doing IT recruitment in his own business.

It transpired, far from being raw and stumbling in my efforts to sell the fuel-saving devices improving the fuel combustion in an engine's cylinders, there were few if any others willing to get out, grit their teeth, knock on doors and sell them. But by that time these devices were history anyway.

If my work clearing and healing myself appears conspicuous by absence of its mention during this period, it certainly was less of a presence in my life. A natural focus on pure survival overtook other considerations, but the relationship between what my body told me, all the time inextricably intertwined with my fragile emotional state, could not be ignored either.

It was a time of wearying, knotted, burning, gut-strangling abdominal pains and releasing it in the best way I could; which meant breaking the solid-clamped knot of tension so often existing there, by the only method I found to reliably work. As already related a number of times, on one level I loathed having to do it, but in terms of creating inner peace for a while, if it meant rolling a face cloth into a plug, sticking it into my throat to force reflexive dry vomiting, immediately breaking the intense contracted intestinal muscular gripping, I was 'happy' if that is the word, to do it as much as I needed to release the agony.

Which was all too often.

The pattern of human body relationships driving it didn't concern me in the least, but vaguely it seemed abdominal regions operated nearly independent of what was going on elsewhere.

I recalled years before when working flat out, building mainframe computers and later teaching new engineers their intimate workings. Studying at night school three nights a week, learning new systems in the meantime; doing night school private study most Sundays, sustaining this for about thirty-two weeks of the year, quite often I drove along in my car in good spirits but a rock-solid knot in my abdomen.

The rest of me operating nearly independent of this acutely stressed area.

If I had stopped to ponder and consider it all then perhaps I would have viewed it in terms of body stress 'mortgage payments' I failed to 'pay' in earlier years having caught up with the rest of me and the stress 'interest' I accumulated finally became an urgently overdue 'repayment'.

All this, as already described, was a far horizon from my boat-of-life existence at the time. I did what I did to survive. 'Doing it' to keep myself 'afloat' was infinitely more important to me than any musings of the intricacies of how my guts-in-turmoil interacted with the rest of me.

Not least, the means to study this didn't exist then anyway. The research had not even been done that now a simple three word key typed in, immediately returns this information from that vast 'brain' of our world; the Internet.

Recruitment became a success and I began to pay my way to a space of relative financial peace.

Over a few months though, it began to dawn why there were empty desks among the company's offices. The person I worked for and with could erupt into an ice-veined rage in a split syllable, which, feeling very emotionally fragile, brought me out in a cold sweat across my forehead.

Material success and money was one thing, peace of mind entirely another and a higher plane of existential need. A few months later, having come across a kindred spirit of an engineering disposition in the IT industry and with an old Jaguar the same as one I had, enthused to me about the company he worked for, which seemed to be a kind of franchise, and of its potential, so I decided to join him.

Only to find I was back metaphorically bridging between trees as when a small boy, repeating the same fateful step into mid-air with my eyes firmly shut, landing with yet another shuddering thud into ensnaring 'briars' of other people's whimsical notions of a network of 'companies' that apart from fantasies doodled on paper didn't exist. Though by then I had begun to develop a certain hard shell of self-protective mentality, and as vaporous as these 'companies' were, even so it was still a great relief to be in an environment where I could tread freely without triggering a landmine explosion and icy-angered verbal shrapnel over some easily resolvable minor issue.

Although I quickly discovered I had landed in a small, family run, commodity computer networking reselling operation and any money I earned was going to be purely through my own efforts, to me it was respite from a daily struggle coaxing significant sums for candidate placement, in a work environment of emotional booby traps.

This is not to say the man completely lacked any warmth or human compassion. He could be and sometimes was very generous. It appeared though, any pressure on sensitive emotional spots, of which there were many, triggered explosions as certainly as blundering about in a mine field.

The Bridge of Trust

Curiously, this period of the summer of 1994 holds poignant memories for me. Extremely tenuous as the prospect of earning money was; purely from my own efforts on a commission basis working in this small family 'umbrella' company, it was a time to heal after my marriage break up. Physically and emotionally I was exhausted. It took me a few days to get over the waves of panic after realising what I had landed in was really just a collection of individuals – though family members – working under one roof.

Fortunately, by this time I had joined another kind of networking organisation; nothing to do with computer hardware, this was selling household and personal products, which really didn't interest me at all. But as it was a 'squeaky' clean business, ethically based and regulated, and used a motivational system based on Napoleon Hill's success principles, and although rather cringingly 'happy clappy' and American in origin and flavour gave me something to hang on to, and – for once – a reliable model of success rather than the one of disaster and struggle I was all too familiar with.

For the first few days when it actually dawned I fitted in with 'the family' about as well as a spare groom at a wedding, I managed to banish the rising waves of panic each morning on arrival, silently reciting mantras of success to myself like a clockwork parrot. They were words I didn't own in any sense; feel or identify with, but like newspapers jamming out frigid draughts of frightening reality, I used them to jam sinking despair and other thoughts out of mind – just.

It might be something like; "I am successful, people I call want to talk to me today, are interested in what I sell and they buy from me."

Or similarly; "Today I find all the prospects I want and business comes easily to me."

As I got out of my motorcycling clothes I would repeat these over and over. Whenever I felt myself slipping down into a pit of brow-moistening despondency, somehow I hauled myself out, reciting my affirmations as fast as I could get the whispered words out, until my heart rate descended to something like normal, I regained normal physical balance, and my physical movements slowed from adrenaline-fuelled jerking marionette to vaguely human.

In lunch hour, especially on fine days, I would leave the converted cow shed in the corner of a farmyard also reincarnated as a courtyard and car park, and walk along the narrow country lane beside it, up a rise to beautiful fields, and sublime, entrancing views over the Berkshire countryside; the Downs in the background with striped para-gliding butterflies circling above them contrasting against the bright green sunlit slopes and clear azure sky. Mesmerised, I would sit under a large oak tree, delighting as always from my earliest times as a child, in the emerald canopy of delicate, newly-spread foliage over me.

In my head, in spite of the continual gnawing uncertainty of what by choice I had got myself into, I felt as if I could talk to my father, or rather I could speak words I recognised as his when a child. Though these were a great deal more encouraging than ever they were as a small boy.

Somehow I found comfort in these, though other people might consider it barking mad, I had a conviction this psychic telephone line had someone at the other end.

The 'conversation' began as soon as I was out of earshot of the buildings where I worked. The gist being I might feel my prospects were very uncertain, but the words that formed were; "Don't worry son; things will soon begin to improve, you wait and see; you may wonder where the next penny is going to come from, it may take a little time, but things will improve much quicker than you think. You will have all the money you need son; you mark my words!"

In my state of constant insecurity as I spoke to myself, I felt them reach a deeper part of me, and speaking as I walked, they continued until the 'line' went dead – from my end.

This wasn't the first time that year I had turned my attention inside myself to connect with something deeper than the cage full of linnets incessantly chirping inside my head all my waking hours.

Around the same time I attended an air display at Middle Wallop in Hampshire; as much for the wonderful energy of the area – being close to Danebury ancient hill settlement and the edge of Salisbury Plain – as for the chance to see aircraft from modern to ancient, which equally fascinated me from when I was four years old.

Wandering around I came across a local car dealer's display and got into conversation. My car badly needed replacing, but the shiny new ones were far beyond my pocket.

Yet *something* inside me didn't seem to care. I found myself, almost against my own will, taking interest.

Some days later one Saturday morning, I sat with the salesman in his showroom 'office' talking over the details and leafing through a book of paint colours, choosing the one I liked. At the same time I was searching for a pool of silent, stillness within. It came; and as if I had already bought the car I 'measured' its frightening cost against a calendar spread out before me in my mind's eye. It was April, and as I 'felt' my way along the months I got to the all important November, when instalments to pay for it would become due. There was no sudden gripping, cold-sweat panic; just a clear neutral feeling. I took it as confirmation; buying wouldn't be a problem.

Then came time to sign and commit to buy. Again for a few seconds, I paused. My low key and un-pushy salesman probably thought I was just going over the details on the document in front of me, mentally checking off the things we had discussed. On one level I was, but on another I was in a completely different place. Sitting there starkly aware of the thousands of pounds of expense I was committing myself to, I let the enormity of this drive me deep within to find again the stillness at the centre of the storm; if there was any.

For a few seconds I searched. Back it came to me and I entered a place of absolute calm.

Silently, I asked the question: if I sign up to buy this car, will I be able to pay for it when payments commence after six months?

The answer was; Yes, you will have enough money to keep you going in the meantime. By then you will have found work. So I signed.

The lane I walked day after day having my 'telephone conversation' became paved with these thoughts and the words I spoke filled the hedgerows with their presence.

I collected my beautiful new, fresh-smelling white gold 'vehicle of my life'. Driving gingerly at first, a feeling of deep relief and equally satisfying sense of heavy history dwindling behind me as the miles smiled their greeting on the odometer like new shoots of springtime optimism, as thoughts of my old car slowly began to fade.

It marked the hardest years of my life. It was filled with an immense amount of every shade of emotion; though so little happiness. Too often it had resounded to cries and tears of burning anguish, outrage and hurt; from my deep past mingled with those of present times.

A golden glow did not suddenly materialise in my life with the first brand new car I had ever bought – or had become my committed intention – but with its increasing miles I seemed slowly, all too slowly, to be entering a new phase of it.

Rather than clock up the miles in my treasured new possession, every week day I would ride my little motorbike the twenty-six miles to work avoiding where possible major routes, through the countryside; small roads and narrow lanes wending my way through scenery I deeply loved at any time of year; and especially in nature's rise of tumultuous breathless joy. The fragile delicacy; first of snowdrops; delightful pearls of optimism, then crocuses; dew-sprinkled clumps of anarchy; rainbow-taunting clusters, rising blades of grass and finally a deafening thunder; an exploding vibrant blush and colours with not a single murmur save the magic thrill of blackbirds and even thrushes singing trees into a thousand shades of joyous leafy green.

Until one day at the doorway of these lanes of tranquillity in which I bathed, came the time when bulldozers, chainsaws and earth-planing juggernauts ripped the silence and the land apart, and police in swarms evicted 'hippies' from trees on 'Operation Prospect' and policemen of six-feet-two punched women a foot shorter to the ground, arresting them 'for assault,' showing passive solidarity with those resisting the growing scar of Newbury's Western bypass.

Fate though, had other plans than to let me ride so close to nature along these roads and one day with a sudden rhythmic rapid coughing, the sump plug I thought screwed securely in place – but taking care not to strip the threads – unwound itself, dropping suddenly off and my motorbike's engine oil, splashing a trail on to the road's grey green stones.

To no avail, I searched for it, finally beginning the four-mile long-push home, just as I had previously pushed it thirteen miles after the battery charging circuit failed. This time though, fate's taxi-rank provided a cab a short distance along the thankfully flat road. A van driver stopped to enquire about my misfortune and quickly I arrived back home. The metaphor of opposite fates underlined by the fact had I travelled a few more yards before the sump plug fell out, I would have descended the steepest hill of any to be climbed back up then or the previous suicide-consumed journey of volcanic inner purgatory.

I sank into the seat and equally comforting smells of my car's pristine interior, and less than half an hour later re-passed the spot where my sump plug lay undiscovered, resting peacefully.

From that day on I drove in luxury, protected from the elements yet missing their direct contact, to and from work each day, wincing every time I put more fuel in the car as the litres and pounds clocked up; mentally seeing the 'dials' of my bank balance turning in reverse.

It never even remotely occurred to me at the time, destiny had decided my transition from aging and Spartan transport was to be total. However insecure and frugal I might feel the need to be, my 'elevation' from poverty stricken outlook and mentality to one of unaccustomed – and as yet unpaid for – comfort, brooked no half measures or compromise, and all summer I basked in trappings of success very conscious of its absence as the weeks went by.

My mentality might not have arrived in my future, but utterly oblivious of it, something far deeper and more powerful propelled me there regardless of what my fear-motivated waking state understood.

The Wisdom of Animals

S TEADILY – IF very slowly – as the months rolled by I began to gain a semblance of calm and with it signs noticed by others of a new and growing confidence in myself. It didn't come for free; like all before it I followed my process established twenty years previously of letting my body's wisdom guide me as to what I needed to do and in doing so – if reinforcement was required – the unshakable bond between clamped suppressed emotions and clamped tensioned body unfailingly, with no exceptions, reaffirmed cause and effect once I cleared what pressed for release, in clear conscious understanding. As more than one clairvoyant reaffirmed; I still carried a great deal of hurt from the history and break up of my marriage and this – just like deep bruising in the body – needed time and patience to work its way out; be released and integrated.

In doing this I had three of the best 'therapists' I could ever wish for; my three cats.

I loved them all equally; but like nearly all the female race they jealously coveted my exclusive affections.

At times of low ebb and crying with deep hurt, they would surround me. Sometimes I would be pinned down in my armchair or bed with bodies on me and right next to me.

Other times I had one each side of me; heads pillowed on my shoulders at the tops of my arms, laying on their backs under the bedclothes with me, purring fit to burst close to my head, as I stroked their bellies.

The third would be close by; not overtly affectionate, due to the horrendous experience of being taken from her mother far too early and very near death when rescued having been abused by children who suffered similarly. Yet of the three she was by far the brightest and acutely aware. Humans frightened her but almost any animal was treated as a kindly parent would a child. She would rub her body round the hooves of a pony utterly without fear. Years later, one night in the early hours, after hearing a sharp bark outside my home, I looked out to see her walk purposefully down the front path and stand nose to nose with a fox.

She knew how much I cared for her. Administering the occasional worm pill, gently wrapping her in a towel so I only had to deal with a set of jaws and not windmilling claws, having swallowed it, I slackened the towel, gently stroking her throat and down on to her belly as she reclined on my lap.

Finger tips reaching her lower abdomen, strong convulsive spasms went through her back legs; kicking out together. Very gently and slowly I continued running them down her white underside; the great jerking shudders gradually slackened and ceased. After this massive release of fear; for it was clearly the trauma she carried from before she was rescued: ears flat to her head, a large bump on it and a hernia on her belly, she became even more completely devoted to me.

If I went for a walk to the woods along the lane beside my house, I would hear plaintive meowing as she hurried after me, appearing from nowhere. Sometimes she accompanied me the whole way, whiskers and senses alert; eyes wide, ears pricked; twitching swishing tail, round the woods and always under her own steam; swearing and struggling if I picked her up.

As I understood her so she did me; though hers was a direct knowing without the manufactured confusion of intellect and judgement.

Together, all three knew my inner state as all animals do, and as I slowly cleared the fog of my own emotions, their behaviour and its motivation became clearer and clearer to me. I began to see, animals although not speaking as humans did, possessed understanding of all around them far surpassing the patronising, mindless, bleating of human kind. There was no self-delusion, constantly rewriting blatantly obvious reality; passing clear perception through an intellectual 'shredder' to arrive at distorted, false conclusions. Just being and knowing.

♥

Whilst my work environment was quite pleasant, and not being paid for anything but the results of my own efforts, I could work and come and go as I pleased.

Finding also the young members of the family saw me as competition for what they were doing reselling networking hardware, I pursued my path through the, by then, well worn familiar process of cold calling; making contacts, obtaining meetings and attempting to develop prospects. But even that was difficult because although there were suppliers who would provide expertise if I sold network solutions, I was simply an agent with no formal ties or agreement. I was merely the 'tail of the dog'.

Fortunately, attending a networks exhibition, I bumped into a previous work colleague and manager from hardware training school days, and we had also shared an interest in the Territorial Army.

He also was involved in networking systems providing management software for large, complex networks.

Once again, it was an informal and very casual arrangement, but I decided if I put my heart and soul into this *somehow* and from *somewhere* fate and the universe would smile on my efforts and it would lead to reliable work from *some* quarter. Where that might be I had no idea.

Three things drove this mentality; first were the success principles set out by Napoleon Hill, reiterated and reinforced by the networking organisation I joined. I didn't mind the 'happy clappy' positive-mental-attitude litanies regurgitated like bovine cud chewing; it might feel foreign but in comparison with my own efforts expended hacking through the jungle of bitter struggle alongside the main arterial road of personal success, its condensed wisdom was clear and unequivocal, having itself only been won through someone else's equally diligent pains-taking struggles over twenty years.

How it might change my life I didn't know, but knowing how the mind adjusts reality through constant repetition, I played the cassette tape summary in my car for endless hours; sometimes for three or four; maybe more, at a stretch until I was punch drunk on it.

Secondly and from a different path but converging on the same wisdom, was Louise L. Hay's book, *You Can Heal Your Life*.

Reluctant to spend precious money on it, I knew I had to; precious or not, the money was inconsequential compared with what I was sure the book contained for me.

This lady, in exactly the same way as myself, had been confronted with a change-or-die choice, finding out she had cancer, and with immense courage and presence of mind refused conventional 'treatment' with body-destroying life-force exterminating surgery, chemotherapy and drugs with sledgehammer 'side' effects diametrically opposed to the body's ability to heal itself, given the right nurturing and encouragement to do so.

Reading it re-opened doors of my own healing process neglected through the sheer weight and even more pressing need to resolve recent personal history reflected in my body and emotional low ebb.

It also opened new doors with its own affirmations of health; visualisations and 'mantras' related to physical, emotional, mental and spiritual wellbeing, coming from a different angle to Napoleon Hill's personal success, related to the business world but ultimately merging like the two Niles to become one great stream of life-affirming consciousness.

Thirdly, was my own intuition which, in spite of all, continued to grow and deepen no matter what obstacles needed to be overcome.

JOURNEY OF A LIFETIME

My experience of 'doing it' gained in twenty years of my own efforts to clear the effects of my personal history on my body was an utterly unshakeable growing source of inner strength; which right from the very beginning had always and increasingly sustained me.

At the same time as this; still working in the reincarnated cowshed alongside 'the family', I learned the lady of the husband and wife couple who ran the business, and could burn paint off steel with her swearing, had been involved in recruitment, and encouraged me to do this if I wished. Also being familiar territory, I took up the challenge following the equally familiar path of making contacts, obtaining job vacancies, finding candidates and making placements.

Fortunately I made one and my bank balance enjoyed a meal in the midst of its prolonged starvation.

It occurred to me to contact another ex-work colleague who I had placed in a technical management capacity of his current employer, and, to use his words I had saved his bacon in doing so.

In his usual somewhat offhand and impatient manner, he told me of a vacancy they had. Gathering brief details from his tight lipped answers, I began putting a specification together. The more I did so, the more it came to me, in spite of the vagueness of his description, it was something I could do very well myself.

The following day, I called him back to ask specific questions to fill in gaps in the sketchy outline he had tetchily given me. This elicited less impatient 'huffs' breathed down the phone and more facts. The more clarification and confirmation I got the more I was certain this was my chance.

Pausing, I said; "Don't laugh; but this is something right up my street!"

Which of course is exactly what he did! After the surprise wore off he promised to 'have words' on my behalf and call me back.

True to this, a day or two later he called to tell me he had arranged for me to meet the sales manager at their office in Maidenhead and it was up to me from there. A location, which although I would miss the healing beauty of wonderful countryside, suited me very well, being exactly the same distance to travel each day ... *if* I was successful. The meeting took place and went well, and shortly thereafter I met the Managing Director and found myself in the first paid work – as a contractor – in months.

In parallel I had pursued marketing the network management system I came upon through my other ex-work colleague, with all the vigour I could muster and found some very good prospects for it and his company. Which he threw away even though one was a name of worldwide renown and was *very* keen to meet and discuss the system!

My conviction the universe would answer my devotion and strenuous – if outwardly pointless – efforts appeared to be answered; but not before one day I reached a point where my forehead moistened with cold sweat and over more than one long lunch hour, I went out and for a solid hour or more, as hard as I could, I repeated 'mantras' of success affirmations walking along a canal path, without pausing until I felt breathless and symptoms of high blood pressure made me feel distinctly light headed, continuing whilst the sheer panic slowly subsided.

Driving this was the onset of payments for my car, and money draining from my bank balance like an opened sluice gate, and if nothing changed I was quickly going to run out of money.

It was with the greatest relief – and pleasure – I picked up the bits and pieces of the work I had done in the cow shed, and departed. Driving home I was sad to be seeing for the last time, in the car headlights, all the things that healed me as, wind against my protective clothing, my little motorbike had carried me along feeling part of nature in a way simply impossible in the comfortable confines of my car.

Only seven-and-a-half months had elapsed, it seemed far longer, recalling when in springtime the road surface sped by under my foot rests and I savoured and even devoured all I saw, outwardly delighting in all around me; inwardly in poor health, poorer spirits and a state of nervous fragility.

I came within a month or two of running completely out of money; but the quiet still pool of inner peace I entered sitting choosing the colour of my new car and contemplating my signature about to go on the contract to buy it, had, infallibly, shown me the way ahead in my life more surely than a thousand miles of dead straight motorway.

The Long Climb To …

On Tuesday 8th November 1994 I began my new work. It was a job I was extremely well acquainted with by then: finding new business prospects for companies.

And another one of those curious 'coincidences'; this is being written/typed on the 8th of a month.

For me '8' has proved to be a number of fate. It has cropped up in various guises; 8, 18, and less obviously 17, and 26 which when the digits are added together reduces to '8'. As the Chinese will say; eight is an auspicious number of good fortune – and why Beijing sought to host the Olympics in 2008 commencing on the 8th of August; the 8th month and the opening ceremony beginning at 8.00 PM.

Perhaps more on this subject later, but I was very clear, it was *no* coincidence I was beginning the work on this particular day. But I knew '8' also had a very dualistic side, also being the gateway to new experiences ultimately turning very sour; as I already knew.

After a perfunctory whirlwind introduction to the sales prospect administration system I was to use, the task of finding new business for the sales staff of the office I worked in began within half an hour.

To the background accompaniment of a howling thermal lance being used in the car park directly outside to burn off incorrect white lines, I found and 'struck' my first prospect firmly on the 'hook'. Very conscious I was there to perform or quickly get thrown out as, in tears, my predecessor had been, like a large and powerful trout on the end of my (telephone) line, I quickly reeled him in. Nearly deafened by the discordant overwhelming howl of the fire-breathing tube outside, the voice in my earpiece either drowned completely or was barely audible above this appalling wailing; with the sales manager who had just 'demonstrated' the prospect system, I agreed a meeting date, confirmed it with him and put the phone down.

In less than an hour from walking in the door I had begun to produce.

Not noted, as I soon discovered, for showering plaudits around on others, the sales manager said quietly to himself as much as in my direction; "I think you've got something there." Repeating the phrase quietly two or three times. I took it to mean he was both surprised and pleased.

By the end of the day I had added to my score in my keep net of arranged prospect meetings and I was absolutely drained.

For the first time since I ran the computer media business five years before, I felt limp as if I'd been put through a wringer. I wondered how I was going to keep going at the same pace; let alone maintain it for a conspicuously unspecified time. There was no probationary period after which I might look forward to a more permanent arrangement.

Over succeeding days my tally of new prospects steadily lengthened, yet apart from a call from the manager I previously placed in the company and who opened the door for me, letting me know in a similarly oblique fashion 'people could see I was doing the right thing', there were no clear words or means to gauge whether my tenure was becoming more permanent; except the growing feeling it was.

On days when the Managing or the Commercial Director appeared from the other company office and sat ostensibly doing their own work, palpably, I could feel ears growing to twice their normal size, tuning in to me; listening to every conversation as, just a few feet away, I made cold call after call. On one occasion, having had a very pleasant friendly conversation with someone, nonetheless having extracted every last piece of information I could to discover his company's 'prospectability', I finished the call and put down the phone. The Commercial Director sitting at his laptop; his severe, angular half-lens glasses perched on his nose, the keys clicking with his typing, said quietly under his breath: "Sucked dry!" Continuing to work as if nothing had happened.

Well aware my performance was being recorded – but no machine being used to do so – this silent vetting would have daunted me before, but finally, I knew from listening to the company people around me, after eight years of relentless gruelling slog, I possessed mental dexterity and a certain panache, though not a word was breathed, they liked and were learning from themselves.

Riding this wave of fate I rode its rolling momentum, like a surfer finally mastering the art of balance and poise standing easily on his board, I relished in my art, once so distant and utterly beyond my horizons or imagining let alone any desire to have anything to do with it.

Although my efforts to heal myself never ceased, indeed from the time I began living on my own again I devoted more time to it than for many years, conscious of the fact if I didn't I was going to be in trouble as without doing it my health was not going to improve; quite the reverse.

Not only was I healing still, it was at two separate although interconnected levels.

Though as told endless times already, as this was my day-to-day life and reality, it never occurred to me this was so. Survival, as ever, was the dazzling light in my eyes, and almost anything outside its glare was either blurred or completely invisible.

Bodily there was no magical instant cure for the all too common gut-gripping discomfort and outright pain for 'IBS' – the utterly meaningless – and downright inaccurate description; 'Irritable Bowel Syndrome' which I knew from years of working with and releasing its sometimes deeply unpleasant sensation, owed everything to powerful emotions sublimated and held deep within me.

Equally – and also with increasing refinement – I was able to break its growling, hollow and sometimes also burning sensation by dint of folding across the corner of a face cloth rolling it into a plug and stuffing it into my mouth as thousands of times before, causing the equally reflexive dry vomit, unerringly breaking the spastic gripping, locking my intestines solid. What began years before as a 'chuckle-sob' increasingly progressed to barking retch, then deeper but louder response somewhere between a retch and a roar; finally, to face-cloth plug induced erupting choking roar as I pursued deeper trauma's more profound strangling grip in the pit of my abdomen. The more complete the releasing the more deafening and explosive it was. And the more instantaneous and complete the subsequent relief.

Drinking any alcohol immediately brought a sensation similar to being kicked in the lower back, also feeling very tight and rigidly tense, and if more than a pint, or even just a pint, resulted in a few hours of the familiar gut-clamped sensations and the inevitable antidote. Not unusually repeated a number of times before gaining release – and for a while at least – pleasant relief.

In case it is still not clear; like the process itself, perhaps yet again I can repeat this was not some bizarre fetish I indulged in for its own sake. To equally repeat my 'mantra' used right from the very beginning; I knew my body possessed a wisdom vastly greater than the squawking birdcage in my head and unfailingly *I knew* it would *always* tell me what it needed to do to release energy locked up in it.

Whether the 'birdcage' understood was utterly irrelevant. *Doing it* was the only thing that mattered, and when enough blocked/locked up energy had been released unerringly effect and cause were unfailingly united in clear, conscious, understanding.

Sometimes it might be quick in coming, i.e., within minutes as my body 'unwound.' Others it might take days or weeks. Sometimes months – and for gut strangling discomfort, pain and outright agony – many levels, with corresponding levels of clearing perception taking not just years but decades.

And a full – or at least a much more complete – understanding of the interaction of my body's interrelated systems driving the changing symptoms, their harmonious resolution and evolution continues to unfold and grow in its completeness. The pace of change and transformation continually increasing.

Work, Survival and Body Wisdom

My tally of prospects rose steadily as the days progressed in my new work, and I was invited in to the next sales meeting to give an account and résumé of the companies and projects I had collected. It was clear from the Commercial/Sales Director's tone of voice he was pleased with the results. Rather than any overt praise, his voice was light, clear and just on the positive side of neutral; the implication being I was doing a good job but under a watchful eye in case results began to dwindle.

It was not easy work.

By about four in the afternoon or earlier, making phone calls felt like the effort of walking in air wearing an old fashioned diver's twill suit, massive bronze helmet with circular windows and cumbersome boots with thick lead weights attached, I was so tired.

Fortunately, as the list of prospects lengthened the need to send introductory letters and company information, also part of my job, meant I could devote late afternoons to this task and the ever growing snowball of updating contact records in the sales administration system I used.

Many were the days; most in fact, whatever strategy I used, I drove home, made a meal and went to sleep in my reclining arm chair, waking later and going to bed.

It enabled me to keep going; very sluggish, and digestive system in far from good condition, tomatoes were a good barometer of how sensitive this area was, or more accurately fried tomatoes were, for if I ate them with my favourite comfort fry-up of egg and bacon I could guarantee to induce the by then familiar sensation of fires being lit in my abdominal regions and the inevitable consequences shortly after.

Also apparent was the slight 'singing' noise in my head, I noticed early on in the year, waking one morning realising the usual silence was disturbed. I knew this was caused by increasing tension somewhere in my neck region but no idea where or how I was tensing up muscles to cause this background head sound. The constant battering away at the phone day after day brought it home there were cumulative stress factors which were not going to improve unless I found some way to relieve the stress and find out how to relax the muscles in this complex area of the body.

Easier said than done, and as a corollary, I also noticed if I stretched my arms clenching my fists I could feel unpleasant pulling sensations in my knuckle tendons in the backs of my hands, which at first – and for a number of years – I could only guess the cause, but as time and my efforts to release deep seated stress and deeper long-stored trauma, I knew meant there was a massive amount of tension throughout my shoulders and it was affecting muscles and sinews in my arms and hands. Exactly what the mechanics of all this were I wasn't clear, but at the outset I knew without a doubt, if I didn't find some way to deal with it the outlook was not going to improve. A stress 'mortgage repayment' moratorium was only going to pile up the 'interest' to be paid back later. Though that too was something I did not really comprehend at all clearly then.

The weeks became months, winter turned to spring and finally warm summer days.

I continued to find business, growing in confidence; not needing to rely on my ability to 'vacuum' up facts about the company's portfolio of expertise and 'hose' it on to people as I had from minute one of my first day's cold calling. Sounding, though not feeling, confident doing it, my knowledge soon deepened, having in any case built and tested computers in the days when every electronic component was visible and worked with and taught software to a depth few others ever reached. A legacy and foundation of fundamental benefit in grasping new technologies. More importantly; for the ability to interpret cryptic responses from IT management I called and talked to and respond intelligently but for which conversations abruptly terminated.

Easy it wasn't; the market place might be much larger in the South East and London particularly, but competition was more numerous, intense and far from easy to dislodge. So it all came down to how convincing I sounded to someone who had probably been pestered by people like myself ten times before that day already; what questions I asked and how I listened, related and responded to his comments on a technical level, and above all sounded human, pleasant, 'unpushy' and alert and not some gormless parrot reading from a script. Something I never *ever* did and a recipe for certain 'death'.

Which became even more important when I began calling large London legal practices to market not only IT systems' skills but work flow or case management software.

There was no change in the demands the work made on me – except they increased in all respects – mental dexterity, technical knowledge, and the ability to read tone of voice instantly and adjust accordingly.

A constant companion in front of me perched on top of my computer screen was a reminder I wrote to myself shortly after I began the work; 'Failure is an intermediate point between beginning and ultimate success'.

Originally I wrote it very keenly aware of what felt like a trail of wreckage and failure in my life to that point, but it served me well. I made contacts with people I'd called and tried to speak to without success not unusually several – sometimes many – times before. Occasionally even a year or two later and making good contact with some of the largest legal practices in the country, and even the world.

Although tenure of my desk and status in the company never

warranted so much as a single line letter, let alone any kind of contract, paradoxically I became a 'permanent' office fixture compared with others. Sales people came and went, including a very attractive female manager whose immaculate turnout and figure made a considerable impact but not as much as a vocabulary capable of melting the galvanised coating off steel when she'd had a liquid lunch!

Finally, with the office secretary, I was the only inhabitant and the cloistered peaceful atmosphere suited me. Like a monk in a medieval scriptorium I could daily pursue my laborious work. Indeed it began to dawn on me the Commercial Director who eyed me over his severe half-lens specs addressing me in a cool authoritarian manner when I began working there, relied more and more on me, and in sales meetings would go for a toilet break when I began my report of current work! A feeling grew that I intimidated him through my work and knowledge.

Simultaneously reassuring and increasingly irritating after one of the transitory salesmen pointed out this habit. It seemed whatever else he might wish to scrutinise, my work was taken for granted, or perhaps there was also a twinge of conscience that my ability to make contacts and find prospects exceeded his own?

Especially when, making my endless daily calls, I called – yet another – large London legal practice. In my usual way I endeavoured to make human contact, and in the brief seconds deciding whether the conversation ended abruptly in impatient dismissal or broadened into real interest, I sought some topic that in lifting the tone of voice at the other end, took the conversation on to a level of attentive interest.

Finding nothing at first, and about to admit defeat, I mentioned a topic put as a question, and suddenly found a door of opportunity opening. Some days later the Commercial Director called me on his mobile having just met the IT Manager of the practice, and in a voice of awed optimism, thanked me and told me how unbelievably well the meeting went.

In a few months this soon blossomed into business valued in seven figures. After that I could probably have sat and played patience on my PC most of the day – as I had seen a guilt-ridden salesman doing once who instantly deleted the screen at my approach. Not being a card player anyway, it never once occurred to me to do so.

Even after my 'reward' for creating an opportunity the like of which seldom – if ever – materialised, was £500; or a little more than the commission I earned on a sales opportunity I created myself doing all the sales work on my own, amounting to just over £13,000 in total. For starters.

I was more preoccupied with finding ways to minimise and reduce the ever present stress of the job, in particular of finding someone who would improve the flow of energy in my spine. Finding a convenient local practitioner, I arranged to see him and was pleasantly surprised to find he did spinal energy regulation as well as cranial osteopathy.

As work wound down on a Friday afternoon I left early for a treatment. Yet *still* feeling guilty for taking time away from my work.

Lying on his treatment table I tried to relax and breathe easily only to be mildly admonished I was doing 'circular' breathing like someone practising meditation; controlling and to an extent, clamping it.

I tried to let it just happen, finding my out-breath short and almost a slump each time, rather than easy and smooth. I found it difficult to lie still, very aware by then of how tense I was.

He asked me what I felt like doing. That was easy; yell!

It was clear this was not a welcome means of releasing my pent up tension, and trying just to let my breath go however agitated I might feel, he began regulating my spinal energy.

It was far from as it should have been. It appeared not a single continuous flow but fragmented or polarised between upper and lower regions.

For some time he worked on this with his hands placed at the base of my spine and at shoulder level. Finally he pronounced he had got it flowing; working as one unit.

Leaving, I wasn't sure what effect – if any – his efforts had produced. Though not for long.

Driving home I was physically in my car and simultaneously somewhere else in the universe. I had physical symptoms as if I was going down with a cold or even the flu. I might be in my car but I was definitely *not* in my body.

Gentle, even ephemeral, as the spinal energy manipulation might have felt when it was happening, for the next few days I struggled to keep going. A great gush of energy – like a river's freeing logjam – broke within me.

Deep sadness and hurt overwhelmed me and closely surrounded in bed by my loyal furry family, I cried in black despair as this maelstrom swept through.

Remarkably quickly, within a day or two, what felt unsurviveable in the midst of it all, the deluge past and I felt lighter, still somewhat fragile, and as on another occasion, sitting down at my desk and realising I was going to have to start all over again.

The person who occupied the seat a day or two before – although it had been 'me' – over a weekend this 'me' had gone; something had been swept away. I was in some sense an observer of my own inner processes like someone standing on the river bank seeing where the logjam had been and the marks left by its breaking tumult. What was left behind was torn, scoured and tossed about, but the river in its path was clean and free. For a day or two I had to sort through those aspects of me and my approach to my work still usable, the rest were left behind and gradually faded away.

Like nature turning cleansing catastrophe into new shoots of vibrant growth, this was the experience and image I had of somewhere within me.

It did not mean though, fate suddenly smiling after a passing cloud. I noticed an unpleasant sensation; almost as though I had been kicked squarely in the middle of my crutch and badly bruised. This region felt distinctly sensitive for months. Whilst I might have shed emotional energy as an unfailing consequence of my body's energy being manipulated, there were very evidently other deeper levels of me far less amenable to releasing their deep stress and tension, even though they were in line with my spine and the energy flowing (better) in it.

In the short run, my spinal manipulation created the gush of body and emotional energy I've explained, but as life is a continuous flow of energy until we die, it was part of a far greater process – just as a river is not what passes in a single instant – and in the succeeding days there were body, emotional, and inner-world changes; some I was aware of and others hidden from clear consciousness. These only becoming 'visible' as part of an evolving continuum of my life, just like the flow of a river.

Perfect Health?

My job security might have improved beyond all expectations and my work recognised throughout the company not without reason as will become apparent later, but there was no letting up in either the accumulation of stress in doing it, or my efforts to find a better means to reduce it.

There were times when temporary diversions requiring different and more creative skills helped lift spirits. To my surprise, in my first summer doing the job, it was decided to advertise for salesmen, and being used to creating advertising copy for recruitment advertisements, I enjoyed doing one for *The Times*. Even more surprising; I found myself entrusted with vetting and interviewing applicants! Proof if it were needed, the never knowingly over-praising Commercial Director showing he did indeed trust me over his own people skills.

It helped considerably – if all too briefly – to lessen the weight; and my shoulders seemed noticeably to ease.

I also found a particularly prestigious prospect, well known in mobile phone circles, and having arranged, attended and headed the company team at the meeting, then found the proposal 'we' needed to create was going to be up to me! Alone!!

Fortunately, having once helped to produce groaningly exhaustive proposals for sales to the Ministry of Defence, although it was hard work, creative muscles not flexed in years could be used and this too brought respite.

But the telephone treadmill could not be neglected for long and warm summer days made me particularly aware of how light-headed and wrung out I felt finishing work and driving home; enjoying the weather but leaden in body and limbs.

JOURNEY OF A LIFETIME

Though always my spirits were lifted as I turned into the lane beside my house to see my devoted little friend who followed me around the woods.

She would curl up on my garage roof on fine days and at the sound of my car, long before it appeared, would jump down and stride purposefully towards the noise as I came into view. Never one to accept a lot of stroking, much less a cuddle; in size, she might be a lot smaller than me but came the nearest of any animal pet to being my equal. I felt she knew me as well as I knew myself; or better.

The months rolled around and one year became two, and still I sat in the same chair at the same desk doing the same job.

Although my feet did not freeze solid as they had a year or two before and energy in these regions was better, I could feel my upper body was tighter, gauged from the noise in my head. The 'singing' was not obtrusive and I did not usually hear it during the day, but equally it hadn't lessened either. I would still roar and let rip sometimes to let out pent up energy as I became aware of bottling it up, and flick my arms and hands to release tightness, clamping and accumulated frustration from work and unlock the energy in them; even more so in my shoulders. But jumping around also doing it to get energy moving in my lower body as well, wasn't enough to make any permanent positive difference. I might be paying off my stress 'mortgage' but the payments were not meeting the interest, let alone reducing the 'principal'.

The load was literally bearing down on my shoulders though there was nothing visible to be seen.

In December 1996 a book by Dr Deepak Chopra entitled *Perfect Health* caught my eye. It was, after all, something I was constantly reminded of the whole time in my waking life, for its lack in me.

Not sure what I might find inside; the cover showing him smiling out, bright eyed, with an intense gaze; though perhaps also as if he had been wiped down with an oily rag as his skin had a slight glaze, I began to read, discovering it was all about the anciently established 'Science of Life' as Ayurvedic medicine means in Sanskrit. The language and the system being incomparably more ancient than anything else including, it appeared, Chinese wisdom on the subject of health.

The combination of Dr Chopra's western and eastern experience and qualifications were especially appealing as they bridged the all too common chasm between the two approaches.

The more I read, the more I felt drawn to investigate and see what benefits there might be in it.

I found a practitioner in London and for several months followed a course of treatment with him.

On a body level, Ayurveda diagnosis demonstrated vastly more acuity than western medicine using the skills of the practitioner to diagnose the *patient* and not merely as a body having *symptoms* then investigated using complex technology subsequently decoded by someone with as much technological expertise as clinical knowledge.

A good example being a case the doctor who treated me – also trained in western and Ayurvedic medicine – telling me of someone whose pulse he took using the Ayurvedic system and told the patient he detected a treatable liver condition. The patient decided to get a second, conventional, western opinion from a close relative and qualified doctor. Which was to say there was nothing wrong with the liver, and there it lapsed. Until three years later, the same person returned to the Ayurvedic doctor saying there was now an abscess on the liver and asking what he could do. The answer being it was up to western medicine to cure the problem as it had progressed too far.

Direct benefit from the doctor's knowledge came immediately. I had been bothered by an itching rash on my feet on the upper side just back from my toes. I thought it was some kind of fungal infection and used a foot bath of diluted bleach, which did not impress the doctor. Taking one look he told me to dose myself with castor oil to clear out all the toxins in my system that had sunk – like mud in water – to the lowest point in my body.

Swallowing this awful liquid, its consequences soon 'cleared' my system – and with it very quickly after went the itching rash. The itching ceasing almost immediately. It was a valuable lesson as later events demonstrated. It also became clear, though it took a long time to dawn, 'Gout' one of the transitory salesmen in the office had suffered from – one foot being so painful he couldn't put a sock on never mind his shoe, one Monday morning – was in reality the poisoning of his system with alcohol he had consumed over the weekend. By the time I realised what the problem and its cure was he had departed anyway.

Over months I followed the doctor's treatments; a combination of 'Marma'/Acupuncture – being also trained in the Indian (Marmapuncture) as well as Chinese methods of applying needles to the energy 'meridians' in the body to adjust and reorder energy flow. Massage and steam baths using spices – principally cinnamon by the smell – to aid healing processes also featured.

Sitting, body enclosed in the cabinet, my head protruding out the top I felt a bit like a broiler chicken that didn't quite fit in the pot.

The massage and steam baths I enjoyed and found very soothing. Being stuck with needles certainly produced effects in my body and also as days went by afterwards, their effects deepened on to an emotional and finally even perhaps a spiritual level, but having also had acupuncture before, I felt increasingly it moved energy around but it didn't deal with root causes.

After a number of needle sessions over months, I suddenly felt extremely sensitive, almost with flu symptoms. On my next visit some days later the doctor took my Ayurvedic pulse, and said my energies – all three major Ayurvedic body energy definitions – had collapsed.

I was not surprised. Instinctively, although I could not say at the time, in retrospect it felt like sweeping energy around like dust. The 'dust'/energy being 'swept' around into different piles but ultimately it did not address underlying root causes. The energy was *not* being cleared out – merely relocated.

The longer I considered it in retrospect, the more convinced I became there was a very big hole in the completeness of Ayurveda. Following my own long established practice of allowing my body to tell me what *it* needed to do, rather than using my – or someone else's 'head' – to decide what I or they *thought*.

Consequently it took me a long time – probably three years – before I had worked through and released enough blocked and sublimated/repressed emotional energy, before my body began to 'unwind'.

Simply said, Ayurveda had no vocabulary for dealing with clamped emotional energy unfailingly shows in the physical body as clamped musculature.

Wilhelm Reich's work – and all those who can trace their 'pedigree' back to him – showed the unchallengeable relationship between rigidity in bodies reflecting rigid suppression of emotional energy in humans. But whether it is a litany and incantation repeated by countless millions makes no difference one way or another. Experience of 'doing it' for myself over many thousands of hours spanning four decades, but fundamentally, of having *lived it* continuously – minute by minute – since I began, means knowledge and authority comes from inner being. The experience and perceptions of others can be extremely useful but no substitute for one's own.

Other people's knowledge is borrowed; ours we own.

Yet even this is not enough, for unless the light of self-awareness illuminates our way it is still like finding our way in the dark.

My own experience right from the beginning of my efforts to clear my own massive burden of unresolved, unexpressed, un-integrated emotional history unfailingly; with no exceptions, has demonstrated the inviolable rule; to release blocked emotional energy is to release physical body energy. Conversely; to manipulate the body's physical energy is to manipulate emotional energy. Continuing to suppress emotional energy and pretend there is no link between the two, changes nothing.

Having repeated needle treatments 'sweeping' energy around inside me created uproar until my whole system went into 'nuclear' shutdown. Because the energy liberated had no channel of release and expression. Or more precisely the channel was far too restricted; I wasn't putting in enough dedicated effort to keep up with what was a deluge of energy the needles had stirred up in my body and being.

Once again in even longer retrospect; over the forty years of releasing and integrating the unimaginable amount of blocked emotional energy and history I carried within me, I am awed utterly beyond expressing, by the staggering capacity nature designs into all its creations – including humans – to 'fail safe'. And in spite of catastrophic injury or failure, to continue to function at a level besides which all the world's most complex failsafe systems combined into one seem as crude as a sledgehammer to maintain the workings of a delicate watch.

Consequently, the sledge-hammering my own being received from repeated Chernobyl events with energy-frigging needles, gracefully shut 'the system' – me – down, to still be able to function more or less as needed.

Which was crucial at the time, playing as I was, a prominent part manning a trade stand at a high profile exhibition.

What is even more incomprehensible about nature's ability to sustain *all* life at the highest possible level no matter what, is that it only began to dawn after a great deal of work to clear the consequences of my inner world energies having been 'adjusted' with sledgehammers – needles, just how much energy had been unleashed with nowhere to go, until much of it was released and resolved.

Although I have lost count of the number of times I have explained 'doing what my body told me' rather than doing what I 'thought my body needed', means, it is my constant experience people respond with vacant-eyed blank incomprehension. And perhaps with fear in their eyes, when I use these words.

Our culture has so comprehensively alienated us from a clear sense of anything other than intellectually centred understanding, that although it is a natural, indeed essential faculty, to have an open dialogue with our bodies, *and consequently our inner being,* the majority would find communication with aliens from a distant planet easier.

The inescapable corollary being we become prone to all the conditions, complaints and diseases which bedevil western culture.

Our bodies are inextricably linked to the wisdom of that part of us which our culture turns into a vast landfill rubbish tip at best or festering midden at worst; our sub/inner conscious. To know what your body is telling you it needs is to be in direct communication with your own inner being.

One of the most profound examples of this was, again as previously related, the work colleague who I got to lay on the mattress I had in my little therapy room in my equally small home.

I gently encouraged him to lay and see what came to mind or anything his body felt like doing without intellectually judging and interfering.

After a short while, not more than a few minutes – probably less than five – a tremor began in his left foot and lower leg. I suggested he let this happen without trying in any way to control it.

It developed until his complete leg twitched in a reflexive kicking motion and steadily involved more and more of his body until he was thrashing from head to foot. He gyrated from side to side with limbs and head flailing. His head moved so quickly the flesh of his cheeks and mouth were like a dog shaking its body to throw water out of its coat. His facial skin lagged behind his head movements and saliva was even thrown from his mouth.

JOURNEY OF A LIFETIME

The trashing rose to a climax and died away again to the gentle foot twitching, repeating the cycle a number of times until his body exhausted its need for that occasion. After which, some minutes later, rising to his feet following this powerful catharsis, he expressed relief after an hour, feeling drained, looking tired and his face noticeably less strained.

Knowing the immense pressure he was under to develop a complex, technical, systems software course, and had been for months, I was not at all surprised.

It was an almost universal departmental joke at work about the fear people felt having to teach a new course, or begin teaching an existing one, by saying it was best to avoid the toilets on a Monday morning as the smell indicated the state of those teaching. The word 'fear' was never used; neither was it needed. Everyone knew precisely what drove this abdominal torment.

He knew only too well what it was like to suffer in this way; the load on him reduced his digestive system to near chaos. He looked pale and stressed, and needed to use my toilet before we began.

This process repeated exactly the same for three more sessions; the last so climactically gyrating at one instant – still laying horizontal – his body actually lost contact with the mattress and had I been quick enough, I could have put a hand between him and it; touching neither.

Trusting my own inner processes, I likewise trusted his, but the power of his movements rose to such a crescendo, I almost intervened – or interfered – but managed to refrain and a few seconds later it passed and quickly died away, and for the first time in four one-hour sessions he lay completely motionless.

Eventually rising – with difficulty – to his feet, looking utterly spent; he shook his head in disbelief and simply said, "I feel absolutely pole-axed." And he looked it. His face was pale and blotchy, but the immense amount of stress had completely gone. Likewise his body had lost its wooden rigidity.

It took quite a considerable time for complete understanding of what I witnessed and its later ramifications to fully form and settle in my mind, but I have never experienced such a colossal amount of body-sublimated fear being released by anyone before or since.

And exactly like my own experience, it was the instinctual need and means of freeing his body from the immense crushing load on him.

The metaphor previously used of a giant elastic band having been tensioned and wound until near breaking point, then suddenly released is a very apt one.

In the days succeeding, his digestive system regained its normal function, as he made a point of telling me with his rapier, impish humour concerning toilets and Monday mornings.

Perhaps finally it may be clear from this, what the words 'doing what my body needed to do' really mean.

Though in my direct experience people will still deliberately confuse this, because if they let the message connect with their inner consciousness it would mean allowing their bodies to do what they have been prevented from doing all their lives until then. At this point fear and panic usually intervene; however much suppressed and denied, as I have observed times beyond numbering.

Choice, it should be remembered, still operates. The human form is not made like a giant toilet cistern with a flushing handle on the side that once used we have no control over, and become an empty husk with nothing left inside. Or reduced to an incoherent, gibbering pool of lard.

The human organism is self-regulating, self-limiting, self-protecting, righting, and self-healing to an extent incomparably greater – as already intimated – than all the 'system protection' and 'failsafe' mechanisms ever invented all rolled together in one.

JOURNEY OF A LIFETIME

Only when intellect begins interfering with inappropriate judgements do problems occur. Our bodies know exactly what and how much they wish to express and communicate. As soon as 'I think' enters the scene, trouble invariably follows. Bodies do not think; they *know*. As does the subconscious to which they link.

The only aspect in question is the culturally instilled lack of self-belief and consequently confidence that freezes so many before they have made the first step along the road of taking back control of their own bodies, concomitantly their own lives, for themselves.

Finally, although for the purposes of illustration I have recapitulated a particular event, humans are not about isolated events; they are about the continuum of the person's life. Once again, as our society is utterly dominated by the intellect – which deals with discrete finite entities; events, facts, logic, ideas, reasons, judgements – life is looked upon from the same perspective, and 'things happen by chance', something was 'just a coincidence' or a 'completely random unrelated event'.

Once inner consciousness attains its rightful place, as our true seat of wisdom, and intellect is pushed off its tyrant's throne to become a wise adviser, a coherent picture emerges that is the difference between treating life in a doll's house as immutable reality, and living in the real world – as part of the cosmos.

As a second year drew to a close and 1997 appeared on the calendar, at work I felt a change in the corporate atmosphere. I had a growing feeling all was not well, and felt there were changes coming and borrowing the words of a Bob Dylan song, 'The Times They Are A Changing', I emailed my perceptions to another colleague and friend.

Another change had also taken place; I replaced my erstwhile brand new car from a couple of years previously, more because I could than any need to replace it. The consequences of which were far beyond any thoughts I had at the time. As will shortly become clear.

My work continued and the relentless pressure of making calls and keeping very detailed logs of every call and its content paid dividends and I made steadily more contacts and inroads into some of the largest legal practices in Britain, Europe and even the world.

Which the Commercial Director came to rely on completely for his own introduction to the practice and IT Manager I arranged for him to meet.

It reflected not only two years of constant and consistent work, and growing experience but inner confidence; not only from growing knowledge of the work itself, but of all my efforts in clearing myself.

Nothing magically changed – far from it – I still had far too little energy and the demands of my work were the same; the need to relate on a human and technical level with IT management who suffered fools for less than ten seconds and expected to talk on their level without explanation for not a lot longer, unless I could create some spark of interest to fan into an expanding glow. Steadily if slowly I worked through the back log of history and fading memory of my marriage, ended more than a year previously. As this progressed it is clear now – but a lot less then – what pressed for expression from within also changed.

Healing of recent hurts and history began to shift into the pattern of deeper, older history; themes familiar from years before pushed to deeper recesses by more pressing needs came back into focus, though the changing emphasis was much more something I did than which occupied conscious awareness. If it did at all as it was happening.

Fate's 'Sat Nav'

It had been my growing intention for some time, to move home. Having begun a new relationship some time before, I grew impatient to part company with the desk at which I had sat for so long. Not least I knew I had to find some way of lightening the load of the daily toil taking so much of my energy and was undeniably wearing me down slowly but surely.

My partner having moved down to the South Coast and countryside I knew well, I began looking for somewhere to live in the same area. Once found, the laborious process all too familiar over the previous decade or so began again, but things seemed to click into place and fate opened doors for me.

In particular one door without which a subsequent one would have been slammed with complete finality in my face.

One bright sunny morning I was following the road to work winding along a route I travelled countless times before.

A Citroen car following me quite close behind as I approached a shallow bend in the road obscured by trees.

Entering this, in sheer horror I suddenly came face to face with an articulated juggernaut. It wasn't straightening out the bend a little and cutting the central white line, or even moderately over into my lane. It *totally* filled my view and blocked my way.

Steering completely on to the grass verge, I stamped on the brakes as hard as I could – and because they were antilock ones in this new car, my previous one had lacked – the pedal vibrated under my foot like a hammer drill, stopping the wheels locking. The car responded; the rear end snaking slightly towards the line of massive lorry wheels. Without antilock, it and I would have gone straight under them as the back end would have swung sideways trying to overtake the front wheels. As this nightmare began I glanced fleetingly in my mirror to see a great cloud of dust, leaves, grass and twigs enveloping my Citroen travelling companion.

With yawning laziness the white bars of the lorry's front grill began veering right with agonising slowness, like a huge open-mouthed shark diverting its attack. I steered further to my left, conscious of a culvert parapet I had to miss or impale the car on its steel tube railings and end up in a ditch the other side of them.

For what seemed eternity, huge wheels the same height as my seated position in my car went by in an endless stream, just beyond the end of my wing mirror and suddenly were gone.

Stopping a few yards further on, the Citroen driver made a comment about it being 'very close'. Which wasn't quite what I called it!

Looking at the left side of my front bumper a black line showed where all the paint had been ground off rubbing hard along the culvert parapet piping. But for which I would have been in the ditch the other side of it. Apart from that and a stress headache I drove on to work.

Fate, it appeared, had whispered in my ear the few months previously to change my car and replace it with one having antilock brakes.

It immediately brought into mind a series of episodes many years before; during a period I was stretched to the limit and beyond, working and studying so hard I reached a stage waking in the early hours, my head filled with a clamouring cacophony of computer hardware technicalities I was teaching; maths and electronics. The latter two from night school, even with my eyes open the uproar continued unabated.

During a period of a year or more I was hit six times in my car – all but the last when it was stationary – and all except the last occasion were insignificant or largely superficial. The final episode being hit from behind; rebounding off a crash barrier, turning over and spinning like a top upside down on the opposite side of a dual carriageway, petrol pouring out of the tank.

After the last occasion fate having intervened to prevent me becoming a 'pinball' cannoned into by oncoming cars. From 1971 until late 1974 I did without one.

These episodes stayed in my memory; something about them reverberated in my mind; was there a pattern? I felt somehow there might be, but all of it remained unresolved for many years.

Cars quite often appeared in my dreams, and usually significant ones – even if I was incapable of grasping the symbolism, or even that they *were* significant. Until recent times.

Pondering many times over these events, I realised a considerable amount of my waking hours over the years were spent driving. The words fitting this seemed to be cars were a metaphor for my life. Finally like seeing how a few previously meaningless jigsaw puzzle pieces related, words began to form. Realisation dawning; journeying far, over long hours and many years, it was as if I had lived my life in cars; or a considerable portion in them.

With a satisfying precision words suddenly locked together forming a phrase and metaphor; a car was the *vehicle of my life.*

I began seeing more of these, until then, inexplicable 'unrelated' 'pieces'.

If a car was a metaphor for my life, what about the metaphorical *road* of my life I was driving it on? Other puzzle pieces began to feel as if they fitted with those already 'snapped' into place. Still pondering I wondered what the connection was between vehicle, road and events of my life at the time?

The inescapable evidence was, several times I – and consequently my car – had been either very gently shunted, hit a glancing blow, attempts made to baulk my way; backed into, or the two most serious and potentially fatal events; either knocked clean from my intended progress, and lastly simply squashed flat; extirpated under rows of a forty-ton juggernaut's great wheels.

There was a clear trend in the first series, from minutely trivial to death confronting, and one catastrophic millimetrically avoided fatal event for the last one.

The fact I had come out of *all* these events without so much as a scratch – even if my shoes had fallen off whilst gyrating around in my car on the roof on the one occasion (fear shrinks the feet) – said something about me/*the vehicle-of-my-life,* and the *road-of-my-life* I was on.

The word puzzle pieces took a little longer to slot together, but writing them down on paper after a couple or so attempts the picture began satisfyingly to emerge.

If the road of my life I was travelling on in my vehicle of life was one I was doing damage to myself pursuing – existing in a state of great intellectually overloaded stress – then 'something' was trying to get the message through to me that I should either take myself off this road of life I was doing deep damage to my vehicle-of-life on (myself), *or get knocked off it completely if I refused to heed this warning from my sub/inner conscious*. The more I delayed doing it the more urgent the warning(s) became. The last occasion being a 'do it *now*' there will be *no* further warnings event.

Fortunately after the first series of warnings I had taken myself – quite literally – as well as metaphorically off that particular 'road of my life', and after the second I moved house and ceased the work steadily grinding me into the ground – as had so nearly the phalanx of wheels; not just one, but to make absolutely certain I got the message *a whole line of them*, all equally fatal in their potential. Or it could be viewed as separate warnings all being delivered at the same time. Either way the message was starkly clear.

Yet again all those of a conventional 'two dimensional' westernised intellectually-dominated mentality and disposition will likely mutter; what utter rubbish! Purely a series of random coincidences – no relationship to each other, and sundry other observations lacking completely in any contact with the fourth dimension; that of the sub/inner conscious mind and its inexpressible power to create in our outer world the allegories, lessons, warnings and even catastrophic events, we are meant to heed. And ignore to our disadvantage, injury and even annihilation, and consequently suffer misfortune, 'accidents' and even death through ignoring inner wisdom our completely crazy culture denies us, and of the means to read and act upon for our own self-preservation and good fortune.

Carl Jung clearly demonstrated this in his work giving an example in his book *Man And His Symbols* of a mountaineer who had a particular image in his mind. He warned the man, saying he needed to unlock what it meant for himself otherwise there could be fatal consequences if he ignored it.

The essence of which was climbing mountains were a symbolic way of escaping the tangle of the shady dealings he was entangled with in his day-to-day activities – literally getting above himself – indulging in dangerous climbs and in one dream image, stepping off into space from a mountain top.

Jung sternly warned him if he did not do something about his life it would have very serious consequences; impressing upon the man if he did nothing, the dream was a death warning.

Six months later a fellow mountaineer on a climb with the man witnessed him just step off the mountain into space and fall to his death as if in a dream-like state, and taking another man roped to him.

It is a crowning irony our 'sophisticated' society is incapable of acting on its own inner wisdom; and worse; deliberately trashing it, and why tribal/native/aboriginal societies find western mentality 'civilisations' so profoundly dysfunctional in being equally blind to the infallibly sound advice and warning messages the inner world presents the whole time, which they unfailingly heed for their protection, nurture and good 'fortune'.

And westernised man in his intellectual stupor patronises and treats as primitive ignorance and superstition.

A final anecdotal example I recall being one the Native American gave, whose workshop I once attended. He was making the point I have been making – yet again – above.

He told the elegantly simple story of a group of Indians who lived in a particular location (in California) and in proximity to westernised Americans. One day, to the surprise of neighbours they packed up and left saying the river was coming, or words to that effect. The ordinary Americans scoffed at them laughing it off as just another of their dopey Indian stories; there was no river and never had been.

Until weeks later when a dam burst and the raging torrent took its course right through the district the Indians previously abandoned and swept away all in its path – including those who sneered at the Indians.

Blind intellect is *such* a wonderful asset.

Without doubt there would have been those amongst the remaining residents who had warning dreams of what was to come. But in the unlikely event they actually recalled them, they would have dismissed them, or not had the faintest notion what their dream meant anyway.

Being intellectually clever – and dead, or injured and homeless – such a great asset also.

Dreamtime

To get some respite from my work, clear my head and literally as well as figuratively get my feet on the ground, after my morning diet of phone work, I made a habit of walking around town. Anywhere, to regain a sense of normality so my head felt connected with the rest of my body and not some pressure vessel sitting on my shoulders. Books always holding an attraction for me, my wanderings quite often ended up in a local book shop. I knew all the places where I might find pleasant distraction for a while.

Returning to one with the odd interesting title from time to time, one lunch hour a book's cover drew me to it. There was a picture of Ayers Rock – or Uluru – the Aboriginal name for this now, and to them, sacred site and naval of their world. Or rather there were two pictures of it; one upright and the other joined to it below – a mirror image – upside down.

I noticed it before, passing it by, but finally, having spent six months in this vast flat continent 'down under' as Australia is often referred to, I succumbed to the beckoning words of its title, *Mutant Message Down Under* by an American Doctor named Marlo Morgan.

To see if it held anything that might speak to me, opening the book at a random page I began to read.

In seconds, I was there with this lady on 'walkabout' in the blistering – quite literally for her – burning barren wilderness of Australia's outback. Not least, for her feet as her shoes and all her clothes had been taken from her. She had been given a simple shapeless robe to wear and all her best clothes burned!

It instantly gripped me because of an event many years before.

At Christmas time 1963 the papers were full of an unfolding story of an English migrant family who decided to leave Adelaide and seek better fortune elsewhere.

Their journey had taken them North, up the Birdsville track, into Australia's most harshly unforgiving interior. At first only brief details were announced on the news; how a broken down car had been found on this deserted unmade track with a note stuck under the windscreen wiper saying, 'Gone to get help'. It did not seem clear where they had gone, but a family of five had left the car and tried to walk to the nearest civilisation twenty miles back from where it had refused to go any further. Then the awful truth became emblazoned across all the British press. The family, having ignored the first principles of bush and outback survival – having left their vehicle – were found under a Coolabah tree all dead from dehydration in the furnace heat – at the full height of the Australian summer at Christmas time – Father, Mother and two sons. The elder third son being found half a mile further on, having crawled on all fours in his desperate quest to find water, his final act being to dig a poignant depression in the ground with his bare hands before he died in the relentless broiling desert, as the sun baked him to a crisp in one of the hottest deserts in the world. Temperatures rising to over 130° Fahrenheit/60°C in this brick oven.

Reading with detached interest, suddenly it felt as if I had been hit with a red hot brick of horror and choking sadness. Even now it is like swallowing one.

The words leapt off the news print column. I read of the Page family; Father, Mother and three sons; Douglas, Gordon and Robert. Or Bobby as I had known him had all been found by a tracker.

I knew 'Ernie' Page quite well – a good hearted man, though one whose feet were not always firmly on the ground; well meaning but more worldly wisdom would have made all the difference to him – and his family.

In those days the Birdsville track was extremely rough and unmade. Even fifty years later, a four wheel drive, high ground clearance vehicle *must* be used, and water, food and spares taken. Ernie with all his family had set out in an ordinary car (and knowing Ernie it would have been one that had known other owners) and without these essentials he was not just courting disaster but issuing an order to share their journey.

This is in no way to point a critical finger at Ernie Page. As a child I felt – though I could not clearly say why then – when he spoke to my engineer Uncle whom I lived with, he did so submissively. My Uncle had a formidably sharp intellect and spoke to him with brusque authority. There was a pleading innocence in Ernie as well as easily triggered anger for his family, and I related to him more as an equal than as an adult. In hindsight one can only wonder what punishments of body and mind he endured as a child to stunt his perceptions; without doubt, from the shape of his head it had undergone considerable compression during birth which meant he already carried an invisible burden to which others had been added later, affecting him emotionally, mentally, and stunting his adult authority. On to which my Uncle raised small wheals of further suffering on Ernie's invisible scars of sublimated inhumanity.

Bobby had been the one – same age as myself – who crawled the half mile further before he too finally gave up the ghost. The family lived next door and Bobby was my best friend as young boys together and at school, before I moved and they later emigrated.

Having gone to Australia myself I knew from stories I was told, its deserts were relentless killers to anyone who went unprepared – and even those who were. Or at least any white man.

I stood reading the book, about this lady who – involuntarily – had gone with a small tribal group on walkabout, her tale of her time with them and all she learned of their ways and their total reliance on their extraordinary powers. How they found food and water unerringly and survived where no other westernised human would dare go; and do it with nothing other than what they could carry in their hands. Or even nothing at all, relying only on what they found; sticks, stones; bits of shell to use as tools.

Their truly incredible skill in healing serious injuries and other conditions; ability to communicate with each other without words and over any distance – near or far.

I was mesmerised by the tale told very simply with few words; the American propensity of never using one word where fifty will do, as someone once acerbically observed, completely absent. It came across with a clear ring of simplicity born of complete conviction – in spite of others who called it fabrication and worse – I felt it spoke from the heart. It certainly spoke to mine.

The essence of her story being shock; appalled seeing young Aborigines stoned out of their minds from glue sniffing, or dead from it, having left their own culture behind and entered the westernised city nightmare. More or less dismissed as mindless 'Abos' by nearly everybody; including colleagues she otherwise found caring. Completely dispossessed within themselves from their own culture's inner wisdom and equally so in their outer; adrift in an alien maze.

Dr Morgan, whose function was health education programmes, created a business so these young people helped themselves to lift their lives out of the deepening chasm of inevitability into which they otherwise sank.

It succeeded far beyond her expectations. Not only was the company financially successful, but she quickly saw how these people worked together was completely different from western mentality. A deep respect for their workmates as humans transcended anything to do with who did what. He who swept the floor and cleaned up was equal with those directly involved in making or selling the products.

In short, *people* came far above what they did. There was no 'pecking order' or rank hierarchy. Equality of shared humanity was the sole *raison d'être*.

Out of the blue an invitation came wishing to give her an 'award' for what she had done for these native Australians.

The 'award' was for her to ineluctably learn for herself the functioning of humans who saw themselves as inseparable from nature, all life, and the Great Mother's nurturing. To show her the true human faculties and abilities western culture has lost in its dependence on intellect centred 'knowledge'. The total lack of their continuum in western 'civilisation' and consequential rapacious devouring of earth's abundance having lost its connection to its Great Mother.

In common with other native cultures the lessons presented to her were by example and living it; no lecturing, dogmas or overbearing superiority.

For me the story's economy of expression spoke its depth of knowledge, for in complete understanding, unfailingly, simplicity *always* transcends complexity. Demonstrating the meaning of the words; 'deceptively simple'.

It especially struck a resounding chord after the dumbfounding revelation I experienced of how invisible influences steered me unerringly into my Uncle Art's field of influence, to my own oasis of healing knowledge.

Just like the ability of the Aborigines to communicate regardless of distance I had been 'magnetised' into Art's invisible field of influence. The world of unseen powers connecting together staggeringly improbable events for me without which I would, with total certainty, not survived.

It was as if I was taken through the life-sapping desert of my own existence by an invisible guiding presence and delivered safely into lands of rejuvenation and transcendence.

Moreover the message of the book could not be more apposite to all this book is ultimately about; how westernised man is a dysfunctional sub-species; a 'mutant' – upside down as in the mirror image on the book's front page, in fact completely unable to function as proper humans – as this Aboriginal tribe did – and *should* function having a full, direct and profound connection with what we label as the 'subconscious' but which in its intended functioning is the *true seat of consciousness.* Not the pathetic, stunted two-dimensional intellect so worshipped as the *only* real 'religion' by westernised culture to its ultimate confounding.

We are far down the steepening slope of self-destruction from which there is no way back unless fundamental change occurs to begin treating our real seat of wisdom with respect, as a real resource and not as a mixture of vast rubbish pit and prison. Instead of worshipping the self-deluding cacophony of 'noise' that is the intellect's specious 'understanding' of all it pretends to know.

The pithy mythical anecdote of Aristotle's encounter with Heraclitus cannot be bettered in its illustration of the difference between real and delusional wisdom. A view buttressed by Robert Pirsig's fascinating book, *Zen And The Art of Motor Cycle Maintenance*. Not least in that the book charts the author's journey into his own inner being and consciousness. Himself becoming a Heraclitus figure clashing with the devious labyrinthine mental contortions of Aristotle he studied. And I owned the same motor cycle as him.

In every way the Pages' journey into oblivion is an exact microcosm of where our mechanistic culture is headed because of our inability to read the signs our inner wisdom constantly reflects back in our *outer world* and prepare properly for our journey into the future on this planet we continue to treat as a treasure-house trash-heap and not a temple-home of residence.

Having stood self-consciously motionless in the bookshop devouring it over a number of lunch hours, I bought *Mutant Message* and devoured it again; this time from beginning to end; twice over.

I related directly to much of the learning and lessons described by Marlo Morgan. The energy given off by plants detectable as a sensation in the hand; the energy of different places and other aspects she mentioned. In any case from an early teenager I taught myself and could divine water – just as my father had – and equally as he had showed someone; my sceptic Aunt – and mentor – in that instance, it wasn't nonsense. As I also did with a non-believer putting my hands over his as they held the forks of a hazel stick with the single limb pointing horizontally forward. As we walked towards an area where I found water, the person felt the stick twisting in his grasp and pulling down towards the ground. When I let go, the sensations disappeared, returning as I replaced my hands again. Slightly unnerved by the sensations he experienced under my influence, his scepticism instantly evaporated.

Decades before immersing – or drowning myself – in sales, marketing, telemarketing and all things inextricably bound up with the dreaded bane of many salesmen's life; cold calling, at that stage still attempting to crush myself under the intellectual load of software systems I taught, I learned on my own how to feel energy flooding off trees, not only experiencing sensations in my hands but as if invisible cobwebs were settling on my face. Also Ley Lines; lines of energy on the earth's surface which ancient tracks followed and which the Romans then used to make their straight roads along.

The most powerful of which is the one running from St Michael's Mount in Cornwall to Bury St Edmunds in Suffolk (also known as the Mary and Michael line) and runs through many well known ancient sites and is the origin of the 'A30' road route.

It also runs through Glastonbury Abbey in Somerset, where I discovered walking out on a raised walkway from the side of the knave to its centre, it felt as if I was being bored through with the pressure of the energy in my back and chest.

Consequently I knew Marlo Morgan was telling the truth about her experiences and how she sensed energy once she stopped using her 'head' and used her body's inner wisdom, to do it under the guidance of her teachers.

It was not surprising then, the work I did was steadily grinding me down under the intellectual load it imposed, causing a steadily increasing imbalance and deep conflict between intellect and creative, intuitional energies, suppressing these and why it had a pronounced and growing effect on me physically. Just as when in previous years I had been completely 'submerged' in hardware and software, not to mention studying as well, the effect over time was to create immense fatigue as my inner conflict steadily intensified.

Not forgetting the steady stream of warning 'accidents' telling me symbolically to get off the damaging road of life I was travelling on.

Having finally convinced even myself I was more than just 'intellect'; in fact first and foremost I wasn't predominantly intellectual at all, but as related; giving up the addiction to intellectual ego-status was far from easy to achieve. It was, after all, what I had been taught to believe was 'intelligence'.

Introducing Groundhog Day

As my intended house move progressed, in parallel with it another 'house move' took place. The company offices in which I spent more than two-and-a-half peaceful, cloistered years in my mental 'scriptorium' were vacated. Monastically, in the silence of completely empty offices save for the secretary, working day after day on my own in the same painstaking, detailed way monks bent over their labours; creating works of value from the most basic of materials with the skills they brought to bear, my own work was not dissimilar.

From my own skills and words I created detailed 'manuscripts' of calls I made and conversations I had, but the 'illuminated parchment' I produced was lit by the glow of an electronic screen on which my notes appeared in the sales administration system I used, as call followed call and their substance recorded.

The new offices were much smaller, lacking in any view other than other buildings across the street and if the window was opened traffic noise made conversations nearly, or actually impossible.

Moreover as de facto Office Manager it was left to me to decide what amongst all the old books, technical magazines and other obsolescent information from corners of the old offices, was kept.

An easy decision; symbolic of my leaving it all went.

Thankfully, as my own house move neared, I followed all the old information out the door, though my imminent departure caused distinct regret to both the Managing and the Commercial Director. They and the company as a whole had come to rely on the results I produced and it was clear all was far from well between the two principals; as I had felt and said months before.

Not for the first time – or the last – my own departure marked the demise of the company itself, in this instance within three weeks, although I had agreed to continue working part-time from my new home.

I seemed to be 'steered' in my life like a figure in early Keystone Cops, or Charlie Chaplin films, where people cheated death by a hair's breadth; driving cars crossing in front of speeding trains, falling out of aeroplanes, off buildings and even from the hands of a clock surviving miraculously unscathed. Not only in the car 'accidents' I had but also organisations I worked for. Time after time I left a job or company only for either – or both – to collapse or drastically change shortly; sometimes immediately, after.

Exactly as happened this time. I learned but for my efforts and the business I created the company would have collapsed at least a year-and-a-half before it did.

More recently, my ability to survive rekindles images from the film Groundhog Day, in which no matter what the news reporter played by Bill Murray does, he survives; repeating the same experiences time after time, the deadpan way past events are relived being extremely funny. The difference between me and all these outrageously implausible happenings being, these were real events in my life and no laughing matter. At least, not as they occurred. Yet again it had happened to me.

Perhaps as in 'Groundhog Day' I was destined, even doomed, to 'relive' the same process – if not the actual event – time after time until I learned from my mistakes and my approach to life. Perhaps even better if I use current tense; because until writing this I never really considered to what extent I have led a charmed life. The words of one clairvoyant who said with feeling years ago I had always been protected, now take on a different perspective.

JOURNEY OF A LIFETIME

Moving house exactly as Princess Diana's life was snuffed out, in the days following, it felt as though there was an indefinable change in the air; not only had I moved from familiar surroundings and predictable – if onerous – work and reliable income, to a new environment, but the deeply tragic events of the time added an altogether greater sense of uncertainty. Not simply for me; the atmosphere felt as if certainties taken for granted by everyone had been swept away forever.

Compounded as mentioned within three weeks by the company collapsing, I began working for nearly three years previously. It seemed ironic, having begun in the most tenuous of circumstances, rather than my services being dispensed with and the company continuing the reverse had occurred. The tail outlasting the dog.

Exactly as in 'Groundhog Day' I was living the same old situations all over again.

What I had taken as dependable was all swept away and the same old all too familiar uncertainties going back nearly a decade, once again went round and round in my mind like continuously revolving doors of fatalistic entrances and exits.

Again with the same old haphazard 'certainty' I found work within a few weeks; on the same old tenuous basis; using my skills sitting on the end of a phone to find new business for a company whom I had helped an employee of the now defunct one find a job in having rewritten his CV opening the door for him, and exactly as before; the person I had helped, in turn helped me.

Not only that but having begun working for the company, the person I found a job for in the defunct company, who opened the door for me, I successfully introduced to the new one!

The revolving doors of fate were more like a vortex in which disparate elements of chance were locked in a greater embrace of destiny.

Again, metaphorically as well as actually, I had to clear the undergrowth of my life; the garden of my new home resembled a rural wilderness. I enjoyed being out in the air removing entanglements of brambles and the previous owner's detritus; it was apparent though, I did not have a great deal of energy. Not surprising; I knew the work I'd done with my erstwhile company demanded a lot of stamina. Indeed, even just after I began, the Managing Director expressed concern I would 'burn out'. Fortunately for him and everyone else as well as myself I didn't, but there was a price to be paid which I well knew. But ironically, it was the company that burned out first!

Satisfying as hacking my way through the jungle alongside the boundary thicket – the 'hedge' – of my property was, I could feel my grip on the hook I used was not as strong as in former years and my arms tired more easily. Stamina was not what it had been either. Perhaps a sign of growing old(er), though deep within I didn't believe it and felt some concern that for all my efforts over many years to liberate my energy as I had done with great effect originally beginning more than twenty years before, other aspects of me were caught in the same circling whirlpool of fate.

Another physical symptom was equally apparent when digging. The sciatic region of my right thigh became painful feeling as if a muscle was really tight and tense, reminding me of a decade previously when I suffered a lot of pain in this region, finally curing it with an intuitive mixture of vitamins.

Taking a different approach, I began doing one or two simple yoga postures. The first with my hands on the floor and my arms straight, keeping my shoulders pushed up, with my legs straight out behind me, toes touching the floor.

I would let my body sag so my legs completely rested on the floor with my body still propped on my arms making a curve or arc. At least that was the intention. To begin with, as soon as I let my legs and lower body begin to dip down towards the floor my suspicions of a tense muscle in my right thigh/buttock area were confirmed with deep agony.

JOURNEY OF A LIFETIME

Over months of daily repetition I gradually got it to slacken until I could make this posture free of pain.

Though not mentioned often, my routine of working through tensions symbolising locked up energy in my body, I continued as I always had, if anything, following the end of my marriage, with increased frequency. It was not pleasant having my abdominal regions knotted in the hollow 'growling' ache I quite often – still – experienced. Or feeling, if I drank any alcohol, a most unpleasant rigidity in my body in latter years that was the price of my second marriage breakup, and the equally unwelcome sensation like the aftermath of being kicked in my lower back.

It took effort to break these rigidifying sensations, but to do so was a familiar and completely reliable process and by then one I had used for years and thousands of times.

To reiterate yet again; I did not enjoy having to roll a face flannel/cloth into a plug and stuff it in my mouth and throat, causing reflexive dry vomiting, but immediately or within seconds my gut-clenched hollow feeling would release. Moreover, increasingly with time, what once began leaning over the back of my car's front seat forcing it into my abdomen twenty years before and emitting a 'chuckle-sob' as the means of dissolving knots in this region, had completely changed. Originally it might have taken half, or a full hour to create relief. It became – as also explained many times – an explosive vomit which, if I took the plug out of my mouth, was a deafening roar. This is no exaggeration; the force was not simply muscular, there was an increasingly clearly identified emotion with it: fear, or so it seemed. The more deafening and explosive the sound, the quicker and more completely the floating, gut-knotting fear was released and pleasant relief radiated throughout my body from its centre.

Also to restate; I didn't care how many thousands of times I had to repeat the process – or if anything *tens* of thousands of times; I was content – not happy – but patient with myself, however long it took I knew my body had its own wisdom far surpassing anything the squawking 'chicken coop' in my head – my intellect – thought it had, *reality* was and is in my *physical self*; not what 'Aristotle' upon my shoulders incessantly pontificated.

This was not – and never has been the full picture of what it took; or may still take, to produce complete relief throughout my body and being. Allowing my body to express itself and unlock the energy stuffed into the subconscious 'junkyard' – as our intellect dominated culture treats this aspect of our real consciousness – *always* results in a harmonious release and integration of what has been deliberately dispossessed by interfering intellect, creating an equally unfailing transformation within.

Our body and the deep intelligence of which it is so ineffably a part, knows how to regulate and heal itself.

This, unerringly is my unfailing experience – with no exceptions – I have found and always followed.

When intellect is servant of this process, harmony follows. When it is master, we enter the world we have created.

I was and am, after all, not just an abdominal region or a collection of isolated elements held together as bits; flesh, bone and offal in a sack of skin. All that is me and the human form which I have and am, possesses a sublime completeness, integrity and elegance of function beside which all the inventions of man rolled into one are as clunking clockwork. Sadly our society with its deeply unbalanced view of itself as intellect in a body, has already long since reached the stage of treating what Great Nature endows humans – and all life – as a 'kit' of parts to be fiddled with, hacked about, filled full of poisons, electrocuted and organismically insulted as 'treatment' in the cruellest betrayal of what creation bestows.

One could easier press mountains of excrement into diamonds with a feather than create harmony in all life and this planet, worshipping 'intellect' as a deity of peerless perfection.

Yet this is what we are doing, and have been since the 'Aristotle' in us was given absolute licence to run amok.

As illustration of what is meant by the body's own intelligence, I have already given the examples of a 'bad back' I was privileged to bring about the resolution of. Also my work colleague's colossal release of fear and deep stress stored in his body when – completely independent of what he was thinking at the time, i.e., as he said; he could be thinking about the price of a bus ticket from home to Hammersmith – his body thrashed and gyrated from head to toe in a catharsis of demonic intensity, unbelievable but for the fact of witnessing it.

In an exactly similar way – if generally not as acutely focused as these examples – I have experienced exactly the same myself. Not once, ten, or a hundred, nor a thousand, but thousands of times over four decades.

Such is the unimaginable force of intellect-dominated indoctrination in our society I should perhaps write this in Mandarin Chinese because people have utterly no idea what body-centred intelligence means. If I try to explain, eyes glaze over, fill with fear and/or fear-impelled anger.

The simple fact is no amount of words substitutes for the experience of doing it; of working *with* our body and finding out what it wishes to express and allowing it to do so.

To repeat also; the human form does not incorporate an external flush handle in its design such that were it so operated it would cause a limitless 'flushing', leaving the person a drained husk like an empty chrysalis.

My work colleague's powerful catharsis I have explained before is an excellent example of the human organism's perfect self-regulation. His body and through it his inner conscious knew exactly what it wished to express, how to express it, how much at a time to express and did so, until finally satiated.

The work pressure he was put under was a very large straw to the camel's back, or put another way it was a slow trigger being pulled; what he released from within himself was energy – fear and immense tension – sublimated in his body over previous years of his life, not just the work pressure he was under for some months.

Exactly as has been and continues to be my own experience. Clearing out from our sub/inner conscious what our society teaches us to treat as a vast midden is not a one time (toilet) flushing event. It is more like archaeology; bringing to the surface and releasing from within the 'earth' what has been buried there. Depending how much has been buried affects how much effort it takes. Similarly it is a painstaking and methodical – no less repetitive – process. The more buried the more there is to deal with.

Just as bulldozers, mechanical diggers and road rollers are not used when dealing with layers of the past, using powerful drugs is equally inappropriate – and can be downright catastrophic.

These broadly split into two groups; the first, those that are designed to suppress symptoms – the ones produced by drug companies – curing nothing and walling up/blocking off manifestations of energy trying to find a way of being expressed and integrated by the sufferer. The second having two major subgroups; those that 'crowbar' off/neutralise the natural inhibitory chemistry of the brain – LSD and other natural and synthesised 'mind expanding' drugs – resulting in the brain being thrown – at worst – into the equivalent of a tropical typhoon/cyclone storm and attempting to reassert normality in the chaos. Also those drugs having the exact opposite effect that 'ice' out the brain's functioning, The difference between being the first generates a psychedelic 'trip', whilst the second 'chills out'. The resulting aftermath of the former being like a riot mixed with desperate attempts to quench runaway fires, and the latter generating exactly the same to reverse the sledgehammer suppression imposed on normal functioning.

JOURNEY OF A LIFETIME

No matter how one explains the healing process, what examples are given or descriptions used, concerning releasing and resolving the blocked energy of our *un*-resolved personal history it is not until one does it for oneself, gaining direct experience, that true knowledge is gained.

The intellect is full of recipes; the sub/inner conscious and all it connects with, is the pudding.

Groundhog Day Effect

Having moved home and changed my life I too might have *thought* I knew it all, but it was clear to me from what my body told me I was deluding myself. Symptoms I had lived with over years didn't magically resolve and disappear. And finding myself back in uncertain territory so far as work and income were concerned brought more abdominal symptoms of fear. Dealt with in the 'traditional' fashion.

Another factor being although I did phone work finding new business for a company, it was much more arm's length. I didn't sit at a desk in someone else's office, which meant I was not subject to the same pressures as previously.

Years before when I gave up lecturing, shortly after I changed jobs, like my colleague who released an immense amount of body energy and with it the stress and fear clamped in his musculature, I experienced a powerful releasing, though this was completely emotional – a back log of all that was 'flattened' in me under the massive weight of intellectual knowledge bearing down on me all the time.

Once this ceased, exactly as my colleague released his 'overload' on a body level I released mine in a powerful emotional outpouring. The end results being very similar; feeling completely drained, and physically and emotionally fragile for a while. Indeed, for me it took years to grow into the massive empty inner spaces I created in the one massive deluge of cathartic outpouring.

With my change of home and way of working, no doubt this was a factor, but there was no avalanche of releasing body or emotional energy. Because I wasn't punishingly stretching myself in opposite directions; intellectually in work and emotionally in clearing my own history and also damaging myself with Rolfing.

What previously had been worked through to completion had gone forever, just as the same bullet cannot be fired twice. Energy spent is energy spent. Period.

Being increasingly aware my upper body was more rigid told me there was something else to be dealt with but exactly what I did not know. Only by following what it showed me I needed to do would clear knowledge come of what the driving forces were buried even deeper within.

In any case this was something I lived with day by day so its presence and effects were not a sudden perception but something becoming more apparent over time. Or more accurately; only when enough blocked suppressed history and its energy was released and resolved do perceptions consciously register in my direct experience.

I continued releasing what pressed for expression but not as a regular routine. If my work was producing no results this often brought up fear – usually centred in familiar abdominal symptoms – and working at home I dealt with it as the need arose not having to stow it away until I was out of a company's premises. Which meant I returned to my little bedroom-cum-office feeling freer, enabling me to work better even if results were no different.

Frustration and anger were no strangers either! In less than three seconds of beginning a call it was clear from the tone of voice what kind of reception it would get. Neutral abruptness generally wasn't a problem. People I spoke to were busy and often called by several like myself during their working day.

What raised hackles was blind, ignorant antagonism at the other end. Though that too provided an opportunity to punch seven shades of frustration out of cushions and roar out its pent up fury – then go back to phoning again.

In this way time progressed but it did not take many months before what had been a very loose working relationship, for any ties to unwind, and I was back to where I had been four years before; only paid commission for the results I achieved.

Just as someone else found who later did the same job as myself for the same company working within their own offices, good prospects he created from his cold calls were simply ignored or trashed by incompetent follow up.

Which increasingly occurred until one day I went into my 'office' as usual and sat down at my desk, and began looking out of the windows each side of me facing towards the back and front of my house, and the greenery I devoured to sustain me whilst making innumerable calls. Unable to focus and finding it impossible to motivate myself to do anything, I gave up, went downstairs, sat in an armchair and it came to me I was certain what the problem was; the company had folded!

It was not quite the sudden death event it may appear.

Over months, people left or were sacked and even I had begun to finally trust what my instinct, intuition and just plain commonsense told me that all was increasingly unwell, and the end was not far distant.

Shortly before the final demise, browsing in a bookshop, I came across an 'I Ching' book; otherwise known as the *Book of Changes*. An inscrutable Chinese means, using 'hexagrams' – six layered symbols of long and short dashes one above the other which when set out and read according to the rules, are capable of predicting 'changes' or the future. At least, for those who understand how to use the system.

Curious to see what it might say about impending change, I opened the book at a random page and read the explanation of the Hexagrams displayed.

Sure enough – by 'coincidence' – it showed everything falling apart!

It would be laborious and extremely pedantic to mention the times and different events over the next two-and-a-half years where my – by then – time honoured tradition of stepping off one stepping stone either just before or just as it was sinking so far as source of work and income was concerned, but it happened a number of times and yet miraculously I stayed dry as the waters of the financial Red Sea closed behind me!

This parting of the waves, or using a previous metaphor; my 'Groundhog Day' existence where whatever 'precipice' of my working life I stepped off, surviving to repeat the process, no matter what, it also had a reverse side to it.

If I was infallibly protected, equally, at the same time I was also limited in my ability to earn.

Having been successful in selling a software system for managing an organisation's documents, which paid the bills for a few months, I found another and much larger prospect which would have kept me afloat for much longer and looked like it could become a good customer. Just as sales discussions were approaching a decision to spend £130,000 on the first phase of acquiring the system, a new Chief Executive was taken on who promptly called a halt on all new acquisitions! The Napoleon Hill effect had struck again!

It may be recalled, in his search, instigated originally by his employer Andrew Carnegie, the steel magnate, Hill found over the twenty years' research of whether certain principles of success existed, if deviated away from this task into other, initially successful ventures, everything eventually collapsed until he resumed his research and normality was once again restored. The same appeared to be true for me.

Provided I stuck faithfully to working through my life's history and its effects on me, reflected in my body and how energy was locked up within and clamped in inner being and muscles, Groundhog Day survival was guaranteed. But, if I so much as dared to make the accumulation of wealth my first priority in activities taking up a lot of my time, energy and mental focus, unfailingly 'fate' intervened; the brakes got slammed on in my vehicle-of-life and I had better heed getting off that particular road-of-life, or, as I had been shown with symbolic, terrifyingly stark warnings before, I should be prepared to get knocked off it – or completely flattened into it if I obstinately persisted!

The corollary being; like Napoleon Hill, I had/have a task to complete – in his case to show beyond question, success *did* have definite, quantifiable attributes not to be fiddled, faked or fudged – and I needed to pursue my own healing and inner development wherever it led me; no deviating into purely personal aspirations. Period!

A marathon gold medal – or goodnight!

Another metaphor I have coined which seems apt is I am shackled to a wagon on rails by very strong rubber reins. If I pull the wagon straight ahead on its intended track it follows my reins exerting a steady tension, but if I attempt to wander off to one side the further I stray the greater and greater the force pulling me back until I can no longer resist or I pull my wagon task-of-life off its rails at which point I get flattened by it.

For those who may still be sceptical or completely disbelieving at delusions I harbour about my 'Groundhog Day' existence, there were occasions when I had no idea where the money to pay the next month's bills was coming from, but each time something turned up and I managed to keep going.

As an example; one time to get away and have a break I went off to Le Mans as I did for a number of years to see the twenty-four hour race, having not the faintest idea where I was going to find more work; or money.

I came back to find my answering machine light blinking and a message from someone I didn't know and a company I'd never heard of leading to work that sustained me for six months. Later, with one foot over the financial cliff's edge, not having enough money to pay the next month's bills, a society I joined which ran a member's weekly subscription to the National Lottery, had quite a nice win – the first significant one ever – and my share meant paying my bills and a bit to spare!

Beginning All Over – Again!

By mid-1999 it was clear to me, however much I wished to pretend otherwise, my hands and arms did not have the energy in them they possessed before, and should have so far as I was concerned, and were not functioning properly; certainly nowhere near as they once did.

The previous year, my left shoulder had become very painful if I laid on my left side in bed. If I put my hands behind my back clasped together with the backs of them resting on the tops of my buttocks, pain in my left shoulder became intense.

If I sat and turned my head to the left for more than a minute or so that too felt extremely uncomfortable, creating a deep unfocused ache right up into my head.

However much work I might have done to free up my body by clearing blocked, clamped and suppressed energy deep within, I was – reluctantly – going backwards so far as having even the energy and suppleness of movement I possessed just a few years previously.

As so many times before, the wheel of fate turned and at the time of year when I originally began working with my body in September 1974 instead of against it as I had all my life until then. A work meeting took me back to Devon; I took advantage of the opportunity to visit places I got to know years before and a reawakening in me of the atmosphere and energy of countryside I came to love.

Visiting scenery in which I did so much work on a body and energy unblocking level back in 1978; a year of tumultuous effort and changes,

I sat in my car seeing familiar beautiful hillside landscapes, conscious so much had changed in my life since then and yet I seemed to be back where I was in those days and the powerfully autobiographical music of Gerry Rafferty.

'Baker Street', which then as now evokes an indefinable chasm of yearning. A haunted deep inner searching; reverberating, unresolved emotions in the combination of voice and musical sounds, so much a part of my life at the time as it was in his song and inner world. Its wailing guitar and musical inner screams of saxophone evoked a strange hidden magic and impenetrable gloom; full of ghouls, whispering formless demons, and deep fear.

It was painful to admit to myself I might have thought I had come so far from those days and all I struggled with in myself and consequently my life. Undeniably I had, but equally my body was telling me whatever I thought, reality was completely different; time had moved on, I had hacked my way through jungles of inescapable personal history alongside the main arterial road of my life and yet as I sat in my car, all around me were surroundings of familiarity and aching poignancy.

The more it all sank in the more it hurt and I cried, realising although my spiral of existence had taken a few upwards turns I was at exactly the same point at exactly the same time of year; the autumnal equinox, as I had been twenty-five years before in September 1974.

I had created changes within myself so far beyond any imagining as to be completely incomprehensible, but if anything I seemed even deeper in the jungle of ensnaring unresolved inner history, there was no other choice than to clear my way through before I was free to travel the arterial highway of my outer world.

This is more than just a metaphor. Years before in previously allowing my body and not my intellect to decide where I walked, I discovered a tendency to take the hard 'path' – in fact no path at all – and not unusually found myself heading for brambles and anything but an easy way forward, and once in a young conifer plantation so dense as to be nearly impossible to get between saplings. The experience got the message through I held this image of my path being a very difficult one, in some subconscious crevice, and finally 'earthed' its power after this event.

Whatever inner motives existed in me I might still have to uncover, one thing was patently obvious; I was going to have to work with my body a lot harder than I had ever done; not when I might 'think-decide' I needed to but pay much more attention to 'feel-decide' what my body was telling me it needed to express instead of overruling it with my 'head'/intellect.

'Thinking' I was in touch with what my body was telling me was fantasy. It was not easy to admit to myself this was so. I *thought* I knew it all but the training I received – just like everybody else in our western society and culture – was still not about to give up its hold without further struggle.

So I went back to doing and following what my body, my emotions, instincts and intuitions told me as I had a quarter of a century before.

To rub salt into the wound of self-realisation I had cut deeper into, a clairvoyant who gave useful advice whilst in trance before, told me I was too complicated in the way I had given healing to others in recent times and I needed to 'streamline' as she spoke it.

Also that 'David needed to start growing!' That *really* rubbed it in!

A deep anguish suffused me, my immediate response was, Christ almighty! I've only been doing it for twenty-five years! What *does* it take? Haven't I done enough already?

Clearly not; otherwise my body wouldn't have been seizing up, but I wasn't about to capitulate to whatever might be the cause. Giving up was not an option.

Following what my body told me was not and is not some muddle-minded swamp of sloshing emotions to wallow in and going nowhere. It is the process of being *aware* something does not feel right and whatever it might be, choosing to deal with it *as the opportunity arises*. During the day telephone work took priority over everything else and only if how I felt really interfered with talking sense and making the best contacts I could, would I stop and take a few minutes to release whatever was pushing for expression.

Not unusually I only discovered what needed to be dealt with once I'd begun, or what it began with; turning into something else.

As an example in 1998 when I found myself in 'commission only' territory again, paid purely for results I achieved on my own, it brought a lot of fear to the surface, sometimes affecting my balance and coordination as it had done more than a decade before having stepped out of the corporate cocoon. Finding myself expected to be a salesman, create prospects and sales single-handed from scratch, not having a clue how or where to begin.

The remedy was simple; I stumbled my way to the bathroom and sat enthroned, honking like a seal except much louder, stuffing a rolled up face flannel into my throat to produce this effect and break the very unpleasant clamping in my abdominal region, and doing it until I felt my body lose its rigidity and I regained my balance and composure. A few minutes, probably five or so, and I would go back to my cold clammy phone and make more sensible human-sounding cold calls.

At the other extreme if goaded past frustration into anger, cushions in the room I cleared for such activities, got a beating and I yelled blue murder muffling my noise in one, so the neighbours did not mistake it all for murder being committed. Once the initial overload was dealt with, it might transmute into hurt and futility and I ended up sobbing until it was dissipated and I went back to my work.

If it seems a deliberate, perhaps even cold bloodedly systematic process, it was. But like pressing a boil to clear it out I was content

– if that is the right word – to deal with my 'boils' within and let the process of my work 'squeeze' them to clear what I carried in me triggering fear, brittle, short temper, and whatever other emotions were linked to what had surfaced, like the conjurer pulling a sausage out of a hat – followed by a whole string of them connected to the first.

Equally coldblooded and deliberate, the wider intention in doing this was to begin tapping within myself what I had pushed deep within and in clamping the door to my subconscious firmly shut, I also clamped my body. Twenty-five years was sufficient time for the equation between the two halves to be joined by an equals sign: clamped/blocked sub/inner consciousness = clamped body energy and musculature.

No ifs, buts, talking around the point, conjecture, intellectual suppositions and other mental 'confetti shuffling'. The rule is inviolable.

As is 'therapy' not fully involving the body not being 'therapy' and unequivocally not permanent healing; words, someone else's methods; what Freud, Jung, Rogers, Reich, Lowen, and legions of others might have said, are sticking plasters for the Titanic. It is in 'listening' and becoming aware of what is carried in *ourselves* the key exists to unlocking, releasing, resolving and *integrating* into outer consciousness cause and effect.

There is *nothing* 'irrational' about the human form as superficial pronouncements on bizarre behaviour and inexplicable 'dis-ease' might insist. There are only buried decisions and the energy associated and locked up with them in order to live life as best we may and *in the absence of a better model*.

Answers may be instant or at the other extreme take a lifetime to discover. Whether real or not is infallibly demonstrated in the liberated flow of energies covering the complete spectrum of the human condition and not intellectual awareness and subscription to someone else's ideas.

A lifetime spent thrashing around, pouring out endless emotion, or talking endlessly for a planetary gold medal or any combination of these, cures nothing, *unless* accompanied by a high degree of *self-awareness*. Without this essential attribute it is exactly as the example already given; attempting to buy a ticket and having no idea of where one is intending to go.

My intended destination in following my own process was and is to release the rigidity and clamping of energy in my arms and upper body increasingly immobilising me. I did not need to know – as also explained before – every step of the way. What possessed me – and still does – was and is an unquenchable desire in releasing blocked consciousness and its energy, learning its driving forces and integrating the complete experience into outer consciousness, to arrive at a destination of freedom in body, mind and being.

Having made the decision to dedicate much more – and more consistent – effort to reversing and freeing my body from its invisible concrete sarcophagus, it was not many weeks spending time each day, before a focus began to form in my body.

It was frightening to feel my hands losing their strength but the deeper I went into exploring the cause releasing more and more energy the more pronounced the symptoms became.

There was one way to find out what the outcome was and that was to keep following my body's wisdom and instinct.

Allowing 'feel decide' and not 'think decide' to dictate what I did, thumping cushions in anger was the direction I was led. Simultaneously, what began as a kneeling process and banging my clenched fists on my cushions soon transmuted into an increasingly prone position until I was punching them stacked up against the wall in front of me. The more I did this the more it turned into absolute fury.

Still my hands did not improve until a few weeks into this routine I detected a flicker of change for the better.

Along with this at night I would wake in the early hours and a deep – initially nagging – pain made its presence increasingly clear.

Night after tiring night I got up, went into my other bedroom and thumped my way into my cushions. Awareness of what I was doing did not take introspection of *Sunday Times* crossword puzzle dimensions; it was painfully obvious I was back at a familiar closed door: my birth.

Indescribable utter fury at being thwarted and unable to progress forwards and out into the world. I knew from my mother I was born a week late.

The knowledge was becoming increasingly clear – not as an intellectual statement – but the burning pain in the tops of my shoulders and base of my neck and incandescent anger with which I tried to punch and push my way out ramming my head into the cushions in front of me, lying prone on the carpeted floor.

Night after night, session after session this alarm clock of pain woke me. Not slackening, but growing steadily in intensity until I awoke at night with a sensation as I gained consciousness, of thinking it was better. It wasn't. As wakefulness increased it became difficult to describe; it was so intense with an almost vibrating quality such was its power.

Weary beyond words at this endless night routine complementing my energy-draining day time phone work, nonetheless the stored outrage of needing to punch and head-push my way out continued unabated.

I noticed another developing trend. Having punched and pushed until I ran out of energy – which wasn't long, putting absolutely everything into the effort – it dawned on me one night, at this point I gave an involuntary shudder in and across my shoulders. In turn my sinuses would clear and mucus flooded out my nose.

I soon cottoned on to what my body was telling me/my head.

The key was when I gave this semi involuntary shudder or 'micro' shudder lasting barely a second or more, I felt relief.

Soon I modified my routine, punching and pushing until the micro-shudder occurred, repeating this usually three times after which I could get at least some reasonable rest and sleep.

This – although minor – was nonetheless a watershed. The energy in my hands and arms slowly, but steadily, increased and I knew I had passed a milestone.

It was utterly exhausting following this routine for nearly two months but I gained the absolute assurance I knew exactly what the process was about because I had worked though enough of the energy I had no other choice at birth than to sublimate and stow somewhere deep within me; my sub/inner conscious.

There are no intercoms or other natural aids to change the mother's disposition and muscles at the time.

There it had remained and been 'walled up' by the brain's staggering ability to sublimate and lock away the energy of events impossible to deal with in any other way at the time. And the consciousness determining the form and expression the energy takes.

But as good as this incomprehensible mechanism was and is, over decades the 'wall' began to crumble and the effects 'bleed' out into my body affecting my arms and hands.

Gradually over months the situation improved; energy not only improving in my upper body but throughout.

Miraculous it definitely was not. It was just a hard, repetitive diligent slog.

For all those who like fairy stories and happy endings, after this everything was fine, I had all the energy I wished for and was never troubled by anything again.

And if you believe this is how the human organism works, prepare to worship at a new altar of reality.

It was a single – if prolonged event – in a continuum of existence.

The human form – and indeed all nature – has the ability to sublimate and survive what would reduce the most robust machine ever made to an unrecognisable flattened wreck.

To repeat a cartoon image already used, the films of Sylvester the cat who survived endless improbable disastrous flattenings, miraculously regaining his full corporeal presence in a twinkling, is not unlike human's natural ability to recover from equally catastrophic inner flattenings apparently none the worse for the experience – outwardly at least.

But as the saying goes; nothing is for free. In surviving inner 'flattenings' there is a cost; overwhelming experiences that cannot be assimilated, their impact humanly 'processed' as they occur, the energy released and integrated on all levels, become embedded and remain; sublimated and held in the deeper regions of consciousness needing to be released and integrated. In humans as in the universe; energy does not disappear or cease to exist, it only changes form. Humans are no exception to the rule.

Put simply; happiness is processed instantly in bucketfuls; misery in thimbles, the rest set aside and stowed within until it can, with conscious effort, be expressed and integrated. If not dealt with, there it remains and its effects are sublimated in the body. Anyone who works with the body therapies soon finds this.

If the examples already given are not enough, perhaps a few more may help.

A case I know directly being a lady whose husband suffers from a long-term illness. She had some foot reflexology done and when the reflexologist pressed on a certain area of her foot she dissolved into floods of tears. The sadness and stress of living with what her husband suffered was something she pushed aside within in order to live her and their lives together, sharing the love they always had, but her body showed what she kept within herself.

I do not know what part of her foot produced this response because her husband didn't know either. But as one who has experienced foot reflex emotional responses, I would say with near absolute certainty hers was when the heart region was manipulated.

Sadly – and years after this was originally written – it transpires lung cancer was diagnosed. The left lung and heart being in very close proximity both actually and the reflexes on the left foot; the heart reflex being within the lung reflex area.

And just as my close relative's inflamed lungs once showed the massive imbalance created by crushing, enervating overwork, so this poor lady's lungs finally could not stand the immense strain in which she constantly existed and endured.

In Ayurvedic medicine, cause and effects on the lungs could not be more clearly correlated or demonstrated.

Which conventional western 'medicine' wouldn't come within a galaxy's width of understanding.

In my own experience, once when a friend manipulated my colonic region reflex – particularly what felt like the transverse colon, it not only had a powerful effect, it drove me straight out of my body.

I simply couldn't stay in my own skin. Paradoxically I was aware of my body but wherever I was it was *not* in my own skin.

It took at least two weeks to get back to earth – and in my own body again. Was I aware of exactly what was happening? Definitely not. Other things occupied my attention. A couple or so weeks later it felt as if I had been powerfully kicked in my abdomen and the familiar very unpleasant clamped gut sensation, as if someone had reached in, gripped and squeezed hard. What wasn't familiar was the strength of it. It took several short sessions with a rolled up 'plug' face cloth forcing reflexive dry vomiting, before the gut agony released and relief was gained. For the rest of the day I hardly moved from my armchair, feeling as if I'd been kicked in my abdomen by a horse.

Did I immediately connect the reflexology session, its overwhelming effect; the time taken for my body to get over the shock and for the manipulated area to respond? Absolutely not! If anything it took me months until I connected it all together.

If anyone still thinks this is whimsical coincidence, perhaps I should also say it reminded me of a reflexology session years before. That didn't get into my abdominal regions. I'm glad it didn't, because it sent me absolutely flying round the universe all night! I only came down to earth after the lady who did the manipulation grounded me again. Being clairvoyant, in holding my hands, she understood exactly how it felt and confirmed what I was feeling. My symptoms were quite similar to flu; hot, flushed, disorientated, heart beating fast, no appetite and general body uproar.

The point I am making is two-fold. Whether we are aware of the direct relationship between stored experience in inner consciousness and outer body 'memory' or not, makes no difference to its actuality.

Secondly, we are taught in our mad society to deliberately ignore the signals and wisdom of our bodies from birth onwards. So it is a vicious circle, the outcome of which is vast profits for companies producing drugs, suppressing symptoms and creating 'side effects' which are actually *the* effects of the drug. 'Side' effects are what can't be got rid of having spent years and millions concocting the patented, high-priced excrement.

If we drove vehicles in the same way, shooting out warning traffic lights, ignoring all signs, crossroads, junctions, lane discipline and everything else, there would be carnage on an unimaginable scale.

Instead we rely on drugs to do the same thing. So that's alright then, isn't it?

♥

Once I gained some momentum having worked through the agony associated with the energy locked up in my upper shoulders / base of my neck, and regained power in my hands and arms, for a while there was peace within.

Not for very long though.

Continuing to work each day on whatever surfaced, which is not especially memorable; meaning that after working through energy powerfully needing to be released and the driving forces understood and integrated into outer consciousness, my body took a 'holiday,' meaning I got some peace in my own skin.

My prominent theme of gut centred trauma surfacing once again was not long in (re)asserting its presence though.

First, over a period of days there were the harbingers of what was to follow; twinges of gut ache or cramp and flickers of sharp pain. I recalled a few years previously the pattern developing into heavy gut pains the like of which were unknown, so I knew I was in for more of this experience. The intensity of this was far greater than the usual clamping discomfort. Progressing from what was familiar, it mounted into deep powerful outright flaring pains. Day after day.

I continued to follow my same method and process of breaking the agony with a 'plug' down my throat and its reflexive result, and whatever else pressed for expression; anger or any other emotion, in the way that *felt* appropriate.

For about three weeks or so I ate little if anything but porridge. Anything else was impossible.

People I knew told me my 'long face' that disappeared after gaining peace in my shoulders, was back.

If that was all, I was happy. Doing almost anything was to risk sudden deep pain almost as if a knife had been jabbed into me. My abdomen stuck out like a malnourished native child. The observation bore undertones of admonishment as if I was slipping back into an old pattern. I saw no point in trying to explain to someone who had no idea of their own body's continuum that far from regressing I was continuing to move forward. I consoled myself with the satisfaction of knowing what was happening within my body and equally, with utter certainty, although it was going to take diligent and very literally painstaking effort, working it through and clearing the powerful symptoms were only matters of effort and time; not of question.

Eventually after weeks more consistent abdomen centred work releasing whatever pressed for expression in the way that felt right, gradually the agony subsided and finally I was free of pain completely.

If I needed any reinforcement I was doing what my body needed to do, this only added to all that had ever gone before, together with the most recent 'reminder' of freeing my hands and body energy.

If it did anything, it gave me even greater perspective of layer following layer of stored body trauma in a way not so clear before, simply because I hadn't worked as consistently hard and so regularly.

I knew I was beginning to make progress.

The first glimmerings came when I was still clearing the rigidity in my shoulders neck and head. One evening driving my car, looking to my left, I suddenly realised I could do so relatively freely without it feeling distinctly tight, and unpleasant.

Instantly, I reconnected to the first few days of my efforts in September 1974. Being utterly consumed with a desire to free my body from the leaden prison of my day-to-day existence; continuing to thrash around and yelling blue murder amongst the detritus of the forest floor to rid myself of the crushing weight of self-suppression I carried. Until finally after ten days of stumbling effort I knew I had shifted a massive weight off my inner self and possessed a key of knowledge to clearing it and with it my body, which instantly began showing vital signs of life in all its deadness.

In the simple act of turning my head, experiencing new, easy movement in my neck I realised how far I had strayed over the years from my original unshakeable perception and purpose. Simultaneously, of the same flooding elation as originally in having reconnected with it, and regaining my lost path.

From beginning again in September 1999 it took about two-and-a-half months before clear signs of progress were evident as just related. Continuing to work daily it took until some time in March 2000 before the signs of surfacing acute abdominal centred pains began and focused in increasingly powerful symptoms. Exactly as with my shoulder and neck pains before, the discomfort worsened as I kept working through the stored emotional energy and its related body symptoms until enough was released to begin abating and diminishing until they ceased altogether. Overall this took about six weeks of steady day by day effort.

It cannot be fudged, pretended into oblivion, intellectually 'magicked' away or banished by any other self-deluding process. To repeat; it takes solid, diligent, committed continuous effort until one's body says it is worked through and the energy blocked in inner consciousness cleared.

Also to repeat, attempting to work through blocked off stored trauma and its associated body symptoms, stumbling around in an aimless swamp of confusion with no *self-awareness* of what the aim is or understanding of what signals your body is giving you is a fruitless process. It means intellect is still interfering rather than acting as a wise observer to the unfolding process; the two aspects of consciousness; outer (intellectual) and inner (subconscious) working together harmoniously as one.

Working with one's stored history – and the energy it represents – is *not* a series of disconnected events bearing no relationship to each other just as the human body and form is not a disparate jumble of bits and pieces held together in a coat of skin. As life from birth to death is a continuous process, a clear continuum exists in working through, resolving and integrating history that has not been completed and resolved previously.

Intellect is an essential faculty in keeping track of, and seeing the connection between, events consequently of seeing patterns emerge over time and being able to read the pictures, signs, symbols, allegories and 'coincidences' the sub/inner conscious projects on the 'screen' of our lives; waking *and* in sleep.

In creating a completely lopsided view of reality in treating intellect as the *only* form of conscious intelligence, we see all the unbalanced characteristics of our society.

In disconnecting from our greatest faculty of consciousness we are disconnecting from ourselves within – and the earth without.

Once we tread this path nothing is ever enough – because there is a fundamental recognition within ourselves *something is missing*!

Undeniably, there certainly is! The part of ourselves we are taught to throw away/stamp on/stamp out/abuse/deny/savage and eradicate from birth; our subconscious or inner consciousness!

As said previously, if someone gave one a saw and telling you, you don't need two legs/arms, ears etc, cut one off you'll be alright, the universal response would be unequivocal and probably unprintable!

So why savage an equally fundamental faculty of essential consciousness?

Were all these perceptions available to me as I began 'growing again' as the millennium came and went?

Of course not! At the coal face, the view of a wider world does not exist. There was far too much sublimated history and its equally sublimated, blocked and suppressed energy locked up within my inner being and body.

It did not take many months of continuous daily effort to realise how little I had done over the previous twenty-five years! As massive an effort as that was, by comparison what I began to see was needed was orders of magnitude greater.

We are back at mortgages and interest again.

I might have been making 'payments' over the years but it was nowhere near enough.

Though this is only part of the picture. It would be crass and simplistic to treat my life's progress in clearing my inner world and changing my outer through it like a bus timetable of inevitability. Even though such was my ferocious determination to liberate and change myself it was a pit into which I stumbled.

It clashed strongly with other human drives and desires.

Abraham Maslow, the American psychologist previously mentioned, formulated a hierarchy or 'staircase' of human needs having seven 'steps'. Encompassing basic survival on the lowest level to 'self-actualisation' at the highest; the pinnacle of fully realised human creativity in all its aspects and ramifications.

I might be driven by an all-consuming desire to liberate myself inwardly and outwardly, but whether I held the wider landscape of my life in focus or not it still existed and acted on me. My own 'staircase' of life to ascend and attain 'self-actualisation' might be something I fondly imagined I was building purely by my own efforts, but it was alongside one I was already treading the stairs of. Human needs, talents, interests, aspirations and creativity were not to be denied either.

Not only was there a 'mortgage contract' to be honoured if I was to improve my quality of life resolving the suffocating effects of my internalised, unresolved history; there were other similar ones no less demanding.

Though I had no idea, I was first shown this as a young secondary schoolboy. It was only when the teacher read out the positions in class of each of us for the first school report we were given. She began with one boy's name followed by mine – adding I had come second by just one point.

Puzzled, never having the experience before, I asked if she meant I had almost come first in one subject. The reply was emphatic; when all marks for all subjects were added up I had missed first place by a single point. Admonishing me over the tops of her glasses for my English, because of uncompleted work, but for which I would have been top.

It was a revelation. No one had *ever* done this before, whether teacher, parent, foster parent, child welfare officer, or anyone else. The irony being I enjoyed English.

It lit a fire not unlike the later one burning in me to change my life. At the end of the first year, I came first in almost every subject, and class.

But my staircase of actualisation I ascended at the time had no perceptible risers!

Perhaps to others; though not to me. It came in the form of the biggest bar of chocolate the child welfare department secretary instructed me to buy and paying for it herself. Apparently self-actualisation was measured in segments and tasted good. That was all.

Other 'mortgages' of my life were and are creative abilities needing to be fulfilled and not knowing where to turn. Each in its way demanding time, effort and concentration; not only personal skills but relationships and family as time progressed.

Self-actualisation can be frustration as well as a plateau of attainment if the energy, time and effort available fails to satisfy all the 'mortgage contracts' of one's life. Whether they are consciously honoured or not.

It is only in very recent years 'actualising' a complete classic car floor in sheet steel as good if not better than the original, I realised what other mortgages of creative ability I had failed to make 'payments' on, choosing electronics instead of silver smithing on leaving school.

The difference between the two being the first I was good at but the latter – and working in wood also – I loved.

Which, to reinforce my own example again, showed the predominance of intellectual kudos over creative expression I was taught to value, and which, aged thirty brought me to the brink of self-extinction.

Consequently finding out which 'mortgage' of creative 'actualisation' to make payments to of my time, energy and talent was not a simple choice and the value placed on intellectual knowledge by our culture meant not necessarily choosing the wrong one but certainly by no means making the most appropriate choice, and trampling my own faculty of essential consciousness in the process.

Old Routines; New Territories

Having returned to my simple routines based on trusting my inner wisdom and what my body told me, I continued doing exactly that.

Once the changes in my neck became apparent I was not suddenly free from all 'inherited' birth history. Being intellectually dominated our culture is consequently addicted to instant fixes; magic pills, 'born again' wisdom and belief in one time wonder cures.

The litmus test so far as whether fundamental change has occurred is in the complete body; not in the head.

Unfailingly the body registers whether what we wish to believe is reflected *throughout our being.*

Yet more evidence and reminders of this came in an unexpected way.

For many years stemming from the time when I began working with my own inner world instead of denying and abusing it, I became interested in the psychic world, clairvoyance and mediumship.

To be honest; it was something I always had been but increasingly denied it to myself before.

Attending a spiritualist church I came to know a clairvoyant who began running a group I joined to develop abilities I had but never realised to what extent I possessed them, which spiritualist mediums kept insisting I had. It was refreshing that the young man running the group was interested in the work I was continuing to do. Talking with him about the relationship between body and mind and how suppressing and clamping energy in a person affects their ability to use psychic faculties every human possesses but which are either diminished or completely repressed by our culture's obsession; treating intellect as *the* centre of consciousness.

For one of the Friday evening classes I arranged to run a very mild introduction for the group, working one to one to become aware of the ways we hold and clamp body and emotional energy and, with some clear guidelines, encouraging expression and release.

Discussing with the group leader and clairvoyant his desire to overcome a block he felt attempting to do trance work, the conversation got into the causes of this and of how we become limited by what we experience in our lives.

Creating guidelines for the group session, I was sitting at my desk putting together a section on 'What Prevents Psychic Development' trying to find examples from memory of how negative suggestion and outright criticism affect confidence and ability. Pondering this, through the open window I heard a baby crying, the sounds of a buggy's wheels and the mother's footsteps.

Quite suddenly a loud voice snapped out: "SHUT IT, DARREL! You're doin' my 'ead in!" The last syllables delivered with falling volume and tone; guilt rising in her voice with the instantaneous incandescent screams of outrage and hurt of her baby.

Not only 'Darrel's' cries assailed me; it felt like red hot pokers had been laid on my ears.

I looked out of my office window to see the very young mother hurrying along below with the child, invisible in his buggy behind a protective cover zipped up against the cold spring air.

I felt like going down and saying he is crying because he wants to see you, he doesn't like being wheeled along not knowing what is happening, unable to see anything, and his cries were to tell you he's angry at not being able to see. Now he's screaming blue murder because you've punished, hurt, and frightened him for trying to get you to let him see you and what's going on.

To me, it could not have been clearer; the example being complete in the mother's instinctual ability having been bludgeoned into hurting incomprehension in herself, was repeating the damage; unable to read her baby's cries having no doubt been told countless times herself to SHUT IT. 'Coincidence' yet again provided an answer exactly as I searched for one.

After that, examples flowed freely into mind; not least the memory of once being wheeled along exactly like 'Darrel'.

At the next meeting in the limited time available, I went hurriedly through the guidelines and set the session in motion, working with another member of the group to equally pair off together. My expectation of achieving anything significant in about an hour-and-a-half were not great. Out of the corner of my eye I could see people bending the guidelines I gave and had gone through with them, but decided something was better than nothing. Doing it was the important thing.

For myself I guided someone who clearly held considerable fear within themselves and was extremely nervous, but for the brief session the trend towards understanding and even the mildest expression of it was positive.

When it came time to switch round and take turn about, as I instructed others; I swapped from being an attentive passively supportive observer, to working on what was uppermost within.

For me it was second nature and very familiar, if perhaps a slightly scary experience as some in the group no doubt found it; reversing our culture's habit of bottling up energy of all kinds nearly all our lives, I began working on what needed expressing. That was easy; more head pushing and punching into cushions and fury at being held back in at birth.

The evening session all too quickly over, I wondered if much had been achieved in so short time.

During the next few days my life continued its normal pattern; working on the phone, and taking time to let my body express what pushed to be brought to the surface and released. If anything I felt heavy and tired. Though not unusual; phone work was very demanding, I and treated it as 'normal', but in any case I was used to the follow-on effects of working through layer after layer of my stored personal history and the consequential inner 'heave' as more suppressed sublimated energy worked its way towards conscious awareness.

It was unfailingly accompanied by body symptoms such as weariness, aches, pains and welling emotions.

Getting up on the following Thursday morning I noticed a rash on my body. It had not been there the night previous and I wondered what it was.

As the day wore on I was conscious of it itching and spreading. I had a sneaking feeling I knew what it was about. As the evening progressed I could actually see the rash spreading on my arms; itching enough to drive me mad.

Not wishing to miss the Friday development group, I spent a tormented night as if my bed was full of stinging ants such was the itching all over my arms and torso. Calamine lotion from a large bottle I was fortunate enough to have, repeatedly slopped on to my body and moved about like mopping up a flooded floor, created relief enough to get some sleep.

I made a precautionary visit to the doctor who looked at the swathes of rash on my chest, back and arms and came to the conclusion I anticipated; she referred to it as a 'non-specific rash'. Adding, "By non-specific we mean we don't know what it is!"

Enjoying her uncharacteristic medical frankness, she might not know what it was but I did! Having checked – as suspected – there was no obvious other cause I was absolutely certain what it was.

As brief as my own working session had been in the group's previous week's body centred therapy, I was convinced it had opened up a powerful change in me.

Once the body rash appeared, the memory of the Ayurvedic doctor came back to me of him telling me the one he diagnosed years before on my feet being caused by body toxins in my system collecting there acting as a 'sump' into which they sank. The cure for which I also – and all too clearly recalled – as being a dose of castor oil. Though I loathed its taste and clinging quality in the mouth making me retch even more than my own self-induced vomiting to break painful gut clamping, it had the desired effect and the foot rash stopped itching almost immediately and disappeared within a few hours, after the 'good clear out' as he called it.

Determined to attend the usual Friday evening class, not knowing how long a serious 'engine flush' would take to work its way through me, I itched my way through the day and made my way to the group.

Wondering what if any feedback there might be from the previous week's group therapy I ran, I was absolutely amazed at the difference in the oldest member. A man in his eighties, the change was simply staggering; he looked about thirty years younger!

The surprise for a short while even overpowered the, by then, soldier-ant bite-strength itching rash progressing down my arms. I had seen people change visibly before, after working through history weighing heavily upon them but *never* anything to the degree his face transformed from its dull expression to being very much alive and eyes gentle beacons behind his glasses.

Meeting him many months later his face showed the fire still burned; against all my low expectations of the brief session I ran, the change seemed permanent.

In fairness it was not quite the complete picture, for in a previous evening of psychic development he talked for a while about his marriage. From his own words he made it clear no bond existed between him and his wife. He also mentioned suffering from angina.

I was immediately and forcibly struck the two were closely connected. I felt these were truly 'pains of the heart.' The metaphor of his hurt and sadness about his relationship having penetrated deep into to the centre of his being; in fact right to his heart. He said very little in reply to my observation and I wasn't sure if he agreed or had politely brushed my comments aside.

The following week I asked how his angina had been. He replied he'd had no pains – and it never returned in the months I knew him.

The young clairvoyant who ran the group made a point saying trance work he wanted to do but had been unable to before, was now accessible to him.

Finally, the person who I worked with showed no signs of any change then, but I learned a couple of months later, from being a person who avoided and disliked criticism of any kind, fearful of stirring up any reaction in others, this had been swept completely away, having both given and risked it in return.

As the session with me had been – albeit very mildly – about fear, in retrospect it took a while for the effects to permeate into deeper consciousness, but in examples already given cause and effect were as connected as forged links of a chain.

Returning to my earlier remark about the litmus test for fundamental change being its registering in the complete body or not, the simple very brief session I ran could hardly have showed this more clearly.

Not least – and most unexpectedly, in me – but also the gentleman in whom such a startling change occurred.

Less obviously in the other two people, but both were able to express themselves in ways previously impossible.

To repeat the words of the tribe who took Marlo Morgan on her involuntary walkabout; their view being, body changes or healing is instantaneous, but as we live in physical bodies – in a physical world – both of which are subject to time, then body changes take time to manifest.

Which meant there were plenty – in fact innumerable – times I still needed to lay prone to release pent up fury, anger and frustration still sublimated from my birth, punching cushions, forcing my head into them to fight my way out into the world. No less also the other side of the emotional equation; underneath fury, anger and outrage; nature's ultimate emergency panic button and *call to action* to resolve and stop the profound hurt we have already or are suffering.

Equally, there was a distinct and definite trend. It was never exactly the same experience twice, and although so many times it seemed – and still does – an interminable process doing the same thing over and over, noticing what *felt/feels right* constantly changes; sometimes quickly, others all too slowly. Either way, over thousands of hours of work over decades, my unfailing experience with no exceptions is, as suppressed/repressed energy is released, expression of it changes and unfolds exactly as inner consciousness decides is appropriate.

Gradually, in sympathy with this, not only was I aware the process was evolving, but so too was my body. As the clamping and rigidity in my neck and head muscles diminished I found – as an example – my sinuses would drain, causing my nose to flood and run as I was actually working through more that needed to be expressed and released.

A vital part of this overall process became what I have referred to as 'micro-shudder.' A certain point was reached where what I was working through resulted in an involuntary rapid shudder almost completely internal and lasting a mere second or two.

Seemingly insignificant, as already characterised, I quickly came to realise it was a crucial sign energy was beginning to flow. It is an unfailing sign of progress no matter how pointless, repetitive and dead-ended the need to continue releasing and expressing locked up energy in a particular way seems. Body is the judge of validity, *not* the head.

Indeed, once 'micro shudder' appears it is an excellent indicator what was clamped solid in the body until then is beginning to unlock.

Shuddering is *not* the body's way – as I have often heard – of creating warmth. It may have this effect in a cold atmosphere by allowing energy and blood to flow, but the primary action is one of muscles holding (gripping) and then letting go (releasing) repeated rapidly a number of times a second. Grip – release – grip – release – grip – release etc.

We hold energy against some internally stored experience or event or unpleasant coldness, not released until then. When shuddering begins it is a clear sign internalised history and/or deep discomfort and its stored power is beginning to flow and loosen. Ultimately be expressed and finally resolved leaving the body and person that much freer.

'Micro shudder' is not an end in itself, it is an indicator of release and change and very much a part of the continuing process of unlocking clamped energy in the complete human organism; mind and body consciousness together.

It may lead to more prolonged and profound shuddering and ultimately complete body thrashing such as described with a work colleague, but in my experience micro shudder shows an immense amount of underlying deep clamping still existing.

Over decades there were periods when this faculty was available to me and reflected a period of accelerating energy release and change within. At others, sometimes for months or even years shuddering was not accessible and unfailingly reflected a great heave of yet more deeply sublimated and locked-in energy gradually rising towards more consciously accessible levels.

Without exception this was also a period of increasing body tensions as our flawless natural self-protection systems with which we are all endowed, seek to prevent being overwhelmed by a massive uncontrollable explosion of cathartic energy. Otherwise known as an epileptic seizure.

Hence as I worked steadily towards releasing more of my own stored history and repression of energy associated with keeping it from interfering in my day-to-day life, getting on with it as best I might; I created a deliberate, though not necessarily conscious, tension between my processes of natural internal protection and my *conscious deliberate desire* to access what Great Nature helped protect me from by locking it away deep within.

Simply put; as I worked through one layer of locked up energy, the subconscious honoured the pact I made with my inner self by bringing to the surface the next layer needing to be released, expressed and integrated into outer consciousness.

And doing it in a way enabling me to function 'normally' as it progressed.

It should not be thought this is an easy process. Self-awareness is utterly essential to understanding trends within of what is taking place as they emerge. There is always a lag between previously suppressed history and its emerging energy rising to the 'surface' of outer consciousness, and understanding the emerging pattern.

As time and the process progresses, as a general rubric one becomes quicker and more acute at divining the trends of inner being. Indeed, to begin with, one initially – in the early days (and years!) – swims around in the emotional energy as it comes to the surface, reacting instinctively to what is pushing for expression from within. Clear perception of what has been worked through only being put in context later; be it weeks, months, years or decades.

This affects behaviour and can be a difficult time to negotiate the way through daily life.

As this is the stuff of which the 'soap opera' of human life is universally made, people treat this as 'normal' human unpredictability. I don't.

There is nothing unpredictable or irrational about the human condition. There are only buried decisions and disconnection from inner motivations. In order to survive as best we may and in the absence of a better model.

In being completely intellectually dominated, our culture deliberately suppresses and disconnects from what by right is ours to know from our inner consciousness or subconscious.

Does this knowing come for free? It categorically does not. Our culture exerts great pressure creating intellectual dominance in us all. It takes equal effort to reverse the process and create an altogether different quality of being and life. Not that I pretend to have all the answers; nirvana is only a name on signposts I pass with many far more accessible destinations pointed to on them.

There have been many times when I told myself I was on the 'home straight' of releasing all there was to be expressed and all my stored history cleared. A year or so into working every single day to steadily unlock my body and free up more energy, I felt free enough in mind and body for this perception to take hold – again! Nonetheless at the same time I was very aware my left nostril was much narrower than my right, telling me I might *think* I was well down the road to nirvana but physical reality said otherwise.

Looking back over my life I knew the left side of my nose had been constricted for at least forty years going back to the early sixties and even well beyond that.

Yet bodily in late 2000 my neck, head and being generally felt better than for many years and more energy was also available.

Even as compared with when I began working with what my body was telling me the previous year, there was a marked improvement in my hands and arms; the energy in them and my ability to grip firmly.

As ever it was not all plain sailing. My left shoulder becoming so painful a couple of years before was still much the same until fairly suddenly over a day or two pains became much more focused and quite agonising.

Doing my usual 'inventory' of my body and how it felt, I decided the work I continued to do to access the driving forces of my body tensions

– such as birth – were shifting, causing changes in my shoulder.

The only way I found of creating relief was to return to an even older skill or faculty by which I released agonisingly tense muscles in my right side many years before.

As then, I concentrated on the area with the command to release whatever was the cause and focus of my shoulder pain. In less than an hour I got to the centre of the problem at which point the agony became much sharper and more focused but was also accompanied by relief absent before.

Then it was a case of repeating the process in stages for as long as I could stand the pain until it began to ease. Gradually it lessened and finally ended and shoulder mobility was better, if still somewhat tentative.

There were definite after-effects though; muscular strength in my left wrist was greatly reduced, which I decided was probably due to trapped nerves being released but suffering the consequences of being clamped previously. It took months for the power to return and be able to push without the wrist buckling under the stress.

Finally shoulder movement was fully restored without pain and wrist strength recovered to almost what it once had been.

It was good to remind myself of this technique I instinctively used from the age of seven, but consistently for some years after beginning to shed my burden of personal history and its life-suppressing effects in 1974.

Feeding back awareness within oneself I found achieved much, but in my experience it is not a panacea in itself.

As already mentioned, Wilhelm Reich clearly demonstrated the relationship between what he called 'body armour,' clamping of musculature in the body and sublimated emotional energy, and from which the whole Bioenergetics/body-mind movement derives.

Ultimately though, it is not about learning other people's methods, practices and theories; this only takes one back into the maze of intellect, diverting from attempting to understand one's own inner processes, instead relying completely on other people's knowledge and experience. Including mine.

There is only one way to gain real knowledge and that is to do it for oneself. It is useful to have a map and a route to follow as guidance to get to an intended destination but there is no substitute for travelling the route.

For at least the first five years of working on my own as well as doing body centred therapy / Bioenergetics, at work I often spent hours when studying new course material either on my own or actually sitting on a course, concentrating on – for example – getting my upper body muscles to release. Wondering how successful I might be, the answer usually took a day or so to come. When it did I usually felt extreme fatigue and aching in the area focused on as I released my habitual clamping I was oblivious of until then.

At night laying awake in bed it was something I often did, sometimes for most of the night if much stirred within keeping me awake. A direct effect of which was often vivid dreaming when I eventually drifted off to sleep, further demonstrating the inescapable link between mind and body.

Though it was no substitute for working in my inner world. The two went together to produce permanent change. Unless the energy held in inner consciousness is released and integrated in conscious understanding, muscles regain their clamping tensions over time.

To repeat; what we sublimate and suppress of past experiences in inner consciousness is unfailingly sublimated in the body. However subtly.

My nearly 'frozen' shoulder experience was a good reminder of how over many years I wandered off the path of following what my body's wisdom constantly showed me, and away into the wilderness of intellect.

JOURNEY OF A LIFETIME

From my 1997 house move, and the simultaneous demise of the company I found new business for, my growing tradition of surviving and finding work like stepping from one dissolving ice floe fragment to another, by the beginning of 2001 I was looking for the next suitable transitory piece of financial security.

The year began working with a company who had done 'proper' market research for a magazine they intended producing. As ever, this entailed continual cold calling to create customers to subscribe to and use it. Apart from gaining an extremely heavy cold working in a room where the recirculating air ensured everyone rapidly acquired the same illness, it was soon very apparent the 'proper market research' indicating a market niche for the intended journal suddenly mutated from incontrovertible fact to being as reliable as the air conditioning for staying healthy.

Once again, after three weeks of fantasy phone work, I found myself back in my little bedroom-cum-office at home, free of other people's germs and free of work as well, wondering what stepping stone of chance would present itself.

With equal improbable certainty it duly arrived within another three weeks but working in an area I would never have considered but for needing to pay the bills.

This was my introduction to the world of hearing aid companies and their ever present need to generate new customers and sell their equipment.

The prospect of phoning not dozens of people – or companies as I was used to – but hundreds to offer them free hearing tests at suitable venues was most unappealing; even daunting.

Beginning this task, two things soon became clear; first, phoning everyone from peerage to pauper was easier and much less onerous than selling complex software or IT systems expertise and products, and second as call followed call I began to realise fate might have steered me – yet again – into this unlikely backwater to learn something of value about stress and the human body a lot closer to my own endeavours, and far more than I could have imagined.

Over hundreds and indeed thousands of calls, some people I spoke to wanted to talk about the problems they had; not only hearing but other head related conditions; tinnitus, approaching blindness, chronic headaches, women's baldness, hair loss and many other variations. Drip by drip a growing pool of awareness began to form.

The more people I spoke to the more the link between the work I had done and continued to do, to make dammed sure I was *not* going to seize up in my neck and head or lose the use of my hands, my growing awareness became rock solid certainty.

In tales of head noise, diminished eyesight, female baldness, and other advancing conditions people related in their desperation, anguish and sense of isolation at their powerlessness to find a remedy, I began to feel like an 'agony aunt'.

More and more I could see this was *exactly* where I was heading had I done nothing and not returned to my process of following what my body told me and releasing energy my muscles were clamping tighter and tighter against.

Working for the company I found new business for previously, I had already experienced the growing effects of stress on me and a part of that was some deterioration in my eyesight, and which with diligent work done to unlock my body, I reversed.

One thing was utterly certain; I was going to stick to my routine every day without fail. To the relief and pleasure I felt in my greatly improved body suppleness, freedom of movement and available energy, was added once again the consuming determination I originally had decades before. There was no possible way I was going to become a basket case locked up in my own body.

It was hard sometimes not to get drawn into long phone conversations with people whom I had great sympathy for, though on occasion I did. But the object of my work was ultimately to get people to venues for hearing tests.

There were, however, times talking to one or two people, when the alarm bells rang very loudly in me at what 'treatment' was suggested to people that – *might? Perhaps?* – help their condition, involving surgery having all the hallmarks of someone let loose in a telephone exchange to perform delicate electronic adjustments with a pair of bolt cutters.

I let them know from all the symptoms they described and I had worked through and cured my own problems they were also suffering from, letting someone experiment on them irreversibly was in my experience something they would live to deeply regret.

There were also numerous times when, sensing something about the person on the other end, I had long conversations about health and the lack of it. In describing their own, a relative or a friend's problems I gave insights from my own experience over more than a quarter century, which they strongly identified with.

It was a very useful sounding board confirming whilst I worked on myself on my own, what I had found, cured in myself and learned, directly applied to a great many people. Common themes cropped up in innumerable calls but with so many, what they suffered from was merely the immutable fate of misfortune or 'old age'.

To suggest otherwise was pointless.

Torn between a sense of genuine compassion and the need to get 'bums on seats' at hearing test venues, increasingly, people I spoke with who needed to feel the impersonal voice on the other end of their phone cared and was not a parrot talking from a script – actual or mental – I often mentioned massage as a means to help themselves.

Almost universally people responded this was something they never had done on them. Some were interested, others sounded wary and many considered it something slightly short of the proverbial massage parlour or dismissed it out of hand as freaky.

Abundantly clear was the almost total lack of contact with their own bodies let alone the very dubious question of letting someone else lay hands on them.

The idea of massaging their own shoulders, necks – back and front – and giving their heads a good rub either never occurred or in any case was something they had never done for themselves let alone anyone in their family either.

If head and shoulders massage was as familiar as quantum mechanics theory then understanding the relationship between chronic tension in these regions and how they came into this world and the effects of birth was something considerably beyond the edge of the known universe.

Even when this was a bona fide service offered in a ladies hair salon done by ladies, some I spoke with treated it with complete scepticism as their tight, matter of fact tone of voice showed.

The exception to this nearly universal rule was speaking to a very small number of nurses from the Indian subcontinent.

I knew from a book by a French Obstetrician named Frederick Leboyer called *Loving Hands* how as a matter of universal practice, massage is accepted by children and adults alike and is performed by both on each other.

Equally almost universally, if I mentioned this to the voice at the other end the tone would lift and a pleasant and useful conversation ensued about the positive effects of this.

Not unusually, the fact many Indian men of advanced age have a good head of hair not whitened by life *and* not needing to wear or use glasses either demonstrating the relationship between upper body massage, circulation and energy in this area is obvious to them.

Talking to those of Indian/Asian origin who lived all or much of their lives in our western culture it usually transpired this connection –

if not completely absent – was nowhere near as prominent or common.

And why I was calling them to speak about hearing tests!

It would be nice to write about all the spectacular changes I experienced as I continued working to free up energy in my upper body particularly, and sympathetically the rest as well. The truth though was more prosaic; there were none; though better to say there were none occurring I could separately identify as having been the trigger for an inner avalanche of body sensations, which infallibly were then followed by the rise to consciousness of emotional energy liberated by the equally infallible link between body clamping and emotional energy clamped or suppressed in the subconscious.

To describe the process would only be to regurgitate what I have already said because it was just a plod, day after day, letting my body 'speak' for itself and allowing sublimated blocked energy expression in the way that felt appropriate.

There was nothing magical in having to work through and clear seemingly endless outrage, fury and anger, from my equally endless clamping, rigidity, holding back and squashing I experienced during my birth. And just as predictably underneath it all an immense amount of hurt, hopelessness, futility and fear, as I worked through more and more of the stored, sublimated energy.

Without exception, as the process continues to unwind, so does the body which unerringly reflects the trend in changes reflecting the unlocking of energy throughout.

It is a continuing process until the energy – and the consciousness driving it – locked up in this, or any other, overwhelming experience, is drained. The experience of working through it continues to evolve until all the energy has been released, expressed and integrated into conscious awareness. When it has *it stops.*

No matter how tediously repetitive it often felt – and still feels – the body is the unfailing barometer of change within. Perhaps better to say barometer of complete being.

There were times when nothing much seemed to be changing except for body sensations; aches and pains, pin-prick and 'spider's feet' sensations easily dismissed but which also unfailingly signified change *was* taking place at a deep level and taking time to work its way to more accessible levels of consciousness and conscious expression.

An example suffices to illustrate.

Approaching one lunch time as I worked away sitting at my desk in my little office, I suddenly became aware of something slightly odd about my eyesight.

It took a few moments to realise I couldn't see out of my left eye. Or rather, I could see but it was like looking into a kaleidoscope of opaque golden light. Blinking made no difference and it increased in intensity so nothing else was visible out of that eye, and began to affect the other.

I wondered if I was going blind, but as ever, deciding to see what my body was telling me, I sat in an armchair and waited to see what would happen.

Some minutes passed as the light show continued, increasing in intensity until finally it began to dwindle, restoring my sight to normal once again.

I experienced no other physical symptoms, sensations, or pains.

I decided the changes were positive, and were a reflection of more energy in my neck and head from all the work I'd done to release the clamping tensions I carried from the effects of my birth. There being nothing untoward I left it at that.

A few months went by until one morning I woke up and tried to move my head. I was instantly consumed by an overpowering feeling of giddiness and sickness, rather like having been on a fairground ride.

Having as ever, continued my routine of working through whatever pushed into bodily consciousness for expression in the intervening period, this time I instantly connected the latest event with the previous one and the trend of my upper body continuing to open up and increasing circulation and energy within this region and evidently affecting my inner ears and sense of balance.

Making my way with considerable difficulty to my room set aside for body work, I lay on a mattress I kept there, having dragged my duvet and pillow with me.

The only means of bringing any relief from the utterly overwhelming feeling of sickness and very unpleasant gut clamping was in forcing dry vomiting by means of the time-honoured face-cloth plug down my throat to try and clear my great discomfort.

I would have just laid there until it all passed but for having promised to help on a stall that morning handing out leaflets, and I was determined not to let others down, particularly as I had been the one to arrange with a shop keeper to use space in front of his premises.

I considered it a powerful event when, for example, I experienced the very unpleasant gut-gripping pain in my abdomen, if I had to use three corners of a face cloth before I was successful in releasing this equally disagreeable symptom and gaining relief.

It took about *twenty-three* corner's worth of repeatedly forcing reflexive retching before I was just able to move. If it is puzzling why I speak of 'corner's worth', the folded over, rolled up corner of a face cloth soon became soggy, cold and slimy with saliva and I did not enjoy having a sensation like a garden slug in my mouth! Once all the corners were used there was no option but to wash the face cloth, rubbing it vigorously between clenched fists to get rid of the saliva then wring it out as dry as I could to reuse it.

It reminded me of being acutely seasick, when any movement

is pure purgatory but if nature demands a visit to the toilet as once happened on a small yacht pitching and rolling in a heavy sea, layers of clothing and working the toilet plumbing had to be dealt with, as well as the indescribable nausea from being thrown about and having to move around.

The recollection of that event helped sustain me as I washed out the face cloth, which was essential as I did not enjoying breaking my teeth either – as once occurred when working through powerful emotions – and was another reason for using this device which kept me from clamping them together and causing back ones with fillings to crack under the pressure.

Eventually, keeping my head as still as possible I slowly dressed, feeling slightly less giddy but my body in a state of general uproar and confusion throughout, managing to drive into town and park, thankful the walk to the town centre where the stall was to be, helped me gain at least some feeling of normality in the crisp autumnal air.

Gradually my head rejoined my body from wherever it was in the universe and the rest of me began to respond with muscular tics and twitches as well as a general buzzing and body sensations throughout. I was very familiar with these when major changes of bodily energy occurred; though never as powerful as on that occasion, nor as complete involving everything from head to feet.

Even hours later I still felt light headed and as if I had been through the human equivalent of a 50,000 mile car service and an automatic car wash at the same time.

These quite extreme symptoms, apart from the feeling of vertigo and acute sickness, I welcomed because I knew beyond any doubt I was achieving exactly what I intended to; releasing and getting rid of the suppressed energy of my life history locked up in my body. And especially neck and head.

It was a milestone and I relished it.

Having been fascinated by aeroplanes from my first encounter close to one at the age of four, it suddenly came into mind I wanted to see them, so I treated myself to a visit of a local airfield just to see and enjoy these machines and watch them take off and land.

Approaching the entrance, I asked myself why I was doing this, feeling there was another dimension that until then I hadn't let myself know about. Before, I simply went wherever I felt like going and wondered afterwards what made me go there. Occasionally I knew; like climbing a high hill with a long steep approach as once many years before when I'd been working and studying at the limit of what I could stand and feeling it was worthwhile when I reached the top, and an allegory of my life then.

In that instance it proved not only worthwhile but prophetic also; out of twenty-three studying only five of us passed our examinations and got the certificate we wanted that year.

This time there was no vagueness, or delay, the answer came immediately. Symbolically, in enjoying my own inner feelings of transformation, I chose its reflection in my outer world in these machines rising gracefully into the air and soaring elegantly as if beyond the pull of gravity.

My body might be subject to it but my spirits soared with them, I knew it was a watershed of change but no idea where it might lead me; content for the time being to bask in all the changes I was aware of in my body, and celebrate with a mug of very average machine-thrashed hot chocolate which was about the only thing I dare trust my digestion with.

Strictly speaking it might well be said this is not one example but two.

As intellectually separately identifiable events they were, but in terms of body and inner consciousness it was very much part of a continuum beginning when I started in September 1999 working every day to unlock the massive muscular clamping in my upper body and the rigidity it caused in my neck and head especially.

Even this though is not the complete picture, because there had been another signpost, if not a clear milestone, before these two directly related experiences.

In early 2001 once I began to earn from my work in the hearing aid sector, I promised myself a head and shoulders massage, or as it was often called Indian head massage because it was very much a feature of Ayurvedic medicine/healing; but in any case something endemic within the Indian subcontinent and culture. Having become familiar with it some years before when I undertook a course of Ayurvedic treatment and studying the subject whilst I did so, in talking to people I called in the course of my hearing aid/hearing test work, a few women I spoke with told me of hairdressers who offered the service.

Locally I knew a lady who had been a hairdresser and who did head massage and duly treated myself.

This lady was also extremely psychic and once she finished the massage she said there was an area at the base of my neck that felt like a big black boil, but this had already 'burst' and was clearing.

From the deep burning pains I experienced as I worked through the effects of my birth leading to the freeing of my neck I felt I was on the cusp of further changes and her perceptions confirmed it.

Knowing also, apparently gentle massage and body manipulation could set in motion powerful changes of body energy, I agreed with her when she said I might experience strong effects after the session.

She was right. For several days, probably a couple of weeks at least, I experienced various symptoms; heaviness and tiredness, sensitive digestive system, sensations, aches and pains throughout my body from head to feet, and also affecting me on an emotional level.

It did not surprise me at all; although the strength of the changes and body energy 'realignment' was even greater than I anticipated.

The point of all this is, although they were separate episodes of experience; the head massage, eye sight, and vertigo, sickness and balance, they were all part of the same continuum. Intellect treats these as unrelated; things that 'happen', but they are *not*. They are as connected as links in a chain when understood from the perspective of the sub, and body consciousness.

In visiting the airfield and understanding clearly it had to do with transformation; of moving on to another level, it might appear I felt I had it all sussed out, did I? Of course not.

At that point I just enjoyed the relief of having got through such an all-consuming body experience. I knew it would lead on to other changes in the future but they would come in their own good time.

Without fail when powerful energy releases occur within, it presages major realignments at all levels affecting total being; mind, emotions and body.

Because we live in a physical body in a physical world subject to time, the inner realignments take time to manifest in mind, emotions and body.

Simply put, it is like clearing bric-a-brac out of a vast building – one big enough to house one of the old great ocean liners – that is stuffed with it. The clearing process opens up space but in doing so creates a certain amount of chaos. Just as it takes time to create a new order of everything left and for new uses of the freed space to be found, in my direct experience over decades the subconscious/inner consciousness follows a similar course, except it is like thousands of such buildings undergoing change; to everything left inside and the building(s) as well.

The dichotomy between order and chaos is not just an aspect of inner consciousness or of our outer world; it is fundamental to the proper functioning of the entire universe and everything in it. There cannot be stability without change and order without chaos.

Consequently a few months went by before I realised I felt rather fragile and following on from the transformation experience was the rise of a great deal of suppressed fear into consciousness, that in its turn took some months to work through leading to further changes.

These also affected me at every level; mind, emotions and body. All of which were in the direction of expanded awareness, emotional and body freedom, and increased strength.

To say thousands of vast buildings may seem wild exaggeration but the more blocked energy I released the more it came to me just how unimaginable is the human ability to suppress and sublimate the effects of experiences and the stored energy they represent.

As the saying goes though; there ain't no such thing as a free lunch, meaning energy does not simply disappear, it only changes form, otherwise the equation $E=MC^2$ would have been disproved.

Though this equation only reflects the physical world. There *should* be one uniting the (non) physical, i.e., consciousness with the physical, i.e., energy, because *consciousness determines form, and FORM is MATTER.*

It may be sublimated and shut away in the brain so we can get on with our lives as best we may but unfailingly it registers in the body and our behaviour. In strictly scientific terms energy sublimated or locked up in the body is potential energy; it is not kinetic and flowing, and the human condition is fundamentally – and should be – about flow and completion.

To repeat; when energy flows freely in humans, like water in a clear stream, we experience happiness, harmony, fulfilment and contentment, and as Abraham Maslow characterised these effects; self-actualisation. When it is blocked and cannot flow to its completion – and again like water – we see stagnation, sterility, lifelessness and ultimately decay.

In summary; this period beginning with the strange effects in my left eye and on to experiencing extreme vertigo were the clearest possible indications working with and through my inner consciousness and body; so called 'body mind', was steadily reversing the trend of clamping off the flow of circulation and energy in my complete upper body. The corollary being but for this I would have gone blind, increasingly deaf and ultimately dead

Energy and the Body's Wisdom

Welcome as the freeing of my upper body was, it was only half the picture, for there were changes throughout and not just in the areas I was most concerned about.

Alexander Lowen in his book *Bioenergetics* talks about the 'narrows' of the body; these being the neck and the waist, and which are focal points for the constriction and blocking of energy in the body.

I was no exception and quite apart from the clamping of energy in the muscles of my shoulders and neck, from my waist down it was, if anything, even more apparent energy did not flow as it once had.

As related previously, if my lower legs and particularly my feet got cold, they stayed cold for hours. The only way to change it was prolonged exposure to heat and warmth.

Such was the clamping throughout my pelvic area in the early nineties even turning over in bed was painful in my lower back and focused in the lumber region, hence the meaningless name for it in past times; lumbago. In my direct experience it comes from a combination of severe disturbance in spinal energy flow, which in turn creates massive tension in musculature throughout this region.

As I steadily released the tension in my upper body and my neck and head freed up, there was a sympathetic improvement in my lower regions, but if I felt particularly tense, the clamping in my crutch area reduced urinating to a trickle sometimes from its reduced flow in any case, not forgetting the sudden painful sensation of needing desperately to go as well.

Gradually as the years of steady, tedious, repetitive effort progressed in the early years of the new millennium the situation improved to become a lot more comfortable. But again, in my direct experience, my genital region was and is a very sensitive indicator of the flow or blockage of energy in my body, as sublimated stress and trauma presses for conscious expression and affects the energy flow or lack of it in my spine.

The amount of muscular stress and tension in this region fundamentally affects the control we have over the body function of urinating; both male and female. The difference being with men it can and does also relate to prostate problems as muscular tension impairs the flow of blood and energy. In women it relates to so-called 'bladder weakness'. In either case though it is primarily the fundamental lack of energy and consequential acute tension in the muscles impairing the normal control we have over this region of our bodies.

In my experience over many years, when the pelvic area muscles become clamped we lose the degrees of easy awareness of the urinary system. Instead of knowing one might need to go for a pee in a while and of the pressure building over time, it results in an all-or-nothing condition. With tight clamped muscles a crisis point suddenly arrives without the gradual growing desire to relieve ourselves.

Over time I developed the ability to consciously release the muscles and proved as I got them to relax, the sudden need to answer the apparent urgent call receded and disappeared and I could feel the muscles release in stages. It was and is, however, not a one-time wonder cure; the unconscious clamping steadily builds up again needing to be repeated, but a fair degree of control is regained benefiting not only this body function but also improving energy generally in the lower body.

To repeat; it is not a cure but it does help to create awareness and confidence one does not need to be driven blindly by one's body even when there is a lot of deep residual stress; it just takes practice and patience.

If there is one faculty above all others making the difference between wandering about in the maze of one's own body and inner being, it is *self-awareness*.

Without it is to be driven rather like a pinball in a machine; when something triggers in inner consciousness and begins to affect the body, to have no self-awareness is to be cannoned around haplessly driven by inner imperatives simply reacting to them – as, for example, the muscle clamping just described.

In the wider context, lack of self-awareness and of one's own body continuum means surrendering it to others and being on the receiving end of other people's perception of it and a myriad of therapies and 'cures' when *we* are our own expert. *No one else is.*

Perhaps better to say we *should* be, but our culture denies us the wisdom our own inner/sub conscious provides us with all the time by treating the intellect as *the* source of wisdom. Consequently we seek wisdom from others instead of our own.

Self-awareness can make the difference between doing/being in all manner of therapies for decades and not creating *permanent* positive change and improvement.

Our bodies are the unfailing barometer and living expression of our total being. If the body does not p*ermanently* improve, all the talk and positive mental attitudes changes nothing.

It has been said the body is like a hologram. The reason being, a hologram shows the complete picture in every part of it unlike a normal photograph which does not. The first is a complex three dimensional representation; the second a flat two dimensional image.

The reason for likening the body to a hologram is, it can be diagnosed from different parts of it. There are many different methods of diagnosis; a few being iris diagnosis – using the iris of the eye, finger nails being another, and in Ayurvedic medicine the pulse, which is taken with three fingers to assess the organs and the energy of the complete body.

JOURNEY OF A LIFETIME

Regarding nails, wives in Arabic harems were allowed no contact with any other male except the King, Sultan or Sheikh they were wives of. The only contact of any kind a doctor was allowed to have in treating wives was using the hand and in particular the finger nails, which was the only part a doctor saw as a woman's hand was thrust through a hole in a wall! As a consequence a complete system of diagnosis was developed.

Over many years I have found nails – finger and toe – to be an excellent indication of not only physical condition but of the deeper rhythms of the emotions and of the subconscious, and how body energy embracing all these levels is unerringly reflected in them.

As one very simple example, I mentioned in 2003 some months after the vertigo experience which signified major bodily changes in energy, I realised a lot of sublimated suppressed fear was working its way into consciousness as I became like a sensitive animal; nervous and (even more) easily frightened. I knew it was from a deep level, but as ever my concern was to work steadily through it as it came to surface consciousness, deal with the emotions associated with how I felt, and moving on.

Whilst this took place, I noticed a white mark rising in the centre of my left big toenail. From early 2003 over the following months it grew in size and shape until by mid-year it looked exactly like a complete crescent moon, the centre of which had an actual hole in the toenail!

The fact it was fully visible I clearly understood signified something rising into clear consciousness in me, though it was only in retrospect as the fog of fear cleared – also affecting my energy throughout – I understood what its significance was.

The moon is a symbol in itself and a reflection of the sun; to be precise 1/250,000 of the sun's light. Just as the sun represents day and the visible world as well as the character we present to the world in waking, and is treated as masculine, the moon's light is purely the sun's reflection and is much more delicate and is associated with night time and feminine aspects, also the 'shadow' and inner part of ourselves; the emotions and the subconscious or deeper unconscious.

This is not purely symbolic either; the word 'lunatic' comes from being affected by the moon. I recall one occasion when a work colleague said a friend of his who was a special constable, i.e., a part-time policeman, was on duty one Friday evening when to use his words, 'It was absolute carnage on the roads'. It happened there was an eclipse of the moon that evening.

I could mention many more but a particularly interesting one told me by a power station designer was boiler de-scaling in power stations produced erratic results. Sometimes it worked well; others mediocre results and at times almost no effect. After research into the phenomenon it was found the phase of the moon had a fundamental effect.

So far as my left big toenail was concerned it could hardly have been a more precise allegory and symbol of the rise into clear consciousness of what had been buried in my inner/sub/unconscious.

Not to mention the fact that this symbolic 'moon', as mentioned, only rose into full view on my toenail by about mid-year at which point the ruling sign of the zodiac is Cancer (21st June to 20th July) – the most emotional and feminine sign whose ruling planet is the moon! Just another 'coincidence' naturally.

Another way of looking at the sign of Cancer is being at the centre of the year and the astrological zodiac of twelve signs, it is also telling us emotions and our deeper consciousness *is at the centre of our total being.*

NOT INTELLECT!

Equally coincidental no doubt being the fact this 'symbol' in my toenail was exactly above the reflexology point for the pituitary gland on the underside pad of the big toe.

This gland controls the functioning of the body's glandular or endocrine system, and is underneath the hypothalamus which links the nervous system with the pituitary. Together they control vital functions of the nervous and glandular systems.

It is also a fact the moon affects women's menstrual cycle. In which case it must affect the endocrine and nervous system.

Where are these elements located? Right in the *centre* of the head underneath the brain!

What does the left big toe and its reflexology points symbolise? The head; with the pituitary gland reflex underneath. Moreover the left side of the body is associated with the emotions, the subconscious and deeper unconsciousness being controlled by the right lobe of the brain. The right side of the body and left brain lobe with the rational and outer levels of consciousness and the intellect.

What were the after effects of the acute vertigo and sickness I experienced about nine months before this 'moon' had fully risen on my left big toenail? There were pronounced profound changes throughout my body.

It seems our bodies have their own deep sense of humour in the way allegories of changes right in the centre of the head and affecting the whole body were then confirmed on the outside of it!

If coins symbolically represented my effort to free up the energy in my body and create *fundamental* permanent, positive, change, cause and effect could hardly have been more clearly demonstrated than the 'coins' having been put into the 'machine' it then 'printed' out a receipt on my big toe! Even if it took a while for the 'printer' to print it!

But all this of course, is just whimsical nonsense as modern medicine and Professor Brian Cox know. The only scientific way to treat the body is, after all, to use the latest techno gadgets to see inside it, take pictures of it, check out its chemistry and having done so; a) fill with allopathic drugs, b) suppress all symptoms, c) chop something off, d) treat as irrelevant, or e); a), b), c) and d) all together.

This one example is far from being the only one so far as toenails are concerned – let alone fingernails.

Ten years before this rising moon of fundamental change within body and being when my second marriage ended, in its wake the *right* big toe also eloquently told the story of changes in my *outer* world just as the *left* recounted my *inner*.

In the aftermath of separating I noticed the inner edge (left side and centre of the body) of my right big toenail changing colour, or rather losing its colour, turning greyish white. At the top of the nail about half its width lost its colour, tapering down to nothing right at the base of the nail. I knew it reflected the events of the time and recent past, but it was only some time later when trimming this nail I discovered it had become completely detached in the colourless area. Underneath, from the base of the nail upwards, was a thin fragile new nail tapering diagonally off towards the top centre, on the left of which there was no nail at all.

The surface of the new nail was also deeply ridged, very uneven and had some holes in it.

Without going into detail, this toenail was a prefect allegory of one way of life having ended (large dead area at the top of the nail) and a new one taking the place of it, the transition taking its time in the physical world – shown in the tapering shape down to the bottom left corner – and that it was all accompanied by considerable changes and disturbance in my day-to-day life (the ridges, unevenness and holes).

There were also white flecks in the nail colouring which was in any case not a clear healthy pink – clear signs of stress.

Observing the changes over the following years, gradually the ridges smoothed and the colour improved, albeit slowly and steadily as I continued to work through my stored history, recent and more distant; particularly from 1999 when I concentrated on clearing the immense amount of muscular rigidity and clamping in my head, neck and shoulders.

By the rise of the 'moon' on my left big toenail in 2003, the right one whilst not completely smooth and a constant delicate pink was nonetheless vastly improved.

One does not have to be Sherlock Holmes, Hercules Poirot or Carl Jung all rolled into one to deduce the symbolism and story of my outer and inner worlds over this time, nor have access to the Met Office's 100,000,000,000,000 instructions per second computer, ultrasound/MRI scanners, endoscopes, thermal imaging cameras, or anything else to see that my toenails infallibly told the story of my complete world – outer and inner over this period.

To summarise what they said; (right big toe) my outer, or day-to-day world, underwent a great upheaval which took considerable time and diligent effort to deal with and work through, *only* once a certain stage of progress was reached, health and wellbeing restored to a sound level, could I *then* begin dealing with what I kept deep within me (left big toe) in my inner world, unlocking the suppressed energy, releasing the stored experiences and integrating into conscious awareness what previously I had had no other choice (as at birth) to sublimate in deep sub/inner consciousness in order to survive.

To re-quote an Aboriginal saying; healing (and change) is instantaneous but because we live in physical bodies in a physical world subject to time, it takes time to manifest in the physical world.

To repeat yet again with no apology whatsoever; our bodies and inner consciousness tell us the whole time what is happening within, but because our culture and society is completely dominated by its obsession with the intellect as *the only* source of intelligence and wisdom we create a fundamental imbalance. And not just imbalance, it is a lack of harmony and in energy terms a split and deep conflict within our bodies and being. It is no exaggeration to say in creating this chronic imbalance within us we are creating a state of organismic warfare.

What a huge surprise it is then, isn't it, that our westernised culture is absolutely riven with wars and conflict?

We are unfailingly projecting out on to the world what is happening/

has happened within.

Or as the ancient saying I thought up recently goes; to abuse others, first you have to be abused.

Our society and culture teaches us to cruelly abuse; to positively trample, suborn and extirpate the immeasurably vast wisdom every living human on this planet has by right of their birth and being; our subconscious and inner consciousness. *This* is the fount and wellspring of *all that we are*.

Not the intellect. The intellect is or should be a guide and wise counsellor who deals with our outer world and who listens and takes the constantly given infallible advice of our deeper consciousness.

To use a superb allegory which is itself deeply rooted in the symbolism of the inner/sub/unconscious – whether the artist Nicolas Poussin knew it or not – there is a picture he painted in 1658 showing the huge blind giant Orion guided by a diminutive human figure – Cedalion – standing on his shoulders showing him the way towards the light of the rising sun – which heals Orion's sight.

Blind Giant Orion being guided to the rising sun by Cedalion on his shoulder
By Nicolas Poussin 1658

In terms of the sun and moon symbolism already used, in the picture, amongst the clouds also wreathing Orion's face, stands Diana. This is intended to be symbolic of the moon's power (with Diana a directly feminine symbol herself) to transmute the earth's vapours into rain. Thus in one picture is united consciousness (sun *and* moon together) and the unifying 'glue' between the two is water – which is also symbolic of emotion. Itself having two aspects; water vapour in air – relating to the intuition and its liquid counterpart which is equated directly with emotion; two aspects of the same substance and links inner and outer aspects of the single consciousness together.

Cedalion helping Orion navigate his way in the physical sensory world could hardly be a better allegory of the physical and intellect centred outer consciousness working in harmony with the sightless emotion and intuition centred inner consciousness towards the light of universal consciousness symbolised by the sun. Both the sun and Orion being gigantic beings. *Both* having immense power. The sun doesn't 'think' how to shine and neither does the light of our own gigantic inner consciousness.

Not forgetting of course; the earth of our being and corporeal reality, without which none of this would exist.

All in all, the picture is deeply symbolic on many levels of how our outer consciousness and physical senses should work in harmony with the colossus of our inner consciousness. Instead of walling off and attempting to deprive it of its colossal power by treating intellect as *the* seat of *all* intelligence; causing the giant in us to blunder *blindly* in confusion and meeting situations haphazardly mirrored in our outer world. When clear, open, communication exists with our inner consciousness we have unfettered access to immense powers.

Knowing Poussin deeply observed the natural world in his late years he could hardly have created a more universally harmonious symbol of healing the schism between outer and inner consciousness and intellect with sub/unconsciousness.

It is a final and fitting irony the picture is from Greek mythology for we owe our completely lopsided consciousness to Aristotle; the arch epitome of Mr Intellect of ancient Greece, so eloquently described by Robert Pirsig in his excellent book, *Zen And The Art Of Motorcycle Maintenance*, and already mentioned in the anecdote of Aristotle and Heraclitus, referred to in *The Hidden Harmony* by Bhagwan Shree Rajneesh.

Even at its most superficial interpretation the picture shows this is *exactly* the relationship that *should* exist between the intellect (outward facing consciousness – and physical senses) and the sub/inner consciousness (inward facing consciousness – without physical senses) but whose access to all the knowledge of the universe is unimaginably vast, direct and immediate. Not simply dwarfing the intellect but in terms of its relative scale is the difference between a pea and the universe. Or even a cabbage and the universe in these times of nurtured gathering dimness, cultivated superficiality and deliberately fostered cult of 'instantism' and thoughtless idiot roboticism. With the physical sense of sight we can *see* but with access to the 'blind' sub/or inner consciousness we have *vision* and *in-sight*.

Why in God's name would anyone want to prevent access to, and repression of, this faculty which is essential to our proper functioning and which makes us *all* giants, if, as tribal and aboriginal cultures and societies do, we are taught to use it rather than attempting to suppress and deny its ineffably promethean wisdom?

Yet this is exactly what our westernised culture does to us from the moment we are born. And each generation bashes the next into this bizarre mould.

Kind words and good intentions make no difference; we are demanding the next generation be as intellectually dominated and incomplete as we are. Just as was passed on to us. Except the momentum and speed of its progress signify the galloping approach of a world prison we may all very soon hear the echoes of its doors slamming shut on us.

JOURNEY OF A LIFETIME

Is it any wonder children cry and scream all too often in our society? For we are forcing them to suppress their proper natures – just as we were forced to go against our own. Like the baby Darrel in the pram; constantly told to SHUT IT!

Having clear understanding of, and unfettered access to, our sub/inner consciousness as a matter of routine – just as we are taught from birth in our western culture to use our intellect – but as *one overall and complete faculty* of consciousness, maintains the state of harmonious completeness and unity we are intended to function as.

What in our culture we differentiate as two completely separate aspects of consciousness is and should be *two parts of singular, unified harmonious whole.*

The Path to Nirvana ... Errr ...?

It should be apparent by now from all I have said and repeated many times, the process of paying attention to what my body, and through it what my inner consciousness was telling me and allowing myself to express and release what pressed for conscious expression – a combination of physical and emotional energy – unfailingly led to new insights and perceptions of the driving forces.

Also to repeat; this was and is no miraculous cure – although sometimes startling positive changes can and do occur as I have related within myself and in other people.

Once again it may appear my experience of seeing and relating the changes in my toenails was a singular event, or as separate events just like snapshots in a photo album. This could not be further removed from the reality or truth.

Human – and indeed *all* nature exists as a flowing continuum of energy. When energy flows in all of nature we see and sense it and as part of that we *feel* it within ourselves.

When energy ceases to flow; consciousness has already flown and it is called death.

In relating my experience over decades my intention has been and is to describe the path and process I have followed and continue to do so; and like Cedalion on the shoulders of blind Orion, I began finally to understand within me was a sustaining force I had 'blinded'. The consequences of which was to crash into the scenery of my life, causing immense hurt and damage. And wondering bitterly; why.

JOURNEY OF A LIFETIME

Just as life doesn't stop and start, once I began to do the exact opposite of all I had been taught by social conditioning imposed by my family and the wider world and begun to release and consciously integrate the unimaginable amount of sublimated, suppressed/repressed emotional energy by convention – like everyone else – I had stuffed my sub/inner conscious with, like some vast landfill site of unimaginable proportions, it did not take long for outer and inner consciousness to synchronise. Just as Cedalion speaking in Orion's ear would cause the giant to instantaneously alter his course, the message from the outer world is instantaneously registered within. It just takes a little while for outer physical reality to catch on because – to repeat – time does not exist in inner consciousness or 'unconsciousness;' it is our physical being that is affected by and subject to time. Hence once we begin to learn a diametrically opposite process to all our life's conditioning, the subconscious responds by starting the 'conveyor belt' of deliberately repressed energy, passing out in an orderly stream all that has been forced into it from birth onwards.

For myself it took just ten days working completely on my own until outer and inner consciousness fused in profound, unshakeable awareness, and I knew how to work with my inner world, embracing it instead of meting out brutal punishment using my own intellect as a cruel prison guard.

The ten days spent floundering on my own felt like being lost in a cosmic chasm; adrift in a vast ocean of time and space, utterly alone. But as the years and experience have lengthened and grown I have come to view this as the greatest asset because I was finding out for myself the workings, rhythms and wisdom of my own being – not other's fables and myths of it. However well intentioned or informed. Knowledge acquired second hand is not knowledge. Knowing only comes from having done it oneself. Everything else is hearsay, as will become apparent later.

Though without doubt describing the route by which one travelled gives others the confidence of events, signs, landmarks and scenery along the way. Just as Marco Polo described his journey opening up new awareness and consciousness of places and peoples unknown. The purpose of describing my journey is the same. Except the 'distance' involved is immeasurably greater and only limited by the perception of the traveller.

The Power of 'Cunning Old Fury'

From all I have written, related and deliberately repeated, of the process and approach of my efforts and resolve to clear the effects so apparent in my body, of the tensions and sublimated stress I carried within, the purpose and practice of how I have pursued my path of inner liberation should be clear also.

To add more examples would serve only to describe the same process over and over, and to disappear in a forest of thickening detail. My purpose was, as I originally described it; to 'anneal' myself; like metal become rigid and brittle through being worked, I deeply yearned to find some way by which I could release the effects of my life's embrittling experience on my body, and which if I didn't I knew beyond any doubt my life was not pleasant nor would be, or long lived.

As the years continued to progress, continuing to clear the weight of sublimated suppressed energy within, I experienced a growing awareness of my inner rhythms; short and longer term. Exactly as described previously and with increasing clarity; like being afloat in a vast ocean and being subject to and feeling the short 'chop' and wind-driven disturbance – the day-to-day feelings and perceptions within body and mind – becoming steadily more aware of the longer 'waves' and inner heave of my sub/unconscious bringing up to outer conscious awareness yet more buried history and the suppressed, repressed emotional energy pressing for conscious expression and integration.

The more powerful the heave I felt in my body and then my emotions; the more I increasingly realised how much or little needed to be expressed and how much it demanded of my energies.

A good indicator I found was when standing up from squatting down or straightening from bending.

If my head began to swim I increasingly understood, it meant I was going to be dealing with whatever emotional energy was pushing its way up into conscious expression in whatever emotions were associated with it. The more intense the swimming head sensation the more powerful the energy of the associated emotions. Sometimes this was fairly mild, others it felt like the precursor to blacking out.

Mild swimminess meant/means effort over a day or two, but more pronounced or even feeling like lead and heavy, deep near blackout sensations were/are a harbinger of a lot of work to be done over weeks and even months.

Another form of 'heave' was/is palpitations similarly announcing something passing across the frontier between inner (un)consciousness and outer world consciousness.

The difference between the two types of symptoms indicating respectively; emotional energy close to and intruding into consciousness (symbolic of it affecting my head), or making the 'leap' between being repressed in the unconsciousness and forcefully making its transition into the subconscious (symbolic of it affecting my heart).

These statements may seem merely arbitrary judgements based on nothing more than whimsy.

The reality is very different.

These symptoms and my consequential experience of them in my body and being span the time from beginning my journey in 1974 until the present.

The first symptom representing dozens of occasions and the latter, hundreds. To begin with I accepted them as things that 'happened' but over years, then decades, the pattern and relationship began to emerge and clarify until symptom, subsequent effects and working through the emotional energy pressing for expression and conscious integration, become absolute certainty.

Always the relationship being the same; my head being affected by what was 'swimming' around in me just under the surface, or a prior announcement of what was coming later, but would only be accessible some time later. The strength and repetition – if any – of palpitation I discovered, signalling how far in the future and how much work involved. Which only as the years became decades, was it possible to gauge what – and when – to expect.

The more deeply buried energy is; and the more of it, repressed into the unconscious, the more potent its power to disrupt normal body functioning.

My personal perception and experience over the same span of time is that our deeper inner being is like an impartial judge. If we steadfastly refuse to acknowledge we are using our inner being and consciousness as a vast midden into which we continually 'throw' unresolved experiences laden with unexpressed emotional energy, there may come a point when the 'midden' is overflowing.

Just as someone creating a tip in their back garden they refuse to do anything about and continue to throw 'rubbish' on it, the 'judge' (our deep inner being) hands down judgement that this will cease forthwith, and clear the rubbish. At which point the person experiences a heart attack / stroke or other serious 'sentence'.

Whimsical nonsense?

A few examples will provide some insight.

Many years ago I clearly recall a study done on (from memory) Filipino workmen who were engaged in breaking ships for scrap metal.

They lived away from home (Bangladesh?) for months in miserable accommodation that were the hulks of ships not yet broken up, saving their wages and sending the money home to their families.

During the time in the ship breakers yard all they did was work, eat and sleep. For weeks / months on end.

The study sought to establish and understand why there was a high rate of heart attacks – serious and fatal – not when the men were actually working, but when they were back in their quarters, i.e., their deep inner selves held them together so they functioned day after day doing endless hours of work, but their inner 'judges' were clearly saying; 'This has been going on for far too long. 'You' – outer consciousness – absolutely refuse to take heed of what 'I' (deep inner self) say, so I have no other alternative but to hand out a heavy sentence for you to cease this immediately.'

The heavy sentence in this example being a heart attack. Once the need to function in, and concentrate energies on work, ceased, the heart attack was the 'rebound' of unsustainable, repeated, compounded accumulation of stress; physical, mental and emotional.

Another clear example being people who endured and survived the Nazi concentration camps of the Second World War.

Inmates said whilst they were in the camps they had vivid dreams of wonderful food as they were being starved to death and brutalised, not of the bestial cruelty they suffered. It was only having survived this utterly unspeakable outrage, attempting to make a normal life again, the horrific nightmares of their experiences exploded from the unconscious into more conscious access with atomic force. And kept on recurring. Without food and water we die. In priority it comes first; whatever other suffering may also be endured.

In my experience our deep inner selves – the unconscious – is an unimaginably powerful sustaining force in us; our bodies and complete corporeal being, to ensure our survival in the best possible way and to the highest level of life achievable in the circumstances.

We are back at Abraham Maslow's Hierarchy or 'staircase' again, the lowest level or 'stair' being food and as different levels of need and creative expression are met and the energy they represent expressed we ascend the 'staircase' up to the highest level he called 'Self-Actualisation'.

But the unconscious's 'patience' is finite in its ability to keep on absorbing energy we stuff into it. After which comes a point when somehow the pressure and organismic crushing burden it represents *has* to be released.

Paradoxically it is our inner selves attempting to correct the unsustainable imbalance we have had to deal with/created in outer physical consciousness and world.

What happens?

Inner consciousness/unconsciousness releases in a single event a huge amount of repressed energy with literally heart-stopping power or explosions into consciousness, strokes and other effects.

The unconscious simply – and as always – attempts to get the message through. Whether our physical bodies and consciousness can actually cope with what the unconscious propels into our physical world and being is not the concern of our unconscious.

It acts independently to correct imbalance and total organismic 'wrongness' exactly as a stern impartial judge might hand down judgement. The effect on the 'culprit' (physical being) is for it to suffer the consequences.

To reiterate an earlier point: Energy is energy – no matter what form it takes – it is a fundamental law of physics and it cannot be magicked away. It can only change its form; in humans and with anything anywhere else in the universe.

It is not for nothing we have simple sayings like 'I'm about to blow my top', and many other variations.

We have an innate knowing what effect having our 'boiler'/inner being stoked with strong emotion(s) has on us even if intellect screws down the 'safety valve' and we pretend it has no effect, as we are socially and morally conditioned to do. Not that humanity and etiquette shouldn't apply, but when it becomes a repressive obsession turned against ourselves, as rule by intellect has, we are deluded if we imagine we can flout the laws of our inner being. Never mind the laws of physics and the universe.

Our unconscious records the truth in storing what we consciously refuse to acknowledge.

However, again in my direct experience, when do we begin to

acknowledge and to reverse the process of sublimating and repressing energy we have previously refused to give expression to, our wise and impartial judge deep within takes a more lenient view.

As I began releasing, expressing and integrating the colossal amount of unresolved and unexpressed energy I had stuffed into my inner being, the symptoms I experienced were the 'judge' saying, 'We recognise you have begun to make strenuous efforts to reduce and clear this unacceptable rubbish tip you have created, therefore you will be kept under observation and from time to time I will issue warnings, noting your continued work but as reminders you should continue to reduce it until the tip is cleared.'

Hence my symptoms of swimming head and palpitations were/are my 'judicial warnings', and also 'approval' of continuing to redress the imbalance and inner 'wrongness'.

There is no doubt whatever in my mind the Reverend Dodgson's/Lewis Carroll's *Tale Of The Mouse in Alice In Wonderland* is a perfect representation of the indirect way (the waves/bends in the tale/tail – not to mention the puns) the unconscious presents its wisdom and warnings (the omnipotent 'cunning old Fury' being judge *and* jury).

If anyone doubts we have a deep fundamental understanding and recognition of our need to not just acknowledge our inner recesses of consciousness, one need go no further than the 19th century's *Harry Potter*. I mean of course *Alice* of Lewis Carroll's brilliant invention.

Our longing to escape the shrinking prison of the intellect's unbridled repressive regime, re-opens in us all, the natural door still swinging freely on its hinges in children between outer and inner world consciousness, but in adulthood is rigidified and shrinks under this assault of procrustean logic.

We *know* there is somewhere in us not ruled by this tyrant. We are captivated by these stories like deprived addicts desperate to satisfy their craving; because that is *exactly* our condition.

It was already Reverend Dodgson's condition; he clearly never lost his connection with the whole panoply of unconscious expression, its contradictory imagery, and with his own inner child. Whether or not he *did* take drugs as some have said.

We crave the unfettered freedom of the unconscious because like Alice in the shrinking doll's house our outer world is repressively confining. Our inner (un)consciousness is endless potential, our outer; constriction and prostration.

Instinctively we know we need to counterbalance this inequality.

If anyone scorns this perhaps they should compare their own bank balance with JK Rowling's and the fact *Alice In Wonderland* has never been out of print since it was first published in 1865.

Following the Signposts

It might appear my perceptions of our inner worlds in the early years of this Millennium were as I have recounted, but the symbolism of Poussin's picture and the way the unconscious communicates was not as clear to me then as it has increasingly, and increasingly rapidly become. It was and continued to be, very much a journey of one foot in front of the other; of living day-to-day in my skin – or when another heave of energy from my inner world/unconscious, pressed into outer consciousness, not so centred in my body but realising something was happening, if not yet clear what was coming.

The process was as always; then and now. Step by step means acknowledging and expressing the emotional and/or body energy, and having expressed this, understanding consciously what in hindsight I had been working through. Once this occurred a point would be reached when I would have to do 'homework' laying awake in bed in the early hours; insights and new perceptions floating into mind and connections of what I had been expressing and working through would spontaneously arise and events in my life that had merely 'happened' I would see were anything but random and unrelated but were a clear continuum as predictable as signposts and scenery on a journey.

Perceptions floating in may have been how it was – and is – at times, but at others it became what I now call a brain race. I would be deluged with new perceptions, not just concerning what I had been working through and wider aspects of my life, but a flood of perceptions about things I had not thought about. It became a veritable gush of consciousness. I began to realise resolving blockages within, and energy locked up/sublimated and suppressed in my inner conscious realms was like unblocking the flow in a river and seeing all manner of things held back upstream, suddenly as the obstacle was released, came boiling by in a maelstrom of energy and things rushing past; some familiar, others not, carried by the liberated flow of consciousness.

Consequently, months or years after working through some unresolved stored past, my experience is, as the process continues, steadily working through, resolving and integrating yet more sublimated history, a trigger point is reached where not only are connections clear between previously unconnected events, but what I took to be the full picture before, suddenly acquire(d) even broader – and deeper – insights and new perceptions stretching back over an even greater span of years. Along with perceptions not limited to me personally at all.

In my long experience the only limitation of how broad one's life view becomes, is determined by social conditioning deeply ingrained in intellect and conscious awareness of what it is possible or impossible to 'remember' and recall.

This in itself can create an inner conflict because what we consciously believe to be an absolute, is nothing of the kind to the un/inner conscious; and it will continue to thrust into conscious awareness the broader picture.

It can be likened to climbing a mountain. If the top is obscured by clouds, if one ascends to ten thousand feet and reaches a plateau just clear of the clouds, considering it to be the summit, this might be accepted as the top.

If suddenly the cloud lifts exposing yet higher reaches – and a perspective from higher up – the inevitable result is the view of the surrounding countryside becomes even larger from a higher vantage point.

The 'clouds' are the consciously indoctrinated limits of our perspective. Their clearing, exposing a greater view, is the acceptance into outer consciousness, of the bigger picture the unconscious has.

If you believe you cannot recall anything earlier than before the age of five, but continue to clear stored experiences and stored emotional history there will come a point when this view will clear like clouds. The more it is resisted, the more insistent the unconsciously held broader 'view' will push into outer awareness.

Having long since given up trying to lash my unconscious to logic's procrustean bed and the intellect's butchery, the consequence is new insights come in increasing number and breadth of vision in 'brain races'.

This is the source of new ideas and true knowledge as so many 'inventions' have proved.

One of, if not the best example, being the scientist and inventor Nicola Tesla. He would actually see visions of the solution to problems and without whom our modern civilisation would not exist in his envisioning of a machine producing alternating current, meaning electrical power could be supplied over great distances and to every home and appliance connected to vast networks that now also illuminate the planet from space.

And a huge number of other inventions modern 'science' has not yet caught up with, due to the suffocating predominance of intellect in modern 'scientific' training.

The rise into view of the crescent moon on my left big toenail and all it signified in more personal history rising and pressing into conscious awareness, meant much effort in working through and resolving the emotional energy this presaged and symbolised.

There is no mystery in this; it meant accepting – as ever – what my body and inner being was telling me and what feelings rose to the surface.

This spanned the complete spectrum of emotions from outrage and anger to fear and everything in between; the primary focus of which were the effects of my birth.

After the great heave of 2003 signified by the ascending 'crescent moon' in my left big toenail, the pace and intensity seemed to slacken and lift, I began to think I was nearing journey's end in working all its affects through.

My body telling me there was more pushing into consciousness was not as insistent, neither was there the pressure needing to be released in whatever emotion was ultimately signified by my body sensations and general feeling disposition.

But 'think' is not reality; merely speculation. I had only to make a mental inventory of my body to know there were areas that were still clamped and/or sensitive.

Basking in my sabbatical hoping it proved to be permanent, the time of year came around to the anniversary of when I began my journey; the 20th of September.

This almost coincided with a Druid ceremony on the 19th I attended to mark the autumnal equinox when the earth is exactly halfway through its annual axial totter on the 21st September.

Just another of those 'coincidences' of course to those of a purely rational bent, who should be present on this 30th anniversary also of beginning my journey, but someone from Nova Scotia where I began it.

I took it as an omen I really had reached the end of a long road.

I was wrong of course.

I soon began noticing the unerring barometer of surfacing energy needing to find its expression, release and conscious integration; my abdominal regions.

There was no denying the all too familiar feelings of clamped, rigid muscles and a tendency for the whole area to be bloated as if I had acquired a beer gut.

In its turn it wasn't long before twinges announced more of what

I had become so very familiar with over preceding years; gripping agony as if someone had reached in and wrung my digestive plumbing like wringing water out of cloth.

Likewise the wearisome time-honoured means of dealing with it; rolling up the corner of a face flannel into a plug and sticking it into my throat forcing reflexive vomiting which as much as I hated having to do it would instantly, or within a few seconds, break the clamping and its consequential agony.

And repeating this for as many times and over as long a period as it took for the next heave of the unconscious of yet more of what in birth I had no other choice than to sublimate and bury in it. To survive the seemingly interminable clamping and crushing of my mother's unyielding muscles, followed by another wave of the underlying residual spectrum of emotions associated with the physical symptoms.

This marked the start of – yet another – phase. To use the simile used previously; another heave of my inner consciousness's oceanic swells I was becoming clearer about, and understanding these weren't simply measured in hours, days or weeks but months and even years.

It took months before – for example – I could risk drinking even half a glass of wine without feeling like an over wound clock spring.

This – equally as ever; and to reiterate yet again – didn't mean sitting sucking my thumb and suffering whatever unpleasantness I felt bodily and emotionally, it meant doing what I had – as a general process – done many thousands of times before; do what my body – and through it my un/subconscious – said I needed to do to; release the stored energy it was pushing into bodily and conscious awareness.

If, as it so often did, mean lying on cushions and shoving my head as hard as I could against and into them, and thumping in outrage and (muffled) yelling, then it was what I did. I might not know beforehand what was coming, but as soon as I began, I knew I was having to play more of the 'tape' of what I had no other recourse than to stuff into inner consciousness during my birth.

It might take many repetitions for the feelings of outrage and fury to be exhausted, extending over weeks and even months but as day follows night, in time it dwindled and ceased.

It was interspersed with and/or then followed by all the other emotions associated with having been put through such an outrage. As predictable as links in a chain there would be hurt, hopelessness, fear – in abundance – despair and the whole spectrum of emotion until, as the storm finally abates and dies; however strong and long endured, finally inner consciousness would announce in calm, peace and undisturbed sleep (at least after a fashion), yet another cyclone of this long lasting weather pattern had blown itself out. Along with the general theme of birth and working though another phase, during this would come 'diversions' from the main theme. These were other events of my later life which had also been stored away, I was unable to deal with at the time. Once the – literally – more pressing need to release another chapter of my birth was resolved, then as is, and infallibly always has been, other events of later life needing resolution would press for conscious expression and resolution and the whole process continue evolving as time passed.

Another good analogy is a reservoir gradually being drained. As the water level (stored, sublimated energy) lowers, other features – perhaps parts of a drowned village (things having no apparent relevance to the reservoir except location) – come into view and conscious awareness that then also becomes incorporated into the overall picture.

Again, as time passed this aspect became clearer and clearer, as did the fact although they related to separate events at different times in my life there was an underlying emotional continuum linking them together.

For example, having released and resolved more pent up energy being denied my right of passage into the world at birth, the seemingly unrelated later life event might – and definitely was at times – the sense of outrage at being dragged around by my Uncle as a young boy, who for a time was my foster father, and spending untold interminable miserable hours in his dingy engineering workshop; or incarcerated in his decrepit old vans for mindless ages whilst he indulged his need for conversation with a fellow engineer. Simply because he wanted company and a distraction from his dismal, unprofitable business. I was like a toy – a human teddy bear – he took with him as a child does his favourite comforter. And who he could berate and shout at with impunity; assuaging his repressed fears and uncertainties in not following his talents in engine design; 'logically' choosing instead the drudgery of agricultural engineering he inwardly hated.

Having suffered this dozens of times, having my weekend playtime confiscated over years, it created the same kind of impotent fury, outrage, deep hurt and misery as being clamped solid and crushed repeatedly during my birth; for the treatment meted out by my Uncle was no less crushing; and a total denial of me.

The threads the unconscious weaves are the same themes of emotions relating to otherwise completely different events.

In reading about Carl Jung's work and his experiences, 'irrational' is a word appearing at times and related to the unconscious.

Whilst the breadth and depth of Jung's research and his work is almost unimaginable, in my experience there is *nothing irrational whatsoever* in the way the unconscious/subconscious works. As stated before there are only buried stored events; the decisions to push them out of consciousness in order to survive, and disconnected motivation; which could not be dealt with in any other way at the time they were experienced. The unconscious delivers exactly what needs to be delivered into consciousness – given the opportunity – exactly when it is appropriate for it to be expressed and as part of a strict continuum of like experiences and emotional energy that are the same, but dressed in different clothes.

The most powerful experiences taking priority over lesser ones of the same emotional nature and content.

JOURNEY OF A LIFETIME

The only thing irrational is the intellect's ability to saw the tree of complete inner certainty, into arbitrary logs of superficial random separateness. Deliberately inventing plausible but wholly spurious myths, palpably *knowing* what the truth really is but deliberately pretending reality is otherwise.

On an individual level this is called protective self-delusion. On a cultural level; scientific theory.

The way I have portrayed the rise into consciousness of changing awareness may appear woolly, lacking in clarity and difficult to grasp over the period of 2003–2004 and extending on into 2005.

The reason is very simple; attempting to apprehend precisely how and in what direction one's consciousness is moving, continuing to evolve and what sublimated experiences are being brought to the 'surface' and outer world expression, is like attempting to look in a mirror, except a mirror only reflects what is immediately visible. This is the world of the unconscious and the emotions which are timeless.

A mirror's ability to reflect images is exactly the way the unconscious / inner consciousness works.

It is only by understanding what emotions, thoughts and dispositions existed previously, trends even begin to emerge; let alone become clear. This is the intellect working harmoniously in concert with the unconscious and the emotions, providing a relational and temporal context to our outer world and consciousness.

Moreover, the analogy of the motions of waves on an ocean and the underlying energy giving rise to them I have used many times before to describe how the unconscious – which I prefer to call inner consciousness – delivers to our outer world consciousness, sublimated and suppressed energy needing to be expressed, is like trying to understand the whole ocean's movement and currents of energy from a single point within it.

It cannot be done.

It is only as a result of living through and experiencing them, patterns of consciousness and suppressed energy rising to the surface; being expressed and integrated into conscious experience, that understanding of the trends – short- and long-term – clarify and become clear(er).

With practice, over many years conscious understanding of inner rhythms, patterns of energy and expression, evolve from vague impressions to steadily more clearly delineated trends, until a new one and a new phase can be spotted quickly; in days, increasingly hours and after an unimaginable amount of work and clearing; instantaneously, that once would only have become apparent in months and years.

Which is exactly like the Polynesian's way of navigating reliably across the vastness of the Pacific to tiny islands. Their method is precisely the same in the outer world as reading the rhythms and patterns of one's inner. They navigated by knowing the ocean swells: the wave patterns, the currents, winds and other signs of the ocean regions they passed through, across vast distances and with great accuracy without a compass or any other navigational aid. In either case with continual practice it becomes completely reliable.

In terms of navigating the immense ocean of the unconscious though, even this is still not the full picture. As conscious awareness expands, new trends become clear looking back over an increasingly long span of years, that were completely unknown before but which provide a greater depth and breadth of perspective on what one previously thought of as the definitive version.

Time passed in 2004 and I continued to work steadily on what pushed up into body and outer consciousness for expression and assimilation. My goal as ever, was to clear body and being of whatever my unconscious said was next to be dealt with.

Ultimately I knew it always took me in the direction of improved function throughout my being. This – as mentioned many times before – did not mean it was a straight, clear and easy path just as navigating an ocean doesn't guarantee fine weather all the way.

As the thirtieth anniversary came of beginning clearing the weight of personal history I carried within me, I thought I had come to the end of it all.

Almost to the day, as explained briefly already, at an autumnal equinox ceremony, I got into brief conversation with someone who it transpired was from Nova Scotia, where I began reversing the process of repression I had been taught to live by. Just another of those many frequent whimsical 'coincidences!'

And as the equinox passed so did the perception of final resolution. It was merely a 'tea break'.

There were – and have always been – times when it was very definitely heavy weather, either feeling uncomfortable; even fragile bodily and/or emotionally.

As with so much of my journey over the decades, my digestive plumbing was an utterly reliable advance warning indicator of minor or major history yet to be worked through.

Though perhaps 2004 was the first year I began to have some awareness of where the trend was taking me.

It was simultaneously welcome and a trial: that I understood body symptoms and perhaps what to expect over succeeding weeks, helped to accept with forbearance difficult periods. Patience though was half the equation; the other half was living with and working through all the trapped and sublimated energy stowed away in inner being until then.

Generally, what started off easily and remained so for months, it became very clear as already mentioned, the going got harder as the year's end approached.

Alcohol provided a good gauge of what to expect. Early in the year, a glass of wine might provide a quiet night or perhaps quite a few dreams but in later months; hence as already described, an over wound clock-spring if I drank even half a glass, I would quickly have a feeling of tightness in my body, particularly in my head and the familiar constricted abdominal knots. By December one glass was sufficient to bring to the surface another phase of unresolved energy locked up deep within from my birth.

There was – and is – no rationalising it, kidding myself and intellectualising it all into a fog of nonsense. If I did what my body demanded I could usually gain relief and inner peace within a few minutes. During this period it not unusually meant repeating the process two or three times over the day. Sometimes more.

The number of times was and is of no consequence to me; the only criteria being resolving energy and my history associated with it so I felt/feel at peace in my body and getting on with whatever I want or need to.

The unfailing result is always to have a great deal more energy available to me because I am not locked in an un-winnable conflict within myself.

As ever, it took a few months but steadily, releasing the sublimated emotional energy until my body felt looser and a glass of wine no longer triggered a gush of energy in need of acknowledgement and release.

Having attempted to explain hundreds if not thousands of times over the years to people, what I do and its purpose, it has proved a waste of time and effort. The cultural conditioning of living completely dominated by intellect, deliberately suppressing if not outright extirpating any dialogue with their inner feeling nature, is so complete it would be easier to communicate with a locked safe.

The problem is, such a huge amount of fear of inner being is created, it does indeed create a sealed prison of implacable resistance.

JOURNEY OF A LIFETIME

It is only by directly experiencing and working with our sub/unconscious or inner consciousness we begin to understand what we truly are. Although I have used analogies and examples to paint pictures of the workings of inner consciousness it is an impossible task simply because this is the world of the intellect and words. The realms of inner consciousness are those of direct knowing, signs, symbols, portents, and images no amount of words can ever illuminate.

This is the gulf as mentioned previously between aboriginal or native, and westernised cultures, and why each sees the other as either bafflingly dysfunctional, stunted, and stupid. Or primitive, simple-minded, superstitious, dim-witted, and incapable of conceptual thought.

The best illustration of this in my experience is to be found in the books of Carlos Castenada, mentioned previously.

In studying anthropology, Castenada epitomised the westernised intellectual academic approach. In looking for a 'case study' he sought out a Yaqui Mexican Indian with a reputation of being a sorcerer or shaman; feared and shunned even by his own people for his powers.

The chronology and progression of his books show Castenada's stumbling progress over years to make sense of 'Don Juan's' teaching. It was only after writing two he began to realise the Indian's wisdom and knowledge could only be imparted by doing and not thinking, moreover had nothing whatever to do with psychotropic drugs.

In putting him through endless experiences, trials and tests, Don Juan worked consistently and systematically through direct experience, to dismantle Castenada's utterly rigid intellectually based view of the world and in particular to open up his access to his inner consciousness/unconscious. Only after years of 'bending' what he directly experienced to fit his brittle intellectual 'knowledge' of Don Juan's teachings, did cracks begin to appear and the divide in Castenada, between intellect and his walled off inner consciousness, begin to crumble.

In reassessing his notes his third book incorporates all he found bizarre and incomprehensible about his experiences he had previously dismissed, and which caused him to begin working with inner consciousness; yet even so, *still* not understanding this is what he was being trained to do; the problem being the workings and world of inner consciousness cannot be explained, they can only be experienced.

These books affect the reader in exactly the same way Castenada himself was affected by his teacher.

The more rigidly intellectual the reader is, the more it engenders the following responses in people: bafflement, incomprehension, incredulity, disbelief, fear, ridicule, irritation, outright anger.

In my experience this also illustrates the order of people's responses, and not just to these books and the completely different approach to life and the world described in them, but *all* new ideas shaking the foundations of intellectually ingrained learning so prized in our western culture.

Not unusually also, radically different new ideas telescope all the emotions up to and including fear into one and the rest as one and finally the two groups altogether; instantly compressing into a reflexive response of blind rage; nature's highest priority overload 'button', resulting in implacable, brick wall hostility and attempt to annihilate the idea and its messenger; literary or corporeal.

Or as Albert Einstein so crisply put it: 'All great ideas go through three stages: Bitter rejection, silent acquiescence, universal acceptance.'

Sadly our culture is at the first stage so far as inner consciousness is concerned. And heading with increasing rapidity in the wrong direction. The inescapable consequences of which will become acutely apparent for humankind within a few decades.

Toenails, Milestones, Trends and New Perceptions

In the years since 2004, dawning awareness of inner patterns has progressed with increasing momentum.

In its turn this has meant focusing less on individual aspects of repressed and sublimated emotional energy and the personal history it represented, and becoming steadily more conscious of the overall trend(s) – exactly like the metaphor of understanding the ocean from continual experience of sailing it.

This may seem a statement of the obvious once read, but to realise this is a trend in itself takes a long time to dawn, because it only becomes apparent by doing it.

To use the ocean metaphor again; the more one sails it the more one puts in context all its elements, from individual waves and swells to a growing understanding of its rhythms. Waves and swells being felt exactly as they were before but their overall context being understood precisely from the greater patterns they signify. The memory of sailing through rough weather and calm seas is not forgotten, but recalled in terms of an overall voyage.

Similarly, 2005 was a 'voyage' of discovery like its immediate predecessor; sailing the same ocean or crossing a vast plain but new experiences, currents and rhythms of inner consciousness being navigated, and, in retrospect becoming understood though only much later put in a greater context for having travelled further a very long way.

As indicated, one of the signs by which I navigated was my left big toenail.

Steadily the 'crescent moon' progressed up the nail until finally it disappeared – rather like sailing over the horizon, out of sight into new aspects of life and being.

Following it, the nail had many lateral ridges and was very uneven.

At the time I simply accepted I was seeing the bodily evidence of what was going on in inner consciousness and reflected wave after wave of personal history and its emotional energy coming to the 'surface' of consciousness, causing the 'waves' and heaving swell of my day-to-day life I steadily sailed on through.

Understanding how to read the ridges (the 'waves' and 'swell') took a great deal longer for it is only as it has progressed over the years can I look back and see what the nail patterns – literally – were telling me.

This is exactly the same as had occurred previously with my right big toenail.

It took me a long time – years – to understand in retrospect, as already described, how my day-to-day life went through a complete upheaval and took a long time and a great deal of diligent effort for it all to be worked through and pass out of my life in the gradual progression from shedding half the nail followed by ridges, pits, discolouration and blemishes before becoming smooth again and regaining a healthy pink colouring.

Taking the two together, they show the trends of personal inner and outer worlds. The right big toenail relating to outer world consciousness and the left, inner world consciousness.

Only as a direct consequence of seeing the changes as they happened and subsequently over a period of years, indeed decades, has it been possible to put them all, or better said; so far at least, in a coherent context.

Useful as they might be – and in retrospect – this is merely confirmation of changes having occurred as a consequence of releasing the sublimated suppressed emotional energy and life history and its integration into a steadily broadening and deepening conscious awareness.

JOURNEY OF A LIFETIME

In retrospect as 2004 reached its end it marked the point where awareness reached (yet) another new threshold. Exactly like sailing on in the ocean and an uncertain night's progress turning into the faintly perceptible glimmers and promise of a new day's dawning.

It did not mark some thunderclap and lightning bolt of sudden miraculous change and transformation in body and mind; in fact at the time I didn't know this was what was happening at all.

The trend over the succeeding years has been the same continuing process. Always open to what inner consciousness announced through bodily and emotional awareness needed to be expressed, released and integrated into conscious awareness.

Not unusually at the beginning of a year I experienced feelings of fragility, feeling very sensitive and having to work hard at 'bailing' – like a boat in a storm – the waves of surfacing emotional energy, wondering at times how to cope with it all. The primary focus of all this was still the effects of my birth.

There were times – equally like being in a storm at sea – when I wished it would all cease. But more and more I learned less and less to try putting intellectual fences of containment around inner consciousness, for without exception what I *thought* made not the slightest difference to the need for acknowledging the energy rising from my inner depths.

Instead, I learned by patterns of dreaming and what emotional energy welled up for expression; dealing with it and moving on, trusting I was on the right course as I had from the very outset, asking myself how I felt; comparing my state of being with months and years previously.

Without fail or exception the general trend was always in the direction of improved physical health, strength, and condition, expanded awareness and improved intellectual functioning.

Over decades I endeavoured to understand my dreams and see what messages my inner consciousness was telling me. Not unusually I recorded them on waking if they hadn't dissolved like fog in bright sunlight as daytime consciousness overpowered the delicate shadows of moonlit inner consciousness.

Sometimes as I wrote them down I knew exactly what they were about. At others the understanding would come weeks or perhaps even months later, having worked through the surfacing energy driving the images.

A good example of a general theme being cars and driving them. As explained previously, it took a long time but I eventually realised cars and driving them was an allegory of me and my life.

Cars got me from 'A' to 'B' in a journey, just as my body and being got me from 'A' to 'B' in my life. Hence as explained a number of times, a car was/is a symbol for my vehicle of life. And not just cars. Many years before I had a series of dreams over succeeding nights beginning with a tank coming graphically squeaking and clanking by in full sound and vision. It was succeeded by more automotive images progressively less distinct, finally culminating with a vague image of Concorde streaking off into the distance.

For some time I wondered what they were all about, realising they were linked but not understanding the theme until about six weeks later I suddenly knew it symbolised the chaotic, 'clanking' uproar of my childhood which became worse and worse, faster and faster until family and all sense of self-disintegrated. Hence a tank (symbolising deep inner conflict) and the mechanistic way in which my life ran – being 'steered' and jerked around by others until it all ended in a roaring image of Concorde (up-)roaring off into nothing. Leaving me with just the blown-to-bits wreckage of what had been me and childhood.

The metaphor of the heat and noise from Concorde's engines was no accident either. For weeks if not months after, when I was on my own and usually walking in the countryside I would feel a sensation of heat all round me. Particularly when it contrasted with being in cool air.

I was very clear at the time what it was about. At some level of my being I felt I was like a piece of metal; repeatedly heated (by the utter chaos of emotional stress) and beaten by the conflicting forces of all I had lived through and a sense of deafening inner clamour for all the cacophony of discordant emotional uproar characterising the whole tumultuous experience.

The same sensation being repeated at other times in my life having gone through the 'heat and hammering' of other powerful emotional experiences.

Inner consciousness/the unconscious always serves up images not just relating to one episode and aspect of life experience either. The images were links in a chain, relating to the same kind of emotional experiences at different times in my life. Hence the tank I saw in one dream was an old one and my father had seen battle in the Royal Navy. At the other end of the sequence of dreams, Concorde and deafening noise from its fire breathing engines also symbolised the same experiences in current times in the break up of my marriage; not least the fact my wife worked for British Airways.

Concorde was not some abstracted tortuous metaphor either; in easterly winds it regularly took off over my house, the intensity of the noise such that, as it approached, it was as if the sound scored a furrow beneath it, like some giant glass cutter cleaving glass; for the sound possessed a sharp edge to its progress. And, but for one pilot, as it passed overhead it did so with a deafening roar, reminiscent of being close to the RAF's V-bombers taking off close by. But their engines were only half the power! So metaphors of excoriating, shattering noise also reverberates with tumultuous shattering emotional uproar. Quite apart from other Concorde symbolism already used.

There is no denying as Carl Jung's work makes very clear, the unconscious – as he calls it – but which to me is inner consciousness, is the vital, strictly independent adjudicator who pronounces on our day-to-day life in the outer world and what corrective action needs to be taken and lessons heeded. And which we ignore – and worse – suppress, to our diminishment at best and avoidable fatal disaster at worst.

In my direct experience though, once one begins working directly with inner consciousness to clear the unimaginable amount of personal emotional bric-a-brac and toxic history our culture teaches us to continually push into it, like some gigantic landfill dump, dreams, though absolutely vital for the wisdom they carry, are by no means the only way to heed, create and maintain health and wellbeing at all levels.

Directly acknowledging what inner consciousness tells us the whole time through our bodies and expressing the underlying emotions previously consigned to our individual 'landfill' dumps, rather than peering through the keyhole in the door to inner consciousness to get a picture of what is pushing into outer awareness through dreams, positively re-owning a natural faculty every single human ever born possesses, means being able to open the door to it and work directly with inner consciousness.

The emphasis being on 'work'.

Meaning working with and through our bodies to release, express and integrate into conscious awareness all we have pushed into our 'landfill' tip of inner consciousness.

It is indeed a great irony it took Carl Jung a lifetime's gigantic research, work and effort to show through intellectual study the mechanisms and 'language' of the unconscious, yet having done so to treat it as purely the province of intellectual knowledge and expertise administered by experts to work with the faculty of (inner) consciousness which functions in a manner utterly dissimilar and separate from intellect.

It is though, entirely understandable Jung strove so deeply and for so long into understanding the workings of the unconscious; first because it fascinated him and was his chosen vocation in any case, but because he also realised unless he established very solid grounds for the conclusions he came to and wrote about, he would get a savage kicking from his peers and elders. Which in considerable measure he did anyway.

Including his erstwhile friend Freud who, like many others since was nothing like as diligent or as open minded as Jung. And far from attempting, without prejudice, to search until he found where to fit a stray piece of the unconscious sympathetically in a context supported by historical evidence spanning ages into antiquity, Freud – rather like a jigsaw puzzle assembler wrestling with an enigmatic piece – having reached a dogmatic conclusion, sought to force it into his intellectually rigid picture of where it had to fit. Meaning it had to be based in sex or wish fulfilment. Or both.

We are back at Einstein's pithy observation again concerning new/great ideas.

In any case the truth is more prosaic than only great ideas meeting with implacable hostility.

Almost any new ideas beyond the light of majority consciousness sends shafts of illumination into its darkened corners arousing uncertainty and fear of what might be revealed. The greater the new ideas' impact the greater the fear and reflexive resistance.

Seen at its most extreme one need only observe the scientific community and those with vested interest in the status quo, to witness the equivalent reaction of pure sodium dropped into water, when a new idea challenging or standing completely outside accepted practice and wisdom appears.

It may still seem to some – perhaps many – simply because our society is so overwhelmingly dominated by intellect, there is no relationship between our bodies and inner consciousness.

Of itself this illustrates the brick wall divide created in treating intellect as *the* centre of consciousness.

Times beyond number over the decades since I very first began working with what my body wanted to express, it has been my unfailing experience that physical symptoms are the messengers of changes in deeper levels of being and inner consciousness.

It is no less true now and in recent times than right at the beginning.

WARNINGS FROM THE INNER WORLD ARE REAL

WORKING WITH OUR inner world instead of against it is not some bookish fantasy, as I can vouch for myself, and as I have already referred to many, many times already.

Having left the chaos of the Air Force behind me in the late sixties, I had a deep hunger and thirst for knowledge; to learn new things and move on in my life. In itself this was an uncanny re-run of my experience as a child. The common theme being to create order, stability and control, based on my own efforts and in my own way, and not a hapless pinball cannoned around in my life by someone else's misperceptions of theirs.

Having entered the computer industry I not only trained and studied for the work I did but academically also.

This lasted for three years and there were times when I worked and studied seven days a week, working alternating day and night shifts week by week, attending night school and studying on my own.

With all I have said about our culture being dominated by intellect and chronically lacking balance by abusing our inner world as a consequence, I became an example *par excellence* of this.

But to be fair to myself, ordered work and study to create meaning and sense of purpose and achievement in my own life was the way I dealt with its polar opposite I had ineluctably lived with for far too much of my life until then.

To re-state again, once I began this increasingly punishing – though intellectually gratifying – way of life I chose, it was not long before my car began to acquire dents from being hit by others. None of these 'accidents' being my fault. People ran into my car whilst I was in it and usually when I was stationary. And even at three in the morning when I wasn't and had just parked it on the very quiet road where I lived in lodgings!

The trend of the collisions was from minute and barely visible – inflicted by a double decker bus – to finally being hit from behind (yet again). And by another car of exactly the same colour, also a Ford but a larger model! Rebounding off a crash barrier and ending up upside down spinning like a top; petrol pouring out of the tank, on the oncoming lanes of a busy motorway in peak hour traffic – and walking away without a scratch, though initially without my shoes, proving the old saying; he was so frightened he jumped out of his boots. Or in my case my shoes just fell off. Either way proving fear shrinks the feet.

In being a car of identical colour and manufacturer the symbolism could hardly be more complete, in effect saying: if you go on being blind to what you are doing to yourself and don't stop doing it, you are sleep walking to disaster; WAKE UP!

If this seems tenuous and contrived, though I could not prove it, I had the absolute certainty I was hit by someone who had dozed off and was asleep at the wheel!

The clear message from my unconscious or inner consciousness was, again, as I have previously said, increasingly urgent and severe warnings I was doing damage to my (inner) self. And I should either take myself off the road of life I was on, or suffer the consequences if I ignored the warnings, continuing to study harder and harder for my work and for night school, then the warning shunts to get off my chosen road of progress would become more urgently severe.

Culminating at the point when I was stretched to my absolute limit; and beyond it – as people remarked afterwards about how I looked at the time – finally, I not only got knocked off my 'road of life' I was so damagingly pursuing in my 'vehicle of life' (a metaphor for my body and being), but so nearly became the proverbial pinball in other people's machinations I was determined to avoid (another metaphor I have deliberately used previously), on the oncoming lanes of a motorway.

But the symbolism, metaphor and warnings do not even end there. Spinning about upside down on the oncoming motorway lanes in effect symbolised: if you insist on conducting yourself in a completely upside down fashion, going utterly and diametrically against the proper flow of your inner self, then you are heading straight for disaster.

This is positively your LAST warning!

If this still seems fanciful, the example given earlier of Jung's stark warning to a man who wanted to escape shady dealings he was embroiled in, should be recalled.

Because the man took no notice and avoiding action to his dream's warning in his day-to-day outer world then its symbolic inner world warning became the overriding operative factor.

The man escaped his nefarious dealings all right! Forfeiting his life in the process; and someone else's theirs as well. Fortunately within a couple of months I finished studying, and the crippling load of learning and teaching new computer systems in minute detail, eased; and perhaps even more fortunately, I did without a car for the next three years and more.

Since those times only on one occasion has anyone ever run into a car I have been driving, because from 1974 I have been working *with* my inner world and self, repairing the self-inflicted damage and clearing also the literally crushing legacy of my birth and other personal history.

Did I understand at the time, these events in my outer world were the warnings from my inner, I absolutely refused to acknowledge?

Of course not. To me they were just a 'phase' I went through of being accident prone.

However, at some deep level far removed from conscious awareness of these warnings, I heeded them nonetheless. The evidence for which is that I am typing these words.

Perhaps those of a purely rational, logical inclination will, if they have got this far, be exhibiting the dispositions listed earlier with all these outlandish ideas, so utterly alien to 'normal' soundly based intellectual reasoning.

However, as the ancient saying goes I recently coined: I don't make the rules, I just make the effort.

Meaning, I have observed over decades and untold thousands of hours of work since I first began giving up rape and pillage slowly: the savage slavery I was taught to subject my inner self to – as a latter day Charles James Fox might characterise our culture's institutionalised slavery of inner being – the body changes accompanying my own gradual abolition of brutalising intellectual dominance within.

Toenails, and indeed finger nails, because they are visible for months, I have found to be a very clear, succinct résumé of what changes of inner self have made their impact visible on a physical level.

Making sense of their temporal, as well as the pure physical appearance is a process involving recollection, reasoning, intuition and instinct, consequently a harmonious combination of intellect and inner consciousness to divine their deeper and broader significance.

They can be likened to a diary of the body's changes to refer back to; the narrative being clearly 'written' in the nail, unlike internal body changes which are hidden and evidence of them made known through aches, pains, discomfort and/or their absence and hence tend to be viewed as separate unrelated events and experiences.

They are as equally part of a continuum as nails indicate but relating them together is more obscure because awareness of them is mostly not long lasting or visible.

A few more examples will illustrate, also previously quoted.

The lungs react very quickly to changes brought about as energy flows more freely in the body.

Right at the beginning of releasing the immense amount of pent up suppressed energy in September 1974 there was no mistaking my lungs were stirring into life. As related I began coughing up clods of yellow mucus and I knew and could feel this was my left lung 'waking up'.

At various times since, as more and more inner liberation took place, they again became a focus of attention.

Consistently from the very beginning and ever since, my experience has always been when blocked, suppressed energy clamped solid in the body is released and resolved, lungs begin clearing out mucus.

In the early years as mentioned, I called this 'coughing up elastic bands' because the mucus was thick and stuck in the throat, requiring effort to clear it, if indeed it was actually possible.

It is not for nothing the old saying of 'getting something off your chest' exists. There is (if only we would listen to it) a deep innate awareness that holding in emotions means holding energy in the body, and the lungs unfailingly show this.

Release the energy/emotion and the lungs respond. Not unusually also the lungs clearing I have found to be advance warning, as well as confirmation of what has previously been cleared, of yet more stored history pushing into conscious awareness for expression and resolution.

This can be short- or long-term and it can either be mild, or when a lot is changing and releasing within, can ache and feel very sensitive or even like being kicked in the upper chest area.

Carl Jung also remarked on miraculous improvements in patients of his suffering from tuberculosis.

We are back again at 'getting something off your chest'.

Once pent up clamped energy is released in inner consciousness, the falling domino effect registers in the body almost instantaneously in the lungs.

Perhaps this also seems like another whimsical assertion; if so, then the Indian system of medicine widely practised in the Indian subcontinent called 'Ayurveda' which in Sanskrit (the language of the extremely ancient Indus Valley civilisation) means 'science of life', and Ayurvedic practitioners/doctors say goes back many thousands of years further than the Chinese systems, is fundamentally flawed.

In Ayurveda, there are three basic body energy types or 'Doshas' exactly similar to the principle of 'Humours' in the Greek system, except it has four.

The Doshas are Vata, Pitta and Kapha. People are grouped within these classifications.

Without going into a lot of detail 'Vata' energy is characterised as being cold and dry and is the fastest registering/reacting energy in the body. Ayurveda associates it with air and the cosmos and particularly with 'prana'; the invisible life sustaining energy one intakes in breathing and pervades the cosmos throughout.

Which 'science' has newly discovered and calls 'dark energy' comprising seventy-three per cent of the total universe.

Whilst we can go without food for a few weeks, water for about three days at a stretch, without air we die in three minutes or so. Hence there is an association between the speed of effect of air and 'prana' in the body.

'Vata' energy is linked with the nervous system in Ayurveda. The nervous system being the fastest operating and reacting in the body.

Consequently Ayurveda links the speed of energy and bodily effects together.

When Vata energy is out of balance in the body, one of the primary effects Ayurveda looks for is in the lungs.

A Matter of Balance

Breathing is fundamental to life and is affected when emotions are clamped; the unfailing corollary being breathing is also clamped.

When breathing is clamped the lungs do not operate at their full capacity and fluid/mucus builds up.

For example, when someone is very seriously out of balance, running on and depleting their nervous and emotional energy the lungs can even become inflamed. Especially if the person is of a 'Vata' disposition.

Also to requote; many years ago a relative was hospitalised with just such a condition.

I was told the hospital were baffled because numerous tests revealed absolutely nothing.

Knowing how this person drove themselves mercilessly and lived on nervous and emotional energy, although this was decades before I heard about Ayurveda, I instinctively responded – with kindness and humour – how terribly unreasonable it was when one worked oneself into the ground, lungs showed their displeasure by becoming upset, angry and inflamed.

She gave a rueful smile and we laughed together but it struck an instant chord of recognition and nothing found, she left hospital and it was not long before her lungs subsided in their outrage and she recovered. Aided by colour healing I also instinctively suggested.

Just as at school whilst rehearsing a school play in free moments I *breathed in* and soaked the beautiful dense blue stream of energy emitted by a spotlight, as previously mentioned.

Leaving a job which not unusually left her emotionally wrung out and prostrated with fatigue was no doubt the crucial factor. Creating profound imbalance in her being and body. Adding to what already existed.

Unfortunately, westernised modern medicine, because it exists in a two dimensional matrix of intellectual facts and categorisations, insists on treating symptoms and not the person; has names for everything and understanding of nothing, treating 'Pneumonia' for example as merely a 'condition' where the lungs become inflamed and consequently nature as part of its healing process, tries to put the raging 'fire' of chronic imbalance out and the lungs fill with fluid. Just as a burn causes the skin to fill with a protective layer of fluid also as part of the natural healing process.

Westernised medicine on the other hand assembles overwhelming force that figuratively speaking would make the greatest barrages of World War One look like a firework party to pulverise the 'dis-ease' into oblivion, hence obliterating the symptoms rather than curing the deep un-ease in the patient.

Having learned in myself the fundamental link between clamped energy and lung/respiratory function; as well as the example given it is clear to me in many people I meet how 'colds', 'flu', 'sore throats', coughs that won't shift and other respiratory affecting conditions, have as their foundation, energy clamped solid in their bodies, because energy is clamped deep in inner consciousness.

So lungs and the respiratory system also I have found to be yet more unfailing indicators of blocked, clamped energy.

People invariably describe the cure for their condition in puns as previously explained, a few examples of these being:

JOURNEY OF A LIFETIME

Condition	Question to ask
'I've got a really **raw** throat'	Who is it I want to **roar** at?
'I can't seem to shift this cold off my chest'	Who is it I need to shift off it?
'I've got this awful honking cough'	What awful person is honking me off?

This is not limited to the lungs; characterisations of headaches are equally illuminating:

Condition	Question to ask
'I've got a thumping headache'	Who do I want to thump?
'I've got a splitting headache'	What/who am I splitting myself away from?
'I've got a raging headache'	Who do I want to rage at?

These 'puns' are inner consciousness/the 'unconscious' presenting the allegory to us as a metaphor/symbol creating in effect an image, because inner consciousness communicates through images, signs, symbols and portents. When we stop intellect from ignoring or deliberately going against our inner wisdom – like shooting out traffic lights at crossroads – inner consciousness unfailingly provides us with the answers.

It is usually only when we are in discomfort or pain – yet another and stronger warning as indicated above – that intellect's interfering activities are moderated or suspended because we can no longer ignore what inner self is urgently trying to get through! So we allow and pass through to our outer world the allegory/pun in words we use. What do we then do? Ignore it of course! That is what this insane culture has taught us to do from when we were born! We shoot out the warning traffic light symptoms with drugs, outright denial and plausible intellectual drivel; in fact anything to avoid opening a dialogue with our demonised inner being.

We are back with 'Alice in Wonderland' again and Lewis Carroll's metaphor for the intellect in the Mouse's Tale symbolised in 'Cunning Old Fury'! Because we treat intellect as judge and jury the whole time and in everything!

The Conservation of Energy, Intellect, Logjams and Palpitations

In *Man And His Symbols* Jung gives the excellent example himself of 'miraculous' recoveries/transformations of tuberculosis conditions in his patients – because the blockage/repression of unexpressed energy had been released through understanding dream messages, like a logjam being released, inner consciousness immediately begins to re-establish and re-assert *balance* in the body through the released flow of energy with 'miraculous' results.

Clearly though, Jung did not fully connect the release of energy blockage in the 'unconscious' with the subsequent restored flow of body energy re-asserting and restoring bodily balance purging out the dis-ease.

If he had he would not have referred to it as 'miraculous', explaining instead cause and immutable effect.

He himself recognised as he said, 'energy is energy'. It cannot be made or destroyed but only changes form as fundamental cosmic laws demonstrate, and what in Physics is called the law of 'conservation of energy'. Humans are not exempt. Yet because Jung's approach was based in vast intellectual study and acquired knowledge of symbolism, he relied heavily on intellect to 'fix' inner consciousness, consequently failing to fully appreciate his own statement about energy.

If he had worked *with* his own body he would have known through *direct experience* the equally direct relationship between creating logjams of stored suppressed energy in inner consciousness and its corollary in the body.

He would also have avoided the near catastrophic heart attack that so nearly killed him which in its turn was his own inner consciousness's way of saying in effect; 'you continue throwing more and more at me; bottling up more and more energy which has nowhere to go, creating a massive logjam. Even you (Jung's own intellect) above all ignore all the signs I give you. You are accumulating such a huge imbalance in yourself by overloading me and won't even acknowledge it, let alone do anything about it. Right! Enough is enough; the limit has been reached. I can't hold back any longer the colossal logjam you have created and now things must take their course whether your body can stand it or not.'

The supreme paradox and irony being inner consciousness's remedial action to restore balance is exactly like someone dynamiting the logjam standing directly in front of it!

It is one stage further than the last warning I got in my car being hit and shoved off my damaging 'road of life', and but for a 'miracle', otherwise knocked into oblivion.

It should not be imagined the foregoing remarks of a conversational nature about Jung's heart attack are coincidental simplistic fantasy.

Earlier mentions of heart effects I experienced and their description were done with the specific conscious intention of expanding them in the light of lengthening experience, my deepening awareness of my own *continuum* and understanding of the relationship between inner and outer consciousness.

Or body/(sub)consciousness and the superficial consciousness our society treats as the *only* level of conscious existence.

Previous examples given should be recalled, e.g., ship demolition workers who died of heart attacks enduring endless months of punishing work and unrelenting dismal existence. Which occurred when the immediate stress of having to function and perform the grinding toil of their work, was relieved for a short time.

Thus the immense cumulative, sublimated stress held back, was finally 'dynamited'. The fuse having been involuntarily lit by the striking match of temporary relief.

Not least, my own direct experiences. Once I began in 1974 to unload the unimaginable (to me) load of repression I carried, December of that year was the first time in years I began to enjoy some sense of rest and peace over Christmas. During this period whilst in bed one morning, as already described, I felt a sudden palpitation like firing and recoil of a howitzer. And as also characterised; like an elephant dancing around on springs in my chest after the initial 'explosion'. I was used to the occasional palpitation but this was of a completely different magnitude.

The point being, had I not even by that time, shifted out and released from body and being, a huge amount of life-strangling repressed, locked up energy, the 'elephant dancing on springs' in my chest would instead have been catastrophic explosions of energy; the detonation of the logjam standing in front of it.

The releasing of buried great inner stress up to that point made the difference between surviving and being hit by a cruise missile of involuntary energy release out of nowhere.

Exactly as described for the Filipino men suffering fatal heart attacks once they were *away* from work.

It has been a pattern of unfailing confirmation with *no* exceptions over almost four decades, when I have worked through yet more sublimated, repressed energy a threshold is reached when still more energy crosses the boundary between inner and outer consciousness and a palpitation occurs.

Thus I have found it both confirmation of release and the infallible indicator of more energy on its way into body consciousness and conscious expression.

Also unfailingly, as more and more history and the energy it represents has been released and integrated into conscious understanding, the trend has always been palpitations have become steadily milder and heart function clearer, more distinct and 'happier' if that is the word.

As a final example – again, one I have given previously – after I stopped lecturing and carrying the massive crushing intellectual overload of computer systems knowledge I burdened myself with, within a few weeks I experienced an involuntary deluge of suppressed, sublimated emotional energy and began getting small palpitations constantly within a minute or two of each other every day for weeks. At the time it was just something I lived with as a dispassionate observer of what was happening within my own body. Because like Jung, I didn't connect cause and effect, simply because I had been so completely addicted to worshipping at the high altar of the Great Jealous Deity of intellect.

Accordingly, to recapitulate; our intellect / superficial consciousness obsessed society tends to view heart attacks as discrete physical unrelated events which they are not, and address them at an almost purely physical level. Concomitantly, to reiterate the universal cosmic law of the conservation of energy; it cannot be made or destroyed, it can only change its form. There are *no* exceptions to this law. Not even intellect dominated westernised cultures that act as though the human form possesses limitless capacity to sublimate and suppress emotional energy are exempt.

In the same book, even one of Jung's most trusted acolytes, Dr Marie-Louise Von Franz, similarly fails to appreciate the link between release of suppressed energy and its bodily expression, i.e., the fundamental link between energy in inner consciousness and energy in outer physical body consciousness. She gives the case history of an engineer who she calls 'Henry', explaining in minute detail the symbolic significance of his dreams and the beneficial gestalt for her patient in their unravelling in outer intellectual consciousness.

After one particularly significant dream analysis, Henry cancelled the next appointment because he had the 'Flu'. There is no recognition of the human continuum and of cause and effect in this case either. Again; unblocking of Henry's particular inner logjam in inner consciousness, energy was inescapably expressed in powerful outer, physical energy body-consciousness, by undergoing the purging, natural healing stress of deep re-alignment and re-balancing.

Intellect sees events as discrete, separate, and unrelated, because that is its function and nature, but our bodies and the consciousness abiding within them operates as a flowing continuum from the womb to the grave. When consciousness ceases to be within, so do we.

The example given of the two people who went out of their bodies may be recalled? When the thermograph machine showed they had left their bodies the machine 'thought' they had 'died' – so it did too; and blew its fuses. Nonsense of course – but absolutely true.

Once again, those of a westernised 'sane', 'level-headed', 'rational', 'logical' intellectual disposition as I was taught to be, will treat these examples at best with bewilderment, or progressing through the responses listed previously, on towards outright rage at what they choose to perceive as fanciful, utter rubbish.

And out of fear at what the reverberating echoes of these words resonate with in themselves.

Equally as pointed out; when intellect's two-dimensional brick wall against inner consciousness is challenged and cultural conditioning since birth is breached or in danger of being, all the denial of our own inner wisdom is challenged as well.

Or in keeping with the metaphor of logjams, anything threatening to dynamite our own logjam of culturally imposed self-denial and suppression, is resisted with varying degrees of inner status-quo-perpetuating antagonism, simply because to admit and accept we have been taught to create painful imbalance deep within, threatens to unleash the complete spectrum of emotional energy locked up in it until then.

The greater the conditioning and the more harshly applied the denial of inner self is, the more pronounced the reaction.

In fact, exactly like when I attempted to help the hitch hiker whose life was a meandering shambles, I once gave a lift to in Australia, who threw my sincere concern and well meant advice back in my face with her rapier thrust response she had 'never met anyone so fiendishly logical in all her life!'

To say it hurt is to say being run through with a sharp blade is somewhat uncomfortable. Deep instantaneous hurt followed, and, having had my inner world pierced so deeply; by near instantaneous anger; the do something *now* overload response to take positive action and either remove myself from the cause or remove it from me. Fortunately for her, my cultural conditioning had been sufficiently repressive. Though sorely tempted, I did not stop the car instantly, in the middle of a storm with which the windscreen wipers barely coped and shove her out there and then!

Plus Ça Change Plus C'est La Même Chose

As the French so elegantly put it; The more things change the more they remain the same.

There is absolutely nothing new in all I have said to the extent that ancient systems of healing have as their fundamental principle re-establishing and maintaining *balance* in the complete human.

It has been fundamental to Indian and Chinese medicine; consequently a third of the world's population, for many thousands of years. Including the use of astrology which 'scientists' treat as nonsense, but they of course know *so* much more than has been known for thousands of years even before the astrological Dendera zodiac.

What is different is instead of looking in the world outside myself for answers in 'isms', therapies, books by the thousand, and all manner of instant intellectual 'sticking plasters' of transformation and instant guruship, I began clearing out the midden of my inner world accumulated during and since birth.

The process in essence is very simple; stop using inner consciousness as a vast tip to store ever more unexpressed emotional energy and reverse it, i.e., start clearing it out.

That is all. But 'science' hasn't discovered this yet.

However, to repeat; simple should not be confused with easy. 'Clearing out' is not synonymous with sloshing around aimlessly in a swamp of emotion. It is not a case of throwing the points and changing tracks from 'all intellect' to 'all emotion', as can often happen, but combining these different aspects of consciousness together, creating and nurturing *self-awareness* and the continuum of one's own inner patterns of consciousness as they evolve over time. And sticking with it for as long as it takes!

The East does not have a monopoly on the philosophy of creating and maintaining balance within oneself. As mentioned previously, tribal or 'primitive' cultures, however incomprehensibly expressed, have as the cornerstone of their intentions, the same fundamental recognition of the need for balance and its maintenance.

Hardly surprising, because living in harmony with, and as inseparable from nature, its balance is the inescapable wisdom they live with every second of their lives.

It is worth reiterating the words of Chief Seattle again; "Man did not weave the web of life – he is merely a strand on it. Whatever he does to the web, he does to himself."

The need for and lesson of fundamental balance *within ourselves* has long since been smothered by the crushing weight of intellectual dominance nurtured in our society from its Aristotelian roots and heritage.

The net result, as Chief Seattle said in so few words, demonstrates the truth imbalance within ourselves creates an utterly devouring need to restore it. The direct consequence being we devour the Great Mother who sustains us with no regard for balance. The culmination will be in Chief Seattle terms: the Great Mother will devour us. And will do so before this century is finished. Unless we change.

In my direct experience of four decades, it is only by 'doing it' insights and perceptions become available. There is no fudging the amount of intelligently applied effort and dedication it takes to clear the unimaginable amount of sublimated and suppressed energy we are all capable of storing through what *consciousness* we suppress in inner consciousness. The two are inseparable.

JOURNEY OF A LIFETIME

Consistently I have found no amount of positive thinking, mantra chanting, living on celery, avocado pears, brown bread and green tea, meditation, deep massage, becoming a trainee pin cushion, all of which I have experienced, or learning other people's words of wisdom, however much one deeply identifies with their perceived therapeutic rewards, all ultimately fail to create fundamental, *continuing permanent improvement* to our body and being *if* we are subsequently still carrying the weight of our past within us, and refuse to acknowledge and release it.

Indeed, the premise of many therapies and treatments is we come to rely on them to just maintain a semblance of inner harmony and health. Maintaining someone else's bank balance doing it.

We can kid ourselves all we like but our bodies and being tell the truth.

The stored history we carry suppressed and hold in inner consciousness continues to act through our bodies as long as we refuse to pay attention to the Great Guru every single one of us has within by right of our human form.

The problem we all have in our culture is we are taught from birth to completely ignore it; or worse; that it does not exist. Hence we are denied the infallible wisdom the Great Creator gave all of us to use.

The insights and perceptions shared so far are not a product of worming through books and pretending the knowledge contained in them is my own, like some steroid driven parrot. It is only by many thousands of hours of diligent work releasing the body and emotional I stored in my own 'landfill tip' because that was the model I was given and learned like everyone else, that understanding dawned of what my inner world was/has been telling me the whole time.

Even this does not express the dedication given to clearing my inner self, body and being. For four decades since Friday 20th September 1974, when I began the process it has never left me for a moment, day and night.

This is no fanciful exaggeration; at the beginning I absolutely burned inwardly with an utterly consuming yearning to free myself from the horrible, profoundly leaden miserable fragility weighing me down the whole time. Once I created the unshakable inner conviction I *knew* I had begun to free my body and being and what I needed to do to sustain it, my burning conviction ignited into a solar incandescence of unquenchable ambition; *nothing* would extinguish except my life's end. Were this not so I would never have possessed sufficient motivation to continue no matter what it took to achieve my goal.

Simply stated, it was and remains, to completely transform my body, being and life. And which has occurred in ways unimaginable even a decade or so ago, let alone when I began.

The inescapable consequences have been the confirmation I have seen in my body, and proof that in working though all I once thought I had no other choice than to bury in myself, I was learning to understand and listen to the benign giant we call the 'unconscious'/'subconscious'/inner consciousness but which is something we should have no name for because there should be *no* barrier between inner and outer consciousness. It is *all one* but which our culture has completely split in two, from what has come down to us from the ancient Greeks and Aristotle in particular.

Making the connection with my own inner being has meant I have unsurprisingly found in the outer world the knowledge and wisdom extant as long as man has recorded it and for millions of years before writing ever existed. Or true to say, the faint whisperings of this incomprehensibly vast source of Everything There Is; to which we have slammed the doors of perception and thrown away the keys.

Recent Times and Recent Signs

Having used big toenails as pointers along my path of progress, especially my left one in the years since 2003, the rising 'crescent moons' ascent out of sight, became a symbol of a new phase on my journey of inner being.

Did things magically change? No. And neither did my life.

I vaguely realised I was entering another phase and another even deeper level of clearing inner being, though as ever I had no idea precisely what this would mean or bring, content to travel my inner journey as its 'scenery' unfolded before me.

The rising moon on my left big toenail was, if one knew how to read the signs, an exact allegory of what to expect within my body and being over the following months.

As one travels any road, a sense of continuum does not fully exist, until one has completed the journey.

Similarly, the toenail 'moon' led as inexorably and predictably to the rise into body and once released; expressed and integrated, to clear outer awareness and body changes.

The fact it was my left big toe – as distinct from right – meant the next phase was central to my deep inner self and of a similar depth emotional energy nature.

Left side of the body is controlled by the right brain lobe which is associated with the emotional, instinctive and intuitional aspects and much else besides. The fact it was my big toenail and not the others, symbolised what was surfacing was of a central nature. Because, the big toe – as already related – is associated not only with the head, but the centre of the left one in reflexology is equated with the pituitary gland. This reflex point being in the *exact centre* of the under side of the big toe.

There could hardly be a more exactly precise allegory of the 'picture' on the *top* (upper side) of my toe – and exactly central to it – of what it was telling me to expect via the pituitary gland reflex on the *bottom* (under side) – and equally exactly central to my toe – as the pituitary gland is *centrally* placed at the base of the brain!

The gland being responsible for nine hormones *central* to the body's functioning. Although only the size of a pea, it is the master control gland in the brain exercising direct control over the body's ductless (endocrine) glands such as thyroid, adrenal and others. Also kidneys, reproductive system and many other aspects of growth, development and general functioning.

It would be difficult not to say impossible to find a more precise correlation and allegory of what I was seeing and the message it carried of what was next to happen within my being was of a fundamental nature directly associated with equally fundamental aspects of body and inner being.

Exactly what I experienced over more than a year as 2003 progressed into 2004 and further into the following year.

Did all this occur to me then? Not at all. It was just another phase and chapter in the unfolding process, as I saw it, of clearing myself; my inner being, and my history showing in my body and governing my daily existence. To me the outward signs my own body pictured for me were intriguing and showed things were changing but like plodding by an interesting feature in the landscape it was simply something I saw and noted, continuing to pass by as I did so.

In retrospect, 2005 signified arrival on a huge new plain with few inner skyline features. It was a time of continuing working to clear whatever pressed for expression without questioning its significance or where it might be leading, like crossing some vast prairie, or trackless ocean.

Equally vaguely, I used my dreams as a rough indicator of what was happening within.

I had no great access to them. Sometimes I recalled parts and wrote them down; occasionally I understood what the message seemed to be, but for the great majority it was the feeling impression of them I used. Over time if their quality seemed involved and for want of a better description, rather dark or heavy in nature I treated this as a sign there was a lot of inner world activity; changes/clearing/working through and resolving things of my inner world. Precisely what, I had no idea but over time – days and weeks; even months – I felt their quality change and go through cycles and becoming lighter, then progressing on to more compressed or heavy inner activity.

This and the changes in toe and fingernails were the signs by which I mainly navigated my ocean of inner being.

Occasionally during this period a few body 'events' made themselves very apparent.

For example, on May Day, I evidently reached a point where it was time for more gut strangling agony to work its way out to a conscious body level.

In time honoured fashion all this sublimated and suppressed energy announced its presence by the sensation I became familiar with over decades when at its worst. That someone had lit a fire within my abdomen and was using a large mole-grip wrench to 'adjust' the plumbing.

Fortunately also, although the remedy was tedious in the extreme to have to endure, I knew how to disperse this intense burning pain in my transverse colon – where I intuited the focus of the agony to be – by my equally time honoured antidote of folding the corner of a face flannel across diagonally, rolling it into a plug and stuffing it into my mouth and throat to force reflexive roaring retching.

As explained before also and not just once, I did not enjoy this bizarre seeming ritual one little bit, but the hundred per cent reliable outcome was I could break and release the involuntary gripping gut spasm more or less instantaneously. Which definitely *was* enjoyable in being able to banish quickly this particularly unpleasant agony. I have known these symptoms reduce people to agony-wracked panic stricken hospitalisation with what I would treat as mild to moderate and dealt with in five minutes.

At least that was the general rule, but this May Day seemed to have brought its own particular colonic 'celebration' and it took several flannel applications with several more agonising spasms before mole wrench and fire were finally removed and extinguished. I spent the day sitting in my armchair watching TV feeling somewhat mollified, the weather outside being horrible, and recalling how my abdominal region felt exactly like being knocked flat by a small, cantankerous young bovine when on holiday once in Tenerife, after I rashly chanced my hand at 'bull' fighting in the tiny open air ring of a night club.

Fortunately my May Day celebration only felt as if I had taken the full force of a small but extremely bony head and horn stubs full in the abdomen rather than the actual event itself. Passing off rather quicker than the after effects of my thirty-second career in bull fighting had.

Humour apart, over the decades I had become very used to the after effects of releasing stored body stress, and the emotional energy sublimated and suppressed in it. A good example being the time referred to previously, when I connected with my childhood desperation and buried decision I would symbolically carry our home and everyone and everything in it on my back if it would only keep my disintegrating family and my own inner world together.

When the deluge of overwhelming aching sadness of it all released into conscious understanding and I finally released the stress in floods of tears, I was wracked from head to foot and could hardly breathe, within minutes my lower back began to feel sensitive and in a couple of hours I could hardly move, and it took three months to regain normal mobility. After which the symbolic load I had carried for years and the sometimes chronic back ache I suffered from since a young teenager left me permanently.

Similarly, it was not for over a quarter-century until I finally connected with the gut-centred stress I stored at an even deeper level, it too released with the power of the bovine metaphor I have used, and force which surprised even me.

The point being, living as we do in an utterly intellect dominated society the *raison d'être* of which is to disconnect cause and effect because the function and nature of the intellect is to see all things as discrete, separate facts, and life's events are no exception to this.

But humans and all life do *not* work on intellect. Its sustaining force and consciousness is a *continuum* from beginning to end.

We may use intellect to push away in inner consciousness what we deny to ourselves because our culture teaches us to do this, but to return to the universal law of the conservation of energy; energy is energy. It cannot be created or destroyed, it can only change its form. Nothing is exempt from this law and humans have no special dispensation. And worth adding; consciousness likewise cannot be created or destroyed; it too can only change its form. For consciousness determines the expression of energy.

So we may treat our inner world as a consciousness and energy midden to throw into it everything we learn to suppress but unfailingly inner consciousness through our bodies carries all the signs, symbols and symptoms and they literally get bent out of shape and break down in consequence.

It should not be inferred I claim any dispensation from the universal law at all. I recall over forty years ago when I was working as a test engineer building up, testing and commissioning computer systems in a factory working alternate weeks of day and night shift at the same time I was studying at night school.

At one point my abdomen swelled up painfully for some days. I let my belt out a few notches, carried on and hoped it would go away, which it did.

Later, when I was stretched beyond my limit in work and study, one morning, after waking in the early hours with a roaring cacophony of computers and academic topics crashing around in my head, I could not stop, I broke the top of my teapot, left the light on in my flat hallway, and the entrance door wide open as I left for work. As a consequence of learning new computer hardware systems, teaching them to engineers and simultaneously studying even harder at night school, I would be travelling along in my car conscious of an independent solid aching knot of tension in the centre of my abdomen. But I just accepted it – and drove on regardless, aware of it but completely detached from it – in the car as in my life.

Well surprise, surprise! What I once steadfastly refused to acknowledge, take any notice of, much less do anything about, when I finally reversed the process and began clearing the 'energy midden' of my past it eventually hit me with the force – without exaggeration – of an irascible, albeit diminutive, rampaging ruminant.

Though so far as intellect is concerned the same considerations and rules apply.

Having stowed away in inner/sub or unconsciousness all the experiences we refuse to integrate, express and release over many years, *if* we then reverse the process and begin the clearing out our store of unexpressed history and the valence of energy it all represents, still being intellect dominated – because a lifelong tradition does not change magically – just as it takes time to learn the rules, it takes time to unlearn them. The effort involved is the same whether we realise it or not.

The net result is we still do not appreciate our own continuum of inner consciousness, consequently still viewing previously unresolved experiences from the perspective of intellect dominated superficial consciousness, as we then begin working through and releasing the *energy* associated with them.

In my direct experience it takes a long time before it begins to dawn there are very definite threads binding them together and for patterns to begin emerging.

What from the perspective of *intellect* when we begin the clearing process and see as *separate events* we work through, gradually deepens into the realm of *inner consciousness* and a whole new landscape slowly emerges from the depths like waters receding to reveal the seabed connecting these islands of 'separate events' in a *complete continuum*.

One of the patterns I began to perceive seemed to connect with each year's passing from January to December.

As 2003 began it took a few weeks before I realised I was somewhat like a rabbit; very sensitive and easily frightened. As the year progressed and I continued to work through and clear out whatever pressed for expression and integration into conscious awareness, I reached calmer reaches of mind and being.

Yet again; by 'work(ing) through' I don't mean sitting around and sucking my thumb, or treating myself to the odd half dozen comforting cream cakes and chocolate biscuits. If I became aware of feeling frightened or tense, and vaguely uneasy, then I would release it in the way my body wished to.

This may cause puzzlement to some; perhaps many, because in this insane society we are taught to deny, suppress and generally eradicate the means Great Nature gives every one of us to express, release and integrate powerful experiences, we all possessed in childhood and which is steamrollered into oblivion as we 'grow up'.

I can almost hear the 'Clive Dunn' (Dad's Army) response –

which he based on an actual person – when something unexpected, outrageous or frightening happened, of going round in a panic telling others not to.

Exactly expressing the way our culture works, as just explained; of suppressing natural reactions to some form of shock.

It is a sad comment on our culture that once, someone living close by was evidently letting out some strong emotions albeit fairly late one evening, as a consequence of which I knew about it when my door bell rang just after going to bed and opening the door was greeted by the police, who enquired what was happening as a passer-by had reported the noise. Yet who lacked the courage to knock and ask at the house if everything was alright.

'Working through' might mean vigorously flicking arms and hands, jumping around like a cat on hot bricks and making a noise rather like stepping outside from a warm room into the freezing cold. Our bodies instinctively react to the shock and release the emotional impact and *energy* generated by it.

Just as children do instinctively but by adulthood our true nature has been steamrollered into oblivion within us by cultural intellect dominated oppression. Called 'growing up', and, God help us! 'Being normal'.

Equally, as not unusually happened if in the course of phone work and cold calling, I got ears full of irritable, bad tempered or downright rude responses until I'd had enough, cushions I kept for the purpose got seven shades thumped and punched out of them with a fair amount of (muffled) yelling, until the anger was spent and I was able to get back on the phone again.

This, however, does not address or express the underlying continuum of which these 'islands' of cathartic expression were a very small part.

Whatever I might begin with, releasing pent up energy, invariably it would evolve into yet deeper levels and more sublimated suppressed energy of my birth surfacing.

Consequently, this may be a good point to weave together the twin themes not infrequently found in these pages of intellect domination and birth.

The Dimensions of Intellect

The whole subject of our inner world and being is treated like approaching a black hole somewhere in the universe; people dare not approach too closely and pass their sensed curiosity event-horizon, for to do so might be to ineluctably disappear into oblivion leaving only a quaking red-shifted shadow of their former self behind.

Or at least, this very understandably, is the perception our culture teaches us to have and my upbringing was in general no exception.

Indeed as described at considerable length, I went a lot further than most in totally immersing myself to the point of destruction in intellectually dominated pursuits, and derived considerable pleasure at times from the kudos it brought because such great store and recognition is placed upon it.

If anyone played devil's advocate with their own true nature, I would claim to be at least a heat finalist if not an outright medal winner.

In those times if someone had talked about the effects of birth we carry with us, and other topics of our inner being and reaches of mind, I would, in all probability have responded with sarcasm and derision in precisely the way I have described people do when something arises to challenge their accepted world view and take them into murky realms of cultural taboo, concerning inner knowledge and consciousness.

Any competent hypnotist knows the human capacity to store personal history. We carry a complete record of life events from the womb onwards. And much, *much* more besides.

The fact our culture teaches us to set arbitrary intellectual limits on what it is possible or not to recall changes nothing. This is cultural horse blinkers territory.

In exactly the same way a psychiatrist and therapist with around fifty years' experience once said after experiencing the 'baggage' of his birth he still carried, thirty-two times; "He was happy with it."

Knowing from direct contact with him that he very clearly *still* carried an immense amount of fear from his birth, he had put himself in his own doll's house of intellectual 'enoughness'.

This is the equivalent of a mother saying she was happy being slightly pregnant or, after thirty-two hours of labour being 'happy with it'.

Intellectually contrived utterances have not the slightest shred of relevance to what the sublime wisdom of Great Nature demands we express through our bodies until the energy has been released to its full and final completion.

My direct experience of accessing and releasing the effects of being clamped solid by my mother's rigid muscles and repeatedly squashed is when the stored energy and the outrage, fear and body agony are finally released and resolved, the feelings are simply of profound relief. And nothing whatever to do with pronouncements of 'being happy with it'.

Being 'happy with his birth' was completely at odds with what showed in his body. The history of his birth was clearly visible there. The shape of his head and upper torso unmistakeably showed how he had undergone a great deal of clamping and compression during his birth, and the effects of it were still locked up within it.

My experience over decades is score keeping and setting arbitrary limits is intellectual 'insulation' against the demands of expression of inner being.

It is not how many times the effects of birth surface and demand expression and resolution, it is working through it – however it needs to be expressed and released – that is the issue and allowing one's body and inner consciousness to speak its truth for as long as it needs to. Difficult at times, tedious, and requiring a great deal of persistence, dedication, grit and determination though it might.

Once the suppressed and sublimated energy has finally drained away the need to express it no longer exists and one is just glad it has finished.

And if anyone 'thinks' bodies can't change shape in later life after working through near catastrophic experience during birth, I state categorically they can and do. Though it might take a long time and hundreds or thousands of sessions over many years to accomplish, but heads and bodies do change their shape as my own head and torso have done. Not to mention the accompanying changes within body and being also, and of such magnitude as to be completely beyond my wildest imaginings even over a relatively short time – five or ten years – let alone the decades since I began the process of clearing my inner midden.

As the weeks past I was aware of changes, not necessarily exactly what they were, because awareness and the consciousness driving it is exactly like the weather. It is the overall pattern and not individual clouds and transitional events one notices, and in recollecting past weeks and months, of how they manifested and perhaps, though by no means certain, spotting trends and the continuum stretching back in one's life.

Outer Wars and Inner Conflict

As a general rule, with the changing seasons, it seemed so did the pattern and tempo of my inner world and no less body changes also. Towards the end of the year – as has happened in years since – there was a sense of work having been done, of changes occurring and having been undergone.

But although December arrived as 2004 dwindled to its close, no Christmas fairy appeared sprinkling 'angel dust' with its wings, having a sparkling wand and saying 'Well done! Now you can be 'happy' with all that.'

The reality was I felt even more fragile than at the beginning of the year, signifying the welling up within of more sublimated suppressed energy and the personal history it represented.

A metaphor coming to mind at the time was the vessel of my life seemed to be springing more leaks and I wasn't sure I knew how to deal with them all.

I knew soon after I began re-reading Major Gordon Corrigan's book, *Mud Blood and Poppycock*, I had done so instinctively initially, to make sense of my own inner struggle, in the way he brought clarity and clear sense of purpose to the hand-wringing emotive blindness characterising so much historical comment concerning the British Army, its campaigns and leadership in the First World War in Belgium and France.

In searching to map the inner terrain of my unseen reaches and the forces pitted against each other in these invisible landscapes, I sought by reading an outer-world allegory of the titanic struggle of armies, to make rational sense of the surfacing, and, at the time, all-consuming inner confusion of my own history, and not aimless floundering in a sea of emotional 'mud' as histories of WWI have floundered in literary quagmires of it.

Progressing through the many topics in the book, it took a few weeks of pursuing my own inner 'campaign' to make my way forward and attain a position of clear vision and perspective, resolving in myself a conflict of my own dominating intellect over long suppressed emotional energy. Just as the British Army and within it, peerless Canadian troops finally overcame the mud and the entrenched German forces dominating the Passchendaele ridge, gaining crucial, commanding dry ground, in the wettest summer for seventy-five years, and in a most difficult year (1917) gave the Germans their 'blackest day'. Whilst strategically, and crucially, keeping pressure completely away from the French army in mutinying disarray. But for which a German assault on it would have broken through the Allied Western Front and rolled up the British Army with it, with profound consequences.

To this can be added the broader symbolism of the British Army, with no other choice then to take over nearly fifty per cent more of the line than originally manned, to reduce and minimise French exposure, constantly interfered with by government keeping it short of men and resources, maintained its morale and its nerve, fighting its way from water-sodden, shell-churned low land, to commanding, dry, high ground, in a drenching summer, overcoming deep defensive German positions and driving them off.

My long buried emotional – watery – energy not only symbolised by the British Army struggling in a confusion of mud, but – intellectual – self-questioning and doubt fighting with my emotions whilst all this took place within. Symbolised by political interference, and the massive, deep German defences and forces equally symbolic of my own deeply ingrained historical tyrannical intellect.

Not least either, my own emotional sensitivity whilst all this unfolded within – symbolised by the fragile French Army – unable to face an assault, as I found emotional demands onerous at the time.

♥

JOURNEY OF A LIFETIME

Whilst I became aware why I was reading the book, I was not, about the symbolism of my inner struggle of surfacing irresistible emotion in conflict with repressive intellect and the many allegories I read in it. These gradually crystallised later and finally, only as this was written.

Unerringly we choose and experience in our outer world that which directly mirrors our inner. For in the book, meeting all the metaphors of the different armies, their dispositions, mud, struggle, conflict, high ground, and clear vision, I was meeting my own 'entrenched' rigid demarcations crumbling into chaos and finally resolving.

Ultimately it is only in releasing, resolving and harmoniously integrating emotion *and* intellect in ourselves, inner wars cease, and no longer projected into the world in conflicts, personal, and such horrific collective ones and their appalling consequences.

As long as our culture teaches and demands we completely shun, alienate and outright persecute vast reaches of our fundamental being and consciousness, nothing will change. The problem is this planet and its populations have been through and almost completely destroyed in terrifying cataclysms and the human race is still living out the resulting collective inherited trauma, which has long since become the embedded cultural norm, expressed in the split between inner and outer consciousness.

And precisely why no matter how I attempt to explain why I began rereading a book that for the first time, put in clear context, and made sense of the First World War, and how events such as those related, had, on a deeply inner personal level, exact parallels with my own unfolding inner turmoil and its resolution, others will read the words but there will be no connection because culturally intellect has become completely dominant.

To repeat yet once more, images, symbols, signs, portents; these are the nature and 'language' of our inner or 'sub' conscious. Intellect deals in logic, facts, and reason *because that is its nature and proper function.*

Our culture teaches us to rely completely on intellect to the complete exclusion, suppression and even destruction of all our vast inner intelligence projects into our outer world the whole time; we have no means to understand, read and act on this flood of wisdom, because we are perpetually hell bent on destroying it.

It is no accident the further back we look in history the more we see the language of inner consciousness expressed in images, symbols, signs, allegory and metaphor, and why writing is not found, or why ancient 'writing' is pictographic.

This is *not* some primitive form of expression as it is so often portrayed and patronised by academics and 'science'. It is as a much a 'language' as this one, C++, mathematical notation, or shorthand. Which are all inventions of the intellect. *But* the only way it can be fully and completely apprehended is by 'reading' it using inner consciousness.

Which our culture destroys the means to use.

Just another one of those 'coincidences'; as I was in the process of writing these words. I watched a BBC programme by the art historian Dr Janina Ramirez about the Vikings, in which she mentioned the Runic language and its partly pictographic, and definitely symbolic nature.

But this is getting far ahead of where I was as 2004 ended and my long voyage across the open reaches of 2005 began and continued on into 2006.

Inner Walls and Outer Armour

There was nothing magical in my progress as 2006 climbed from the depths of winter into fresh green optimism; except bursting daffodil buds and delicate miniature smiling faces of primroses in which I delighted and derived immense pleasure in the sheer perfection of their colour, form and subtle fragrance.

The only other harbingers of change were completely beyond my senses focused on my outer world. Perhaps the only awareness was a growing dissatisfaction and unease with the work I had been doing for five years to keep at bay the wolf from my door and pay the incessant bills.

Through my sink or swim baptism twenty years before into sales, I learned to turn the telephone – a device I once feared and shunned – into a means not just of making calls but of genuine communication out of desperate necessity.

As I embarked on the work I did for the hearing aid industry, I began to get the feeling fate had steered me in this direction for a reason. Like the slow steady drip of water imperceptibly filling a vessel within me, a perception formed as call followed endless call and hundreds quickly became thousands and tens of thousands over days, months then years, it dawned there were distinct patterns emerging in the contacts and occasional conversations I had with people with hearing problems.

More and more it became apparent it wasn't just ears that were the problem; it was one manifestation of a complete range of head and neck related ones.

Steadily the mists of uncertainty resolved into sharply focused clear understanding, based on my own experiences trying to clear the growing tensions in my upper body and especially up into my neck and head.

By 1999 I knew I was heading for deep trouble unless I made strenuous and continuous efforts to release the growing tensions I was increasingly affected by.

I found it hard to accept and even harder to believe, in spite of the staggering amount of work I had done over decades to rid myself of the invisible – but no less prostrating burden of the load of personal history I carried – I was inexorably seizing up in my upper body. The strength in my hands and arms was diminishing, and generally throughout it.

As told already, I went back to doing what I had intuitively done from the beginning; letting my body and its own sublime intelligence lead the way and dictate what I needed to do to, to unlock it, free it up and restore my energy and strength; and not just once in a while but every single day, which by 2006 I had been doing and created positive changes inconceivably beyond anything I might have imagined when I began. Not only in my upper body but throughout body and inner being.

Having released unimaginable amounts of muscular tensions and their underlying cause in my struggle to escape my mother's rigid muscles and crushing birth contractions, I became more and more acutely aware of how much I had had no other choice than to sublimate in inner consciousness, the colossal stress; physical and emotional, in my fight to survive and be born. Or die in the attempt.

The witness to all this I carried – and always will – being my upper jaw and particularly the bone of my left side literally squashed sideways in an 'L' shape out into my cheek, as I fought and pushed with my head, body and with all my might to get out of the nightmare prison, which unless I succeeded would be the end of me.

Yet having spent thousands of hours, releasing the trapped, sublimated energy in inner consciousness and but for which otherwise, my upper body was clamping tighter and tighter against this massive invisible burden, I began to realise something even more profoundly stowed away in deep inner recesses was becoming a vague presence as the year unfolded.

In short, I became increasingly aware it felt like I was wearing an invisible close-fitting outer layer. The sensation on my upper body being like a diving suit pressed against it with the pressure of water.

If I jumped up and down, I could feel this heaviness there.

Casting off the increasingly oppressive burden of my outer world and daily work seemed to be mirrored by the rise into growing conscious awareness of something I seemed to be pushing out from depths within me I simply could not fathom; or even knew existed.

Did this clarity of expression exist at the time I was living through all of this?

Not even remotely. As ever, on my continuing journey to free my inner being and body from the tensions and clamped muscles, or as Wilhelm Reich so aptly called it 'body armour', I continued to plod on.

Not unusually I would wake around the time of my birth in the early hours with a washing machine head-full of tumbling dream images, with my breathing clamped and body tensed up; hot and uncomfortable, which I knew from decades of experience was more outraged agony surfacing.

There was no intellectualising it away in theories of it might be this, or it might be that or some other plausible – and completely specious – rationalising. I knew from the beginning this 'kidology' was just a way, figuratively speaking, of turning the telescope of focused awareness around and reducing the charging elephant of inner outrage to a small speck. Putting it in a mental matchbox with intellectual tweezers, closing it, and doing what our bizarre culture teaches us all to do from birth; namely, pretend reality is other than it is!

The tediously infallible consequence being the need to thump cushions and (muffled) yelling in teeth-clenched fury, no matter how tired I might feel or what time of night it might be and whatever images might have floated in to begin with of situations/people/things that had annoyed me in the past.

Equally infallibly, these I knew were merely instances when I had 'match-boxed the elephant' previously and were signposts pointing in the direction of suppressed anger.

Finally, I also knew no matter who or what might be the trigger, the more I stopped interfering with my intellect and let my body and inner being express what it needed to, the more, and more quickly, it focused into the utter fury of being subjected to the interminable clamped-solid crushing experience of my birth.

It was not a matter of once, a few times, twenty; or the famous thirty-two times of self-deluding 'being happy with it'. Nor yet dozens but hundreds, and on into thousands.

How many thousands I have no idea, nor do I care in the slightest. The unavoidable consequence with no exceptions whatsoever ineluctably being the opening out and opening up of every conceivable aspect of body being and inner consciousness. And far beyond this, the opening out of consciousness in ways utterly undreamed of as time and repetition of this simple, unimaginably tedious process has progressed over years and decades, in all its different shades and aspects.

For different people the journey and the experiences along the way will be uniquely their own but the common denominator of energy suppressed in inner being and needing to find its expression, release, resolution and integration into conscious awareness is the same.

The immutable cosmic rule that energy can only change its form and can neither be created or destroyed cannot be contradicted, fudged or fiddled with by intellectual 'smoke and mirrors,' however much our society pretends otherwise.

To repeat, with no apology yet again, this is no St Vitus stuck-in-the-same-groove fixated blind obsession followed for its own sake.

Although the same process, and having a very definite theme overall, it is never completely and identically the same twice. As musical themes evolve into different areas, returning once more to the original in a new context, the same is true of working through energy sublimated in inner being.

The fundamentally essential ingredients are a burning desire to succeed and *self-awareness*. To possess them is to look for and notice the changes that keep on coming in body, being and consciousness. To lack them is to have no idea of origin, direction or destination, and at best to travel like a pinball in a machine and at worst to become lost in a maze of hapless confusion.

As two examples previously mentioned, when I first began in 1974, completely alone with no guidance or help from others, and sustained solely by the unshakeable belief my body and being knew how to heal itself, after ten days I created the absolute certainty beyond any expressing, it was beginning to happen. Confirmed as days turned to weeks; my left lung and left kidney stirred back into life and the increasing flow of life's river within steadily purged out the 'sediment' clogging my barely functioning body.

Then in 1999 I decided if I didn't make determined, consistent efforts to reduce the increasing tensions steadily making it more and more uncomfortable to turn my head, and reducing the strength in my hands, I was going to be in even more serious trouble.

After three months of daily effort returning to the infallible simple wisdom I trusted right from the outset; that my body and inner being knew exactly how to undo what rational, reasonable, intellectually-dominated existence was destroying, one evening driving my car and turning my head to check no one was coming out of an obscured side road, I realised my neck felt free and took considerable pleasure in repeating the movement, relishing the increased ease of movement.

Both these milestones marked the beginning of different stages on the same journey of a lifetime I had embarked upon. And continue to travel.

Very likely it all makes for dull, laborious, repetitious reading, but the reality was incomparably more dull, repetitious, nit-pickingly detailed and not unusually wearisome, than the superficial description of it here.

Exactly like archaeology, in order to reveal and fully understand the sense and meaning of previous existence, the past is uncovered sometimes in great bucketfuls. At others, by diligent effort layer on painstaking layer; sometimes with the emotional equivalent of a soft brush, only picking out inexplicable fragments of no consequence and putting them to one side.

A good example being the one already referred to, of sitting in bed at a low ebb, thoughts drifting in of my sojourn in Australia; my Uncle's life there, and all that had led me to the key to healing myself. Like puzzling many times over little shards in a collecting tray; pondering on what I thought of as just a jumble of events and purely my own journey. Until 'coincidences' suddenly erupted in an incandescent flash of understanding; it was the palpable unseen influence of my Uncle Art related in the anecdote of just seven words: 'Let's all go mad for five minutes', preserving his and his fellows' sanity in the endless nightmare of the First World War, instantaneously fusing together so many small, 'random' fragments of 'chance' into a complete vessel of profound understanding.

But as it took nineteen years for that one revelation to arrive my progress owed more to brushes than buckets.

As the year progressed, 2006 seemed to be the antithesis of sudden transformational leaps in understanding; nothing seemed to change much. The only noticeable one being the toe on my right foot next to my big toe.

I knew from previous experience, toenails were a clear reflex and outer manifestation of inner events and their pushing into consciousness for expression and release, but a sensitive and mildly painful one puzzled me. I knew it was also a reflex for, and related to, my upper body but had to content myself with this becoming clear as time and my efforts continued.

What was increasingly apparent after years and many tens of thousands of phone calls to those with hearing problems, I decided I'd learned all I could about them. Not just of hearing but the underlying fundamental one of tremendous and increasing muscular clamping causing a whole range of symptoms in the upper body, and how, if I'd done nothing about my own condition, I would otherwise have suffered exactly the same way they were. As had become crystal clear from the many conversations discussing symptoms and causes I had with people whose situation I felt great sympathy with. Though sadly, if I suggested they massage their own shoulders, necks and heads, not unusually my comments were met with wary responses and incomprehension at best, and at worst were seen as being one stage removed from the proverbial massage parlour, such was the unfamiliarity of their own bodies and the puritanical tradition they had been brought up in.

At first a grumbling dissatisfaction, increasingly I felt a growing awareness and desire to move on and find other work.

Not least for the reason more and more calls with increasingly onerous deadlines and qualification of those agreeing to a hearing test, for less money. Meaning also, 250 calls in a day became more like 350 and once 450 Easy to do using a computer and software to dial the number each time, but hand dialling each one resulted in feeling absolutely punch drunk after the latter tally of contacting increasingly canvassed people who not unreasonably became increasingly irritated as a consequence!

From working as a subcontractor for five years it was a very tenuous step into the unknown to go completely freelance and work on my own, but the need to escape the head-banging drudgery of no other reward than being able to pay the bills had become intolerable and although it brought to the surface a great deal of fear, feeling as if I was on some kind of stimulant, which in a sense I was; adrenalin! I knew I had to make a change to preserve my sanity, come what may.

Having made the change and working completely alone continuing to do it on the phone, each day by mid afternoon, I felt so weary I could barely stay awake, never mind make more phone calls. There were times when I felt like an 'ME' or Chronic Fatigue Syndrome sufferer; absolutely drained of energy when even moving was like wearing an old style twill diving suit with heavy lead-weighted boots on my feet and weighty thick bronze helmet, having to lay down feeling so heavy, for a while I was completely inert.

At the time I accepted it was how I felt and as it passed after a couple of hours, I shrugged it off and carried on.

It took a long time for it to dawn in hindsight; some years in fact, that doing the telephone work constantly under pressure as I had been for years, I had stored a considerable amount of stress. Moreover once the load was lifted, the backlog of fatigue became the proverbial releasing logjam.

But also as had happened many years previously, when I stopped teaching, and shed the massive intellectual load I had carried for nearly six years, within a few weeks not only did I experience an engulfing deluge of backlogged emotions releasing, for weeks after I experienced a great many minor palpitations day after day.

Only very recently has it become clear to me just how much more sense my inner being has than the twittering birdcage of intellectual 'consciousness' I took for my own reality, ignoring my real nature.

Borrowing a pithy phrase, it was only when I finally stopped banging my head against the wall, I found out just how much it hurt. Though breaking my addiction to doing it was not easy!

To be fair to myself, I needed to earn a living and pay bills, like millions of others, but also like millions of others in our intellectually dominated culture, by doing so in the way I did, was going directly and deeply against my real nature even when I 'thought' I was in touch with and connected to my inner world.

Only when I stopped – or at least greatly moderated – ignoring my real self did my body and being erupt in remedial outraged protest at the profound conflict I created within, in refusing to acknowledge my true nature.

Well, well; what a surprise! As part of the corrective 'instruction' I received for my transgression, in mid-2006 I experienced another gut-strangling abdominal event for a complete day. Although without doubt I suppressed and stored up a lot of energy doing the grinding, pressurised, bill-paying telephone work previously, its release would surely not have been so intense had a well-meaning friend not vigorously done reflexology massage on my feet in the area relating to my colon and particularly the transverse part. The perception being one of releasing constipation which was not the case.

But bodies do not exist in isolation from our inner being. What I was holding back and *blocking off* in inner consciousness manifested in blocked energy in my abdominal regions.

As the massage took place I had the sensation of being unable to stay in my body, and although very aware I was there nevertheless, some part of me went elsewhere in order to make the experience bearable. Evidently it took time to get myself back together again; for the shock to pass and then for the sublimated energy to be released in a sudden, cramping, cathartic deluge.

Had I not known what was happening and how to deal with it, ordinarily I would have been frightened and in agony – as I have known of others be; sometimes for hours or even longer – but as explained a number of times already, I knew exactly what was happening and more importantly how to break the sudden involuntary deluge of releasing energy causing an equally automatic; and involuntary, spasm of intense colonic cramp.

It took years to fully understand the instinctive procedure I automatically used, and to repeat it again; that of forcing myself to retch, using a rolled-across diagonally folded corner of a face cloth and sticking it in my throat, and repeating the process, until, more or less instantly, or within a few seconds the agonising feeling of an iron grip on my colon and a dry-mouthed unsatisfiable desire to vomit, released. If necessary repeating the process until my body 'smiled' – even if the aftermath felt like having been butted in the abdomen as once described.

Resorting to this infallible, if slightly less unpleasant remedy, than the problem itself, times beyond number and over decades, I finally understood cramp – of any kind – including gut cramp – is in effect, energy imploding. And also to repeat yet again; energy can only go two ways. It either implodes or involutes – which is always bad news on a human level, because muscles reflexively clench solid trying to control and prevent being overwhelmed by the sudden gush, or it flows successfully and evolutes moving outwards from its source, producing relaxed muscles and pleasant sensations within and throughout human bodies and a sense of inner harmony.

The staggering intelligence of our inner being expressed through our bodies knows infallibly how to regulate them. It is only when we start interfering with intellect – which in our culture we are taught to do from birth or occurs even before we get into the world through our experience of it – that the harmonious flow of energy is affected and symptoms such as gut cramps and so called 'Irritable Bowel Syndrome' and a myriad of other conditions begin to occur.

Without doubt, having had a holiday and recovered from the reflexology session whilst on it, a lot of the residual stress not only from my telephone work, but much deeper levels of what I still carried, buried

JOURNEY OF A LIFETIME

through no other choice during my horrendous birth, the combination of both together produced the result it did. Yet the continuum of cause(s) and effect in my own inner being and body still took a long time – a few years – to connect together as all part of the same overall process.

All of this was what I lived through and dealt with at the time. Doing it was the important part. Creating a lot of intellectual traffic noise, doing the work I did, did not help my healing process, but changing deeply embedded personal and cultural upbringing was a slow, continuous, and sometimes tedious journey.

Times beyond recall I might think I had it all buttoned up, but as always in this situation I took inventory of my body and I could feel blockages and tensions still remaining, knowing it was going to take a lot more time and effort to clear them. Intellect's stop-start perception is not the continuous reality of inner being and body.

To quote again the words of the eighteenth century MP and anti-slavery campaigner, Charles James Fox, who likened a proposed gradual abolition of the slave trade to giving up rape and pillage slowly, and my own slavery through my upbringing and cultural indoctrination, would be no miraculous repeal of my entrenched personal disposition. Far from it!

Fortunately, whilst some part of me knows security may be important, survival and sanity are still sufficiently powerful instincts to throw caution to the winds and step off the beaten track of convention.

In any event, I was becoming used to a growing tradition of metaphorically spurning the easy path for the tightrope of an uncertain future not knowing where, or even if, it was tethered at the distant end!

Like the film 'Groundhog Day', fate seemed to conspire no matter what I did, somehow I survived each time.

The Wisdom of Animals

Perhaps the high point of my year was having my young black and white female cat who I doted on, give birth to her kittens beside me.

I neglected to get her spayed and that spring it wasn't hard to tell what was coursing in her veins. The Emperor Claudius's wife Messalina – equally an irresponsibly promiscuous teenager – showed a similar degree of chastity as this little four-legged strumpet. Though on reflection the latter was driven by Great Nature's seasonal madness rather than pathological, psychotic insatiability. After disappearing for two days she reappeared and I instantly knew in some indefinable change in her flanks, she was pregnant.

I seemed to be programmed to wake in the early hours when she – and my previous cats – often called to be let in. As I did so some weeks later, although I could not see her clearly I once again knew with absolute certainty her time had come.

I laid down on my bed of cushions in my healing/therapy room, and she snuggled up as close as she could on my left side just below shoulder level, and sure enough within a few minutes I could feel her contractions start.

I felt very privileged she trusted me enough to forsake her instincts and find a secure hidey hole to bring her litter into the world. Or perhaps more apt to say her trust in me was strong enough to want me with her as protector, comforter and 'midwife'.

The latter role, on further reflection, might be closer to reality than I ever realised at the time or, for that matter, until now. Perhaps she knew me far better than I ever imagined. Without twittering human intellect to get in the way, instinct may have told her directly, I understood what she was going through and this caused her to snuggle up in the energy she felt from me. In hindsight it certainly feels like it to me.

Over the next hour or so – and initially with cries of agony – first one then another little body arrived until there were four. All boys. She lay right up beside me with them, and I was a happy 'father'. But I made the mistake of switching on the light and she erupted in a recoiling blue fit of swearing and paranoia, because cats normally have their young in a small secure place and a huge expanse of room freaked her out completely.

Next morning, although I tried to make a small secure 'cave' of cushions for her she moved them downstairs where I found her with them in a small cramped cardboard box under my upright sideboard.

So I 'upgraded' them all without a murmur from her, to 'first class' in a Sainsbury's banana box suitably lined and an at first strange clicking sound got steadily more audible over succeeding days, which I realised was four little purring bodies suckling on their mother.

This as I discovered to my surprise was not a scene of automatic feline bliss. Exactly the opposite. Bonnie – her name – having got out to feed herself, as she re-entered the room where her 'nest' was, began deep throat-growls and swearing with great feeling. Which I had never known any cat before do. It appeared the demands and responsibilities of being a teenage mother were more than she cared for or wanted! Though having expressed her resentments at her 'bloody kids' she climbed back in the accommodation suite and dutifully lay down for her litter to plug themselves back in without another murmur. But each time she got up for her own needs the same routine was re-enacted.

Perhaps she got relief because she knew I would understand this as well! Which I definitely did.

As years had passed and I freed myself more and more of the burdens I carried within my body and being, I discovered an increasing affinity with animals and they with me. Even when some distance away some would respond in an unafraid manner, proving if it were needed, animals know instantly the 'vibes' someone gives off. Equally, they are also very aware when someone is edgy or hostile.

In retrospect, the process of freeing myself from all my history I carried within me reflected throughout my body and being may have been like breaking stones in its struggle, tedium and monotony, but this little animal showed me more about myself and all I had changed in me than I was within light years of appreciating at the time.

More of the Same

To make the point thinking has nothing to do with reality, having decided I must have surely reached the end of colonic events; this time without any obvious cause such as the previous reflexology manipulation, another even more powerful wave of gripping abdominal discomfort heaved into unavoidable awareness as nature's awakening did the same the following year; dealt with the same way, and from feeling as if I'd been run over, normality was restored by the following day.

As the seasons changed the landscapes of my outer world, so did those of my inner being; whether I understood them inwardly or not or even whether I was aware of them.

Increasingly, as I had learned to over years, it wasn't so much the details of dreams, if I could recall them, I steered by, so much as the general impression of whether they were heavy or light, insistent or quietly present.

Though on occasion the messages they brought were easily apprehended.

In any case by far the most accessible guide was how my body felt.

To my growing awareness, whereas in previous years my efforts to unlock and release energy were clear to me; more physical energy and strength and general body mobility, the trend in 2007 seemed to be much less so. If anything, tensions in my head and upper body seemed to be more rather than less.

In particular, the effects I had lived with at night for many years, in fact for about twenty; clamped muscles in my head causing symptoms such as my nasal passages clamping closed and my eyes dry such were the tensions throughout it, if anything, and much to my irritation, no matter what my continuing efforts were to release these, causing sleep to be interrupted and waking hot and uncomfortable with clamped breathing, the trend was to become more pronounced.

I realised after a while; it was very much a case of deciding which was chicken, and which the egg. It was feelings of deep outrage surfacing into awareness causing involuntary muscle clamping throughout my upper body.

The evidence was very clear; I simply followed my feelings, waking in the early hours, my body very tight and tense unable to get any peace or rest and trusting them as I always did, instantaneously I felt the need to push with my head and lash out with my clenched fist thumping a cushion I kept beside my bed, bringing my fist down like a hammer, not forgetting to put a rolled up face cloth between my clenched teeth to prevent splitting back molars as I once had.

Pondering what it might mean was completely unnecessary; I *knew* exactly what it was the moment I allowed my body the freedom to do what it needed.

Like hundreds and probably thousands of times previously I was having to deal with the sublimated, suppressed fury and outrage at being clamped solid by my mother's unyielding muscles in my fight to be born. Though that is adding perceptions which weren't available at the time.

It was simply a case of dealing with what I felt knowing in its own good time, as I cleared more and more of it, exactly like a draining a reservoir, features of my emotional 'landscape' came into view. Meaning clear understanding of exactly what drove this huge store of blocked energy.

There was and still is no fudging it. Only by following what inner/real/body consciousness was telling me to do and doing it, did the extremely unpleasant clamping of my extra ocular muscles – those around the eyes – deep in my sinuses and head, release. Once the surfacing outrage was expressed, that during birth I was completely unable to do, then my body relaxed, I got some peace and eventually went back to sleep.

The infallible tell tale signs of this release were my eyeballs regaining their lubricated state, my nasal passages popping and clearing; opening out again as the muscle clamping in my head released and my digestive plumbing resumed its normal gurgling peristaltic activity. The latter being the rhythmic contractions of the colon which are very sensitive to stress.

Trying to explain all this to anyone – including those who have indulged in 'therapy' – invariably brought/brings the same responses in varying degrees from inside their intellectual 'fortress'.

The spectrum being everything explained previously; from absence of any reaction at all, blank, uneasy silence; a widening of eyes, a noticeable tightening of body posture, head/face scratching, nervous fiddling with hands/objects, nervous humour, combative contradictory comments to kill the explanation, outright antagonism, and usually a combination of these and more. All simply to stop the rising tide of awareness in themselves and ultimately all having their roots in fear. And the suffering they too had once endured.

A clearer demonstration, if one were needed, it is impossible to formulate of just how effective intellectually centred westernised cultural indoctrination is.

We are taught to ignore, disbelieve, shun, abuse, and destroy our true inner *real* consciousness from the time we are born. No surprise then, anything attempting to open the barred, bolted, barricaded doors to our inner world are implacably resisted.

In fact the indoctrination begins before birth, because the infallible consequences of treating intellect as the sole seat of consciousness is bodies tighten up and become tense, and energy no longer properly or harmoniously flows in them.

For mothers giving birth it means the muscles Great Nature exercises and uses in the process to stimulate and aid the baby's progress into the world do exactly the reverse.

Pedantic or tediously repetitious this may all appear to experience and explain to frightened, defensive people, but almost four decades working to clear my own inner blockages increasingly demonstrated the massive wall the indoctrination our intellectual dominated culture builds within us beginning for many in birth in the repressions of the mother's true nature and fear of her own body.

Whilst on the subject, one of the conversations I vividly recall in the tens of thousands of calls I made to people with hearing difficulties, a lady I spoke to on the subject of the causes of hearing and head problems generally, was open minded enough to actually listen.

Talking about the fact our entry into the world makes a huge difference to how well or otherwise the energy flows in our bodies and especially in our upper body, I mentioned how unlike in India where babies are massaged as a matter of course, and massage amongst all family members is the norm, in our culture massage is almost never done by people on themselves let alone on babies or anyone else within families from the youngest to the oldest. In fact to use the word 'massage' with many people is to immediately associate the word with massage parlours, loose morals and deviant sex.

I mentioned to her a French obstetrician called Frederick Leboyer who wrote two books, one called *Birth Without Violence,* showing the brutal mechanistic treatment of babies – and mothers – often experience being seen, and too often treated as, mere objects during birth, and after the baby's arrival, and the shattering traumatic effects this has on the newborn and the mother. Contrasted starkly with a caring, gentle, loving and humane welcome of babies into the world; who actually smile with happiness. Moreover who are much more peaceful and less inclined to cry than babies who have been subjected to brutal, trauma inducing mechanistic inhumanity being brought into the world.

The second book called *Loving Hands* shows precisely the way babies are massaged on the Indian subcontinent, and how this makes a fundamental positive difference to their suppleness and the flow of energy in their bodies. Not least in the shape of them as well.

Mentioning how vital it is the mother's muscles are not tight and tense and aid the baby as nature intends, I said I often saw people whose heads clearly show in their shape the massive unrelieved stress they carry into adulthood, and their bodies also.

The lady immediately responded with force and feeling, saying how she once walked past a crèche of newborns in a maternity ward and was amazed, horrified and disbelieving at the shape of some of the babies' heads that had clearly been subject to massive pressure and stress during birth.

I asked her how much attention as a culture we pay to massaging ourselves, never mind infants and family members? None!

She understood and was completely sympathetic to what I said, but as the call and conversation ended, I had the clear feeling she still did not connect with cause and effects in her own body.

It is only when we begin working *with* our bodies and not ignoring or working directly *against* them we begin to understand the difference between superficial intellectual awareness and fundamental, direct body and inner consciousness-centred deep understanding, concomitantly the huge effect our completely intellectually dominated upbringing imposes on us all through our culture.

Changing it is not a 'born again' one-time-wonder of Damascenian transmogrification. Far from it. It takes as much time, energy and effort to undo this deeply inculcated, daily spun hawser of habit as it does to weave it within ourselves in the first place. We add a thread a day at a time; and unwind it the same way.

But *only* if we make unrelenting efforts to do so. Above all, with a *clear aim* in mind of what we want to achieve.

This is not some arbitrary fanciful notion of mine. On a personal level it is only as a consequence of the thousands of hours of diligent effort beyond counting and more than this; living it every minute since

I began forty years ago, fundamental changes to inner reality so far beyond any imaginings I had, have occurred and continue at a steadily accelerating rate.

Ultimately it is only in doing it for ourselves we learn the difference. Learning from others and books is hearsay and story telling. It is not until we pick up the cudgel of effort and striving and begin using it, we instil in ourselves a fundamental *belief* based in absolute certainty from direct experience, the difference between understanding and direct knowing becomes clear, in living the reality.

Coughing up Elastic Bands – Again

The months progressed and continuing daily to release whatever tensions and the welling emotional energy driving them, a really irritating condition I had experienced numerous times in the past, reasserted its presence.

No matter what efforts I made to work through – in the small hours at the time I originally entered the world – tensions and the clamped emotional energy driving them, I found it impossible to clear my throat. It really felt exactly like having an elastic band stuck there. I could gargle, make the usual throat clearing noises, try 'huffing' air forcibly out of my mouth to dislodge this sticky mucus, but to no avail. This time it wasn't for a few weeks as had occurred; this went on for months. Equally as times before, I knew it was symptomatic of changes within, but exactly what, I couldn't clearly say beyond knowing my lungs were the source of this mucus. Or more precisely I associated it more with my left lung, which had come a long way from its state of near – if not total – non-functioning back in 1974 when I began reclaiming ownership of my own body.

A clairvoyant I knew well picked up on the 'sticky throat' and the energy imbalance in my body between upper and lower and moved it in my legs using vigorous pressure with his hands to drag it downward. For a day or two I got some relief, but then it returned as before.

It took near enough another couple of years before I regained more or less normal conditions and could – for the most part – clear my throat and spit out what felt like a great clod of mucus, but was only a small white button of it. But that too passed and it was back to living with this for years; sometimes unbothered by it. Others, no matter how or what I tried, life became misery.

That it *would* finally clear, I lived in hope of. And just as hope springs eternal it took years before 'elastic bands' became thinner and finally viscous fluid, and with its clearing the equally growing perception of how much deeply sublimated fear needed releasing and resolving before an epidemic of coughing, throat clearing, hacking and spitting lasting weeks brought increasing relief. But years passed before this was possible.

And like almost all else in this story, when the change began it was not a one-time five-minute wonder. Five days; months or years but a continuing process, reflecting the ebbs and flows of inner progress and changes.

The Art of Gargling

Easy! Just fill your mouth with water and expelling air, at the same time usually making a sound with vocal chords through the liquid, clearing the back of the throat, and spitting it out.

This I call 'intellectual' gargling. All very civilised, neat and tidy and terribly refined and genteel but doing absolutely nothing for the energy in the body.

From somewhere about the mid '80s I instinctively began opening up my throat and involving my body. Not as easy as it may seem. The key being the balance between pressure of air keeping water out of my throat and ending up choking and coughing it out of my oesophagus.

It took some practice, but once I got the balance right, gargling took on a whole new meaning and dimension.

The difference between clamped neck and throat muscles 'intellectual' gargling and allowing them, or rather consciously releasing them and pushing energy into them and up into my head at the same time was a completely different experience.

When it first happened, I was surprised and somewhat intrigued to discover it felt like the onset of blacking out, such was the rush of energy and blood to my head. As my head began to 'sing' and awareness of my surroundings to blur, I stopped and normal vision and sound were quickly restored.

This did not happen every time because it also depended on how relaxed or tensed I was. The more tensed; the less effect. Which as time and repetition continued understanding of my exercise – for that it became – I was able to regulate the effects I produced and to learn more about energy in my own body.

Like everything else I did on an emotional and a physical level or any other level for that matter, this was consciously and deliberately towards unblocking my body and being and getting energy to flow.

It was very much a ratchet effect.

The more I focused on getting energy moving in my body, the more blockages I became aware of. The more blockages I found the more I concentrated on opening up my body.

In parallel with this over months and years, it began to dawn there was some sort of pattern emerging. For many years not clear at all; then vaguely – like mist slowly clearing to reveal hints of a landscape – then in recent decades and latter years and thousands of times following this procedure, understanding of the flow of energy in my body has become more and more acute.

Easy, eh? Just gargle 'properly' and the world opens up magically, the sun comes out, birds sing and everything is lovely and life is a breeze.

This is actually when the work really begins.

As Wilhelm Reich used to refer to it, once energy begins to flow and 'body armour' begins to release in clamped rigid muscles the inescapable fact is emotional energy stowed in and blocked off in inner consciousness, i.e., what we are taught to use as a rubbish tip of our unresolved personal history in this lunatic culture, which teaches us to ignore, suppress, deny and disown our emotional nature, we find ourselves back once more, standing in front of the logjam we have been taught to create in our being.

So over years this see-saw process of opening up my body to find there was a direct relationship between physical energy and emotional energy release and emotional energy release and physical symptoms, gradually as my unrelenting efforts continued, like mists clearing, inexorably, perceptions became clearer of this see-sawing *and changing of balance* throughout my being and body.

The point of all this being seemingly insignificant routines can, if followed, with the utterly essential ingredient of self-awareness, lead to massive cumulative *positive* changes throughout our complete being.

Meaning deep inner consciousness, body consciousness and intellectual faculty, taken altogether produce a vastly increased flow of energy in every possible part of us.

This of course comes as easily as gargling, clipping one's toenails or drinking a quick glass of instant wisdom and enlightenment guaranteed 70° proof.

Or is what 99.9999% of people would like to happen, and just as certainly it can be said 99.9999% of people would rather sit back and dream about doing it rather than make the effort to change their inner world.

Learning to gargle and use it to open up my body was – and is – just a very small part of the regime I follow, and as I discovered over time, one with cumulative results I have learned and benefited greatly from.

'Coincidence' and Gathering Momentum

One day in 2006 I got a phone call from someone living locally who like myself had attended group therapy weekend workshops run in London many years before. He was going through big changes in his life and wanted to work with someone on clearing his emotional landscape. Having contacted a therapist he knew and had worked with as I had also, in the remote hope of finding someone who understood the forum he was familiar with he was surprised to find someone on his doorstep who was from the same culture I had known over a quarter of a century previously.

In parallel with this it also transpired I regularly attended a group doing 'shamanistic' evenings which were very pleasant, being a mixture of meditation, guided imagery and generally sharing one's experience in doing this. What made it even more pleasing in summer, these events were held in a Yurt – a frame supported, domed-top circular tent used by nomadic Mongolians on the plains of Asia where they roamed with their horses and animals. Being situated in a wood added measurably to the delightful energy suffusing the atmosphere.

One evening whilst sitting quietly before activities commenced, a newcomer came in to join the group and sat down beside me.

I instantly recognised him as someone I knew from a mediumship and clairvoyance development group I had been in at the turn of the Millennium.

To earn his living, as I had known him do previously, he still did a number of different jobs to keep the wolf from the door. One of these, he told me, was looking after rehearsal rooms for bands, which registered, but was not something I really took notice of … until the exactly coincidental phone call from the chap who wanted to work one to one to clear emotional baggage he had accumulated.

The need to find a suitable venue where any sound and fury could be freely vented without disturbance was resolved exactly as the question of where to find such a place arose.

Just another of the endless 'coincidences' or synchronistic events cropping up regularly along the way of clearing my inner world.

The room in what appeared to be a nearly derelict warehouse on an industrial estate, having sufficient sound insulation to muffle a deafening rock band seemed ideal – at least in principle. Though on entering it appeared it was actually used for fumigating them as well, as it stank of cigarette smoke; the atmosphere having an almost viscous quality as if there was a stratified fog of tobacco tar filling the space.

No less, the place was unkempt; even filthy and looked like the corner of a rag and bone man's yard.

Nonetheless, it proved very useful in a year of many changes and uncertainties to be able to rage against the frustrations created by the machinations of others for and with whom I had worked and without doubt also the legacy of interminable telephone work and many thousands of calls.

Working on my own every day for about seven years by then, it also proved very useful to be able to make comparisons with someone who had not done any 'sessions' for many years.

This was not about scoring ego points off someone else but realising just how much I had liberated and resolved in myself, and thankfully, my greatly increased amount of energy to sustain the momentum created within body and being.

I was very clearly aware by this time, taking a sabbatical or not bothering to do any clearing of the energy welling up from what was still sublimated, suppressed and unresolved in inner consciousness, was simply not an option.

If I did so the consequences quickly exerted their influence in the increasing muscle and body tensions and other symptoms I had become all too familiar with, becoming more insistent.

Dismantling the brick wall between intellect and real consciousness, our culture forces us to build as 'normal' is like starting a conveyor belt.

Outer consciousness – our day-to-day superficial reality – becomes and is like a worker on the line. He works with regard to the speed of the conveyor belt and woe betide him if he slows down; for the conveyor won't. It continues to move by and his uncompleted tasks create a backlog whose effects become cumulative until chaos ensues. Our real/inner/sub conscious never sleeps. It continues to function every second. If it didn't that would be the end of us. Intellect can switch off when it likes. Indeed it is not built to withstand unceasing continuous use. If it is the likely destination is a stroke or heart attack, depending respectively on how far we stray from our real being and/or how brutally we burden ourselves with post-it note 'knowledge'.

Decades before, I soon learned when studying at night school three nights a week, learning new computer systems at the same time as teaching other ones, and doing night school study all day Sunday, what intellect could stand. Or rather the limits of intellectual absorption and obvious bodily damage it inflicted, as a circle of brown blotches devoid of any feeling appeared all round the base of my neck and under my arms, turning to itching bright scarlet wheals later, and I had gone to work in a feverish daze leaving my flat door wide open and the hall light on.

In short, using intellect as a brutal battering ram to assault the *real* consciousness of my body and inner being.

I knew there was a great deal more work to do before the deep-seated tensions I could feel in my body – not least in my head – began to ease and release, and I had no intention of ending up blind or deaf as so many of the legions of people suffered, I had spoken to in the course of my telephone work

Once, it had been sufficient to release and clear blocked energy much less frequently, but by that time my 'conveyor belt' of inner consciousness delivered daily a steady stream of blocked energy to be worked through, resolved and integrated into outer awareness. But my partner in our fumigation room sessions felt one – lasting an hour each – each week, was more than enough so it was agreed to meet once a fortnight.

During one of these sessions, he brought some pictures to use as cues for or to himself to explore; what they meant to him; and meanings he had not yet divined within himself and what wisdom and useful insights they provided him for his daily life.

This was very much a session by himself for himself with me as a receptive, passive, presence, offering no suggestions, insights or any other comments unless specifically requested to do so.

Indeed, this was the invariable rule of the way we had originally learned to work in the weekend groups – and one to one sessions within them – decades previously.

It was at this time I first saw Nicolas Poussin's picture referred to previously, of blind Orion being guided towards the sun to heal his sight. I never felt much sympathy, interest or understanding before for works of art by famous painters showing scenes derived from ancient Greek myths and writers, but this positively leapt off the page, hitting me instantaneously with its powerful symbolism. What really surprised me was my instant ability to read this very visible and clear imagery of true / inner / 'sub' consciousness.

In particular the relationship intellect should have with true consciousness our culture has turned upside down, making true consciousness not the benign giant in us it really is, but turning intellect into a puny yet despotic tyrant – attempting to dictate to the real giant within us what true reality is. Which is what happens all the time in our 'real' world.

The real revelation for me was in realising, far from being a tedious, grinding, even pointless slog, the work I was doing to clear my inner world and with it my body and being, was bringing about changes in me far beyond my expectations or day-to-day awareness, as the wall within between intellect and true consciousness crumbled to a far greater extent than I realised until that moment.

Poussin's picture should be on the wall in front of everyone making this journey, for it exactly personifies the harmonious relationship that *should* exist between inner and outer consciousness.

Rhythms, Patterns and Future Trends

Over the decades of clearing my own 'landfill tip' of suppressed and disowned history, a pattern or rhythm soon became apparent. Within each day as already related, overnight rest restored body energy also meaning anything my inner consciousness had placed on the 'conveyor' needed to be dealt with. Though by no means was, or is ever such a simplistically ordered process as this.

It was and can be as if someone has forgotten to switch the conveyor belt off when much is pressing for conscious expression, resulting in nights of little rest and feeling as if it wasn't so much a conveyor belt as a washing machine full of tin cans clattering endlessly around inside my head. The 'programme' was/is dictated by inner consciousness – and intellect has no access to the stop-start switch. On these occasions getting up in the morning felt as if I had been working all night; which in many respects I had.

Which is where the condition called 'Sleep Apnoea' comes from. It is simply inner consciousness trying to release and rid our inner being and body of experiences and the suppressed energy they represent we refuse to admit because we are taught to ignore, suppress and treat our inner consciousness as a giant landfill tip.

Morning time therefore, as our inner consciousness determines, is when personal history and the emotional energy represented by it pushes most for conscious expression.

Why also – as an example – statistically, early Monday morning is the time when the greatest number of heart attacks occur. Powerful conflict existing between inner consciousness and being trying to release and resolve suppressed history and the energy it represents, and outer consciousness and being diametrically opposing this need.

Reflecting for many another week of creative self-denial in a job and life they dislike, and worse; detest.

Hardly a surprise then, such powerfully driven conflict of energies results in a heart seizure. Or stroke.

If the energy is released, as the day continues and body energy diminishes there is less need or ability to release more. When rest once again recharges our body and being the cycle repeats.

When a lot of suppressed energy needs to be released, each day may well bring the need to do so, and if a great deal needs to be expressed then the pattern may continue for weeks or even months.

Ultimately the sublime intelligence of our inner being is a perfect regulator and as much or as little as needs to be released and consciously integrated will push for expression. It is only when we interfere using our intellect – as we are taught to do the whole time – problems occur. If and when we let our bodies release and express *freely* the energy we constantly suppress and repress, it will run to its completion. Just as our bodies know when they need to sleep and wake up, the same consciousness within them knows exactly what and how much needs to be expressed and released that as a culture we constantly and continually use intellect to prevent and deny. The energy does not disappear. To repeat once again the universal cosmological law of the conservation of energy; energy cannot be made or destroyed, it can only change its form. And to repeat again also; humans and westernised culture in particular, are *not* exempt. There are *no* derogations or exemptions from this law. To which can be added; energy can only move in two ways; it either *evolutes* – moving outwards or away from a point, or it *involutes* – moving inwards towards a point. In a state of equilibrium the two are in perfect balance.

In human terms, balance equates with harmony and happiness, imbalance either way means depletion and exhaustion or suppression, clamping and rigidity. The latter three attributes describing what happens in our bodies when we use intellect to prevent permanently the release of energy from inner consciousness.

The result is, at times I find myself working overtime or even flat out on my own conveyor belt of consciousness to clear a backlog of blocked consciousness and energy. Once resolved, like a conveyor belt becoming clear, nothing needs to be done, until inner consciousness decides more history needs to be resolved, and the stored energy it represents released and expressed.

The cycle repeats both in the short and longer term – exactly also as likened to sailing an ocean with its weather, individual waves, longer swell and much more subtle and extended rhythms of our complete life's time; the whole ocean's currents.

Like everything else it takes practice to understand our own rhythms which in my experience is where one begins to learn the difference between our much or completely neglected inner being and consciousness, and the twittering 'birdcage' of intellect on our shoulders we are taught, falsely, to regard as consciousness.

Or returning to the symbolism of Nicolas Poussin's picture, the difference between Cedalion standing on Orion's shoulder – intellect – seeing in the outer world acting as a guide; also in this outer world, for Orion himself – this gigantic inner consciousness; seeing in the inner world, and when the two aspects of consciousness act in harmony together *as one* as they are designed to do and to be, we become giants because we have access to and understanding of our total being, and the vast power all of us have at our disposal, not the barricaded, butchered, emasculated divided self in a state of profound conflict we call 'normality' in this bizarre culture of ours.

Understanding our inner rhythms, and the constant stream of wisdom delivered to our outer world in images, signs, symbols and portents, is out natural birthright but our culture, from the very outset, as I have said many times already, teaches us at best to completely ignore it and at worst to actively savage it.

Small wonder then becoming tuned to and learning to trust and act on this limitless fount of wisdom within us is not a one time wonder – however much gurus, seminars, courses, workshops and all the rest of the get-it-here-now instant results brigade might have us believe. Because if they do they are still trapped in the delusion of 'instant results' intellect as their *only* reality.

My direct experience is it takes a great deal of work, time, diligent, intelligently-applied effort before one begins to recognise how the 'Orion' in each of us communicates this wisdom, and a lot more time and effort to maintain constant contact and still longer to act consistently on what our inner giant tells us.

It is not a matter of hours, days, weeks or months; it is a process of years and decades. There is no final point of arrival; it simply continues to improve, expand, growing in strength and power with use and practice.

Which meant the lessons or more correctly the patterns of my life in 2007 were of continual steady inner work, and accepting what the 'conveyor belt' of inner consciousness continually delivered to my outer reality to be acknowledged, released, expressed, integrated and understood.

Whatever shade of emotion pressed for expression was what I worked through day by day, or as so much of what I seemed to be dealing with were the effects of my birth, night after night, when I finally fought my way out in the early hours.

There were no particular themes of which I could say I knew where they were leading because it would have meant free access to inner consciousness and the ability to know the future – which is what I was and am still, working towards – that inner consciousness possesses unlike intellect which is limited to the rules of the physical world including time, and was still the world I dwelt in like everyone else; taught from birth onwards intellect is the only reality.

JOURNEY OF A LIFETIME

It did not mean I blundered blindly around in an aimless, purposeless, emotional maze either. Though I might not know the destination to which I travelled in my day-to-day efforts, I trusted inner being as I had done from the very outset to reveal the scenery of my journey as I progressed, and to take me on past milestones of reflection on how I felt in body, mind and being and the unfailing positive changes accrued as compared with the last occasion.

Understanding what I was working through as it happened was very much like being in a mist; able only to perceive where I was from my immediate surroundings, these being the bodily sensations and emotions I experienced.

Just as my left big toenail had shown me in 2003 with the rise of the 'crescent moon' in it, there were profound changes taking place in inner being; in 2007 on my left hand the nail on my second finger – the one next to my index finger – began to reveal a shape that to me looked uncannily like the matter I was dealing with at the time. The shape arising as a hole in the nail resembled the general shape of a house, the plans of which I had drawn up!

This was connected with property and literally, the actual place where I had been born.

As this symbolised, quite apart from my own birth I barely survived, almost every conceivable kind of family break up, breakdown and final disintegration by the time I was nine years old – including my own sense of self and childhood with it, and the death of my father.

It brought to the surface a great deal of fear over months previous, and by the beginning of the year manifested in the shape I saw becoming more apparent and morbidly fascinating as weeks and nail growth progressed.

It did not show me the future except to the extent it confirmed what I knew; I was facing and working through history of mine I buried deep within as a child simply in order to survive and live my life the best I could, and as this symbol edged in slow motion out of my nail with the passing months, so I was resolving at yet another and deeper level this buried history which had such a shattering effect on me at the time it occurred.

The broader symbolism of which finger and hand this apparition applied to, also struck me; it was the middle digit of five, i.e., it was central to my hand – as the history I was dealing with had been central to my life – when it occurred. No less it was my left hand, which is the emotional side of the body controlled from the right lobe of the brain dealing with the instinctual, emotional, intuitive, creative aspect of being.

In palmistry it is called the Saturn finger, and Saturn is seen as the inner world or inner aspects of being and it is associated with fear. As it is also associated with healing; and just another of those whimsical 'coincidences', a newspaper magazine article I read back in the seventies came up with the fact there are more physicians born under the astrological sign of Capricorn than any other zodiac sign. Capricorn, being ruled of course by the planet Saturn.

The fact it was a finger and not a toenail on which the 'slow-mo' picture (but quicker than on a toenail) symbolism rose in sight and consciousness, also struck me in that at a standing position feet are the lowest point in the body and in contact with mother earth; hands higher above. Which reads symbolically to me as the big toenail is not only central to inner being, but at the deepest level, whereas fingernails show a more accessible level of inner consciousness and being – and a (much) shorter time span also. And as said elsewhere; feet are connected to our Great Mother; the earth, whilst hands are connected to the cosmos. Also, as 'scientists' and particularly physicists it seems, develop selective amnesia on the subject, in quantum physics there is *no* separation between subject and object, so if middle/central digit of five is synonymous with Saturn in palmistry, then this digit shows what is happening in the centre of our being.

Those of an intellectual two-dimensional disposition might regard it all as whimsical coincidence but as those who have connection with their inner consciousness understand 'coincidence' is like Japanese knotweed. There is nothing showing on the surface linking one isolated knotweed plant with the sudden emergence of another many feet away. But the hidden root tendrils tell a different story.

Just as Saturn is equated with the deeper, hidden, aspects of our inner world.

Meaning the continuum binding events together in unseen inner consciousness is as dependable as the invisible roots connecting 'isolated' plants together. Though only for those the colossal culturally constructed wall built between intellect and real consciousness has at least some points of access through it.

Which rules out physicists and mathematicians it seems. And without doubt; solicitors.

But it does not prevent – in my direct experience – a palmist decoding your life from your hand with laser point accuracy – and detail – of events of life which the person may have forgotten and/or not even be aware of. And most certainly including when life ends.

There was nothing magical about my life that year. Dealing with the property matter and the deeply disturbing personal history it represented for me I found anything but easy. Like the image of climbing Everest I used to friends who helped me deal with certain aspects of it, I could only deal with it a stage at a time. Reaching one emotional 'camp' higher at a time and wondering how I was going to 'climb' to the next.

Coming home from holiday in France in late summer my ferry was cancelled and I spent the night camped in my car. Next morning I watched the early sun light up vast billowing reaches of cumulus clouds rising to great heights high in the sky above me.

Deep within it stirred feelings to match these thunderous ranges piled up over me; made more imposing as the sun lit shining summits like vast sparkling snow fields; casting disquieting canyons of gloom where it did not penetrate, all etched vividly against the flawless blue.

For some time these images haunted me even though a few weeks later I realised in these clouds I was seeing an allegory of the mountainous task whose weight I felt upon my shoulders. And this was by no means purely metaphorical. I had a gathering awareness no matter how much I worked through my own history – whether it was connected with property or not – my upper body, far from freeing up as I wished, was doing the reverse. It was as though I was encased in an invisible rigid carapace.

I knew and was certain it meant more, still deeper, personal history sublimated deep in reaches of inner consciousness as yet inaccessible, was rising closer to expression in my outer world and I would find out in due course, however long it took, and whatever the driving forces were as first physical expression then evolved into the deeply suppressed emotional energy driving this clamping and bodily rigidity.

With this also, the unshakable certainty, born of decades of experience, the outcome would ultimately and unfailingly be resolution and further freeing up within body and being.

Though attempting to explain this to anyone I had long since ceased to try because understanding only arises by going on the journey for oneself, and our culture teaches us to shun and fear it in ourselves.

The continuum of inner consciousness can only be experienced, it cannot be described.

Which is why knowledge was passed on in ancient times in this manner. Written systems of learning can only ever be a description; it is only in doing it and living it for oneself that real knowledge is something other than 'post-it' notes to the intellect.

Why as an example, it took twenty-one years to train a Druidic priest and no written records exists of their knowledge. Though all the descriptions of the Druids' remarkable and miraculous faculties show they had no barrier between outer and inner consciousness; meaning also why they could and did transcend time and space as they wished.

Perhaps holding a doctorate in quantum physics should also require training as a Druid priest. Then they could 'tunnel' anywhere in the universe – this or others – instantaneously exactly as certain quantum particles are known to do – and electrons can be in different places simultaneously. But that's just being silly …?

Then again, consciousness the Druids and all other practitioners of 'magic' – the fabled power of unified consciousness – used, enables humans and so far as I'm concerned, a lot of other life forms, to do the same as quantum particles do because it's their nature and they don't screw it up as we do: exist simultaneously in different places.

Humans though, take a lot more training, because the more 'matter' involved, the more rigorous the training of *consciousness* required to be able to transmute form into pure consciousness, especially when sobriquets such as 'dim', 'dense', and 'degenerate' characterise our culture that has spiralled so low aided by 'education'; the Albert Hall would have been demolished long ago if someone had put an expired 'use by' date at the entrance, having confused it with a large swede / rutabaga.

From Part Time to Continuous Working

OVER THE YEARS, one pattern becoming reasonably familiar was periods of activity; some times extending over weeks, seeming interminable whilst working through all the surfacing energy and emotion, followed by periods of relative peace and calm within, when sleep provided real rest in contrast to times of suppressed history and energy pushing into outer consciousness for expression and resolution.

In mid-2008 it all changed.

In the way I have become used to, and at an increasing tempo, an intuition and clear perception came to me one day having to take a few minutes out to release the pent up energy I could feel simmering away within, causing me to feel physically and emotionally uncomfortable.

In this instance it meant letting out more thumping fury, bringing the side of my left fist down like a hammer on suitable padding underneath, lying flat on cushions or a mattress in my meditation-cum-work room. Usually also at this time it often meant ramming my head into cushions and/or pillows and punching with both fists into them alongside my head, and occasionally (muffled) yelling at the top of my lungs into them also. Though something which puzzled me was a general absence of vocal expression.

But as ever and always, also being satisfied my body knew exactly what – and when – it wanted to do and how it wanted to express my releasing pent up energy, and no amount of intellectually driven 'boil squeezing' and interference of what I *thought,* made the slightest difference to what infallible inner consciousness knew needed to be resolved.

JOURNEY OF A LIFETIME

Did I know what the thumping fury was about? Of course!

I knew from times far beyond number or counting, it was more of the incalculable outrage I had no other choice than to go through and suffer being repeatedly squashed and crushed by my mother's contractions and inability of her iron rigid muscles to dilate and let me out into the world. Though hardly surprising considering the immense suppression she endured as a child through Victorian social condition and a mother who had been savagely smashed into the mould of social civility in her turn, poor lady.

It is impossible to overstress intellect has no part whatsoever in deciding how many times the process needs to be repeated until the energy is released and finally spent. And the origin of this deadly inculcated pattern becoming clear. Meaning in turn not only the energy has been unlocked, but the consciousness driving its expression.

To repeat yet again the example given earlier of someone being 'happy' with their birth after thirty-two times experiencing it. Or for that matter someone who was amazed at *actually* thrashing around *once,* and for a few days was astonished about ending up on the floor doing it.

Golly! Wow! Shock and amazement! How extraordinary! *Once!* How unbelievable! Thirty-two times! How unimaginably astonishing! How whimsically intellectual!

Once is a whisper of surfacing inner conscious presence. Ten times is confirmation of presence; a hundred, statement of serious intent, and thousands; statement of serious commitment, and final *conscious* resolution, complete acknowledgement, intent and commitment have been fully satisfied.

IF that is the magnitude of the stored need to release suppressed energy, then no amount of intellectual score keeping, suppressive interference changes anything. When allowed, energy flows until it is exhausted, however large or small is the need to release it.

The fact is we are taught to become disconnected; cut off from the sense of natural continuum we are all endowed with before birth, and consequently strangers to, what our bodies and the inner consciousness sustaining them needs to express through our culture's totally intellect centred domination. Unsurprisingly, we are dumbfounded, confused and not unusually frightened; even terrified, when our bodies – like a dog kept too long indoors, taken out for a walk and let off the lead – releases the suppressed energy in manic activity until the need has been sated.

Decades before, I ceased to keep an intellectual 'rule book' of what my body should or should not do, how it did it and how often it needed to repeat the process, though not without reluctance I learned to switch off my 'head', get out of the way, and let my body and its infallible wisdom speak for itself, having let it off my own 'lead' of suppressive, regimented, logical, how-much-was-reasonable-and-how-much-wasn't, intellect.

Like water in a reservoir, lake, inland sea or any other metaphor of stored energy finding its release, it will continue to flow until it has been spent and there is no more left.

Intellect is the finger in the dyke, or the sluice/floodgate, wall or dam; we have free choice to allow or prevent the flow of energy within our bodies. The trouble is we are taught in this barmy culture, suppressing the flow of energy is the *only* option we have and *no other*. Which is completely false. As well as downright damaging.

I did not enjoy the clear perception coming to me after one such session, a break – however long or short I had become used to – was a thing of the past, and the 'conveyor belt' regulated from inner being was now set to run twenty-four hours a day.

What my body and its driving consciousness decided it could now sustain, meant balancing the need to release suppressed energy bottled up since birth – or whatever time in my life the need prevailed to suppress and sublimate within what was impossible to deal with at the time – I had to walk my own tightrope of available energy, suitability and opportunity of place and time.

Simply put, I was having to find a more delicate and finely tuned harmonious balance between what rational, logical, intellect wanted to insist was 'reasonable' – as well as what I could physically sustain and was convenient – and what my body and its pressure vessel of stored energy said must be given release, expression and free reign of.

It was not a new experience balancing on the tightrope of what inner consciousness demanded and the physical resources I had to deal with it.

From the beginning as previously explained, there were periods when 'sleep' was like having a launderette of washing machines filled with tin cans, nuts, bolts and rocks all running full tilt inside my head in a ceaseless clattering cacophony of thoughts, images, and scenes I was ineluctably a part of at night; and dead on my feet with during the day. Particularly in the early days, only concentrated time spent working through, on my own in some conveniently remote woodlands or a weekend group workshop, would this incessant racket cease, having released the energy represented by my pressing backlog of unresolved history. After which I was equally often absolutely exhausted for a day or two, and not unusually either, so stiff throughout my body free movement was impossible, but the washing machines had been silenced, sleep brought real rest and peace, and the stiffness wore off as the massive release of deep body stress demonstrated the state of acute tension I had existed in before.

Although the same general pattern of peaks and lulls of activity continue, the huge pressure originally driving them has long since been released, which is why I have used different metaphors to describe the process as it has progressed over years and decades.

Hence originally so much suppressed energy and the personal history represented, pressed for expression the 'launderette syndrome', or as also explained what medical 'science' calls sleep Apnoea but hasn't a clue what causes it, much less how to permanently resolve it, took me to the limit of physical endurance at times, but as I drained more and more energy away, it progressed through 'logjam' phases when a crucial experience having been resolved, like the 'king log' in a logjam having been freed, all the related 'logs' – events, history and the energy blocked by the particular 'log' of experience holding the rest back – moved into consciousness with a powerful surge of energy expressed as a variety of cathartic 'logs' suddenly on the move in a boiling chaos. A complete spectrum of emotions and the physical energy trapped as part of them. Feeling pounded and tossed around by the force of my own expression, but like the jam having scoured the river and banks leaves a clean unimpeded steady flow in its wake and bed and banks soon recovering and bursting into vibrant new life.

The metaphors of waves, swells and currents also, as, with time a sense of rhythms of consciousness began to emerge but not understood or even comprehended at all to begin with. Dealing with one's inner consciousness was/is having to work from trust in one's insights and perceptions to build a body of personal experience totally lacking in our culture, which seeks to deny, damage and even destroy this vast and crucial faculty absolutely essential to health, happiness, individual organismic *and* collective cultural harmony.

Similarly as time and experience progressed, becoming increasingly familiar with the flow of insights, new and clarifying perceptions – like a 'conveyor belt' between inner and outer consciousness – which before, existed as occasional thoughts and ideas whose sudden appearance in outer consciousness seemed 'random' and of no particular significance, but in fact is inner consciousness's *vital* way of saying what we should know (but blot out/destroy with intellect) and even more so what is coming next if we would only listen/knew *how* to listen to this 'conveyor belt' of continuous wisdom and things still needing to be resolved. Which no longer have such immense force behind them of massive suppressed personal history and blocked energy, yet still need to be acknowledged, expressed, resolved and released, together with new perceptions and direct knowledge inner consciousness brings to outer consciousness. Like a 'Sat-Nav' enabling us to find our route forward in our life *because this is the faculty of inner consciousness which being time-less is not subject to past, present and future; time does not exist in inner consciousness.*

Inner consciousness delivers to our outer world a constant stream of what intellect sees as 'random' daydreaming dross but which is the utterly crucial relationship and *continuum* in which the past, present and future relate in the *context* of our lives and we ignore to our disadvantage at best or worst; outright peril.

So what are we taught in our culture to do with this stream of wisdom and our own inner nurture?

Response: Errrrrrr, what do you mean; 'listen/how to listen', 'inner wisdom', 'direct knowledge', 'continuum', 'no past, present or future', 'context of our lives', etc?

The metaphor of conveyor belt I have used has come *after* the others because the sense of awareness of a continuous stream of inner wisdom only begins to be clearly apparent when a massive amount of blocked repressed energy has been released and with it the near impenetrable wall has been at least partially cleared away between intellect/outer consciousness and real/inner consciousness our insane culture demands we create and call this 'normal reality'.

It is the equivalent of being given a vast mansion, having thousands of rooms as our birthright, and living in a toilet in the basement because others tell us physical functioning is our only way of being; there is nothing else. Which is simply and completely untrue.

At the time I became aware inner consciousness had cancelled tea breaks and time off and dealing with blocked suppressed energy had become a twenty-four hour process without breaks of days or weeks between releasing whatever pushed into consciousness for expression, it was still very much a case of dealing with it and moving on. Understanding of my wider and deeper continuum I have added here, was not available then; the need was to keep clearing my inner world for as long and until new perceptions came floating into mind showing me a broader view. Consequently a more complete picture and understanding of what I had been working through and the thread of deeper consciousness binding it all together.

I only knew then of having to work harder. I did not understand what my own 'conveyor belt' of inner consciousness was, only that it existed and having started it working, outer/physical world consciousness had to deal with what I had previously stuffed into inner consciousness – my own vast reservoir or 'landfill' tip – of suppressed emotional energy I refused to acknowledge, or even realise, that was what I was doing because, as I have said many times our whole culture teaches us from birth to suppress and deny this vast aspect of ourselves and we learn for suppression to become the 'norm' exactly as we learn control over our bodily functions and no longer need nappies. It takes a massive and concerted effort to reverse this process; just as it took a massive and concerted effort to learn to do it in the first place. It becomes so deeply learned and ingrained it is automatic, and in its turn leads to the myriad of complaints/conditions/symptoms and diseases we see around us and suffer from. In our culture as in ourselves.

This is not some cerebral intellectual statement whimsically dreamed up – or borrowed from anyone else. It is my direct experience over thousands of occasions and thousands of hours over decades, it requires consistent effort, dedicated self-awareness, determination and energy to reverse, drain and dismantle the dam our culture teaches us to build in ourselves.

JOURNEY OF A LIFETIME

We all understand the consequences if a boiler has its safety valve blocked and pressure goes on building until it explodes. Yet to repeat again; our culture teaches us to block our own safety valves and go on pouring more and more energy into our inner world in defiance of the universal law of energy conservation; energy cannot be made or destroyed, it can only change its form. Energy we bottle up within us does *not* disappear. It goes on building and building and if not released in outer consciousness – our ordinary waking world – the strain begins to show mentally, emotionally and physically, which is nature's way of telling us through our bodies something is wrong, but because we disconnect and block off our inner world from our outer we also disconnect cause and effect in bodies and being. We're back at complaints/conditions again.

Once this new pattern of being and releasing blocked energy was established, which, after all, was what I had been working towards for decades anyway, i.e., clearing my own inner being and massive backlog of suppressed, blocked off energy, it was a case of devoting the time, energy, effort and resources my inner being was telling me I had to, whatever my superficial feelings were, and get on with the job.

The question might be asked; so what was different from before?

The answer, of course, is only the tempo. Since mid-2008, that has been the pattern. As the second part of *Journey of a Lifetime* relates.